Slaves, Spices & Ivory in Zanzibar

Slaves, Spices & Ivory in Zanzibar

Integration of an East African Commercial Empire
into the World Economy, 1770–1873

Abdul Sheriff

Professor of History
University of Dar es Salaam

James Currey
LONDON

Heinemann Kenya
NAIROBI

Tanzania Publishing House
DAR ES SALAAM

Ohio University Press
ATHENS

James Currey Ltd
54b Thornhill Square
Islington
London N1 1BE, England

Heinemann Kenya
Kijabe Street, PO Box 45314
Nairobi, Kenya

Tanzania Publishing House
Independence Avenue, PO Box 2138
Dar es Salaam, Tanzania

Ohio University Press
Scott Quadrangle
Athens, Ohio 45701 USA

British Library Cataloguing in Publication Data
Sheriff, Abdul
Slaves, spices and ivory in Zanzibar: integration of an East African
commercial empire into the world economy, 1770–1873.
——(East African studies)
1. Zanzibar——Economic conditions——To 1964
I. Title II. Series
330.9678′102   HC885.Z7Z3
ISBN 0–85255–014–6
ISBN 0–85255–015–4 Pbk
ISBN 978-0-8214-0872-8
Library of Congress Cataloging-in-Publication Data
Sheriff, Abdul
Slaves, spices and ivory in Zanzibar
Revision of the author's thesis.
Bibliography: p.
Includes index.
1. Zanzibar——Commerce——History——18th century.
2. Zanzibar——Commerce——History——19th century.
3. Slave-trade——Tanzania——Zanzibar——History.
4. Spice trade——Tanzania——Zanzibar——History. I. Title.
HF3897.S54 1987   382′.096781   87–12339
ISBN 0–8214–0871–2
ISBN 0–8214–0872–0 (pbk)

Typeset in 10/11pt Baskerville by Colset Private Limited, Singapore
Printed and bound in Great Britain

To Suhail

Contents

Preface

The publication of a book so many years after the completion of the doctoral thesis on which it is based requires an explanation, if not an apology. African historiography has been going through such rapid changes since the coming of independence from colonial rule in the early 1960s that any extended piece of research has had to contend with strong intellectual eddies if not outright contrary currents. History has become one of the battlegrounds for contending ideological forces trying to interpret the past in terms of the present, and vice-versa. The perspective depends very much on one's vantage point, not only in geographical terms between Africa and the Western metropoles, but even more importantly in philosophical terms.

The research for the thesis was done in the late 1960s partly in the United States, France and India, but largely in London which has a well-established scholarly tradition and unrivalled research facilities. I owe to Professor Richard Gray, who supervised the thesis, as well as other scholars at the School of Oriental and African Studies, University of London, an enormous debt in initiating me into what may be termed the SOAS school of African history which has obtained its fullest expression in the *Cambridge History of Africa*.

Halfway through my research I went to the University of Dar es Salaam to teach for a year, and I found myself in the middle of an intense philosophical debate on the nature of African history, reflecting the changes that Africa was then going through. It had already given rise to what came to be called the Dar es Salaam school of nationalist history which was bent on discovering the African initiative in history that colonialism seemed to have obliterated. The approach is best summarised in Professor Terence Ranger's inaugural lecture and demonstrated in the *History of Tanzania* edited by I.N. Kimambo and A.J. Temu. But the school was already being challenged by the emerging 'radical' school influenced initially by the Latin American theory of underdevelopment and dependency, and later by Marxist theory. The atmosphere was vivacious and from it emerged Walter Rodney's *How Europe Underdeveloped Africa*, and a series of three conferences on the history of Tanzania, Kenya and Zanzibar under colonial rule of which the proceedings of only the first, unfortunately, have so far been published.

My encounter with this new trend during that first year at Dar es Salaam was of too short a duration to allow me to digest it, and yet long enough to impress upon me the need to come to grips with the fundamental philosophical questions in the debate. Although I went on to complete my thesis at London using all the empiricist skills I had learnt, I began to carry out a thorough critique of my own work upon my return to Dar es Salaam. This led me to the decision, perhaps unfortunate in hindsight, that I should refrain from publishing the results of my research, even with the fresh dust-covers of a new introduction and conclusion to gloss over the intellectual dilemma that I, and some other scholars at the time, faced. I decided instead to try to bring harmony to my mind first and revise the thesis accordingly to maintain its unity. Laudable as this was, I was to realise rather painfully with time that a new philosophical tradition cannot be learnt overnight and used as 'a tool of analysis'; it has to be developed and internalised through endless debate and struggle. This meant participation not only in strictly academic activities, including the teaching of new areas of history such as Tanzanian economic history, and contributing to various textbook projects of which Tanzanian schools as well as the University of Dar es Salaam were then in need, but also extra-curricular activities in which an academic comes face to face with the realities of life.

During this long period the various chapters went through several revisions, and the present work had to be almost entirely rewritten. While the primary research done for the thesis still forms the bedrock of primary data, a greater theoretical clarity has enabled me to interpret and bring out the full significance of the historical trends I had tried to analyse. One of the more significant dimensions that was poorly developed in the original thesis, which was conceived as 'a purely economic history', was the political aspect, both internally in connection with the political role played by the various classes in the commercial empire, and externally in terms of the long-term subordination of Zanzibar to British over-rule, and the interconnection between the two.

It has not been easy over the last few years to keep up with ongoing research, especially that carried out in the United Kingdom and the United States. Although certain aspects of the economic transformation of East Africa in the nineteenth century have undoubtedly been picked up for detailed analysis by other scholars, I nevertheless feel that there is enough merit left in what I did to warrant the publication of the broad interpretation of the history presented below.

The honours list of people who have directly or indirectly contributed to the formulation and execution of the present work has grown to such lengths after all these years that it would be impossible to list them all;

Preface

sometimes it is difficult for me even to remember where I picked up a particular fruitful lead. But the main source of ideas that have fashioned the present work has undoubtedly been the University of Dar es Salaam. Interdisciplinary barriers were breached in many places during the 1970s to permit a lively and very fruitful cross-fertilisation of thought to understand social change which, after all, is hardly divisible into neat academic compartments. A partial list of people who have contributed to the development of my own thought may be an unsatisfactory one, but it would be unforgivable not to mention my colleagues Mr Ernest Wamba, Professor Issa Shivji and Mr Helge Kjekshus, as well as Professors Steve Feierman, Ned Alpers and David Birmingham with whom I have had intense exchanges of ideas at various times.

Although a long period separates the present work from the original research, it would be unfair to forget the librarians and archival staff who had contributed to the success of the research, at the Public Record Office and India Office in London; in Paris; at the National Archives in New Delhi and the Maharashtra State Archives in Bombay, and particularly at the research institutions in Salem, Massachusetts, where personal attention to a researcher's needs has left very fond memories. I should also record my appreciation to the Rockefeller Foundation for support during the initial research for my thesis, and the Ford Foundation for support during the year I spent at Madison, Wisconsin, when I began the revision. My gratitude to the University of Dar es Salaam, and the History Department in particular, which provided the milieu and direct and indirect support during all these years, however, remains immeasurable.

Finally, the revision of my thesis has encompassed so much of the early life of my son Suhail that it is only fitting I should dedicate this book to him to record my appreciation for his patience and companionship, and to make up for any neglect he may have suffered.

A.S.
Dubai

Illustrations

Acknowledgements for illustrations

Plates 1, 3 and 6 from R.F. Burton, *Zanzibar: City, Island Coast* (2 vols, 1872); Plates 2, 9, 11, 13, 14, 17, 23, 31 and 33 from The Peabody Museum, Salem, Massachusetts; Plates 4, 5, 12, 19, 22 and frontispiece from Carl von der Decken, *Reisen in Ost-Afrika* (1869); Plate 7 from Abdul Sheriff; Plate 8 from H.H. Johnson, *The Kilima–Njaro Expedition* (1886); Plate 10 from *The London Illustrated News*, 18th June 1842; Plates 15 and 16 from V. Giraud, *Les Lacs de l'Afrique Equatoriale* (1890); Plate 18 from 'The Stone Town of Zanzibar: A Strategy for Integrated Development', a technical report commissioned by the UN Centre for Human Settlement, 1983; Plate 21 from J.R. Browne, *Etchings of a Whaling Cruise with Notes of a Sojourn on the Island of Zanzibar* (1846); Plates 24, 25 and 26 from Baur and Le Roy, *A Travers le Zanguebar* (1886); Plate 27 from R.F. Burton, *The Lake Regions of Central Africa* (2 vols, 1860); Plate 28 from H.M. Stanley, *How I Found Livingstone* (1872); Plate 29 from M.G. Alexis, *Stanley L'Africain* (1890); Plate 30 from H.M. Stanley *In Darkest Africa* (1890); Plate 32 from P.H. Colomb, *Slave Catching in the Indian Ocean* (1873); Plate 34 from *Harper's Weekly*, 5th July 1873.

Maps, Graphs and Tables

MAPS

GRAPHS

TABLES

xv

Abbreviations

Adm.	Admiralty Records at Public Record Office, Kew
ANSOM	Archives Nationales, Section Outre-Mer, Paris
BHS	Beverley Historical Society, Beverley, Massachusetts
BM, Add. Mss	Additional Manuscripts, at British Museum, London
BR	*Selections from the Records of the Bombay Government*, New Series
CCZ	Correspondance Consulaire et Commerciale: Zanzibar, at Ministère des Affaires Etrangères Archives, Paris
Cust.	Customs Records, at Public Record Office, Kew
EI	Essex Institute, Salem, Massachusetts
FO	Foreign Office Records, at Public Record Office, Kew
FOCP	Foreign Office Confidential Print, at Public Record Office, Kew
HSBA	Harvard School of Business Administration, Baker Library, Cambridge, Massachusetts
IOR	India Office Records, London
LC	Library of Congress, Washington, DC
MA	Maharashtra State Archives, Bombay
MAE	Ministère des Affaires Etrangères, Archives, Paris
NAI	National Archives of India, New Delhi
NAW	National Archives, Washington, DC
OI	Océan Indien series, at Ministère des Affaires Etrangères Archives, Paris
PM	Peabody Museum, Salem, Massachusetts
PP	*Parliamentary Papers*, United Kingdom
PRO	Public Record Office, Kew
PZ	Correspondance Politique: Zanzibar, at Ministère des Affaires Etrangères Archives, Paris
RIHS	Rhode Island Historical Society, Providence
SCHR	Salem Custom House Records, at Essex Institute, Salem, Massachusetts
T 100	American Consular Records, Group 59, on microfilm at National Archives, Washington, DC

Note: For more details see Sources, pp. 259–65 below.

Glossary

Imam   Spiritual title of the Ibadhi ruler of Oman traditionally elected by the *ulema* and the tribal *shaikhs*. It declined in significance during the latter part of the eighteenth century with the secularisation of the Omani state, but was revived in the late 1860s.

Seyyid   Lord, used in Oman and Zanzibar to refer to the more secular ruler, and to members of the ruling dynasty.

Shaikh   Heads of tribal and clan groupings in Oman; also a term of respect used more generally.

Shamba   A Swahili word for plantation or plot of land.

Sultan   Secular title of the ruler of Oman and Zanzibar emphasising the temporal aspect of his position.

Ulema   Religious experts in Islam; played an important role in the election of the Imam in Oman.

Currency and Weights

CURRENCY

Cruzado (Cr) A Portuguese silver coin with a fluctuating value: 1777: 3.75 Cr = 1 Piastre (see below); 1813: 2.60 Cr = 1 Piastre.[1]

Maria Theresa Dollar (MT$) A coin known as the Austrian Crown, the 'Black dollar', *Kursh* or *Rial*. Current on the East African coast until the 1860s when it began to be replaced by the American dollar. 1 MT$ = Rs 2.10-2.23 during the first half of the nineteenth century. £1 = MT$ 4.75. Spanish, Mexican *Piastres* or dollars and American dollars were exchanged at Zanzibar at 1 per cent to 6 per cent discount.[2]

Rupee (Rs) The Indian unit of currency. Before 1836 different parts of India had their own coins. The universal rupee was established in that year, but the value fluctuated until 1899: 1803-1813: 1 Spanish Dollar = Rs 2.38-2.14. 1841-1868: 1 Spanish dollar = Rs 2.10-2.18.[3]

WEIGHTS

Arroba (Ar) A Portuguese unit equal to 14.688 kg.[4]

Frasela (Fr) A unit widely used along the East African coast varying from 27 lbs or 12.393 kg in Mozambique; 35 lbs in Zanzibar; 36 lbs on the Benadir.[5]

Maund An Indian unit, of varying weight. The Surat *maund* used to weigh ivory equalled 37½ lbs.[6]

Sources:
1. Freeman-Grenville (1965), p. 88; Milburn, Vol. 1, p. 60.
2. See p. 136 below. Milburn, Vol. 1, p. 198; Burton (1872), Vol. 1, pp. 324-5, Vol. 2, pp. 406, 418-19; MAE, CCZ, Vol. III, pp. 344-9; Bennett and Brooks (eds) (1965), pp. 477, 499, 534-5.
3. Phillips (ed.) (1951), p. 62; Milburn, Vol. 1, p. 116; Hamerton to Bombay, 3 January 1841, MA, 54/1840-1, pp. 20-2; Churchill to Bombay, 28 October 1868, MA, 156/1869, pp. 120-1.
4. Alpers (1975), p. xiv.
5. ibid.; Fabens to Hamblet, 10 October 1846, PM, Fabens Papers, II.
6. Milburn, Vol. 1, p. 159.

Plate 1   Zanzibar from the sea, c.1857

Introduction

The Commercial Empire

Zanzibar developed during the nineteenth century as the seat of a vast commercial empire that in some ways resembled the mercantile empires of Europe of the preceding centuries. Unlike them, however, it was developing at a time when capitalism was already on its way to establishing its sway over industrial production and was subordinating merchant capital to its own needs. In the capitalist metropoles this entailed the disintegration of merchant capital's monopoly position and the reduction of its rate of profit to the general average. It was thus being reduced to an agent of productive capital with a specific function: distributing goods produced by industry and supplying the latter with the necessary raw materials.[1]

But capitalism was simultaneously developing as a world system as it gradually drew the different corners of the globe into its fold. In this historic process merchant capital played a vanguard role. As a form of capital it shared the dynamism arising out of profit maximisation and the drive towards accumulation of the capitalist classes. This drive, therefore, pushed it to encourage constant expansion in the scale of production of exchange values without itself participating in actual production. Existing as it did at the periphery of the expanding capitalist system, it seemed to enjoy its pristine position and relative autonomy. Backward conditions here enabled it to monopolise trade and appropriate a handsome rate of profit that appeared to guarantee primacy to the merchant classes. That primacy, however, was illusory, for capitalism was close on their heels, subverting them step by step, and ultimately subordinating them to its own rule. In examining the history of Zanzibar during the nineteenth century, therefore, it is necessary to consider closely what Karl Marx termed the 'historical facts about merchant capital'.[2]

Zanzibar was essentially a commercial intermediary between the African interior and the capitalist industrialising West, and it acted as a conveyor belt transmitting the demands of the latter for African luxuries and raw materials, and supplying in exchange imported manufactured goods. Economic movements in East Africa from the eighteenth century onwards were primarily based on two major commodities and two

1

fundamental transformations. Increased Omani participation in Indian Ocean trade, particularly after the overthrow of Portuguese hegemony over their coastline, had given impetus to the emergence of an Omani merchant class which began to invest part of its profit in the production of dates using slave labour. To this important but limited demand for African slaves was added during the last third of the eighteenth century a substantial French demand for slaves to be supplied to their sugar colonies in the Mascarenes[3] and even to the Americas. But the period characterised by European mercantilism, of which the slave trade was an aspect, was rapidly drawing to a close. The strangulation of the European slave trade after the end of Anglo-French warfare in the Indian Ocean, however, provided an unexpected opportunity and a new lease of life to the slave mode of production in East Africa at the periphery of the world system dominated by capital. A vital transformation of the slave sector was therefore initiated during the first quarter of the nineteenth century as Arab slave traders began to divert slaves to the clove plantations of Zanzibar, and later to the grain plantations on the East African coast. Thus the sector was metamorphosed from being primarily one dominated by the export of slave labour to one that exploited that labour within East Africa to produce commodities to feed into the world system of trade.

The second economic transformation was activated initially by the collapse of the supply of ivory from Mozambique to India towards the end of the eighteenth century as a result of the rapacious Portuguese system of taxation. However, the ivory trade became a vibrant force with the enormous expansion of demand by the affluent classes of the capitalist West. The supply of such a commodity of the hunt demanded a constant expansion of the hinterland. So rapid was the growth in demand that throughout the nineteenth century it almost always outstripped supply, and resulted in a constant increase in the price of ivory. The price of manufactured imports, on the other hand, remained steady or even declined as a result of technological improvements and the development of the productive forces. These divergent price curves constituted for East Africa a powerful and dynamic motive force for the phenomenal expansion of trade and of the hinterland as far as the eastern parts of present-day Zaire. The extremely favourable terms of trade were able to cover not only the increasing cost of porterage but also to permit an enormous accumulation of merchant profit at the coast.

The trade of Zanzibar grew enormously during the first half of the nineteenth century as a result, but it owed its motive force primarily to the process of capitalist industrialisation and the consequent affluence of the well-to-do classes in the West. Through the export of ivory, cloves and other commodities, and the import of manufactured goods, it was therefore inevitable that the predominantly commercial economy of Zanzibar would be sucked into the whirlpool of the international capitalist system and be subordinated economically, and eventually politically, to the dominant capitalist power.

As a mercantile state Zanzibar sought to monopolise the trade and appropriate the profit at the coast. An attempt was made to centralise the whole foreign trade of Africa from eastern Zaire to the Indian Ocean at the major entrepôt of Zanzibar; this included prohibitions on foreign merchants trading at the mainland termini of long-distance caravan routes from the African interior. This was particularly true of the Mrima coast opposite Zanzibar, which was reserved for local traders. On this system was constructed an elaborate fiscal structure that sought to squeeze a maximum amount of the surplus from the different stretches of the coast. The most heavily taxed area was of course the Mrima coast since it had little alternative except to use the entrepôt, while areas further to the north and south were induced to channel their trade through the commercial centre by lower rates of taxation. The system permitted the appropriation of part of the surplus by the Zanzibar state whose revenue rose more than sevenfold during the first seven decades of the nineteenth century.

The commercial system was also extremely profitable for the merchant class which, taking advantage of the highly favourable terms of trade, accumulated an enormous amount of merchant capital. Commerce, in fact, was so profitable that there was little inducement to divert that surplus from circulation to production except initially. Until the 1830s clove production was rendered attractive by the high prices of cloves as a result of the Dutch monopoly over the commodity, and many Arab traders did invest their profit from the slave trade in landownership. But with overproduction the plantations became a trap for the Arabs; they had invested much of their capital in them and now had little hope of a favourable return. For the Indian section of the merchant class, the declining profitability of clove production and prohibition against their use of slave labour, as British Indian subjects, meant that this avenue for investment was blocked except in the form of merchant and moneylending capital to extract much of the surplus that remained in that sector. In the process they undermined the landowning class economically.

In the interior merchant capital induced expansion of commodity production, diverting labour from subsistence production to hunting for ivory and slaves. The result was the undermining of the existing pre-capitalist modes of production. In his discussion of merchant capital, Marx showed that commerce – which has existed in all modes of production other than the purely subsistence-oriented natural economy – is not confined to exchange of actual surplus, but bites deeper and deeper into subsistence production, converting entire sectors of production into producers of commodities, making not only luxuries but even subsistence increasingly dependent on sale. Commerce therefore has an erosive

3

influence on the producing organisation. By subordinating production increasingly to production for exchange, it begins to transform the economic basis of the social formation originally founded primarily on production of use values, and sooner or later it disrupts the social organisation of production itself. It progressively dissolves the old egalitarian or feudal relationships, and expands the sphere of monetary relationships. It permits the emergence of a merchant class which begins to exert its apparently independent influence on the political economy of the social formation. Despite the fact that this class depends on the existing dominant classes which organise production, it undermines their economic as well as political position by constantly pushing for production for exchange and appropriating an increasing share of the surplus product. Although merchant capital undermines the existing mode of production, it is 'incapable by itself of promoting and explaining the transition from one mode of production to another.'[4]

In the case of Unyamwezi in what is now western mainland Tanzania, merchant capital contributed not only to the depopulation of elephants as they were killed for their ivory, but also of its people as the Nyamwezi turned to a life of trading to as far away as eastern Zaire, and to porterage to transport ivory and imported manufactured goods between the coast and the interior. In a sense it may have begun the process of dissolving the old mode and preparing it to be remoulded by colonialism as an underdeveloped area. It is not, therefore, commerce that revolutionises production but, rather, production that revolutionises commerce. Far from promoting the transition, merchant capital – which is dependent as preconditions of its own prosperity on the old classes that organise production, and on the old system of production – may play a reactionary role in preserving or buttressing the old classes and production system against change even while draining them of their vitality. It cannot by itself contribute to the overthrow of the old mode. Accordingly, Marx formulated the law that 'the independent development of merchants' capital . . . stands in inverse proportion to the general economic development of society.'[5] What new mode will replace the old one, therefore, does not depend on commerce but on the character of the old mode and, with the rise of the capitalist mode as a world system, increasingly on the impact of this vibrant mode from abroad.

The Zanzibar commercial empire that developed during the nineteenth century and encompassed much of eastern Africa was like its European predecessors in that it did not evolve elaborate administrative and political structures. Fiscal administration was provided by the custom master who farmed the customs for five-yearly periods. The Sultan had a number of governors at the major ports on the mainland, but his flag did not follow trade into the interior. The empire was largely sustained by the Sultan's monopoly over the coastal termini of trade routes from the interior, and a system of common economic interests with the emergent merchant classes and chiefs in the interior to keep trade flowing. Such an informal system suffered from competition and contradiction between the merchant classes from the coast and the interior, leading to several wars. At the coast the state itself was subverted by its indebtedness to the most powerful group of Indian financiers and by the conversion of the Indian mercantile class into an instrument of British influence. But from the end of the eighteenth century the compradorial[6] state had also been politically dependent on Britain to protect itself from its rivals, particularly in the Persian Gulf, and to gain access to the British Indian market. By the middle of the nineteenth century it could no longer safeguard the political integrity of the Omani kingdom and prevent its partition between its Omani and African sections. This was a prelude to the partition of even the African section during the Scramble for Africa, and eventually to the subjugation of Zanzibar itself to colonial rule.

Previous historians of the East African coast tended to approach the subject of economic expansion during the nineteenth century with the empiricist tools of political history, ascribing to Seyyid Said, who presided over the commercial empire, all sorts of initiatives, and taking little account of the nature of the Omani 'monarchy'. They rationalised all economic changes then occurring in East Africa in terms of the economic policies of the most prominent political figure. Sir Reginald Coupland attributed to Said, among other things, the exploitation of Zanzibar for cloves, the expansion of the hinterland, the development of the Indian community to finance economic expansion, and the encouragement given to foreign merchants to trade at Zanzibar. Kenneth Ingham went so far as to assert that the history of East Africa was moulded by the personality of Said, arguing that the transformation of Zanzibar from a small and relatively unimportant village to the most important trading centre along the coast was 'almost entirely due to the initiative and powers of organisation of Seyyid Said.'[7]

As will be shown in the following analysis, many of the developments with which Said is credited were set in motion long before he first set foot in East Africa in 1827–8, although as a merchant prince, when he jumped onto the bandwagon, he gave that wagon a powerful push. But the argument against the Coupland–Ingham thesis is not merely empirical but also philosophical. As Marx shows, the theory that history is moulded by some 'great men' is but a variation of the idealist conception of history which began to develop with the division of labour at its highest stage, the division between mental and manual labour. Henceforth men's ideas appeared to emancipate themselves from their earthly roots, and to rise to the rarefied atmosphere of philosophical idealism, only to return to earth head first to impose a pattern, an order, on material conditions, and to attempt to explain historical phenomena with the help of their idealistic derivatives.[8]

Plate 2   Seyyid Said bin Sultan, Ruler of Oman and Zanzibar, 1804–56

In practice, as Marx shows, the attempt to prove the hegemony of the spirit in history involves, first, an effort to separate the ideas of those ruling from these actual rulers and thus to recognise the rule of ideas in history. Secondly, it involves bringing an order into this rule of ideas and proving a mystical connection between successive ruling ideas, thus providing the world of ideas with its own independent laws of development.· Finally, in order to remove the mystical appearance, it involves personifying the various stages of development of the idea in certain philosophers and 'great men' who are seen as makers or manufacturers of

6

history. But as Georg Büchner aptly put it, 'the individual personality is only foam on the crest of the wave'.[9] He may betray the turbulence in the bowels of history but he is not its explanation. The explanation lies in the economic infrastructure of relations of production and exchange and the appropriation of the surplus product. On this foundation arises a legal and political superstructure to which correspond definite forms of social organisation,[10] such as the Busaidi state at Zanzibar.

Notes

1. See Marx, Vol. 3, ch. 20; Mukherjee, ch. 3.
2. Marx, Vol. 3, ch. 20.
3. The Mascarenes refer to the small islands to the east of Madagascar. Under the French they were known as Ile de France and Bourbon. The former was renamed Mauritius after its capture by Britain in 1810; the latter was renamed Réunion.
4. Marx, Vol. 3, p. 328.
5. ibid., pp. 327-8.
6. *Comprador* is a Portuguese term for 'purchaser'. In the East it referred to brokers or commission agents, and in China to substantial agencies which carried out commercial activities on behalf of foreign traders and supplied their needs, and even workers to the trading factories. In Chinese Marxist literature the term referred to local agents of foreign capital or interests. See Yule and Burnell, pp. 243-4.
7. Coupland (1939), pp. 4-5; Ingham, pp. 19, 73, 80.
8. Marx and Engels, Vol. 1, p. 33.
9. ibid., Vol. 1, p. 50; Büchner quoted in Plekhanov, Vol. 1, pp. 608.
10. Marx and Engels, Vol. 1, p. 503.

One

The Rise of a
Compradorial State

The East African coast was a part of the commercial system in the Indian Ocean for at least two thousand years. But its role in that system for most of that period was largely that of an intermediate zone of exchange between various producing and consuming zones around the ocean. Commerce, rather than production, formed the basis of the civilisation that flourished there. It was cosmopolitan and urbane; it was prosperous but compradorial. The coast was a zone of interaction between two cultural streams, one coming from the African interior and one from across the Indian Ocean, from which emerged a synthesis, the Swahili[1] civilisation, that at every step betrays its dual parentage. But that civilisation was mercantile. It gave rise to city-states that were like beads in a rosary, each forming a distinct entity, and yet threaded together by maritime communication and a common culture and language. Their mercantile ruling classes prospered from the middleman's profit which they cornered. They were utterly dependent on international trade, with no control over either the producing or consuming ends. The rhythm of Swahili coastal history was not internally generated but was synchronised with the wider rhythm of international trade in the Indian Ocean, and of some of the dominant social formations in that system.

The East African coast forms a fairly distinct geographical entity, bounded on the west by a belt of poor, low-rainfall scrub known in Kiswahili as the *nyika* (wilderness). The *nyika* runs just behind the narrow coastal belt in Kenya. Further south, it is more broken, being penetrated by the eastern rim of mountains and by river valleys which form corridors into the interior. The *nyika* recedes further into the interior, virtually disappearing in southern mainland Tanzania. The character of the narrow coastal belt, especially in the north, meant that it failed to provide an adequate productive base for many of the city-states, some of which were confined to offshore islands. Moving from north to south, however, there is a progressive enlargement of the immediate hinterland, and the

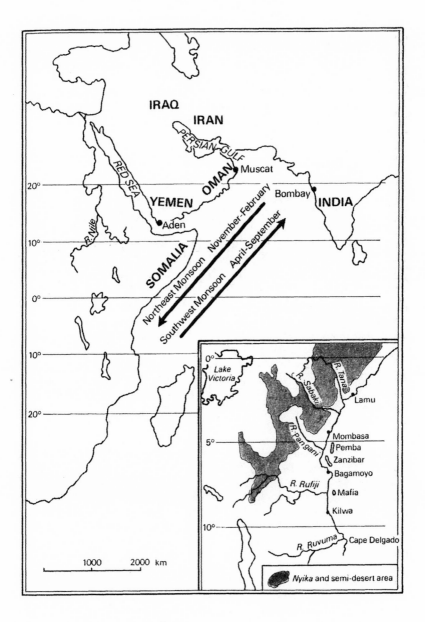

Map 1.1   The western Indian Ocean

potential for production and trade. On the other hand, the *nyika* imposed not so much an absolute barrier as a premium on the costs of communication between the coast and the interior, a price that could be paid only at certain times and places in the history of East Africa.

The sea defines the eastern border of the coastal belt, but it is the end of the world only to an incorrigible landsman. To coastal people it is an arena of production, an avenue of communication, a zone of commercial contact and cultural interaction. Such interaction, of course, presupposed the development of a suitable technology which included not only marine engineering but also the harnessing of the winds and the currents. In the Indian Ocean this meant, above all, the monsoons. They are marked by a seasonal reversal of winds showing great regularity, forming a highly dynamic system of which the East African coast forms only a fringe. The north-east monsoon begins to build up from November when it covers the western Indian Ocean as far south as Mogadishu. The winds are steady and light, and they permit the departure of the early dhows from the Arabian coast, taking thirty to forty days to reach their destinations in East Africa. With a greater frequency of tropical storms in the eastern half of the Arabian Sea in October and November, suitable sailing conditions from India occur in December. By then the monsoon is well established as far south as Zanzibar, allowing for a faster and more direct voyage taking twenty to twenty-five days. This pattern of circulation is reinforced by the equatorial current which flows southwards after striking the Somali coast, thus facilitating the voyage from the north. But since the African coast is at the fringe of the monsoon system, the constancy of the monsoon decreases dramatically as it encounters the south-easterlies blowing towards Mozambique. The convergence of the two wind systems creates a region of variable winds and unstable weather prone to tropical cyclones in the Mozambique channel, making the voyage both arduous and dangerous south of Cape Delgado.[2]

By March the north-east monsoon begins to break up, and it does so earliest in the south. By April the wind has reversed to become the south-west monsoon. The equatorial current at this time strikes the coast near Cape Delgado and splits into the strong north-flowing current which facilitates the northward journey, and the south-flowing current which hinders exit to the north from the Mozambique channel. This is the season of departure from East Africa, but there is an interruption between mid-May and mid-August when the weather is too boisterous for Indian Ocean shipping. Dhows therefore sail either with the build-up (*Musim*) of the monsoon in April, if commercial transactions can be completed in time, or with the tail-end (*Demani*) in August. The latter strategy becomes increasingly necessary if dhows have to proceed south of Zanzibar.

10

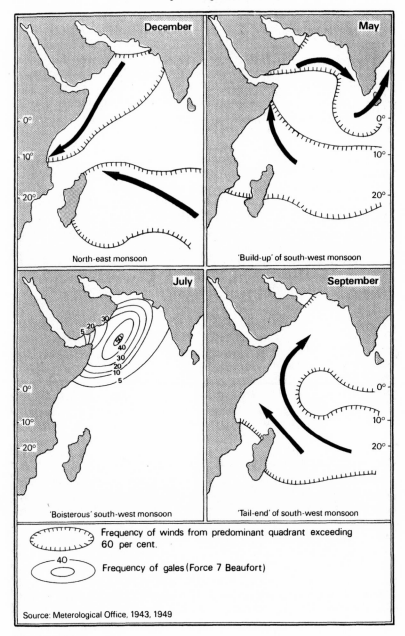

Map 1.2   The monsoons

The spatial extent and the differential pattern of the monsoons thus helped define the normal radius of action of Indian Ocean dhows. They tended to favour the northern part of the East African coast which enjoyed a longer trading season between the two monsoons, especially for Indian dhows. The southern coast, on the other hand, is at the extreme periphery of the monsoon system, and it thus experienced a shorter trading season, forcing dhows to 'winter' in East African waters and sail back with the tail-end of the south-west monsoon in August or September. This required a more elaborate entrepôt system for effective exploitation of the commercial resources of the southern coast, especially that beyond Cape Delgado.

On the one hand, therefore, the narrow coastal belt failed to provide an adequate productive base for the economies of the city-states. They were thus dependent on the transit trade between the African interior and the regions beyond the Indian Ocean. On the other hand, the longitudinal alignment of the coast accessible to the monsoon, even if access was differential, provided the various ports with potentially independent commercial bases. This imprinted on the coastal economy and politics a generally acephalous and even fissiparous tendency, and a spirit of political independence despite, or because of, the individual economic dependence of the city-states on international trade.

The mercantile civilisation of the Swahili coast

From the beginning of the Christian era African social formations along the East African coast, which were initially geared to production of use values for direct consumption or barter, were induced by international trade to produce surplus products for exchange. A surplus of food grains and mangrove poles was exported to the food- and timber-deficient south Arabian coast and the Persian Gulf at various times, though these mundane staples are hardly ever mentioned in the few available sources before the sixteenth century. External demand, however, also induced the production of certain luxuries for which there was probably no local use. While new sources of wealth were thus opened up, they may have entailed the diversion of labour from other essential economic activities. Early Greek and Roman demand for ivory induced south Arabian traders to extend their commercial activities down the East African coast as early as the second century BC. After the collapse of the Roman empire its place was taken by India and China which remained the main markets until the beginning of the nineteenth century. Gold was procurable in sufficient quantities only from Zimbabwe. As demand in Asia increased at the beginning of the second millennium AD, greater amounts of labour, including that of young females, were mobilised to mine gold. Coastal shipping was extended south from Kilwa to Sofala where it met the land routes from Zimbabwe. The medieval glory of Kilwa was directly dependent on this entrepôt trade.[3]

International trade induced not only the diversion of labour from one economic activity to another within the same social formation but, at various times, even the physical transfer of that labour. The *Periplus of the Erythraean Sea*, which was probably written in the late first or early second century AD, mentions the export of slaves, but only from the Horn of Africa. From the seventh to the ninth century, however, there was a massive demand for slave labour to reclaim the marshlands of southern Iraq. Severe exploitation and oppression of a large number of slaves concentrated near Basra led to a series of slave revolts from the end of the seventh century, and culminated in the famous 'Zanji rebellion' in the ninth century when the rebels controlled southern Iraq for fourteen years (868–83). The revolt was suppressed but, by their resistance, the slaves had ensured the failure of one of the few cases of agricultural exploitation based on slave labour in Muslim history. The subsequent economic decline of the Middle East meant that the slave trade did not again attain such massive proportions until the eighteenth century.[4]

In return for African products merchant capital made available to the East African social formations manufactured goods and luxuries which helped expand the sphere of circulation. During the first century AD, imports included metal tools and weapons, but also wine and wheat 'to gain the goodwill of the barbarians'. By the thirteenth century they included beads, Chinese porcelain and cloth, part of which was consumed by the affluent merchant classes in the city-states themselves. Such imports may at times have offered stiff competition to local bead and textile industries. These industries, which apparently flourished at Mogadishu, Pate, Kilwa and elsewhere, showed signs of decline, although at Kilwa they were killed only with the coming of the Portuguese.[5]

While merchant capital thus helped to expand the production and circulation of commodities, it may also have helped to impart to East African economic structures a certain lopsided character, with over-developed commercial, mining and hunting sectors, and a more stunted industrial sector. Moreover, international trade appears to have been conducted on the initiative of foreign traders to supply the needs of their own homelands, and generally in their own ships. As late as the eleventh century, al-Idrisi commented that 'the Zanj have no ships to voyage in, but use vessels from Oman and other countries'.[6] This suggests inequality in the level of technological and socio-economic development between the trading partners. Under these circumstances there may have been an imposition of a pattern of development on the East African social formations that made them dependent on international trade, and that was more beneficial to the more developed social formations across the ocean. This tendency, however, should not be exaggerated for the period before the rise of capitalism since commodity production, largely of luxuries, played only a limited role in total production.

13

International trade stimulated the growth of market towns, some of which may have been initially established by the indigenous people themselves. In these market towns trade provided a base for the emergence of a ruling merchant class which appropriated its middleman's profit from commodities passing through its hands. It ruled over a coastal population that was no longer undifferentiated. In the first century AD the *Periplus* talks of 'men of the greatest stature, who are pirates, inhabit the whole coast and at each place have set up chiefs'.[7] Commerce may have begun to undermine the tribal constitution, paving the way for the emergence of a class society and a state. By the second century, Ptolemy talks of Rhapta, one of the market towns, as a 'metropolis', which Gervase Mathew suggests meant the capital of a state. A thirteenth-century Chinese source describes a stratified society along the coast consisting of the 'bareheaded and barefooted' commoners who lived in 'huts made of palm leaves', and a ruling class whose stone habitations are alone visible among the coastal ruins today. The populations of some of these city-states are said to have numbered several thousand, and yet none of the ruined cities seem to have more than about fifty stone-built houses.[8]

In these coastal city-states flourished a civilisation which was prosperous but not self-reliant. The cultural level attained surprised the early European visitors, one of whom was moved to compare the mosque at Kilwa with that at Cordova. A modern archaeologist has been impressed by 'the complexity, luxury, variety and sensitivity' of design of the Husuni Kubwa palace at Kilwa. The merchant class, according to the early sixteenth-century Portuguese factor, Duarte Barbosa, exhibited great opulence and luxury:

> The kings of these isles [Pemba, Mafia and Unguja] live in great luxury; they are clad in very fine silk and cotton garments, which they purchase at Mombaça from the Cambaya merchants. The women of these Moors go bravely decked, they wear many jewels of fine Çofala gold, silver too in plenty, earrings, necklaces, bangles, and bracelets, and they go clad in good silk garments.[9]

But that civilisation was mercantile and dependent, as evidenced by the storage rooms which backed the Husuni Kubwa palace. Its dependence on the international connection was not confined to the economy, but permeated the whole range of cultural and social life of the Swahili city-states. Religion and the fundamental bases of culture generally came from abroad, though they were gradually indigenised. The standing architecture appeared on the coast 'fully fledged' in the earliest known buildings, and thereafter, according to Peter Garlake, only 'a slow deterioration in the standards of workmanship is discernible'. This occurs not only when cultural links with the motherland weaken, but also when commercial connections are strengthened, permitting new imports

14

to extinguish some indigenous workmanship. Thus increased imports of Chinese porcelain began to replace the exquisitely carved coral decorations on mosques and tombs. The reliance of the coast on the international connection was so complete that when the Portuguese cut the economic lifelines across the ocean, the mercantile civilisation suffered a major setback. Some of the most prosperous city-states, such as Kilwa, never recovered their medieval glory.[10]

Portuguese intervention

In 1497 the Portuguese inaugurated what K.M. Pannikar has described as 'the Vasco da Gama epoch of history'. It was characterised, first, by the ruthless destruction of the pre-existing system of international trade in the Indian Ocean and its forcible integration into the emerging international economic system dominated by Europe, then in transition from feudalism to capitalism. It was also characterised by the dominance of maritime power over the land masses of Asia, and by the imposition of a foreign commercial economy over social formations originally mainly based on agricultural production and internal trade. In their crusade, 'commerce and Christianity' were closely intertwined, the former providing the material motivation, the latter the ideological justification. Royal instructions to Portuguese captains enjoined them 'to conduct war with the Muslim and trade with the heathen'. Should the infidels prove unwilling either to be converted or to engage in trade, then the spiritual weapon of the cross was to be augmented by the carnal weapon of the sword.[11]

The Portuguese objective was to capture the Indian Ocean trade and divert it from its traditional paths across western Asia to their own maritime artery round the Cape of Good Hope, thus outflanking the Italian-Muslim monopoly over the spice trade. Their geopolitical strategy involved the blocking of the Red Sea and the Persian Gulf by capturing Aden and Hurmuz, the capture of Malacca and Goa to control and centralise the Far Eastern and Indian trade, and the establishment of a provisioning station at Mozambique. The threatened interests of Venice, Egypt and the Indian Ocean merchant classes combined to thwart Portuguese designs commercially, by attempting to deny them access to spices, and militarily, by trying to defeat Portuguese naval power. The latter strategy failed at Diu in 1509, but the Portuguese, with their limited human and financial resources, failed to supplant the pre-existing system in the Indian Ocean completely.

Along the East African coast, the maritime and mercantile Swahili city-states were vulnerable. Their economic and political foundations were based on the transit trade. By the end of the fifteenth century the coastal mercantile economy was bifocal, dominated in the north by Mombasa as the most convenient port for the northern, especially

Indian, dhows and in the south by Kilwa which controlled the gold trade from Sofala; and there was considerable collaboration between the two.[12] But the Swahili merchant class was fragmented, both between and within the competing city-states. This provided the Portuguese intruders with a golden opportunity to divide and rule, allying with the weaker puppet sections to subjugate Mombasa. Despite valiant resistance, the power of Mombasa was broken, and the town was twice razed to the ground, in 1505 and 1528. In the south the Portuguese took advantage of the cleavage within the ruling merchant class in Kilwa to impose a puppet regime in 1505. A couple of years previously they had severed its southern lifeline by establishing a factory at Sofala. Under this double blow Kilwa declined precipitously, never to recover its medieval glory.[13]

Although the power of the Swahili merchant class was broken, the Portuguese lacked the resources for effective control of the whole coast and monopoly of trade. Their power north of Cape Delgado was restricted to the occasional collection of tribute, and the 'Captaincy of Malindi' to serve as a centre of the Indian trade so crucial to Sofala. They tried to control sea traffic with a pass system, and granted a monopoly over certain commodities to the Captain of Malindi. They also tried to cut out Swahili traders from the Sofala trade. All these measures helped to kill the goose that had laid the golden egg. Trade in both gold and ivory declined. Although the Swahili merchant class, legally or otherwise, was able to circumvent these restrictions, it was embittered and felt oppressed, creating a fertile ground for disaffection and revolt.[14]

By the 1580s the Portuguese empire had already embarked upon its century of decline, caused by both internal decay and external attacks. Portugal proved unable to make the transition from feudalism: high birth and connection with the court remained the main qualifications for high office; and the corrupt monopolistic system of administration and trade in the East hindered the development of mercantile capitalism. Portugal proved no match for the burgeoning English and Dutch mercantile bourgeoisies which began to carve their spheres out of its preserve. It was also unable to resist the revitalised and expansive Iran and the Ottoman empire.[15]

Turkish incursions in 1585–8 and the instantaneous Swahili revolts shook the foundation of Portuguese rule in East Africa, and led to the building of Fort Jesus at Mombasa to guard Portuguese possessions there. But the oppression of the Swahili merchant class continued, culminating in the alienation of the closest ally of the Portuguese, the Malindi dynasty, which had been transferred to Mombasa. Swahili resistance was fuelled by the revolt of Sultan Yusuf of Mombasa, despite his Portuguese and Christian upbringing. Pate emerged as the standard-bearer of Swahili resistance. It had developed as a centre of Arab and Indian shipping, and had successfully forged commercial links with the interior. The consequent prosperity of Pate seemed to threaten Portuguese hegemony. The closing of the custom house in 1645 converted Pate into a centre of anti-Portuguese insurrection all along the coast. However, the spineless Swahili merchant class was unable to overthrow the Portuguese yoke on its own.

The external ally to whom it turned had a similar history of Portuguese domination over its coastline and of participation in oceanic trade. Omani raids into the Portuguese domains in East Africa may have encouraged Pate's insurrection, and Omani dhows became an annual feature in East African waters during the second half of the seventeenth century, trading and raiding. By 1652 the whole region was infested with Omani raiders and in open rebellion against the Portuguese. The chronicle of Mombasa specifically states that the Swahili called on the Imam of Oman to relieve them from Portuguese bondage. The rulers of Zanzibar, Pemba and Utondwe repudiated their allegiance to the Portuguese in 1653, though they were soon re-subjugated. In 1661 the Omanis and their Swahili allies briefly occupied Mombasa town, though not the impregnable Fort Jesus. In 1670 they went so far as to attack Mozambique and pillage the town.[16]

In this struggle between the Portuguese and the Omanis for dominion over the East African coast, different factions of the Swahili merchant class appeared merely as junior partners of the two combatants. For many of the smaller potentates the only practical policy was to remain on friendly terms with both, swaying with the shifting political winds, and sometimes getting flattened by the whirlwind. It is quite clear from the various engagements during the second half of the seventeenth century that the Swahili ruling classes were themselves unable to stand up to the Portuguese on their own. In 1678 Pate, Siu, Lamu and Manda were reconquered by the Portuguese and their rulers beheaded, but with the appearance of an Omani fleet the Portuguese and their Swahili allies abandoned their positions precipitously, though they took with them considerable loot. In 1687 Pate was again conquered and the captive king prepared to renew his allegiance to the Portuguese and exclude the Omanis, but his country was soon to be liberated without him with the mere appearance of the Omani fleet. The end of the Portuguese era in East Africa came with the capture of Mombasa. In 1694 Pemba, the granary of Mombasa, had rebelled against the Portuguese. In 1696 an Omani fleet, supported by the Swahili of Pate and Lamu, began a three-year siege of Fort Jesus. The less than a hundred Portuguese in the garrison were supported by at least fifteen hundred well-armed Swahili refugees from Faza, Malindi and elsewhere, led by the compradorial Prince of Faza who 'wished to show the world that even the Muslim vassals of your Majesty have Portuguese loyalty'. When the Portuguese relief expedition arrived in December 1698 it found the red flag of Oman flying over the fort.[17]

Oman, however, was undergoing a fundamental socio-economic revolution and consequent civil war. This external drive could therefore not be sustained. The Swahili ruling class, so soon after being relieved of the Portuguese yoke, did not look with favour on the imposition of an Omani yoke. The Omani garrison at Fort Jesus was driven out soon afterwards. The prolonged interregnum in East Africa contributed to the commercial renaissance of the Swahili coast during the eighteenth century when there was a revival of building activities on the coast and a flowering of Swahili commerce, penetrating deep into the Portuguese domain south of Cape Delgado. This tended to confirm the false sense of security the Swahili city-states felt in maintaining their independence by playing off the two external vultures against each other. They failed to realise that in the absence of a more secure and unified economic base than the transit trade, the power vacuum could not be long maintained. The temporary Portuguese reoccupation of Mombasa in 1728–9 emphasised the point, but failed to teach the lesson. This time the Swahili ruling classes were able to expel the Portuguese by themselves though, for good measure, they requested Omani naval support. They were ultimately unable to stand up to the renovated Oman when it came to demand its pound of flesh. The Swahili merchant classes had to accommodate themselves the best way they could as coastal traders and shippers within what was emerging as the Omani commercial empire.[18]

The transformation of Oman

In view of the dominant role that Oman was to play in the history of the Swahili coast during the next two centuries, it is necessary to trace the genesis and nature of the Omani state. Oman's heartland, unlike that of the Swahili coast, was in the interior, in the Green Mountains, the *wadis* or dry valleys irrigated by subterranean canals (*aflaj*), and the desert. The main occupations were agriculture and pastoralism, and the main source of revenue was the produce tax. Such was the economic base of the continental theocracy which was often little more than a tribal confederacy. It was presided over by the Imam, a religious leader rather than a monarch, 'the most considerable' among a number of petty sovereigns who ruled Oman. He was elected by the elite of the society which consisted of the 'chiefs', the 'nobles' and the 'learned', but he had to be confirmed by the 'commons'. Although the imamate represented the unification of Oman and a triumph over fissiparous tribal structures, it was still ephemeral. According to Ibadhi ideology, the post did not need to be filled at all times.[19]

The weakening of Portuguese power in the Indian Ocean permitted this continental theocracy to extend its political control over the coast and to assume a larger role in maritime trade. In a series of wars the Portuguese were forced to surrender their fortified posts one after another, and to permit the Omanis to trade freely in the remaining Portuguese-held ports. In 1650 they were expelled from Muscat, their last stronghold on the Omani coast. Sultan b. Saif (1649–79), the conqueror of Muscat, incurred the odium of the religious party for his worldly activities – he had sent merchants as far as the Red Sea, Iraq, Iran and India to trade on his account – and he had to justify it as part of the holy war 'to supply the demand of the Mussulmans for horses, arms, etc.'[20] His son no longer needed any religious cloak in the pursuit of wealth. These imams, who owed their politico-ideological role to the theocratic constitution, began increasingly to be transformed into merchant princes, diverting part of their profits to date production based on slave labour. The dates were grown on large plantations of 3,000 to 5,000 palms or more, some of which required irrigation and a considerable amount of slave labour. Saif b. Sultan (1692–1711) is said to have owned 1,700 slaves and one-third of all the date palms in Oman, planted 30,000 date and 6,000 coconut palms, and renovated or constructed 17 *aflaj*. This created a demand for agricultural slaves from East Africa, numbering more than a thousand a year, to produce dates for export. During the first decade of the nineteenth century MT$50,000 worth of dates were exported from the Persian Gulf to Bombay.[21]

The emergence of this class of merchant capitalists and landowners who employed slave labour began to transform the political economy of Oman. An important indication of this transformation comes from the Arabic chronicle of Oman, Salil b. Razik's *History of the Imams and Seyyids of Oman*. Whereas during the seventeenth century he repeatedly refers to 'nobles and commons' as the dominant powers in the Omani social formation, which still retained a strong egalitarian element, during the eighteenth century this formula is replaced entirely by a new one, 'merchants and nobles', and consistently in that order, indicating the rise of this new class and its dominant influence in the Omani state. Rival groups within the Ya'rubi dynasty offered commercial privileges to the merchants to attract their support.[22]

The concentration of wealth in the hands of the merchant prince made it incompatible with the Ibadhi politico-religious ideology of an ascetic imam. The growing secularisation and tendency towards temporal power ran counter to the Ibadhi principle of an elected imam. With Saif b. Sultan a ruling dynasty and the principle of patrilineal succession were established. The accession to the imamate of a mere boy who had not even reached the 'age of discretion', and who was elected and deposed four times, made a mockery of the Ibadhi principle. Gradually a glaring cleavage between religious authority and temporal power appeared, with the appointment of a series of regents as de facto rulers.[23]

19

Omani participation in maritime trade was imposing a great strain on the traditional society. The fabric of the essentially tribal society was unable to incorporate these innovations without a social revolution. During the first half of the eighteenth century Oman consequently went through one of the fiercest civil wars recorded in her annals, a war that contributed to the downfall of the Ya'rubi dynasty. The Busaidi dynasty which replaced it in 1741 was quite frankly mercantile and maritime, drawing its strength from oceanic trade rather than from territorial or spiritual overlordship. The founder, Ahmed b. Said (1744–83), was 'first and foremost a merchant and shipowner'. As the traveller C. Niebuhr commented, 'to eke out his scanty revenue, the prince does not disdain to deal himself in trade.' Under this dynasty the separation between spiritual and temporal authority was completed when the spiritual character of the ruler was quietly renounced. Hamad b. Said (1786–92) did not even care to depose the Imam when he assumed the reins of power. Instead he adopted the title *seyyid* (lord), to distinguish the ruling family, giving them corporate dignity and pre-eminence over all other chiefs and grandees. Said b. Sultan (1804–56) underscored the irrelevance of the spiritual post by never seeking an election, and instead he adopted the unabashedly secular title, *sultan*, which signified temporal authority and power. To emphasise the new basis of this political power, Ahmed b. Said had formed a standing army of 1,000 free soldiers, including Baluchi mercenaries, and 1,100 African slaves, rather than rely entirely on the tribal rabble. The seal to this social revolution was set towards the end of the eighteenth century with the shift of the capital from the traditional seat of the imamate at Nazwa in the interior to the metropolitan mercantile seat of the sultanate at Muscat.[24]

This internal transformation manifested itself in the foreign relations of Oman, economic as well as political. Its character correlated with stages in the internal transformation of Oman. Initially Omani activities abroad were characterised by periodic raiding of Portuguese settlements in India, the Persian Gulf and East Africa. The Omanis weakened Portuguese hegemony over the Indian Ocean but apparently made no systematic attempt at conquest and sustained commercial expansion. In East Africa they encouraged Swahili insurrection against Portuguese domination, and their dhows appeared annually with the monsoons, ostensibly to trade, but not averse to raiding the Portuguese and their local allies.[25]

While the first stage of the transformation turned Oman into a raiding naval power, the second stage was to convert her into an expansionist commercial power. The character of Omani ventures abroad increasingly began to take the form of sustained commercial expansion and territorial aggrandisement. The long siege of Mombasa from 1696 to 1698, and the establishment of an Omani administration there upon its capture were a clear indication of this change. A large number of armed merchantmen which had taken part in Omani raids reverted to peaceful commerce by the mid-1730s. Their trade, apart from slaves, was in the less ostentatious commodities of the age-old commerce between East Africa and Arabia and the Persian Gulf, such as food grains and mangrove poles. In return they offered dates, dried fish and Muscat cloth. More lucrative, however, was probably the carrying trade in the western Indian Ocean, exchanging African ivory for Indian cloth, and transporting Indian and British manufactured goods to the Persian Gulf. It was during this period that the Omani merchant class is said to have captured the lucrative trade between Gujarat and Iran.[26] The long-term prosperity of this class, with the Omani ruler at its head, depended therefore on international trade and on the success it achieved in monopolising sections of this trade. Not only was such dependence on foreign trade compromising the economic integrity of Oman but, as we shall see below, its success in monopolising the trade came to depend on the overall British hegemony that was developing over the Indian Ocean.

Although commercial and diplomatic contacts had earlier been established between Oman and those European powers that were competing for hegemony in the Indian Ocean, it was the spillover of Anglo-French rivalry into Asia that began to undermine the political independence of Oman. Struggle for monopoly over the trade of the East involved concessions from oriental potentates. The chartered East India companies, both British and French, were therefore backed by the political power of the European mercantile nations. Rivalry between them was particularly virulent during the second half of the eighteenth century, partly because of the disintegration of the Mughal empire which exposed the naked struggle for political control in India and the Indian Ocean. For Britain, which had emerged as the dominant power in India, the defence of its empire and its arteries of trade became a constant preoccupation. Two of these arteries were the Persian Gulf and the Red Sea, and for both of these Muscat was a regular port of call. For the French Muscat was strategically located: in wartime it was a potential base for overland attack on British India by way of Egypt and as a base to attack British trade routes from Bombay, in peacetime it could be used to undercut British trade pursuing the longer route round the Cape of Good Hope. Thus in January 1799, Napoleon wrote from Cairo to the ruler of Oman that 'as you have always been friendly you must be convinced of our desire to protect all the merchant vessels you may send to Suez.'[27]

However, the British had already struck the preceding October with a treaty whch has been described as 'a decisively pro-British' and 'virtually unilateral treaty.' The Sultan of Oman bound himself not to allow the French or their Dutch allies to have an establishment in his territories, while the British obtained a concession to build a fortified factory. The

Omanis had thus abandoned their long-standing veto against foreign factories on Omani soil. During the war, moreover, the Sultan bound himself not to allow the French to enter the inner cove of Muscat to water, but to anchor outside, and the Omanis agreed to take part with the English in any naval engagement against the French in Omani waters, though not on the high seas. It was stipulated that 'the friend of that Sirkar [the East India Company] is the friend of this [Oman]; and in the same way the enemy of this is to be enemy of that.' The Omani state had thus been induced to surrender its neutrality, at least on paper, and to recognise its subordinate position vis-à-vis Britain. What were all these concessions for? As Captain John Malcolm, who renegotiated and extended this treaty in 1800, put it to the Omani governor:

> What . . . was to become of the famed commerce of Muscat if the harbours of the whole Indian peninsula were to be closed against the merchant-ships of Muscat by the fiat of the paramount power?[28]

The independence of Oman had been sacrified at the altar of commercial profit. The compradorial character of the Omani state had been confirmed.

However, the collapse of Napoleon's Egyptian expedition in 1799 reduced the threat to British India, and many of the concessions wrung from Oman in these treaties were not immediately taken up. Instead, Oman was allowed to assume 'neutrality' during the Anglo-French war so that British trade could continue to flow. Omani shipping was considerably augmented by the purchase of English prize ships at French ports. British Indian ships, which could not be protected by the overstretched navy, adopted the neutral flag of Oman. Two of the best Surat vessels formerly employed in the trade with the Persian Gulf passed into the hands of Muscat Arabs, and one prominent shipowner of Surat held 2,000 tons of shipping at Muscat. It was reported in 1803–4 that Omani Arabs, 'in the course of ten years have increased their tonnage from a number of Dows and Dingeys, and two or three old ships, to upwards of fifty five ships' with a total displacement of between 40,000 and 50,000 tons. Some European merchants at Bombay reported that 'the present shipping of the subjects of the Imam including domiciled Arabs of our own settlements, exceeds the British tonnage of this port.' With this augmented shipping the Arabs had become not only 'the carriers of that part of India which lay between the eastern shores of the Bay of Bengal and the western extremities' of the Persian Gulf and the Red Sea, but also controlled the carrying trade between Indian ports, and threatened to capture the lucrative China trade. At the height of the boom about five-eighths of the whole Persian Gulf trade passed through Muscat. Apart from neutrality the reason advanced for this Omani success was their great competitiveness in freight charges, for it was claimed that they could carry freight at a price between a half and one-third of what a British ship could.[29]

The lamentations of British shipping capital in India, harking back to the monopolistic Navigation Laws of yesteryear, received scant attention from the representatives of British industrial capital at the beginning of the nineteenth century. The neutral flag of Oman not only provided protection from French raids but also lowered transportation costs for British commodities. And for all these services the Omani compradorial state demanded only 5 per cent import duty, and even less if Muslim or Arab agents were used.[30]

However, this commercial boom at Muscat, especially between 1798 and 1806, was based on the shifting sands of Anglo-French warfare over which the Omani merchants could have had no control. While the war lasted the Sultan's exchequer prospered with an annual revenue of MT\$112,500 from import duties alone. The merchant class at Muscat flourished, 'some of them possessing capitals of a million dollars.' But with peace came a massive desertion of the Omani flag by Indian vessels and the drying up of the sources of cheap English prizes. By 1817 the old ships had begun to decay. The balloon had burst. The restless merchant prince was again in search of new commercial monopolies, new niches in what had become a British lake.[31]

One of these niches was the Persian Gulf where maritime Arabs on both the Arabian and Iranian sides, poorly endowed with means of livelihood, had been supplementing their incomes with an active role in commerce from time immemorial. By the late eighteenth century these Arabs, under the leadership of the Qawasima, had begun to challenge Oman's commercial dominance in the western Indian Ocean. The ruler of Oman, on the other hand, sought to enhance Omani dominance over the Gulf, aiming 'to create a tightly controlled maritime state' embracing both shores of the Gulf of Oman, the major Persian Gulf islands and the Arab coast, and to make Muscat the sole distribution centre for goods from abroad. This maritime commercial rivalry ran parallel to the struggle on land between the expanding Wahhabi power of Saudi Arabia and the Omani sultanate.[32]

British government policy towards these struggles astride one of the major arteries of trade was governed by its position in India. For the British the Persian Gulf was an area which had to be kept open for their commerce and free of any power which could threaten their empire in India. As regards the strictly commercial rivalry between the Omani merchant class and the Qawasima, the British government was not particularly interested in underwriting Omani monopoly any more than it had been to support British shipping capital. In fact the Secretary to the Government of Bombay argued that it was the Omani drive to monopolise the trade that was primarily responsible for maritime warfare in the Persian Gulf, and that this had given a stimulus to piracy and had endangered British trade. Thus, when in 1804 the ruler of Oman called on the British to help him sweep the Gulf clear of the Qawasima, Bombay turned a deaf ear, and he paid with his dear life in the unsuccessful campaign that he conducted unilaterally. The British studiously avoided hostilities with the Qawasima unless they were fired on first, and when they did get embroiled in the conflict in 1806, they quickly concluded a treaty that, among other things, made a provision allowing the Qawasima to frequent British Indian ports directly. In 1809, when they were again involved in military action against the Qawasima, a conflict that led to the destruction of a large portion of the Qawasima merchant fleet, the British tried a temporary ban on timber exports to the Gulf from India. However, since the object of the expedition had been to safeguard and not destroy commerce, the ban was not enforced for long.[33]

Nevertheless, the British government's concern for the security of India meant that it was vitally interested in the 'independence' of Oman from either French or Wahhabi control, and in her dependence on Britain. The Governor General of India wrote that the independence of Oman was important in Britain's interests for political and economic reasons, and since the Qawasima had allied with the Wahhabis, 'the preservation of that independence appears to turn upon the cooperation of the British power against the Joasmee [Qawasima] pirates.' An additional consideration was the need to counteract the influence of the French, who had signed a commercial treaty with Oman in 1807. While the British government refused to accept the Sultan's interpretation of the Anglo-Omani treaties as amounting to an offensive and defensive alliance, it was nevertheless prepared to underwrite the survival of its surrogate to ensure British dominance over the area. Between 1806 and 1820 the British, with the ready cooperation of their junior partner, the Omanis, attacked the Qawasima three times, finally breaking the backbone of their resistance against the Omanis and their British overlords. The subordinate role played by the Omani forces in all these engagements further confirmed the depths to which the Omani state had sunk by 1820. The General Treaty of Peace with what were called the Trucial States concluded at the end of these hostilities excluded all reference to the Omani role in the Persian Gulf.[34] The British had finally decided to come out from behind the Omani veil.

The subjugation of the Swahili coast

Oman was a monsoon-using alien power dependent on easy communication with the homeland. With the fragmented commercial economy of the Swahili coast, and with each city-state controlling its own narrow hinterland as well as sharing in the coastal trade, the Omanis needed control over strategic points along the coast to dominate its trade. Mombasa appeared to be an ideal headquarters, with the impregnable Fort Jesus and a secure harbour dominating the northern approaches to

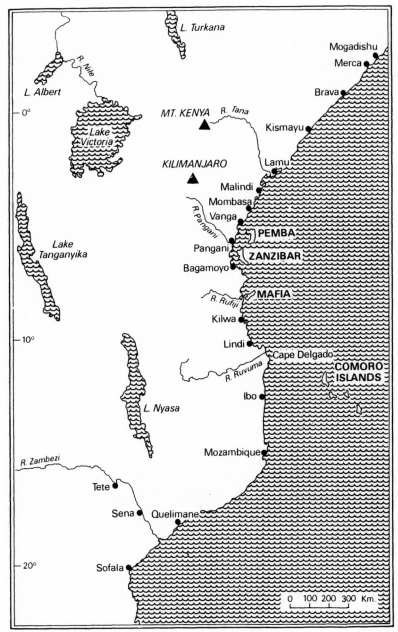

Map 1.3   The East African coast

25

the coast. It was in fact the first seat of Omani governorship. However, the spillover of the Omani social revolution to East Africa was to deprive the new Busaidi dynasty of control over this port. The Mazrui governors of Mombasa appointed by the previous Omani dynasty, the Ya'rubi, refused to offer their allegiance. Instead they attempted to indigenise their power base and to embark upon their own Mombasa-based expansion to resist the inevitable Omani invasion. The most stable base of Mazrui rule rested on an intricate hierarchy of relationships between the Mazrui dynasty and the rival Swahili confederacies of Mombasa between whom the Mazrui held the balance, and on a system of patronage that linked the various Swahili and Mijikenda 'tribes' of the immediate hinterland on whom depended the economic well-being of the city.[35] These relationships proved sturdy enough to withstand nearly a century of struggle, but without a more secure economic base, and before long-distance trade links were forged with the deep interior, the immediate hinterland of Mombasa provided too narrow an economic base to withstand the full weight of Omani pressure.

Unable to dislodge the Mazrui from Mombasa immediately, the Busaidi were forced to turn to Zanzibar which offered good sheltered harbours and a weak Shirazi dynasty which had learned during the preceding century to swim with the changing political tides. After initially resisting the Portuguese in 1509, Zanzibar is said to have remained friendly to them, even during the 1631 revolt by Mombasa. However, in 1652 the kings of Zanzibar and Pemba destroyed Portuguese settlements and asked for help from Oman, though they were subdued the following year. With the capture of Mombasa by the Omanis in 1699 Zanzibar fell under Omani control, but when Mombasa was reoccupied in 1728 Zanzibar is stated to have offered allegiance to the Portuguese once again. However, this was short-lived. The following year, Zanzibar joined the other Swahili city-states in the final overthrow of Portuguese rule over the Swahili coast.[36] By 1744 the Omanis had installed their governor but the local ruler, the *Mwinyi Mkuu*, was retained as the chief of the indigenous subjects. From their Zanzibari base the Busaidi continued their struggle against the Mazrui. During the eighteenth century they were unable to subjugate Mombasa militarily, though the latter was forced to pay tribute more than once to the Busaidi. But it was the economic struggle for hinterlands that was to prove decisive in the nineteenth century for the subjugation of Mombasa and the whole coastline, and the erection of the Omani commercial empire.[37]

The Kilwa area was not as critical in the Busaidi–Mazrui struggle though it was to form one of the bases of the commercial empire.[38] The Lamu archipelago, on the other hand, was much more critical, and it was here that the tide turned in the struggle. This was the heartland of Swahili resistance to the Omanis just as previously it had been a centre of opposition to the Portuguese. The extension of the conflict into the archipelago set off disastrous internecine warfare during which, according to the 'History of Pate', 'for five years they were not able to cultivate or to trade or do any work whatsoever. So a great famine raged.' The decline of Pate culminated in the disastrous battle of Shela in 1813 when the Busaidi-backed Lamu routed the combined forces from Pate and Mombasa. As a result Mombasa had to surrender any pretence to control the rich hinterland of the Lamu archipelago, though the Busaidis found it by no means easy to assert their dominance. Calamities at home may have driven the people of the archipelago to seafaring pursuits, acting as coastal traders all along the coast, and even settling abroad. During the first half of the nineteenth century they were found settled along the coast of southern Tanzania and northern Mozambique, as 'the most recommendable' local merchants, and in places as chiefs.[39]

The final act of the struggle was to be played out at Mombasa itself, and it was to demonstrate once more the proverbial weakness of the Swahili merchant class, but also the compradorial character of the Omani state. In 1823 the Omanis captured Pemba, Mombasa's granary, a move which a British naval officer, Lieutenant Boteler, believed was 'a great step towards the subjugation of that power by the Imam'. In 1825 they captured the northern Mrima ports, Mombasa's last commercial outlets outside its territories; this deprived Mombasa of a share of the lucrative trade of what was to become the centrepiece of the Omani commercial empire. The bell of Mombasa's independence had begun to toll loudly in the ears of the Mazrui who began desperately to look around for external allies. Johanna in the Comoros was itself too weak to be of much help, and the Qawasima of Ras al-Khayma had just been subjugated by the paramount British power. The Mazrui, who in essence differed little in their economic interests and world outlook, therefore, did not hesitate to embrace the same foreign power. They had offered to place themselves under British overlordship as early as 1807–8, and in 1823 they again begged for the British flag so that

> beneath its protecting shade we may defy our enemies. As the lamb trembles at the lion's roar, so will the Imam shrink from that which is the terror of the world.[40]

This was a rather neat analogy of the relationship between the Mazrui, the Busaidi and the British.

Through the impetuous mouth of a Royal Navy captain, W.F. Owen, the British lion did indeed seem to roar. In 1824 he negotiated with the Mazrui an unauthorised declaration of a British protectorate over Mombasa. Under the terms of the convention Owen not only guaranteed the 'independence' of Mombasa and the perpetuation of the Mazrui dynasty under British suzerainty, but also promised to reinstate it in its

27

Plate 3   Fort Jesus, Mombasa, overlooking the town and the harbour, c.1857

former possessions, Pemba, Lamu, Pate, and the Mrima coast as far south as the Pangani river. In return the Mazrui agreed to abolish the slave trade, a policy in line with what had become the constant preoccupation of the rising industrial capitalists in Britain. They also offered the British half the customs revenue of Mombasa, and freedom to British subjects to trade with the interior. This seemed to offer the prospect of a new market for British goods. As the British Governor of Mauritius, Sir Lowry Cole, put it:

> I am inclined to consider it as presenting a favourable means for putting down the Slave Trade as well as for opening a commerce with the eastern coast of Africa which might ultimately be of advantage to the mercantile interests of Great Britain. . . .[41]

For good measure Captain Owen used the old and potent argument of the threat of French intervention, and he capped it all with an ideological justification that barely camouflaged the material interests of the rising British capitalism of which the philanthropists and the British navy were objectively the vanguard:

> It is to me as clear as the sun that God has prepared the dominion of East Africa for the only nation on the earth which had public virtue enough to govern it for its own benefit . . . I have taken my own line to the honour of God and my King and to the benefit of my country and of all mankind.[42]

28

Owen, however, was a premature manifestation of British capitalism; it sought at this stage an empire without boundaries, economic domination through free trade, and indirect political control through subordinate states rather than the heavy burden of a colonial empire.

Abolition of the slave trade was certainly high on the agenda of the British government at this time. It had just negotiated with the Sultan the Moresby Treaty which prohibited the export of slaves to the Americas and European colonies in the Indian Ocean. But the Omani governor of Lamu seems to have understood the British strategy of restricting and ultimately abolishing the slave trade better than Owen himself. As he shrewdly put it, the unification of the East African coast under the Sultan was essential, 'for not until then will the British have power to put an effectual termination to the Slave Trade.'[43] As regards the wider strategy in the western Indian Ocean, the British government had already chosen its surrogate. It therefore had little interest in jeopardising a laboriously constructed strategy for British paramountcy, in which Oman played a central role, by supporting a smaller power in East Africa. In 1823 the Governor of Bombay had replied to the Mazrui request for British protection by saying that 'fidelity to our engagements with His Highness the Imam of Muscat would prevent our acceding to your proposal.' When Owen declared the protectorate anyway, the Bombay governor argued strenuously that the Sultan of Oman:

> has always been our faithful and cordial ally and not only has he cooperated with us in all our attempts to put down piracy in the Persian Gulf, but has on more than one occasion refrained from enterprises that promised to be profitable to him, because we represented to him that his engaging in them would be inconsistent with our policy.[44]

Faced with the outstretched hands of two suitors clamouring for protection under their hegemony, the British accepted that of their old and faithful protégés, the Busaidi, who were not only already subservient to British power, but were also still capable of subjugating Mombasa to their own, and ultimately, therefore, to British overlordship.

British protection over Mombasa was therefore withdrawn in 1826, but anxious not to provide an opening for the French the British government recommended a policy of conciliation with the Mazrui to the Omanis. Deprived of British support, the Mazrui were now forced to compromise. They were prepared to acknowledge formal Omani suzerainty and resume payment of tribute, but they demanded a confirmation of their hereditary claims to the governorship and refused to surrender Fort Jesus. Although the Sultan was unable to take Fort Jesus by force of arms, and unable to keep it when he took it by treachery, the economic blockade that he imposed on Mombasa began to create severe strains in the network of alliances which had formed the basis of Mombasa's independence. Its collapse facilitated the final coup de grace in 1837. The leading Mazrui were either deported or fled to establish their own petty states along the Kenya coast. However, the merchant class of Mombasa, consisting of the other Arabs, the Swahili and their Mijikenda allies, were incorporated within the emerging Omani commercial empire.[45]

Conclusion

The common experience of Portuguese oppression had brought together the Swahili and Omani merchant classes in a partnership to overthrow Portuguese rule north of Cape Delgado. But that partnership was unequal. Though they pretended to walk on high stilts of political independence, the Swahili merchant classes were politically too fragmented and economically too dependent on international trade to stand on their own feet. The Omanis, on the other hand, had started from the interior which provided a more secure economic and political base for their independence. However, with the rise of the merchant class to political dominance the centre of economic and political gravity shifted to the coast, and the economy and the state became increasingly dependent on international trade. This shift, moreover, coincided with the rise of capitalism in Europe and the inauguration of an epoch of world domination by capital. The merchant class flourished with the expansion of international trade that the rise of capitalism entailed. But the Omani state that they ruled was simultaneously subordinated, being converted into a compradorial state that acted as an economic and political agent of the foremost capitalist state of the era, Britain.

Through the agency of Omani expansionism the East African coast thus began to be integrated, if indirectly, into the international capitalist-dominated system. However, other economic forces, emanating also from the development of capitalism, began to impinge directly on the East African coast from the last quarter of the eighteenth century, more effectively integrating it into the system, economically and ultimately politically.

Notes

1. The word 'Swahili' is derived from the Arabic word which means the coast. It is used to refer to Kiswahili, a Bantu language with a considerable number of Arabic, Persian and Indian loanwords, betraying its maritime and mercantile history. It is also used to refer to Waswahili, coastal people who speak the language and are generally Muslim, and to the coastal Muslim culture generally. See Nicholls, p. 19; Prins (1965), pp. 24–7, 38–49; Whiteley (1969), p. vii; Krumm, p. 2.

2. Kirk, pp. 263-7; McMaster, pp. 13-24; Datoo (1974), pp. 23-33.
3. Sheriff (1975a), pp. 12-13.
4. ibid., p. 11; Martin and Ryan, p. 73. Martin and Ryan have gathered evidence to show a continuation of the slave trade between the tenth and the eighteenth centuries. While this is indisputable, there is little evidence to show that the *scale* of the trade was comparable to the two major periods of the slave trade, the seventh to ninth centuries, and the eighteenth to nineteenth centuries. Austen's attempt to quantify the slave trade is based on inadequate data, and has little virtue other than its provision of a total figure for the East African slave trade of dubious authenticity with which to compare the West African slave trade. See Chapter 2, below, for a fuller discussion of Austen's figures.
5. Strandes, pp. 89-94; Sheriff (1975a), pp. 17-18.
6. Freeman-Grenville (ed.) (1962a), p. 19.
7. ibid., p. 2.
8. Mathew, p. 96; Chau Ju Kua, p. 130; Wheatley, p. 97; Strandes, p. 90; Garlake, p. 89.
9. Freeman-Grenville (ed.) (1962a), pp. 133-4.
10. Garlake, p. 2; Sheriff (1975a), pp. 15, 19; Strandes, pp. 88-91.
11. Panikkar, p. 13; Strandes, pp. 56-8.
12. Datoo and Sheriff, p. 102; Strandes, pp. 97-8.
13. Strandes, pp. 71-3, 119-26, 39, 45, 106-10.
14. ibid., pp. 114-30; Boxer and Azevedo, p. 28.
15. Strandes, pp. 312, 319.
16. ibid., pp. 228-30; Boxer and Azevedo, pp. 47-8.
17. Strandes, pp. 232, 237-8, 240; Boxer and Azevedo, pp. 50-1, 57-69.
18. Miles, pp. 221, 250; Strandes, p. 291; Alpers (1966), p. 156.
19. Wilkinson (1972), pp. 69, 75-6; Salil, pp. 46, 51, 53, 78, 84; Niebuhr, Vol. 2, p. 113; Halliday, p. 267.
20. Salil, pp. 65, 69, 89, 92, 100; Bathurst (1967), pp. 137, 205-6.
21. Salil, p. 93; Bathurst (1967), pp. 205-6.
22. Salil, pp. 51, 57, 84, 90, 100, 176, 200, 216-18.
23. Bathurst (1972), pp. 103-6.
24. Salil, pp. 152, 202, 342; Wilkinson (1972), pp. 77-8; Kelly (1972), p. 109; Bathurst (1972), pp. 101-2; Phillips (1967), p. 66. Said b. Sultan, however, continued to be referred to, incorrectly, as the Imam in British sources well into the nineteenth century. Nicholls, pp. 22, 101. Frederick Cooper seems to reject this whole analysis of social transformation, but presents little evidence to refute it or an alternative interpretation for the overthrow of the Ya'rubi dynasty (unless it is merely one of a series of 'communal feuds'), and for the secularisation of the ruler's title. See Cooper (1977), pp. 30-3.
25. Strandes, pp. 239-40.
26. Miles, p. 237; Strandes, p. 266; Bathurst (1967), p. 137.
27. Mukherjee, pp. 110-12, 118; Coupland (1938), pp. 84-6.
28. Coupland (1938), pp. 95-8; Phillips (1967), pp. 70, 72; Nicholls, p. 105.
29. Nicholls, p. 98; Maurizi, p. 30; IOR, P/174/16, nos 60-71; P/174/8, nos 58-72; P/419/41, nos 49, 52, 54.
30. Gavin (1965), p. 19; Nicholls, pp. 97-9.

31. Gavin (1965), p. 20; Miles, p. 270; IOR, P/174/28; Smee, in IOR, MR, Misc. 586, entries for 23 February and 1 April 1811.
32. Nicholls, p. 98; Winder, p. 35.
33. Winder, p. 37.
34. Coupland (1938), p. 116.
35. Berg (1968), pp. 35–56.
36. Strandes, pp. 111, 118, 136, 199, 211, 228, 275–6, 285–93.
37. Nicholls, p. 126, Gray (1962a), pp. 83–5. The existing histories of the Mazrui seem to pass over the less glorious periods in silence. A version of it appears in Freeman–Grenville (ed.)(1962a), pp. 213–19, but see also p. 193; Alpers (1966), p. 155; Freeman–Grenville (1965), p.128.
38. See Table 5.1.
39. Nicholls, pp. 122, 125; Alpers (1966), pp. 226–7; Loarer, 'Ports au sud et au nord de Zanguebar', in ANSOM, OI, 2/10.
40. Coupland (1938), pp. 225, 221–2; Boteler, Vol. 2, pp. 1–2; Nicholls, p. 132; Gray (1957), passim.
41. Coupland (1938), pp. 244, 236.
42. ibid., p. 238.
43. ibid., p. 235.
44. ibid., pp. 260–1; Nicholls, pp. 141–2.
45. Coupland (1938), pp. 272–3; Berg (1971), pp. 133–7.

Two

The Transformation
of the Slave Sector

The process of integration of East Africa into the world capitalist system from the last third of the eighteenth century onwards distinguishes the modern history of East Africa from the preceding eras. It is this specificity that tends to be ignored in colonial and neo-colonial histories, especially when dealing with the so-called Arab slave trade. The British imperial historian, Sir Reginald Coupland, for example, argued that the slave trade runs 'like a scarlet thread' through nearly two millennia of East African history, without paying any attention to the historical specificity of the different phases of that trade, the different modes of production to which they were linked, and the specific nature of the slave sector at different times. He went on to conclude that although the annual volume of the East African slave trade never rivalled the numbers involved in the West African slave trade during the seventeenth and eighteenth centuries, the total number of Africans exported from East Africa during the two millennia 'must have been prodigious'. 'Asia, not Europe', cries Coupland, 'bears the chief responsibility for the damage done by the slave trade to East Africa' – a neat apology for the capitalist role in that trade at its height in the nineteenth century. It was the Arab slave trade, he asserts, that 'intensified . . . barbarism' in Africa, and 'closed the door to all external aids they [Africans] needed to stimulate their progress' – a justification, to cap it all, for European colonialism.[1]

Although writing forty years later, Ralph A. Austen prefers to stick to the well-trodden path blazed by Coupland. He tries to quantify Coupland's assertions as is the modern vogue. Although he admits that all the sources before the last quarter of the eighteenth century 'tell us virtually nothing about the absolute quantity of slaves', he nevertheless proceeds to assign 'relative indices' to different periods on the basis of the more precise figures for the nineteenth century. We are thus presented with a formidable table of the slave trade from East Africa since the rise of Islam, translating Coupland's softer prose into apparently more solid

33

statistics. The only virtue of this exercise in the 'numbers game' is to conjure up a figure for the 'Islamic slave trade' from East Africa over the thirteen centuries that totals over four million. When added to the estimates of 'the Islamic slave trade' from West and North-east Africa, Austen has the satisfaction of arriving at a grand hotel of 17 million over a period of thirteen centuries as compared with 12.5 million taken by the Europeans from West Africa during two centuries.[2]

Although Austen adds contours to Coupland's 'scarlet thread', they are based on flimsy empirical evidence for the period before the eighteenth century, and they take little account of the different modes of production articulating with the East African coast at different times. By laying emphasis on the 'continuity' of the so-called Islamic slave trade, both have failed to recognise the fundamental transformation of the slave sector from the last third of the eighteenth century, and its vital link with the rise of capitalism in the North Atlantic region.

A more promising reappraisal of the East African slave trade was undertaken by L. Sakkarai within a more explicit theoretical framework. Unfortunately his analysis for the period preceding the nineteenth century is marred by a conception of merchant capitalism which is both theoretically unsound and empirically unsupported. Merchant capital has undoubtedly operated on the East African coast throughout the past two millennia. However, Sakkarai's attempt to associate this throughout the period predominantly with the operation of the slave trade – a specific form of merchant capitalism – is incorrect. He argues that the slave mode was the earliest mode of production and that slaves were the first form of commodity, that throughout the period the principal reliance of merchant capital was on the slave trade, and that it was only in the latter part of the nineteenth century, with the Industrial Revolution, that other commodities began to displace slaves as the principal commodity.[3] All these assertions are quite obviously contrary to all the available empirical evidence for the East African coast.

Sakkarai, however, is not oblivious to the connection between the slave trade and the rise of capitalism and he makes his most positive contribution to the understanding of that relationship in East Africa during the nineteenth century. He shows how slave and 'legitimate' trade were so intertwined that the former could not be abolished without jeopardising the latter; hence British prevarication about the suppression of the slave trade in East Africa during the nineteenth century.[4]

The period from the last third of the eighteenth century onwards was one during which the slave trade did play an important, though not necessarily a dominant role in the economic history of East Africa. In analysing the slave phenomenon during this period we have to bear in mind two important considerations. The first is the assimilation of the East African economy, including the slave sector, into the expanding world capitalist system. The second is the fundamental transformation of the slave sector as a result of the restrictions placed on the export of slaves; this had the effect of internalising that sector, transforming it from one that was primarily based on the export of slaves to one based predominantly on production by slave labour within East Africa of commodities for export, to self-righteous England as well as to other parts of the world. This transformation was accompanied by a shift in the character of the Omani commercial bourgeoisie which, though it persisted in commerce and even found new outlets for it, was nevertheless gradually being converted into primarily a landowning class. Few of its members, however, realised that the plantation economy they were establishing, though lucrative at the time, was a treacherous trap which would result in their impoverishment and indebtedness within a few decades.

The northern slave trade

To the colonial and neo-colonial historians, as to the British abolitionists, Arabia was a convenient bottomless pit that allegedly consumed any number of slaves that their lively imagination cared to conjure up. The abolitionists, of course, were trying to sustain the anti-slavery campaign to clear the decks for the maturation of capitalism, and to mobilise their people, benumbed by the vast dimensions of the West African slave trade, to support their crusade. A series of wild estimates of the export of slaves to Arabia thus grew up in the fertile minds of the crusaders where they seemed to flourish more wonderfully than in the deserts of Arabia.[5] No serious examination was attempted to see where such numbers could have been absorbed, and what economic conditions would have permitted the absorption of such large numbers in the sparsely populated areas of Arabia and the Gulf. A British naval surgeon, J. Prior, who visited Kilwa in 1812, commented that 'at present the demand is confined to the Arabs, who do not take many', and a report in 1826 asserted that 'the present export of slaves from the . . . possessions of the Imaum is very trifling'.[6]

To determine the dimensions of the northern demand for slaves, it is necessary to understand the uses to which slaves were put. The social transformation of Oman into a mercantile state and the expansion of slave-based date production from *c.* 1700 had created a demand for agricultural slaves. It is extremely difficult to arrive at an estimate of the annual demand for such slaves in Oman. The only clue is the statement in the Omani chronicle that Imam Saif b. Sultan (1692–1711) owned 1,700 slaves and one-third of all the date palms in Oman.[7] As the biggest landowner and perhaps the individual most involved in commerce, the Imam probably had a higher proportion of slaves to date palms than the smaller peasants and interior tribesmen. He may also have had a proportionately

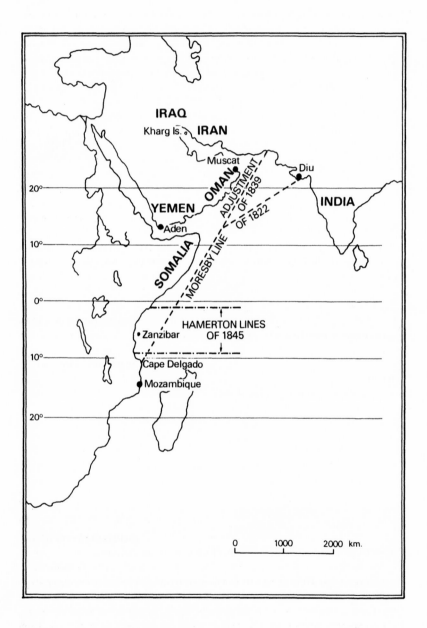

Map 2.1   The East African slave trade

larger number of domestic slaves, who were presumably included in the total number of slaves owned by him. Assuming, nevertheless, the ratio of 1:3, the slave population of Oman at the beginning of the eighteenth century would have been about 5,000. Assuming further an attrition rate of about 10 per cent[8], the annual demand for slaves in Oman would have been about 500. There are no precise quantitative data for the trade except a reference to between two and four large Omani ships which bought slaves from East Africa apparently on royal account, apart from about '300 blacks' exported on ships locally built in East Africa.[9] The numbers may have grown during the eighteenth century as the social revolution was consummated. Whatever may have been the absolute figure for the eighteenth century, however, there seems to be little evidence for any significant increase in the demand during the nineteenth century when Oman appears to have been economically stagnant or declining, particularly with the migration of many well-to-do merchants and landowners and the transfer of the capital to Zanzibar.

African slaves were apparently not used in agricultural production in Iran, although they were widely used in maritime activities in the Persian Gulf. Africans were ubiquitous among dhow crews of the western Indian Ocean during the nineteenth century, but there is little quantitative evidence for the number of slaves absorbed in seafaring and in the docks to service Indian Ocean commerce. Africans also constituted a sizeable proportion of pearl divers in the Gulf who were estimated to number between 27,000 and 30,000 in the mid-nineteenth century. An early twentieth-century survey suggests that about one-third of the divers were Africans.[10]

Slaves were also used in the army. Although warfare in Oman appears to have been based primarily on tribal levies, the secularisation of the Omani state and the weakening of religious and tribal loyalties did suggest the need for a loyal standing army under the Busaidi. Thus Ahmed b. Said purchased 1,000 East African slaves at one time in the 1740s. However, the standing army appears to have been small, and the more prominent component, especially during the nineteenth century, appears to have been Baluchi mercenaries. In 1802 it consisted of 300 slaves and 1,700 Baluchis, Sindhis and Arabs, and in 1809 there were 2,000 mercenaries, but there is no mention of slaves at this time.[11]

A larger number of unproductive slaves were absorbed in the domestic sector to perform menial domestic chores or as concubines. The demand was for young slaves to be groomed in the household. In 1831 their ages ranged between 10 and 14, and evidence from slave captures suggests a fair balance between the sexes.[12] We have no estimates of the size of this population. During the eighteenth century it may have been growing as Omani society was being transformed with the emergence of a wealthy merchant class. The migration of part of this class to Zanzibar after the

37

commercial crash in Oman at the end of the Napoleonic war may have led to stagnation or decline in the annual demand for such slaves.

The rough estimates for each of the uses of slaves are intended to provide only an idea of the magnitude of the demand for slaves against which the scattered numerical estimates by contemporary observers may be judged. We are fortunate in possessing some very precise quantitative data about the slave trade at the receiving end collected by British officials who cannot be accused of trying to minimise the Arab slave trade. According to these officials Muscat and Sur were 'the principal, if not only primary ports to which all slaves . . . were brought, and whence they are carried into Turkey [i.e. Turkish-controlled Iraq], Persia, Scinde, the Arabian states', and even India.[13] The British Resident in the Gulf reported in 1831 that normally 1,400 to 1,700 slaves were imported into Muscat, although during the preceding season only 1,150 to 1,200 were imported, including 250 to 300 who were smuggled. Of these slaves three-quarters were imported from 'Sowahel or the coast of [East] Africa', the remainder being Ethiopians. In 1830 over half of the slaves, i.e. about 500 East African slaves, were re-exported to the Gulf, while the remaining 400 were absorbed within Oman.[14]

In 1841 the British kept a register at the strategic island of Kharg of all the slave dhows passing to the northern end of the Gulf. Although the Gulf slave traffic normally started from around the beginning of July, the register itself began on the nineteenth of the month. By the end of the slave season 118 boats had passed, carrying a total of 1,217 slaves of whom 640 were females and 577 males. Most of these slaves were re-exports from Muscat and Sur or via third ports, and only one boat with twelve slaves apparently came directly from 'Sowahel'.[15] The register does not make a distinction between East African and Ethiopian slaves, but assuming the proportion given in 1831, and after making allowance for the first eighteen days of July, we get about 1,000 East African slaves reaching the northern end of the Gulf.

A most unfortunate gap remains in the data for the trade of Sur, the other, but smaller, port importing slaves directly from East Africa. However, its re-export to Kharg Island in 1841 was roughly in the proportion of 7:10 compared with Muscat. Assuming that such a proportion held true for the total slave trade, it would appear that the total number of East African slaves imported into Muscat and Sur in 1830 was about 1,500, or 'normally' between 1,800 and 2,200. Since these were the 'only primary ports' for the slave trade from East Africa to Oman and the Gulf, the dimensions of the Omani slave trade were much more modest than hitherto assumed by colonial and modern historians.

East African slaves were also imported into the Red Sea region. Some were later re-exported to the East. For example, in 1835 three Mahra dhows were intercepted at the Gujarat port of Porbandar carrying

Table 2.1 *The northern slave trade, 1831 and 1841*

Muscat, 1831	*No. of slaves*	*Kharg Island, 1841*	*No. of dhows*	*No. of slaves*
No. of slaves re-exported to:		Imported from:		
Qawasima ports	180	Qawasima ports	21	168
Bushire/Basra	245	Muscat	30	390
Bahrain	210	Sur	29	279
		Lingeh	23	253
		Sohar	7	82
Total no. of slaves retained in Oman	515–565	'Sowahel'	1	12
		Others	7	33
Total	1,150–1,200	*Total*	118	1,217
Minus estimate of 25 per cent imported from Ethiopia	288–300	Allowance for eighteen days not recorded		120
Total of slaves imported from East Africa	862–900	*Grand total*		1,337
East African slaves retained in Oman	386–424	Minus estimate of 25 per cent imported from Ethiopia		334
		Total of slaves imported from East Africa		1,003

Sources: Wilson to Norris, 28 January 1831, MA, 1/1830–31; Robertson to Willoughby, 4 March 1842, MA, 78/1841–2, pp. 346–62.

39

seventy-nine slaves.[16] Some, however, were locally absorbed, and they formed pockets of African population in southern Arabia. The former headquarters of the National Liberation Front of South Yemen was at a place called Zinjibar which, as the name suggests, was formerly populated by black people. However, the number of slaves imported from East Africa was probably small, partly because the region was closer to Ethiopia, another major source of slaves. In 1840 the French Consul at Jeddah reported 500 East African slaves entering the Red Sea.[17]

The demand for slaves in the more densely populated India, which had its own fairly large poor population, was probably very small. In 1838 only twenty-six slaves were imported into the main Kutch port of Mandvi which, before being superseded by Bombay, was the Indian port with the largest trade with East Africa. They were for the most part domestic slaves brought by returning Indian merchants from East Africa.[18] In 1809 Henry Salt had witnessed the export of 500 slaves from Mozambique to the three Portuguese colonies in India, and in 1841 it was reported that 'in former years the number of slaves imported into the three Portuguese settlements . . . averaged from 250 to 300 per annum'. But this trade appears to have suffered a decline, so that by the late 1830s the annual import amounted to only thirty-five slaves. The small dimensions of the East African slave trade to India are confirmed by the size of the African population in Indian territories with closest contact with the East African coast. In 1837 the total African population in the province of Kathiawar was only 550, and the Portuguese port of Diu had an African population of between 200 and 225 in 1841. Various censuses and other reports for the whole Presidency of Bombay between 1848 and 1881 give an African ('Sidi') population of only 700 to 1,200.[19]

If we allow for an annual total of about 1,000 slaves from East Africa for the Red Sea and the Indian markets, we shall arrive at an aggregate of about 3,000 slaves being annually exported north from East Africa during the first half of the nineteenth century. This estimate comes fairly close to that of E.B. Martin and T.C.I. Ryan, based on slightly different data. They estimate an average of 2,500 for the period 1770–1829, and they suggest an increase to 3,500 for the 1830s. Austen's estimate is also fairly modest for this period, giving an average of 2,250 per annum for the period 1700–1815.[20]

What is contentious, however, is the rising trend of the export of slaves to the north during the nineteenth century which both Martin and Ryan as well as Austen attempt to project. The former suggest a rise to an annual export of 4,000 during the 1840s, and to 6,500 during 1850–73. Austen, on the other hand, suggests an annual average of about 6,625 for the whole period 1815–75.[21] I find little evidence for any increase in the prosperity of the importing region, and a lot suggesting stagnation and even decline in mercantile prosperity especially in Oman after the

Napoleonic Wars. On the other hand, there is quite substantial warming up of British anti-slavery sentiments under Palmerston from the 1840s onwards, and with it the bloating of slave trade estimates. For example, the actual figure of 1,217 slaves who passed through Kharg Island in 1840–1 is successively blown up to 4,000 to 5,000. Martin and Ryan quote the British Consul in Zanzibar, C.P. Rigby, writing in 1861, giving his estimate of 4,500 for the 1840–1 period. Both Austen, and Martin and Ryan indiscriminately use all these figures in their statistical exercises.[22] The use of more numerous bloated estimates, compared with the single actual count, naturally has the effect of shifting the average towards the inflated figures. Curiously, neither Martin and Ryan nor Austen take account of the evidence presented by slave captures during the fairly comprehensive anti-slavery campaign launched by the British navy in the late 1860s (see Table 6.1). What is remarkable is that the number of slaves liberated annually during three consecutive years remained fairly constant at about a thousand. These figures suggest, if anything, a declining curve for the northern slave trade compared with the early part of the nineteenth century.[23]

The northern slave trade, therefore, appears to have reached its plateau during the eighteenth century when the demand for slaves in the productive sector was at its peak. In the unproductive domestic and military sectors, the demand may have peaked during the commercial boom that the Omani merchant class experienced during the Napoleonic Wars at the end of the eighteenth and the beginning of the nineteenth century. With the bursting of that bubble by 1810, and the migration of a considerable section of the Omani merchant class to Zanzibar, conditions were hardly auspicious for the northern slave trade to thrive.[24]

The French slave trade and the re-subjugation of Kilwa, 1770–1822

The northern slave trade which had developed within the pre-capitalist modes of production in south-western Asia had a fairly limited potential for expansion beyond the dimensions attained during the eighteenth century. Communities of people of African origin are scattered along the non-African parts of the littoral of the western Indian Ocean, but they do not constitute substantial national minorities in any of the countries of this coast as they so conspicuously do in the Americas.

On the other hand, from the 1770s eastern Africa was drawn into the vortex of the genesis of capitalism, and experienced what Marx has described as 'the rosy dawn of the era of capitalist production'.[25] The development of sugar plantations in the French Mascarene islands of Ile de France (Mauritius) and Bourbon (Réunion) was an extension of similar developments in the West Indies which fed into the infamous

41

Atlantic triangular trade. These developments sapped the vitality of East Africa's trade with the north, initially sharpening the contradiction between the northern and the French slave trade. The northern slave trade could not ultimately withstand the tide of nascent capitalism, and the Arab merchant class therefore had to accept the new compradorial role being assigned to them in the new global capitalist system.

French demand for slaves was modest in the first decades after the 1730s and was largely met by Madagascar, and intermittently by Mozambique and the East African coast. It was not until the 1770s that the supply from the African coast reached significant proportions. However, with the decreasing profitability of the West African slave trade a tremendous demand for slaves was added in the 1770s and 1780s for the American market as well. That market became even more attractive as the small Mascarene islands became 'so well stocked with blacks' by the mid-1770s. An annual average of about 3,000 slaves was then being traded by the French from Mozambique.[26]

The rapidly rising French demand for slaves began to cause a major dislocation of the Arab trade along the East African coast. Previously, during the middle of the eighteenth century, Omani demand for slaves had been responsible for the penetration of Swahili traders of Mombasa and Pate into the ports of southern Tanzania, and they even encroached on the Portuguese sphere along the northern coast of Mozambique. By the mid-1770s this northward flow of slaves had been partly reversed. It was stated that Swahili traders were taking slaves to the south 'when they do not have to sell to the Arabs'.[27]

The French also began to encroach directly into the Omani sphere north of Cape Delgado. Mongalo, or Mgao Mwanya along the southern coast of Tanzania, was located close to the Makonde plateau where, it was alleged, the Makua, Makonde, Ndonde and Yao were 'continually at war, solely to make each other prisoners, whom they sell'. By the 1750s it had become a regular port of call for Swahili traders in search of ivory and slaves.[28] To secure their supply of slaves, the Omanis had imposed their suzerainty over Mongalo in 1776, although they had no permanent political representative there, and no tribute was exacted. The Omanis were more interested in economic control over the trade which was channelled through Kilwa. They were seasonal traders who deposited their merchandise with the local ruler who collected slaves and ivory for them while they continued their voyage to Mozambique or Zanzibar according to season. The French sought to encroach upon this Omani sphere through various schemes to establish a factory there by forming an alliance with the local ruler. In 1786 an agreement was concluded with local authorities to supply slaves at 25 piastres each, a price far below that prevailing·elsewhere along the coast. But in view of the acute demand, this low price could not be maintained, and the following year the price was reported to be equal to that at Kilwa, though the tax was kept to 3 piastres to attract French traders there. However, Mongalo had a fairly restricted hinterland, able to supply a smaller number of slaves than Kilwa. Most of the French schemes, however, failed to attract French governmental support and appear to have all fizzled out.[29]

A more serious encroachment was attempted at Kilwa which was 'the entrepôt of the slave trade for all the coast of Zanzibar.' The French slave trader, Morice, had made two voyages to Zanzibar in 1775, taking off 1,625 slaves, most of whom probably came from Kilwa. The following year he shifted his trade to the source, buying 700 slaves, and negotiating a 100-year treaty with the Sultan of Kilwa to buy 1,000 slaves a year at a fixed price of 22 piastres each, including tax, and regardless of sex.[30]

This was not merely a commercial transaction but also a conscious entry into the local politico-economic struggle along the East African coast between the various Swahili polities attempting to maintain their independence, and the expanding Omani hegemony. Previously the Omanis had exercised a rather loose control over the Swahili ruler of Kilwa. But they were seasonal traders – apparently including the Omani governor – who visited Zanzibar from January to March to buy merchandise from the monsoon dhows. Taking advantage of the temporary absence of the Omanis in 1771, the local ruling class informed them that they would no longer be tolerated as rulers, though they quickly added that they would always be welcomed as traders.[31] Their eager invitation to the Omanis to continue to trade at Kilwa pointed to its economic dependence on the Omanis and their rising entrepôt at Zanzibar.

Kilwa is located towards the periphery of reliable monsoons, and the consequent lengthening of the voyage and the shortening of the trading season at Kilwa led to a preference for Zanzibar as an entrepôt by the monsoon dhows. As Morice explained:

> It is to them [Arabs] and to their centres in Zanzibar that the ships from India go in preference to unload their cargoes for distribution all along the coast. When the ships from India arrive in December, January or February, all the Moors from Kilwa, Mafia, Mombasa, Pate, etc., go to Zanzibar to buy cargoes and distribute them subsequently in their districts in exchange for ivory tusks, provisions and slaves. In March and April all the Moors and Arabs come to the Kingdom of Kilwa to trade these for slaves.[32]

Kilwa's dependence on the Omanis was also partly explained in terms of lack of deep-sea shipping, capital and commercial know-how, while the Omanis, according to Morice, 'being richer, more business-like, and more commerical', were able to attract the trade to Zanzibar. Whatever the merits of these arguments, Kilwa's economic dependence was a stark reality. As Morice commented, 'the well-to-do today cannot do without all the materials that the Moors have been bringing them for 300 years'. Consequently, he said, though the people of Kilwa were capable of driving the Omanis back to Muscat, 'they will never do it so long as some European nation [does not bring] them Surat goods which they need and can take in exchange for their slaves and ivory'.[33]

The northern circuit of trade on which Kilwa remained dependent, even while expanding the slave trade with the French, thus consisted of the export of ivory, primarily to India and China, and slaves. The imports included Indian textiles and beads of great variety; particularly coarse but durable handwoven textiles, such as bleached *basto* or *bafta*, dark indigo-dyed *kaniki* that was popular in the interior, and *dhoties* which originated from the Gujarati port of Surat. In addition, striped loincloths were imported from Muscat and the Portuguese Indian port of Diu. Morice was quite eloquent on the role of Indian textiles and beads which sustained the whole trade of the East African coast at this time.[34]

It was precisely this economic dependence of Kilwa on the Omanis at Zanzibar that Morice sought to break in his schemes. He proposed to provide Indian goods directly, thereby eliminating the Omani middleman and making Kilwa dependent on the French instead. Under his plan of operations he envisaged sending a cargo of French merchandise to Surat to buy there goods suitable for the Kilwa market. In exchange he expected to buy slaves for the Mascarenes and the Americas, and ivory which could be sold at a good profit in India, China or even France. The project called for a capital outlay for the first year of over 170,000 piastres, and Morice also felt he needed the sanction of the French government; neither the capital nor this assistance apparently materialised. The project was therefore abandoned.[35]

Morice was a monopolist who sought to exclude all European rivals, but not yet the Omanis whom he did not wish to alienate before his project materialised. His monopoly and the freezing of the price of slaves at Kilwa in the agreement may have dampened the growth of trade. With his death in *c.* 1781 the agreement apparently lapsed, and Kilwa now witnessed intense competition between the French traders. In 1784 one slaving captain, Joseph Crassons de Medeuil, bitterly complained about the lack of planning for the trade as a result of which 'three or four ships find themselves in the same place and crowd each other out.' He listed eight vessels which, over a period of 28 months, made a total of 14 voyages and carried off 4,193 slaves, apart from others which may have escaped his attention. This would give an annual average of nearly 2,000 slaves. The Swahili traders were fully aware of this high demand and could therefore dictate the terms, forcing the French to take away slaves without selection. Moreover, the price doubled to 40 piastres and the duty increased threefold to 6 piastres, and even to 10 piastres.[36]

The consequent commercial prosperity at Kilwa is recorded in the

Swahili chronicle of Kilwa. 'The people and their sovereign enjoyed great profit', and the period 'was one of great prosperity for the country.' A tangible monument to this is the Makutani palace which was enlarged during this period by the addition of a second storey and the enclosure of a large courtyard to the east.[37] Kilwa's prosperity must have appeared to the Omanis as a multiple insult. The shift of the French slave trade to Kilwa from Zanzibar not only deprived the Omanis of part of their middleman's share, but also buttressed a rebel city-state that threatened to nip in the bud the nascent Omani hegemony. Moreover, the intense competition for slaves in the first half of the 1780s had sent prices skyrocketing not only for the French but also for the Omanis. This underlay an attempt by the Omanis to prevent the Europeans from buying slaves at Zanzibar that led to M. Clonard's 'petite guerre' and to the difficulties that Dutch ships from Cape Town had in obtaining slaves there in 1776 and 1777.[38] European competition threatened to deny the Omani date-growers their labour supply. The Omanis were apparently not yet prepared to make the transition, as had the Swahili merchant class, to a more purely mercantile existence from which they might have derived considerable commercial profit by the expansion of the French slave trade. Therefore they had to act.

The French had excited fissiparous tendencies along the coast but, by failing to provide their favourite with adequate protection, they left Kilwa powerless to resist the inevitable retribution. The Omanis may have exploited both the territorial and political weaknesses of Kilwa to subdue it. Since the expulsion of the Omani governor from Kilwa in 1771 Kilwa had been ruled by a diarchy of a Swahili sultan and a family of 'amirs' of Malindi origin who represented the interests of the increasingly powerful mercantile class. The latter had successfully resisted the imposition of a tax on them by the ruler in *c.* 1774, while the agricultural section of the population had to pay the dues on grains and other products. The Omanis may also have taken advantage of the territorial and political fragmentation that was so endemic on the Swahili coast. It seems that many of the Swahili city-states along the southern coast of Tanzania asserted their independence from Oman when Kilwa overthrew Omani rule in 1771, but they were unable to unite against an external invader. By 1784, Mafia, Kilwa's 'foster-mother', on which it had depended for cattle and provisions, had begun to assert its independence from Kilwa, perhaps with Omani encouragement. In desperation Kilwa turned to the pretender to the Omani throne, Saif b. Ahmed, who was seeking a share of his patrimony in East Africa, and together they probed the possibility of French aid, but to no avail. A similar drama was to be enacted at Mombasa four decades later. Kilwa, however, fell under a 'swift and fierce' Omani onslaught.[39]

The Swahili ruler of Kilwa was left with his title and dominion over the

45

mainland section of the kingdom, while the Omanis appropriated half the revenue from the slave trade. The Swahili merchant class had thus once more been subjugated to the demands and control of its Omani counterpart. It was accommodated within the structure of the emerging commercial empire, with both the ruler and the Malindi 'amir' being given an annual present of cloth by the Omani ruler. The Omanis, moreover, sought to remove any advantage Kilwa may have had as a source of slaves by charging a slightly lower duty at Zanzibar. The French thus began to shift their trade to Zanzibar though Kilwa was only gradually abandoned by them. Kilwa and the Swahili merchant class there were thus gradually impoverished. In 1804 the customs of Kilwa were farmed out to an Arab merchant for only 6,000 piastres. It had thus become merely an outport of Zanzibar. By 1812 Kilwa Kisiwani (Kilwa on the Island) was described as a 'petty village', and was surpassed during the second quarter of the nineteenth century by Kilwa Kivinje, the mainland terminus of long-distance trade routes from the interior.[40]

Having tasted the nectar of commercial profit, the Omanis were by no means united in their resolve to strangle the French slave trade. The Omani date-growers may have been interested in removing French competition to lower the price of slaves, but the commercial section was apparently too strong to allow the diminution of its profits. The French were therefore permitted to trade 'in complete safety', and the duty was increased initially by only half a piastre to 6½ piastres, though by 1804 it had risen to 12 piastres. The date-growers had to be content with a much lower duty on slaves going to the north from Zanzibar, amounting to 1 piastre in 1804.[41]

The Napoleonic Wars – almost continuous between 1793 and 1810 – were a catastrophe for the Omani and Swahili merchant classes in East Africa. They were not confined to the western Indian Ocean but were global, disrupting the previously lucrative slave trade to the West Indies. In 1804 it was reported that all trade except that between Madagascar and the African coast had been suspended. The French slave trade with Mozambique declined precipitously from an annual average of 9,000 in the late 1780s to just over 2,300 in 1794. For the coast north of Cape Delgado, only five vessels traded at Kilwa and Zanzibar in 1803–4 compared with at least eleven in 1788. French slave vessels, moreover, were subject to capture and were thus kept away from Zanzibar by the presence of British warships. To beat the British blockade around the Mascarenes the French had to devise a circuitous route via the Seychelles, or to encourage the Arabs to transport the slaves in their own dhows to the Seychelles or directly to Mauritius, under the neutral Omani flag. Portuguese entry into the conflict, and the consequent cessation of the French trade at Mozambique, may have given a fresh stimulus to the French slave trade with Zanzibar. The Omanis were able to buy many of the

Portuguese and British prizes at low prices and use them to conduct their trade. However, the new opportunities could hardly have been fully exploited under conditions of war. The fall of Mauritius to the British in 1810 dealt a stunning blow to the trade. Although slaves continued to be smuggled into the Mascarenes in later years, the slave trade to the south was clearly a spent force.[42]

The trans-Atlantic slave trade from Mozambique to Brazil revived after the shift of the Portuguese court to Rio de Janeiro in 1807–8, and especially in the 1820s when up to 16,000 slaves were exported in a single year. It is not unlikely that some of these slaves were obtained from the coast north of Cape Delgado either directly or by transhipment from coasting dhows from Kilwa. However, assertions of the British naval officer, Captain Fairfax Moresby, in the early 1820s that twenty-four slave ships had been fitted out from France to export slaves from East Africa, and that there were more than 20,000 slaves awaiting them at Zanzibar, were grossly exaggerated. Even if all these vessels had carried an average of 300 slaves, they could not have carried more than one-third of the alleged number of slaves. Moresby was a British anti-slavery crusader making a case for the prohibition of the slave trade to the south from East Africa. This was ultimately formalised in the Moresby Treaty of 1822 which prohibited the export of slaves to the east and south of a line drawn from Cape Delgado to Diu Head in western India.[43] Seyyid Said claimed that this concession cost him MT$50,000 in lost revenue. This figure may well have been exaggerated, and in later years he continued to inflate the figure to impress the British with the enormity of his sacrifice, in the hope of precluding further demands of that nature and to extract the maximum concession in return. However, even if these figures were accurate, they would represent, at the rate of MT$12 in duty, only about 4,000 slaves per annum.[44]

The Omani and French demand for slaves during the eighteenth century had served the important function of expanding Zanzibar's entrepôt role in the supply of the imports, and of developing a large hinterland behind Kilwa. By 1785 developments at Kilwa had reached the stage where they threatened to pull the economic centre of gravity towards Kilwa and revive its medieval glory, in this case based on the French slave trade. The Omanis effectively intervened to prevent the French from supplying Kilwa with an economic base independent of Zanzibar. They also set about converting Kilwa into Zanzibar's outport, but by the end of the century Kilwa's well-developed hinterland was still Zanzibar's only limb, and the French market for slaves was still very important in the economy of Zanzibar. It had given rise to a powerful group of merchants at Zanzibar who had flourished by the slave trade and who were exerting a great deal of influence in the politics of Zanzibar. According to Captain Tomkinson, it had been 'a lucrative trade for the Island and the people in office made a great deal by it'. Zanzibar was farmed to 'black merchants connected with the French', although they were, in fact, mostly Omanis. The strangulation of this branch of the slave trade, therefore, was not only disrupting the economy of Zanzibar but also eroding the economic base of the Omani mercantile class at Zanzibar. It is precisely members of this class who began actively to look for alternative markets for their slaves since the slave trade to the north could not be expanded.[45] Perhaps there could have been no better substitute than the agricultural exploitation of the East African littoral using slave labour, for the Omanis were soon to discover that the tender conscience of the British abolitionists was not yet troubled by the consumption of slave-grown spices. Thus the stage was set for the transformation of the slave sector from one that was merchantile, based on the export of slaves, to a productive one based on the use of slaves within East Africa to produce commodities for export.

The genesis of the slave system of production in Zanzibar, 1810–1840s

The collapse of the southern slave trade during the first quarter of the nineteenth century posed a grave crisis for the mercantile classes operating along the East African coast. Before the extension of the European slave trade to eastern Africa the Arab traders had enjoyed a monopoly over the slave trade in the Indian Ocean system, and prices remained low. By integrating the Indian Ocean system into the international commercial system dominated by the Atlantic slave trade, the European slave traders had subjected Indian Ocean consumers to the higher prices that were current in West Africa. As a result the price of slaves at Kilwa had doubled by the mid-1780s. The amputation of the link with the Atlantic slave trade system meant not only the loss of a market for about 2,000 slaves per annum, but also the removal of the higher floor prices. By 1822 the price of slaves had halved to MT\$20.[46] This must have appeared calamitous to the Omani merchant class which had grown dependent on the trade, and which had every reason to look for an alternative. In a letter to his agent in Bombay in 1828 Seyyid Said put the case succinctly:

> In consequence of the abolition of the slave trade the collections [revenue] of Zanzibar have been diminished; it has therefore been deemed necessary to make plantations of sugar cane in the islands.[47]

And, he might have added, of cloves as well.

It was members of the Omani merchant class who were in a position to initiate the transformation of the slave sector of the economy of Zanzibar. From their acquaintance with the Mascarenes they realised that if slaves could not be exported, the product of their labour could. They witnessed in those islands the employment of slave labour for the production not only of sugar but also of cloves, which had been introduced from the East Indies in 1770. The clove trade was particularly lucrative as a result of the Dutch monopoly over the spices. As late as 1834, when that monopoly had already begun to crumble, it was still yielding a profit of over 1,000 per cent on the original cost of production.[48]

Contemporary French observers attribute the introduction of cloves to various Frenchmen, probably all slave traders. M. Guillain attributes it to a M. Sausse, a creole from the Mascarenes who is known to have been trading in slaves since 1785. Richard Burton says that Sausse was the first person to extract clove oil, subsequently a universal favourite with the Zanzibar public. F. Albrand credits M. Desplant with the initiative.[49] While the Frenchmen probably played a role, no evidence has come to light of French landholding on the island at this time. It is more likely that they did so in conjunction with members of the Omani merchant class.

Zanzibari tradition, current at least from the end of the nineteenth century, attributes the introduction of cloves to Saleh b. Haramil al Abray who appears to have been the doyen of the Omani merchant class. He is probably the same individual who is referred to by several early nineteenth-century accounts simply as Saleh. Born at Muscat in *c.* 1770, he left his native country young and visited the Seychelles, Ile de France and Bourbon. He is described by Albrand as 'a perfect Frenchman' who spoke 'the creole of Mauritius passably' and who appreciated 'the superiority of our arts', presumably including the use of slave labour in the production of sugar and cloves. He was a friend or a relative of, as well as an interpreter for, the governor of Zanzibar whom Albrand names as Said. As early as 1804 a Frenchman, Captain Dallons, mentions an unnamed interpreter, 'a subtle and pliant man on whom all success depends' in the conduct of the slave trade. In 1857 Burton refers to probably the same individual, whose share in a single venture in the southern slave trade was worth MT$218,000, and he credits the introduction of cloves to this same Arab. At the end of the nineteenth century W.W.A. Fitzgerald recorded what was then becoming a tradition; that Haramil b. Saleh (*sic*) accompanied a French officer from Zanzibar to Bourbon at the end of the eighteenth century and obtained permission to take back a small quantity of seeds and plants with him. These were planted on his plantation at Mtoni and, according to Guillain, at Kizimbani. The contemporary Albrand dates this introduction more precisely to *c.* 1812 and adds that by 1819, when he visited Zanzibar, they were already 15 feet high. This is confirmed by another French visitor in 1822 who found cloves growing on two plantations belonging, according to him, to the governor who 'is almost the only person on the island who has on his lands these precious trees.'[50]

Saleh was the leader of one of the factions at Zanzibar competing for power. He was opposed by the Harthi clan, long established at Zanzibar, who may have been more identified with the northern slave trade, though undoubtedly also profiting from the French slave trade. It was led by Abdullah b. Juma al Barwany, a very rich man who had been governor of Zanzibar, and controlled Kilwa at the time of Albrand's visit. Saleh's faction may have played a part in the removal from the governorship of Abdullah b. Juma whom Seyyid Said allegedly feared. Within three years Saleh's relative was awarded the governorship. Saleh himself fell victim to this factional struggle, probably during Seyyid Said's visit to Zanzibar in 1828. He had apparently continued to participate in the southern slave trade despite the Moresby Treaty of 1822. Seyyid Said imprisoned the governor and confiscated Saleh's properties, profiting thereby 'with all the appearance of justice'. Saleh apparently escaped to the mainland and, though he was eventually pardoned, he died a pauper.[51]

What was particularly interesting about Saleh's properties was that they included Mtoni and Kizimbani. Seyyid Said also bought a plantation at Mkanyageni from the sons of Saleh, and inherited another at Bumbwini from his slave 'Alkida Jengueni'. It was probably from these plantations, all planted with cloves before Seyyid Said's first visit to Zanzibar in 1828, that the first crops came. Bombay trade figures show that between 1823-4 and 1832-3 small quantities of cloves were already being imported from East Africa.[52]

While Seyyid Said can no longer be credited with introducing cloves to Zanzibar, as so many historians have maintained, he was a sovereign of Zanzibar and a merchant prince who felt the pinch even more acutely when the southern slave trade collapsed. He claimed that the Moresby Treaty of 1822 cost him MT\$40,000 to MT\$50,000 in lost revenue alone. Therefore, when he jumped onto the clove bandwagon, he gave it a most royal push. The American trader, Edmund Roberts commented in 1828 that the government of Zanzibar 'for some time past have turned their attention to the cultivation of spices, the sugar cane, coffee, etc. all of which . . . will shortly be articles of export'. By 1830 an American vessel was able to buy 127 *fraselas* of cloves from the governor of Zanzibar, the first known cargo of Zanzibar cloves sent to the United States, at the still handsome price of MT\$10 per *frasela*.[53] Seyyid Said took a direct lead in this expansion by extending the cultivation of cloves on the plantations he had confiscated or otherwise acquired which, by the time of his death, numbered forty-five. In 1834 W.S.W. Ruschenberger saw about 4,000 cloves trees at Kizimbani, ranging in height between 5 feet and 20 feet, the smaller ones having been planted since the confiscation. In 1840 production of cloves from Seyyid Said's plantations alone amounted to between 5,000 and 6,000 *fraselas*, and, by the late 1840s, to between 20,000 and 30,000 *fraselas*. Each of his numerous children, concubines and eunuchs also had their plots, and one of his elder sons, Khalid, owned 'the grand and superb plantation "Marseilles" ', so named because of his 'predilection for France and everything French'. Seyyid Said's kinsman and governor of Zanzibar, Suleiman b. Hamed al Busaidi, was one of the richest landowners, whose plantations at Kizimbani, Bububu, Chuwini and elsewhere, were furnishing 5,000 to 6,000 *fraselas* worth over MT$10,000 by the late 1840s.[54]

The ruling Busaidi dynasty was at the head of what was developing as the landed aristocracy. Seyyid Said is said to have compelled his Omani subjects, under threat of confiscation of land, to plant a certain proportion of clove to coconut trees. By the mid-1830s it was reported that:

> the easy profits which clove plantations yielded made all the inhabitants of Zanzibar turn their eyes towards the crop . . . almost everybody on the island is now clearing away the coconuts to make way for them.[55]

A French naval officer, Captain Loarer, aptly described this as a clove 'mania', and it was still raging in the 1840s. Members of the second most powerful Omani clan, the Harthi, participated in this feverish expansion and its leader, Abdullah b. Salim, who traded extensively, possessed great wealth in land and 1,500 slaves. Hasan b. Ibrahim, who had been a captain in the Sultan's navy and had been appointed in 1832 as the agent to transact business for foreign merchants at Zanzibar, also owned by 1839 a plantation with 12,000 clove trees at Bububu. It was named Salem after the American port that had initiated American trade with Zanzibar. Between 1841 and 1843 the United States Consul and commercial agent, R.P. Waters, made contracts with at least eight other Arab producers for the supply of cloves.[56]

Though the Omani ruling class undoubtedly dominated landownership at this period, members of other ethnic groups began to join it fairly early on. As early as 1811 a British naval officer, Captain Smee, mentioned 'some considerable Arab and Soowillee landholders' possessing from 200 to 400 slaves.[57] Sadik b. Mbarak, described as a Swahili born at Merka, who had acted as an interpreter for the anthropologist C. Pickering and as a clerk for Waters, had a *shamba* (plantation) in Zanzibar, though it was probably small. On the other hand, Burton heard in 1857 of an unnamed Swahili who had purchased an estate for MT$14,000, which suggests that it must have been of considerable size. The most important among the Swahili landowners was probably the ruler of the indigenous Shirazi population, *Mwinyi Mkuu* Muhammad b. Ahmed al Alawi, who lived on the proceeds of plantations at Dunga and Bweni. When he died in 1865 his plantations were inherited by his son Ahmed, who died of smallpox in 1873, and by two daughters who married into prominent Arab landowning families, unions that emphasised the confluence of the different ethnic sections of the landowning class.[58]

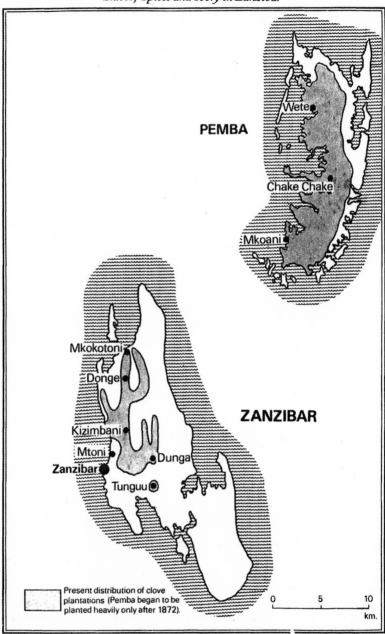

PEMBA

Wete

Chake Chake

Mkoani

Mkokotoni

Donge

ZANZIBAR

Kizimbani

Mtoni

Dunga

Zanzibar

Tunguu

Present distribution of clove
plantations (Pemba began to be
planted heavily only after 1872).

0   5   10
km.

Map 2.2   Clove areas of Zanzibar

52

Plate 4   Mwinyi Mkuu Muhammad bin Ahmed bin Hasan Alawi, the Shirazi Ruler of Zanzibar, with his son, the last Mwinyi Mkuu

By the 1840s some of the Indian merchants had also begun to pay 'their tribute to this mania', according to Loarer, each having his small *shamba*. Ibji Sewji, brother of the custom master of Zanzibar, acquired a new *shamba* in 1844, and another merchant had 3 plantations and 175 slaves when he went bankrupt in 1846. Production of cloves on non-Busaidi plantations had initially lagged behind, partly as a result of those early confiscations, but as the 'mania' gripped the population, production jumped, surpassing royal production in 1845 by two to one.[59]

By the late 1840s, therefore, a landed aristocracy had emerged which, though predominantly Omani, was not exclusively so. And it was as a class that it enjoyed economic privileges, the most important of which was freedom from taxation, although members of the ruling dynasty also enjoyed exemption from duty on the import of slaves. It was only when overproduction threatened the prosperity of the class that Seyyid Said imposed a tax of MT$¼ per *frasela* on cloves from Pemba in an effort to slow down expansion there. The source of capital for the clove economy was primarily commerce which provided most of the Sultan's revenue and the merchants' commercial profit. Some Arab merchants involved primarily in coastal trade, such as Muhammad b. Abd al Kadir, diverted their capital from commerce into clove production, especially during the highly lucrative phase in the early 1840s, as did members of the Indian mercantile community. And many caravan traders into the interior of Africa, after three or four journeys, settled down to a more leisured life in Zanzibar. The most outstanding case was that of Tippu Tip who reportedly owned 7 *shambas* and 10,000 slaves, worth MT$50,000 at the end of the nineteenth century.[60]

It was during this same lucrative period that cloves spread to Pemba. Loarer reported in 1849 that two-thirds of the island had been, until a decade before, 'a very good forest' which was then being cleared by Busaidi and other rich landowners of Zanzibar to establish clove plantations. By 1848-9 Pemba was producing 10,000 *fraselas* of cloves, but the imposition of the tax on Pemba cloves, coupled with the fall in the price that accompanied overproduction by the late 1840s, postponed the rise of Pemba as a major producer until after the hurricane of 1872.[61]

So feverish had been the spread of cloves in both Zanzibar and Pemba that they had begun to encroach seriously on areas better suited to other crops and to undermine the islands' self-sufficiency in foodstuffs. Traditionally Pemba had been a granary for Mombasa and Arabia, and even Zanzibar had exported large quantities of foodstuffs to Arabia and the mainland as late as 1819. But as Burton put it in his characteristic style:

> Requiring little care, [cloves] speedily became a favourite, and in 1835 the aristocratic foreigner almost supplanted the vulgar coconut and the homely rice necessary for local consumption.[62]

Loarer adds cassava, sweet potatoes and grains to the list of foodcrops displaced by cloves. While it is questionable whether cloves could have displaced rice from the flat swampy valleys where they cannot thrive, the higher price enjoyed by cloves may have led to a diversion of labour from foodcrops. This contributed to the transformation of Zanzibar into an importer of foodstuffs. By the 1860s Zanzibar was importing large quantities of rice and other cereals, only a small proportion of which was re-exported, as Table 2.2 shows.

The displacement of coconuts by cloves was probably more dramatic. Thriving in the more sandy soils, coconuts were apparently widespread on the foothills of the four longitudinal ridges situated in the western half

Table 2.2 *Imports and exports of grains and cereals from Zanzibar, 1859/60–1866/7*

Year	Imports	Exports
	(MT$)	
1859/60	204,600	7,000
1861/2	95,800	6,700
1862/3	48,900	9,400
1863/4	129,000	56,456
1864/5	103,200	50,000
1865/6	100,000	
1866/7	145,000	

Sources: MA, 73/1861, pp. 7–25; Webb to State Department, 10 March 1869, NAW, T100/5.

of Zanzibar where the soil is not as fertile and deep, and where rainfall is moderate. It was in these areas that from the 1830s the landowners began to cut down coconuts to make way for the more lucrative cloves rather than incur the expense of clearing new land. In 1845 the French Consul feared that in three more years the export of coconut oil would decline to insignificance. According to statistics for the early 1860s, an average of about MT$372,000-worth of coconuts were annually imported into Zanzibar and only MT$143,000 exported. Unfortunately these peripheral sandy areas proved to be the most unproductive clove areas in Zanzibar, yielding less than a pound of cloves per tree. Once planted, however, inertia and the higher price of cloves compared with other crops allowed them to retain their hold on the land well into the twentieth century.[63]

The development of the clove plantations contributed to the marginalisation of the indigenous peasantry. Many of the food-producing and coconut-producing areas which cloves encroached upon had apparently been previously settled by the indigenous people. They held this cleared or *kiambo* land under a communal land tenure system in which ownership was shared by all who were patrilineally descended from the man who originally cleared the land. Although there is evidence for transactions in land and a freehold system as early as the beginning of the nineteenth century, there are widespread traditions of expropriation of land of the peasantry by the intruding landowning class. J.M. Gray went so far as to assert that 'a great deal' of the development of the clove industry 'was brought about by expropriation of the original landowners', though, with the characteristic legalism of a former Chief Justice of Zanzibar, he added 'that many of these changes of ownership were brought about by means which would have borne scrutiny by a court of law'.[64]

Plate 5   Coconut oil milling using camel power, Zanzibar, c.1860

However, the best clove plantations were established along the ridges themselves which enjoyed a heavier rainfall and had deep and well-drained soils. Albrand claimed in 1819 that large portions of the island were still covered with forest. John Middleton was informed that 'although the Shirazi sometimes planted plots in the forest area, these were covered with weeds so fast that cultivation became impossible. These *misitu* were therefore used, before the expansion of cloves, primarily as places of refuge in times of trouble, or to hunt and collect firewood.' He adds that the large villages in the plantation belt are not indigenous since they lack the social characteristics of native villages such as Donge, Chaani and Dunga. In these areas expropriation of cultivated land may not have been widespread. However, the loss of access to the forests to

56

Plate 6   Chake Chake Fort, Pemba, c.1857. Note the hilly terrain

which the peasants could claim some rights may have upset the peasant economy in the surrounding foothills, and thus may have contributed to their displacement from the clove areas into the less fertile areas to the east such as Bambi and Uzini.[65]

Topographically Pemba is more dissected than Zanzibar and consists of a series of small hills divided by deep swampy valleys suitable for rice cultivation which made the island famous as a granary. Villages were established throughout the island on top of the ridges where the forest was less dense, and Middleton believes that they are mostly indigenous, dating to the period before the introduction of cloves. On the other hand, the hillsides, which were fertile and received a heavier rainfall, offered the same problems for cultivation as in Zanzibar. As mentioned above, two-thirds of the island was forested until the late 1830s and was being cleared in the 1840s specifically for cloves. However, because the major expansion of cloves in Pemba occurred after the hurricane of 1872 and the abolition of the slave trade in 1873, the indigenous peasantry was able to share in the clove industry, and landownership in Pemba was therefore ethnically more heterogeneous than in Zanzibar.[66]

As the cultivation of cloves spread there was an increase in the demand for labour. Contrary to the assertion of the British Consul, Atkins Hamerton, in 1841, the indigenous Muslim population of the islands was not enslaved. Seyyid Said appears to have attempted to obtain a share of

57

*Plate 7   Clove picking in Pemba. Note the tripod scaffolding used before the abolition of
slavery*

the traditional tribute in labour, amounting to a fortnight a year (*siku arbaatashara*), which was due to the *Mwinyi Mkuu* for public works, such as cutting and transporting timber, for which workers were given a supply of grain for subsistence. However, the supply of labour from this source was not adequate since the Hadimu population appears to have been small. In the 1830s two American visitors estimated the free indigenous population of Zanzibar at 17,000, and in 1857 Burton computed the adult male population at between 10,000 and 12,000. Increased demand on them for labour sharpened the contradiction between the Omani ruler, the *Mwinyi Mkuu* and the Hadimu peasants. As early as 1811 there is evidence that this tribute may have been converted into one in kind, 'the Macauduns' paying MT\$4,000 annually in grain to the government. By 1834 this tribute had been converted into a poll tax. Peasants were thus marginalised even further from the clove economy, preferring to produce other commodities for exchange to pay the tax.[67]

With the ever-limited source of non-slave labour drying up, the plantation economy came to depend entirely on slave labour. Contemporary sources are replete with various estimates, often merely wild guesses, about the size of the slave population of Zanzibar at various times during the nineteenth century. Martin and Ryan have attempted a statistical exercise to bring some order to these disparate figures. This exercise, however, is based on three assumptions which are clearly unacceptable. The first is 'arbitrarily assuming', as they readily admit, a slave population of 30,000 in 1770. In support of this assumption they merely mention that there were then 300 Omani Arabs in Zanzibar, as if Omani Arabs in all places and at all times represent a certain proportion of slaves.

Martin and Ryan's second assumption is a 5 per cent mortality rate for a sexually unbalanced and oppressed slave population, a figure not much above the more than 3 per cent death rate among the free population of Zanzibar in the 1910s. Slaves were taken to Zanzibar without regard to normal sexual proportions. Rigby noted in 1860 among 3,000 of the slaves he emancipated from the Indians that less than 5 per cent of adult females bore children. Miles's estimate of 8–12 per cent in the 1880s is probably much closer to reality, and would halve Martin and Ryan's estimate of the total population, assuming the validity of the other two assumptions.

The third set of assumptions made by Martin and Ryan is their estimate of the number of slaves retained in Zanzibar which suggests a curve steadily rising from an annual figure of 1,250 in the 1770s to 15,000 in the 1870s. Based on these assumptions they suggest that the slave population of the two islands rose from 30,000 in 1776 to about 183,000 in 1876, the peak year.[68] In view of the fact that the first major spurt in agricultural development based on slave labour occurred in the 1810s, that the 'clove mania' gripped the islands during the 1830s and the early 1840s, and that stagnation set in by the end of the that decade with overproduction and the collapse of clove prices (see p. 61), I find little justification for the suggested curve, and especially for the steep rise proposed for the early 1870s.

Any attempt at estimating the number of slaves annually retained in Zanzibar and the size of the slave population in the islands will have to consider the general pattern of economic development of the islands and the more realistic of the contemporary estimates. Curiously enough Martin and Ryan ignore Albrand's and E. Burgess's first-hand accounts which suggest a slave population in 1819 and 1839 of 15,000 and 17,000 respectively, which may be reasonable in view of the fact that the clove economy was still in its infancy. On the other hand, the American traders, Horace B. Putnam and Captain Loarer, suggest a slave population of between 60,000 and 100,000 during the 1840s at the height of the 'clove mania'. In view of the stagnation which set in by the end of that decade, I would suggest that the peak in the slave population was attained during the 1840s or 1850s when clove production itself reached its plateau at about 140,000 *fraselas*. Custom house figures for the 1860s suggest a figure of about 10,000 slaves being retained in Zanzibar and Pemba annually during that decade, just the numbers required to replenish slaves lost through the high rate of mortality.[69]

The growth of the slave trade during the nineteenth century was due, therefore, not to any expansion in the demand for slaves in Asia where they were to a considerable extent articles of unproductive consumption, but was the consequence of the development of the dependent slave mode of production along the East African coast. This had a much greater potential for expansion, and slaves were a vital means of production in it. In fact, British measures to prohibit the export of slaves to the south in 1822 and to the north in 1845, contributed, ironically, to this development. But the slave mode had its own momentum once it began to develop, more than making up for the loss of the external markets. At the beginning of the nineteenth century, when the French slave trade had been badly shaken but not yet entirely stopped, the total volume of the East African slave trade was estimated at between 6,000 and 13,000, of which a substantial proportion was for export to the north as well as to the south. By the 1840s the estimate was still only 13,000, but, with the southern slave trade virtually blocked, a large proportion of the slaves were already being absorbed in Zanzibar, coinciding with the onset of the 'clove mania'. Thereafter, the volume continued to increase, to between 14,000 and 15,000 in the 1850s and to about 20,000 in the 1860s. But by then the clove economy had already entered a phase of overproduction and economic stagnation in Zanzibar.[70]

The development of the slave system on the northern coast

As the cultivation of cloves spread in Zanzibar and Pemba, so production increased in line with the yield characteristics of the crop. After a five- to seven-year gestation period, small quantities are produced during the subsequent early years, leading up to a mature crop when the tree is about twenty years old. Apart from small quantities of cloves inter-mittently imported from the East African coast, probably transhipped from the Mascarenes, Bombay trade figures show the importation of cloves on a more regular basis from the African coast, and from the Persian Gulf and Kutch, both areas in close commercial contact with East Africa, from 1823–4 onwards. During the first decade or so the quantities were limited, averaging about Rs10,000 in value (about MT\$4,600), evidently the initial crops from plantations established before Seyyid Said's first visit to Zanzibar in 1828. As the trees matured and more were planted, imports from East Africa to Bombay rose to an average annual value of over Rs54,000 (MT\$25,000) during the late 1830s and early 1840s. During this period also, increasing quantities of cloves began to be exported directly to the United States, reaching about US\$24,000 in 1839.[71]

However, the full significance of the 'clove mania' that raged during the 1830s began to be felt only by the late 1840s. Production increased tenfold between 1839/40 and 1846/7 when it amounted to nearly 100,000 *fraselas* (about 1,500 tons). Though production characteristically fluctuated widely from year to year, it seems to have reached its first plateau of about 140,000 *fraselas* (about 2,200 tons) by the early 1850s as most of the trees planted during the 1830s attained their maturity. By the early 1870s production had risen to 250,000 *fraselas* (3,900 tons) (see Table 2.3).

Such a rapid expansion of this export-oriented economy brought in its train a host of problems typical of a monoculture which have continued to plague the economy of Zanzibar ever since. The most immediate effect of breaking the Dutch monopoly over the spice was a precipitous decline in the price of cloves on the international market. Already by 1834, as a result of expanded clove production in Zanzibar, the Mascarenes and apparently in Guyana, the profit margin had been nearly halved. By the 1840s the monopoly was more or less dead and buried. Whereas an American captain had bought cloves from the governor of Zanzibar in 1830 at MT\$10 per *frasela*, by 1840 the price had declined by about half. By the 1860s the price had fallen to less than MT\$1.50 per *frasela*. The collapse in the price is confirmed at Bombay where it declined from Rs65 per *maund* in the early 1820s to about a tenth of that amount by the late 1850s.[72]

61

Table 2.3 Cloves: production, export and prices, 1830–79

Year	Production (fraselas)	Value (MT$)	Price (MT$ per frasela)	Source
1830			10.00	PM, W.C. Waters Papers, Osprey. See Note at end of table
1836			5.25	
1839			5.04	
1839/40	9,000		5.00	Burton (1872), Vol. 1, pp. 364–5
1841			4.00	
1842			4.54	
1843			4.53	
1843/4	30,000		3.75	Loarer, 'Girofle', ANSOM, OI, 5/23
1845			3.79	
1846/7	97,000			ibid.
1847/8	35–40,000		2.85	ibid.
1848/9	70,000			ibid.
1849	120–150,000		2.88	Burton, (1872), Vol. 1, pp. 364–5
1851			2.98	
1852			2.71	
1852/3	128,840		2.81	NAW, RG84/Z/C-3, Misc. Rec. Bk. 1852–60
	119,470			
1853/4	140,356		2.17	ibid.
1856	142,857		2.13	Burton, (1872), Vol. 1, pp. 364–5
1857			1.75	
1859	138,860	250,500	1.56	Rigby to Sec. of State for India, 1 May 1860, PRO, FO 54/17
1860			1.45	
1861			1.25	

Year	Production	Value	Price	Source
1861/2	(168,200)	201,840	1.20	Playfair to Bombay, 1 May 1864, MA, 58/1864, pp. 16–33
1862/3	(247,826)	332,087	1.34	Playfair to FO, 1 January 1865, PRO, FO 54/22
1863/4	(149,636)	206,498	1.38	ibid.
1864/5		315,132		Seward to Bombay (1865), MA, 73/1865, pp. 7–25
1864/5	(415,398)	469,400	1.13	Ropes to State Department, 31 July 1865, NAW, T100/5
1865/6	(246,890)	293,800	1.19	Jablonski to MAE, 31 December 1866, MAE, CCZ, Vol. III, pp. 43–5
1866/7	(192,125)	228,629	1.19	same to same, 31 December 1867, MAE, CCZ, Vol. III, pp. 71–2
1867/8	(220,923)	262,898	1.19	Bure to MAE, 25 April 1869, MAE, CCZ, Vol. III, p. 108
1870			1.39	
1870/1	249,987	347,177	1.39	NAW, RG/84/Z/C–83, Misc. Letters Recd., 1871–5
1872			4.44	
1872/3	80,000	480,000	6.25	Prideaux's Report, *PP*, 1876, Vol. 74, p. 181
1873/4	50,000	400,000	8.00	
1874/5 (est.)	80,000	720,000	9.00	
1876/7		954,750		Kirk's Memo, 21 April 1882, PRO, FO 84/1657
1877/8		1,538,050		(Values given in £, converted at the rate of $4.75 = £1)
1878/9		807,500		

Note: Unless otherwise indicated, prices are calculated from numerous invoices at the Peabody Museum and the Essex Institute. Prices are given for calendar years. Whenever production or value of cloves are given for financial years, prices relate to the later year. Production figures in brackets are calculated from values and prices.

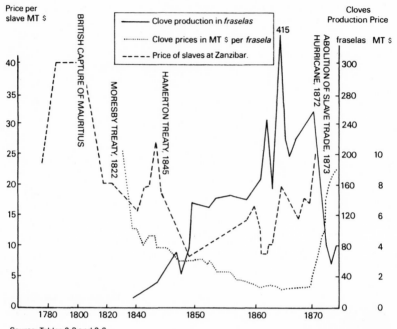

Source: Tables 2.3 and 2.6
Graph 2.1   Cloves and slaves: production and prices

Seyyid Said himself 'saw with pain the depreciation of his beautiful plantations'. Loarer proposed to him that he should control further planting by imposing a tax on each new clove tree and by prohibiting the destruction of coconut trees. Seyyid Said replied that the measures proposed 'will need surveillance which will cost money, whereas he wishes to save money'. Nevertheless, he threatened to confiscate plantations which did not replant a certain proportion of coconut to clove trees. He also imposed a duty of MT$¼ per *frasela* of cloves from Pemba to restrict expansion there. The duty was onerous because cloves were then worth less than MT$3 per *frasela*. Coupled with declining prices, this effectively prevented the emergence of Pemba as the larger producer of cloves until after the hurricane of 1872. During the late 1850s and the 1860s Pemba contributed less than one-eighth of the total (see Table 2.4). The low prices also discouraged plantation owners in Zanzibar from replanting dying clove trees as J.A. Grant noted in 1860.[73]

With the decline in the price of cloves there was a substantial decrease in the profitability of clove production. British officials at the end of the century estimated that the desirable proportion of slaves in a plantation was about ten to every hundred clove trees, and at an average of 6 lbs of

Table 2.4 *Value of cloves from Zanzibar and Pemba, 1859/60–1864/5*

Year	Zanzibar	Pemba	Total	Export
			(MT$)	
1859/60	200,320	20,030	220,350	250,500
1861/2	170,265	15,027	185,292	201,840
1862/3	250,395	40,065	290,460	332,440
1863/4	144,228	20,030	164,258	206,498
1864/5	200,315	40,060	240,375	315,132
Average	193,105	27,042	220,147	261,182
Percentage	88	12	100	

Source: Seward's Report on the Trade and Commerce of Zanzibar for the Year 1864/5, *PP*, 1867, Vol. 67, pp. 284–5.

dry cloves per tree, this meant 60 lbs per year per slave. At MT$10 per *frasela* of cloves in 1830 this meant a gross financial return of MT$17 per slave per year. However, when the price of cloves had plummeted to MT$1.50 by the mid-1860s, the gross financial return per slave declined to about MT$2.60 per year. Clearly, therefore, investment in slave-based clove production had become unprofitable by the middle of the nineteenth century.[74]

The collapse of the clove market was bound to affect the economic well-being of members of the landowning class. They had invested a substantial amount of their capital in clearing the land and establishing clove plantations during the period of the 'clove mania' when prices of slaves as well as of cloves were high. With overproduction the volume of their investment and their incomes progressively diminished. This inevitably led to indebtedness, mortgaging of plantations to moneylenders, and even loss of land. As early as 1843 Hamerton reported that many Arab plantation owners were mortgaged to Indian moneylenders 'who cultivate [the plantations] and in this way repay themselves'. Burton similarly reported in 1857 that 'the Indians have obtained possession from the Arabs, by purchase or mortgage, of many of the landed estates'. In 1860–61 Rigby emancipated over 8,000 slaves owned by Indians who had been declared British subjects and were therefore not allowed to own slaves.[75] A partial register that has recorded more than one-third of the emancipated slaves, indicates that about one-third of these were domestics owned by more than three-quarters of the Indian slave-owners, who possessed an average of three slaves. The remaining two-thirds of the slaves were probably employed on plantations owned by the remaining quarter of Indian slave-owners, who owned an average of about thirty slaves. The largest owner was none other than the most prominent firm of merchant financiers and farmer of the customs, Jairam Sewji, who owned 400 slaves.

Table 2.5 *Emancipation of slaves held by Indians, 1860–1*

No. of slaves per owner	Zanzibar		Mainland ports		Total				
	No. of owners	Total no. of slaves	No. of owners	Total no. of slaves	Owners No.	%	Slaves No.	%	Average no. of slaves per owner
1–9	259	771	40	72	299	77	895	30	3
10–19	56	841	16	225	72	19	1,066	36	15
20–99	11	472	3	105	14	4	577	19	42
100+	1	460	–	–	1	–	460	15	460
Total	327	2,544	59	402	386	100	2,998	100	8

Source: Zanzibar Archives: Secretariat G.I. I am indebted to Martha Honey for the list from which the analysis has been made.

However, the actual transfer of land to moneylending capital represents only the tip of the iceberg of indebtedness of the landowning class. By 1873 a prominent Indian firm of financiers, probably that of Jairam Sewji, had loaned out nearly MT$285,000 to Arab landowners on Zanzibar and on the mainland. Moneylenders were typically not anxious to be involved directly in production, especially with the declining profitability of the clove economy, and foreclosure was therefore a last resort. With the emancipation of slaves held by the Indians, foreclosure was virtually ruled out. Moneylenders, therefore, may have sought security for their capital in high rates of interest and by establishing their claim directly on the crops, retaining the landowners as little more than managers. In 1873 Sir Bartle Frere was 'assured that few of the larger Arab estates in Zanzibar are unencumbered by mortgages to Indian capitalists, and that a large proportion are so deeply mortgaged as virtually to belong to the Indian mortgagee'.[76]

The precipitous decline in the profitability of clove production was bound to have an effect on the price of the producers, the slaves. Captain Colomb, one of the Royal Navy's 'dhow chasers' in East African waters, commented that there was no 'considerable rise in the price of slaves at Zanzibar between 1844 and 1870'. In fact, available data, imperfect as they are, suggest a *decline*. At the height of the French slave trade in the 1780s the price of a slave at Kilwa had been about MT$40. As a result of Anglo-French warfare, the capture of Ile de France by the British, and the Moresby Treaty which prohibited the export of slaves to the south, the price had declined to about MT$20 by 1822. Thereafter, the price may have recovered somewhat, or at least stabilised during the 1830s and early 1840s with the onset of the 'clove mania'. But by the late 1840s, with the collapse of clove prices and the prohibition of the export of slaves to the north, the price at Kilwa had fallen to as low as MT$4 to MT$5 according to Loarer. During the early 1860s, according to a number of fairly reliable British consular and naval sources, the average price was between MT$8.50 and MT$10 (see Table 2.6).[77]

Though the decline in the price of slaves was primarily a response to the collapse in the price of cloves, the decline in the price of slaves was not as precipitous as that of cloves. The price of slaves declined by about 50 per cent between the early 1820s and the early 1860s whereas the price of cloves declined by 85 per cent between 1830 and the 1860s. This incongruence was apparently due to some success in diversifying the economy. With declining prices of slaves, other more mundane commodities stood a better chance in competing for slave labour. Guillain and the American agent, William E. Hines, record, for example, a greater interest in the production of indigo and coconuts. The relatively poor quality of the former, however, prevented it from penetrating the prime Indian market. On the other hand, French demand for vegetable oils led to an increase in the production of coconut products for export from about MT$50,000 in the late 1840s to about MT$200,000 in the 1860s.[78]

Table 2.6 *Prices of slaves at Zanzibar, 1770–1874*

Year	Average	Adult (MT$)	Juvenile	Child	Source
1770	22				Freeman-Grenville (1965), p. 70
1776	25				Ross
1777	24.50	24–25	22–25	10–22	ibid.
1784	40				Freeman-Grenville (ed.) (1962a), pp. 196–7
1802	40				Nicholls, p. 201
1817–19	15–25				ibid., p. 202
1822	20				Cooper, (1974), pp. 87–8
1840	15	17	20–21	7–10	MA, 78/1841–2, pp. 7–9
1841	19	25	18.70		Harris, pp. 135–6
1842	14–25				Bennett and Brooks (eds) (1965), p. 253 (MT$7 at Kilwa)
1843	25–30				Hamerton to FO, 27 April 1843, PRO, FO 54/4
1844	19	17–30	15–30	7–15	MA, 88/1844, pp. 215–16
1846	12–15				Loarer
1847	4–5				ibid. (at Kilwa)
1849	8	15–25			Bennett and Brooks (eds) (1965), pp. 427–8
1856	12.50	7–18			Burton (1872), Vol. 1, p. 465
1859	14				Russell, p. 333
1860	16		10–35	6–13	Devereux, pp. 70, 104
1861	13		8–9	4–5	ibid.
1861/2	8.50				MA, 54/1864, pp. 16–33
1862/3	8.50				ibid.
1863	10	15		9–12	Colomb, p. 57
1863/4	10				Devereux, pp. 368–9 *PP*, 1863/53, p. 176

Table 2.6   *Continued*

Year	Average	Adult	Juvenile	Child	Source
		(MT\$)			
1865	20				MA, 52/1865, pp. 11–15
1868	14.50		20–25	5–8	Germain, p. 551–3
1869	17.50		14–23		Colomb, p. 57
1870	17				Christie, p. 32
1871	25–30				ibid.
1873	6–10		At Kilwa		Kirk to FO, 6 November 1873, *PP*, 62/1874, p. 102

After 1873 Treaty at:	Dar es Salaam	Pangani	Kenya	Brava	
1873	12–15	25–40	40–45	60–80	ibid.
1874		20–25	25–40	35–45	Cooper (1977), p. 123

The sugar industry in Zanzibar also received a fresh stimulus. As we have seen above, Arab landowners, including the Sultan, had turned to sugar production to compensate for the collapse of the slave trade to the south during the first quarter of the nineteenth century. By 1819 there were already two sugar mills which had recently been established, one of which belonged to the then governor of Zanzibar, a relative of Saleh b. Haramil who had introduced cloves to Zanzibar. Seyyid Said sought to expand this industry by importing technology and personnel from the Mascarenes, and even from England. In the early 1840s Seyyid Said went into partnership with an Englishman under the terms of which the latter provided machinery and supervision while the former supplied land and labour, i.e. slave labour. In 1847 about 10,000 *fraselas* of sugar were produced which Seyyid Said wanted to send to the United States or England for refining. The Americans, fearing penetration by their commercial rival into the United States market, tried to discourage him. On the other hand the British imposed an embargo on the importation of sugar, though not cloves, from the 'slave states'. As a result the industry may have suffered a setback. By 1860 only about 20,000 kg of sugar was being produced and it had difficulty finding a market.[79]

During the 1860s, however, interest in the production of sugar revived, attracting European and even Indian merchant capital. British Consul Pelly reported in 1862 that two Indian merchants had offered to put up Rs100,000 (MT\$45,000) each for the establishment of sugar plantations, but were apparently prevented from doing so by their inability as British subjects to hold slaves. This limitation, however, did not hinder H.A. Fraser, a former Indian Navy officer who had retired to Zanzibar and established sugar plantations. Fraser resurrected the ingenious formula of the 1840s under which he supplied machinery and supervisory staff, while the new Sultan Seyyid Majid supplied land at Mkokotoni and 500 slaves. When the agreement broke down, Fraser contracted with four Arab slave-owners for the supply of 400 'labourers' who were to be 'at the sole disposal' of Fraser & Co. for five years and were thereafter to be freed. The Arabs received their 'wages' for one year which amounted to MT$24 per 'labourer', a good price for an experienced slave. When the British law officers pronounced the contracts to be a subterfuge for the employment of slave labour, the British Consul induced Majid to pay for and then emancipate the 711 slaves on Fraser's plantation, and suggested a gift in return of a portrait of Queen Victoria.[80]

However, attempts at diversifying the economy were less successful on Zanzibar, where cloves had already established their tenacious grip, than on the mainland coast where, with the decline in the price of slaves, production of food and oleaginous grains became competitive. Along the southern coast there appears to have been considerable development of agricultural production after the end of the slave trade to the south, and especially by the late 1840s when overproduction of cloves had led to a glut in the market for slaves. Loarer reported that of the 20,000 people in the Tungi region, three-quarters were slaves, and some of the slaves exported from Lindi were absorbed along the coast. The coast between Tungi and Kiswere produced annually about 7,000 tons of millet and 3,500 tons of sesame, apart from the unstated but 'large quantities' from Lindi, exported to Zanzibar and Arabia. Slaves also appear to have been used in digging up copal, and the region exported about 8,500 *fraselas* of the resin each year.[81]

On the coast of Kenya the agricultural base was always important, and in 1826 Lt J.B. Emery recorded that many of the inhabitants of Mombasa had their plantations on the mainland where they were employed in cultivating grains after the departure of the monsoon dhows. However, production appears to have been small, and Mombasa was then dependent on grain imports from the northern coast of Kenya, the Mrima coast of northern Tanzania, and from Pemba, primarily for re-export to Arabia. The loss of Mombasa's political independence in 1837 and the consequent decline in its direct foreign trade as it was absorbed into the Zanzibar commercial empire (see Tables 5.2 and 5.3) seem to have transformed it from a mercantile metropolis into an agricultural backyard. The dispersed members of the Mazrui dynasty and others turned their attention to agricultural production all along the southern coast of Kenya. From the 1840s there was a marked expansion of grain production, and J.L. Krapf lamented the encroachment on Mijikenda land and an increase in the employment of slaves on the plantations. In the 1860s about 700 slaves were annually re-exported from Zanzibar to Mombasa and Malindi apart from those taken directly from Kilwa. By the late 1840s 3,000 tons of maize and small quantities of rice, millet and sesame were annually exported from Mombasa; in 1860 MT\$94,000-worth of grains were being exported; and by 1887 production had risen to 9,000 tons.[82]

More spectacular, perhaps, was the rebirth of the medieval town of Malindi after it had been abandoned since the seventeenth century. It was revived in the late 1850s or early 1860s under the direct encouragement of the Sultan of Zanzibar specifically for the production of food grains for export to Zanzibar and Arabia. By 1873 John Kirk, the British Consul, estimated an annual importation of at least 600 slaves just to maintain Malindi's stock of 6,000 slaves. He estimated an annual export of grains worth MT\$166,000, though H. Grefulhe, a French commercial agent directly involved in the trade, estimated it at between MT\$80,000 and MT\$120,000.[83]

A similar development occurred in the Lamu archipelago where many of the merchants, including the governor, had extensive plantations worked by slaves. Emery's journal of 1824–6 contains numerous references to dhows and *mtepe* from the Lamu archipelago which brought grain to Mombasa. In the late 1840s it was said that there were 40,000 slaves belonging to the people of Lamu involved in the production of sesame and other grains on the mainland, largely for export to Arabia. In 1853 it was reported that cultivation was on the increase, and that many dhows were being sent south as far as Mozambique to procure slaves. This was apart from an average of about 5,000 slaves who were being re-exported officially from Zanzibar to Lamu in the late 1860s, though not all were necessarily retained in the Lamu area. These slaves were used to extend cultivation on the mainland opposite Lamu. An important stimulus was given to agricultural growth in the area by French and German demand for sesame for the production of vegetable oil, and orchilla weed (orchil) used in the production of dyes, for export to Europe. During the 1860s Zanzibar exported an average of about MT\$170,000-worth of sesame and other oil seeds, 70 per cent of which went to France and Germany.[84]

All these areas were within the legal limits of the slave trade before 1873, but the economic factors which lay behind the expansion of the slave system of production on the East African coast exerted their influence on the southern coast of Somalia as well. The most important geographical feature of the coastal belt is the Shebelle river which runs parallel to the coast for nearly 200 miles, and which overflows its banks seasonally to irrigate a vast fertile riverain plain. This was the traditional breadbasket of the Benadir ports of Mogadishu, Merka and Brava. There appears to have been a marked expansion of agricultural production during the nineteenth century. W. Christopher reported in 1843 that the Benadir had become the 'grain coast for the supply of South Arabia', and Guillain observed thriving agricultural communities along the lower Shebelle. There was also an expansion in the production of cotton for the Benadir's own textile industry from the 1840s in an attempt to lower the cost of production and compete with the cheap *merekani* using local resources instead of imported cotton from India. A fresh impetus to the expansion of agriculture was also given by French and German demand for sesame and orchilla weed which was also exported to England in the 1860s.[85]

This expansion of production was based on the exploitation of the subordinate class of agriculturists, probably descendants of the region's earliest cultivators called the *habash*, and slaves imported from the coast to the south. It was in the 1830s and the 1840s, after the abolition of the slave trade to the south, and later with the decline in the price of slaves, that importation of slaves into the Benadir reached sizeable proportions. When the slave trade to the north was also prohibited in 1845, particularly when British warships began to blockade the Benadir in the 1860s, slaves began to be marched along the coast or smuggled by sea from the Lamu area. Marguerite Ylvisaker estimates that during the early 1870s as many as 4,000 slaves were thus taken to the north, while Kirk suggested that 10,000 slaves were crossing the Juba annually, which may be an exaggeration.[86]

Lee V. Cassanelli suggests that this development tended to encourage individual Somalis to take up tracts of land, and this new wealth in slaves and land tended to increase their clients, following and prestige. He argues that few landholders, however, had more than ten or fifteen slaves, and that they continued to use kinship ties to obtain land and protect their property. They therefore functioned within the traditional political system rather than creating new centres of power. Cassanelli may be exaggerating the theme of continuity. That a rising class seeks to use elements of the pre-existing socio-political system to consolidate its position is a widespread phenomenon, and it should not be allowed to camouflage the transformation in the social system along the southern Somali coast. As Cassanelli himself shows, the wealth of this class of landowners enabled it to turn the tables on the coastal merchants who often became indebted to the former, a fairly unusual phenomenon along the East African coast during the nineteenth century.[87]

Thus with overproduction of cloves on Zanzibar and Pemba, and the consequent decline in the price of cloves and of their slave producers, a tremendous impetus was given to the spread of the slave system of production along the mainland coast. As we have seen, this process was given a powerful shot in the arm by the steep rise in the European demand for oleaginous grains and orchilla weed. The coast of Kenya and southern Somalia, therefore, had developed as a considerable market for slaves, contrary to Austen's estimates,[88] though some of the slaves officially imported into the coast of Kenya were smuggled north to Arabia.

Notes

1. Coupland (1938), pp. 4, 34–5.
2. Austen, p. 33.
3. Sakkarai, passim.
4. ibid., pp. 67–77.
5. Alpers (1967), p. 11; Coupland (1938), p. 500; Sulivan, pp. 444–5.
6. Freeman-Grenville (ed.) (1962a), p. 210; 'Memo on the Principal Parts of the east coast of Africa', 15 February 1826 in MA, 20/1826, pp. 132–5.
7. Salil, p. 93.
8. See p. 230 below; Nicholls, p. 203; Cooper (1977), p. 160n.
9. Freeman-Grenville (1965), pp. 85, 93, 107–8, 163; Auten (1977), Table I, D.
10. Austen (1977), Table IV, B.
11. Salil, p. 202, 342; Nicholls, pp. 101, 257.
12. Wilson to Norris, 28 January 1831, MA, 1/1830–2, pp. 18–21; Robertson to Willoughby, 4 March 1842, MA, 78/1841–2, pp. 346–62.
13. Wilson to Norris, 28 January 1831, MA, 1/1830–2, pp. 18–21.
14. ibid.
15. Robertson to Willoughby, 4 March 1842, MA, 78/1841–2, pp. 346–62.
16. Rana of Porebandar to Long, 6 November 1835, MA, 19/1835–6, pp. 59–63.
17. Austen (1977), Table III, B.
18. Resident, Kutch, to Political Secretary to Government, 26 July 1838, MA, 106/1838–9, pp. 131–4.
19. Salt, p. 82; Bombay to Court of Directors, 20 April 1841, PRO, FO 54/5, p. 374; Political Agent, Katteewar to Willoughby, 1 December 1837, NAI, 18/7/1837, p. 50; same to same, 4 December 1840 and 18 March 1841, MA 111/1840–1, pp. 153–5, 159–60; Austen (1977), Table IV, A.
20. Martin and Ryan, p. 79; Austen (1977), Table V.
21. ibid.
22. Martin and Ryan, p. 78; Austen (1977), Table III, 13.
23. Sulivan, pp. 307–8; Colomb, p. 47; *PP.*, Vol. 7, Session No. 420, p. 52.
24. See p. 47 above. This interpretation is challenged by Cooper, but he produces little evidence to the contrary. See Cooper (1977), p. 43n.
25. Marx, Vol. 1, p. 703.
26. Alpers (1966), p. 172.
27. Freeman-Grenville (1965), pp. 64, 92, 152.
28. ibid., pp. 163–4, 202; Datoo (1968), pp. 222–3.
29. Datoo (1968), pp. 235–8; Alpers (1966), pp. 228–32, 238.
30. Freeman-Grenville (1965), pp. 64, 87–8, 92, 152, 169, 207.
31. ibid., pp. 76, 135–6, 151.

32. ibid., p. 82.
33. ibid., pp. 82, 148, 151.
34. ibid., pp. 107, 121-2, 142-4, 172-87, 191; Alpers (1966), p. 119.
35. Freeman-Grenville (1965), pp. 186-7.
36. Freeman-Grenville (ed.) (1962a), pp. 196-7; Alpers (1970), p. 109; Datoo (1968), pp. 234, 238.
37. Freeman-Grenville (ed.) (1962a), p. 223; Chittick (1959), pp. 186-9.
38. Ross, passim; Hall, p. 47; Freeman-Grenville (1965), pp. 13, 87, 141.
39. Freeman-Grenville (1965), pp. 115, 135; Freeman-Grenville (ed.) (1962a), pp. 193, 222-3.
40. Gray (1964a), pp. 20-4; Gray (1964b), p. 224; Freeman-Grenville (ed.) (1962a), pp. 194-5, 200, 203, 205, 210, 224-5; Albrand, p. 83; Owen, Vol. 2, p. 3; Krapf, p. 423.
41. Gray (1964b), p. 225; Freeman-Grenville (ed.) (1962a), pp. 194, 199, 200; Datoo (1968), pp. 18-19.
42 Alpers (1966), p. 238; Datoo (1968), p. 264n; Report of Captain Tomkinson 1809, and Fisher to Bertie, 31 December 1809, PRO, Adm. 1/62-63; Theal, Vol. 9, p. 13; Freeman-Grenville (ed.)(1962a), p. 210; Coupland (1938), pp. 193-7; Farquhar to Moresby, 5 April 1821, BM, Add. Mss. 41/265 f. 17.
43. Salt, pp. 122-3; Coupland (1938), p. 189; Klein and Engerman, Table I; Moresby to Farquhar, 4 April 1821 and 7 August 1821, BM, Add. Mss. 41/265, ff. 12-18.
44. Memo. from the Persian Secretary, 11 April 1834, NAI, 29/5/1834-PC-6/11; Cogan's Memo., 5 January 1838, PRO, FO 54/2; Hennel to Bombay, 10 January 1838, MA, 990/1838-9, p. 226; Hamerton to Bombay, 1 February 1842, PRO, FO 54/5, p. 422.
45. Report of Captain Tomkinson 1809, PRO, Adm. 1/62-3; Freeman-Grenville (ed.) (1962a), p. 210.
46. See Table 2.6. Cooper (1977), pp. 38-9, 44, disagrees with this interpretation, arguing that the Arab decision to invest in clove plantations reflected 'a choice of life-style'. What I argue is that the crisis in the slave trade at the beginning of the nineteenth century led a number of Omani traders to plant cloves from the 1810s and particularly in the 'clove mania' of the 1830s as shown below. See Sheriff (1971), pp. 175-84.
47. Said to Shoostree, n.d., Consultation 9/7/1828, MA, 8/1828.
48. Ruschenberger, Vol. 1, pp. 73-5; Crofton (1936), p. 80.
49. Guillain, Vol. 2, p. 49; Gray (1964a), pp. 21-3; Burton (1872), Vol. 1, pp. 363-4; Albrand, p. 69.
50. Albrand, pp. 78-9; Fisher's Report, PRO, Adm. I/62; Freeman-Grenville (ed.) (1962a), p. 199; Burton (1872), Vol. 1, pp. 294-5, 361; Fitzgerald, pp. 553-4; Guillain, Vol. 2, p. 49; Cooper (1974), p. 99.
51. Albrand, pp. 78-9; Farsy, p. 29; Guillain, Vol. 2, p. 49; Burton (1872), Vol. 1, pp., 294-5, 361.
52. Guillain, Vol. 2, p. 49. See Appendix A below.
53. Bruce of Warden, 25 February 1822, MA, 82/1822; Roberts to Woodbury, 19 December 1828, LC, Roberts Papers, VI; Invoice of the *Osprey*, 3 July 1837, PM, W.C. Waters Collection.

54. Ruschenberger, Vol. 1, pp. 70-1; Ruete (1929), p. 87; Loarer, 'Girofle', ANSOM, OI, 5/23/4 & 5; Guillain, Vol. 2, p. 48; Ward to Ward, 22 November 1847, EI, Ward's Letter Book, 1848-9; Bennett and Brooks (eds) (1965), p. 256; Burton (1872), Vol. 1, p. 98.
55. Loarer, 'Girofle', ANSOM, OI, 5/23/4 & 5.
56. Ruschenberger, Vol. 1, pp. 27, 51, 54; Rigby to Bombay, 4 April 1859, NAI, 17/6/1859-PC-5; Bennett and Brooks (eds) (1965), pp. 162, 212-13, 444; Waters's journal, 21 July 1842, Waters's Notes, 23 March 1844, Waters's contracts, PM, Waters Papers, IV.
57. Smee's Journal, 5 June 1811, IOR, MR Misc. 586.
58. Burton (1872), Vol. 1, pp. 278, 432; Gray (1962a), p. 168; *Zanzibar Gazette*, 592/2; Waters's Notes, 15 June 1844, PM, Waters Papers, IV; Pickering, p. 181.
59. Loarer, 'Girofle', ANSOM, OI, 5/23/4 & 5; Waters's Notes, 8 September and 22 November 1843, PM, Waters Paper, IV; Bennett and Brooks (eds) (1965), p. 376.
60. Russell (1935), p. 328; Waters's contracts, PM, Waters Papers, IV; Mackenzie, pp. 92-3; Brode, p. 48; Cooper (1974), p. 143.
61. Loarer, 'Pemba', ANSOM, OI, 2/10/2D.
62. Burton (1872), Vol. 1, pp. 361-2; Loarer, 'Girofle', ANSOM, OI, 5/23/4 & 5; Albrand, p. 69.
63. Broquant to MAE, (1845), MAE, CCZ, Vol. I, pp. 220-31; Burton (1872), Vol. 1, p. 363; Christopher, p. 377; Tidbury, pp. 108-9; Ruschenberger, Vol. 1, p. 51; 'Principal Articles of Commerce at the Port of Zanzibar', MA, 73/1861, pp. 7-25; Cooper (1974), p. 123.
64. *Zanzibar Law Reports*, Vol. 8, pp. 282-92; Gray (1962a), pp. 176-8; Jabir, pp. 35, 58-9.
65. Albrand, pp. 66, 70; Middleton, pp. 11, 42; Prins (1961), p. 62; Smee, in Burton (1872), Vol. 2. p. 500.
66. Middleton, pp. 62-3; Loarer, 'Pemba', ANSOM, OI, 2/10/2D; Tidbury, p. 163; Jabir, p. 35; Sheriff (1986), passim.
67. Ruschenberger, Vol. 1, p. 64; Burgess, p. 118; Burton (1872), Vol. I, p. 414; Gray (1962a), pp. 161-2; Gray (1956b), p. 10; Hamerton to Bombay, 2 January 1842, PRO, FO 54/4; Jabir, p. 37; Hardy's Journal, IOR, MR, Misc. 586.
68. Martin & Ryan, p. 82. See note 8 above.
69. Albrand, p. 73; Burgess, pp. 118-21; Bennett and Brooks (eds) (1965), p. 400; Loarer, 'Girofle', ANSOM, OI, 5/23/4 & 5.
70. Smee, in Burton (1872), Vol. 2, p. 493; Albrand, p. 75; Martin and Ryan, p. 74.
71. See Appendix A below. Loarer, 'Girofle', ANSOM, OI, 5/23/4 & 5; Burton (1872), Vol. 1, pp. 364-5; EI: SCHR, Inward Invoices (1839).
72. Burton (1872), Vol. 1, p. 219; IOR, P/419/1801/2-1859/60; PM, Waters, Shepard and West Papers.
73. Loarer, 'Girofle', ANSOM, OI, 5/23/4 & 5; Grant, p. 15; Seward's Report on the Trade and Commerce of Zanzibar, 1864/5, *PP*, 1867/67, C. 3761, p. 285.
74. O. Sullivan Beare's 'Report on the Island of Pemba, 1900', *PP*, 1901/81, C. 2653, p. 11; Tidbury, p. 106.

75. Hamerton to Bombay, 9 October 1843, Rigby to Anderson, 14 May 1861, PRO, FO 84/1146; Burton (1872), Vol. 1, pp. 316-17. However, as late as 1869, the French Consul mentions Indians owning slaves. Bure to MAE, 4 March 1869, MAE, CCZ, Vol. III, pp. 93-6.

76. Frere's 'Memo. regarding Banyans', *PP*, 1873/61, C. 820 p. 102. Frere, unfortunately, does not give a precise figure, but says that 'a somewhat smaller amount' than £60,000 (MT$285,000) had been loaned out to Arabs in Zanzibar and on the coast. See also Mangat, p. 19.

77. Colomb, p. 57; Devereux, pp. 70, 104, 114, 368-9; Freeman-Grenville (ed.) (1962a), pp. 196-7; Cooper (1974), pp. 87-8; Loarer, 'Esclaves', ANSOM, OI, 2/10/B & 5/23/5.

78. Bennett and Brooks (eds) (1965), pp. 528, 553; Seward's Report on the Trade and Commerce of Zanzibar, 1864/5, *PP*, 1867/67, C. 3761, p. 284; Cooper (1974), p. 123.

79. Albrand, p. 76; Hamerton to Palmerston, 24 September 1846, PRO, FO 54/10; same to same, 13 April 1844, PRO, FO 84/540; Memorial of W. Henderson & Co. to the Treasury, 20 May 1842, PRO, FO 54/8; Said to Palmerston, 30 June 1847, PRO, FO 54/11; Bennett and Brooks (eds) (1965), pp. 253, 257, 384, 390, 398; Loarer, 'Sucre', ANSOM, OI, 5/23/5; Derche to MAE, 2 May 1860, MAE, CCZ, Vol. II.

80. Playfair to FO, 3 May 1865, Seward to Gonne, 14 July 1866, PRO, FO 84/1261; Seward to FO, 20 February 1867, PRO, FO 84/1279; Frere's Memo, 10 February 1873, *PP*, 1873/61, C. 820, pp. 105-6. See also Bennett and Brooks (eds) (1965), p. 525.

81. Loarer, 'Lindy', ANSOM, OI, 2/10/2A.

82. Emery's Journal, passim, PRO, Adm. 52/3940; Berg (1971), pp. 196, 202, 216-23, 245, 263-6, 277; Loarer, ANSOM, OI, 2/10/2 & 5/23/5. See Table 6.3 below.

83. Cooper (1974), pp. 173-85; Martin (1973), ch. 4; Kirk to Granville, 6 November 1873, *PP*, 1874/62, pp. 101-2.

84. Loarer, 'Lamo', ANSOM, OI, 2/10/2D; Sunley to Clarendon, 23 August 1853, PRO, FO 84/919; Grefulhe, pp. 328-31; Rigby to Anderson, 11 February 1860, MA, 159/1860, pp. 219-53; Ylvisaker (1971), passim.

85. Cassanelli, ch. 4; Christopher (1844), pp. 85-7; Alpers (1983), pp. 449-50.

86. Ylvisaker (1971), p. 118.

87. Cassanelli, ch. 4.

88. Austen (1977), p. 12, n. 7.

Three

Commercial Expansion and the Rise of the Merchant Class

The decline in the export of slaves from East Africa from the end of the eighteenth century onwards had initiated the transformation of the Omani merchant class at Zanzibar into a landed aristocracy. However, the slave relations of production that had developed on Zanzibar, Pemba and the Kenya coast required the continued flow of slaves from the African interior and the marketing of the slave-produced commodities. These activities, therefore, ensured the survival of the commercial sector and of the merchant class in East Africa.

The commercial sector, however, received a greater boost from the end of the eighteenth century with the development of the ivory trade. This was sparked by the collapse of the ivory trade at Mozambique which had created a gap in the supply of ivory to India. A greater and longer-term impetus, though, was given by the steeply rising demand for ivory and other luxuries from the affluent classes in the industrialising countries of the West from the 1820s onwards. What made the ivory sector of Zanzibar's commerce so vibrant and expansive was the fact that, whereas the price of ivory and other luxuries rose steeply in response to the demand in the West, the price of manufactured commodities used in exchange declined throughout the nineteenth century as a result of capitalist competition in the industrial countries. The diverging curves of prices of the exported luxuries and imported manufactured commodities was the dynamic factor in the phenomenal expansion of the commercial hinterland of Zanzibar and the prosperity of the entrepôt.

In this expanding trade the Omani and Swahili sections of the merchant class found a new lease of life, especially in coastal trading and in the caravan trade into the interior. However, the ascendant section that initially captured the ivory trade with India and later came to monopolise the trade at the entrepôt was of Indian origin. Merchant classes are typically compradorial, accommodating themselves to the prevailing dominant modes of production and classes. Initially these seemed to be the slave mode and the Omani landowning ruling class but, as the century wore on, it became increasingly clear that both were themselves subordinate to the capitalist mode which was becoming a world-wide system. While, on the one hand, the merchant capitalists undermined the landed aristocracy by appropriating a major part of the surplus in the form either of commercial profit or usury, they could not, on the other hand, avoid being subjugated to and becoming a tool of British capital in the Omani commercial empire in East Africa.

The ivory trade to the end of the eighteenth century

Ivory has been an export from the eastern coast of Africa from as early as the second century BC, initially directed to the Mediterranean market. From about the seventh century AD India and later China emerged as the major market. Asian demand for East African ivory arose from the fact that Asian elephants are poorly provided with ivory and are rarely hunted for it. Asian ivory, moreover, is 'hard' and brittle, harder to polish and tends to yellow with exposure to air. The East African variety, on the other hand, is 'soft' and polishes much better. As local supplies of ivory in Asia diminished, African ivory found an easy market. As al-Mas 'udi wrote in the tenth century:

> It is from this [Zanj] country that come tusks weighing fifty pounds and more. They usually go to Oman, and from there are sent to China and India. This is the chief trade route, and if it were not so, ivory would be common in Muslim lands.[1]

In India much of the ivory was used in the production of bangles which were considered indispensable bridal ornaments, especially for upper class women, though cheaper sets were worn by almost all Hindu women of the lower classes as well. These bangles were exclusively the adornments of marriage and married life, and among Hindus they did not survive the termination of that state by the death of either of the partners. In the days of *sati*, the widow followed her dead husband into the funeral pyre bedecked with her bridal ornaments. After the abolition of *sati*, the bangles were nevertheless broken as a demonstration of the widow's grief. If the wife happened to predecease her husband, she was of course cremated together with her bridal ornaments. Thus there was a steady demand for African ivory in India well into the twentieth century.[2]

Before the nineteenth century, however, Asian demand for ivory was still fairly limited, and the coastal belt of East Africa was initially exploited to meet the demand. But as these local sources began to diminish, there were attempts to tap the ivory resources of the interior along one of the corridors across the *nyika* wilderness, such as that along the Tana, but it was not yet economic to brave the hardships of the *nyika* itself. Until the end of the eighteenth century, therefore, the alternative was to extend the trade to Mozambique where, even in the pre-Portuguese period, long-distance trade routes had already been forged with the deep interior for the supply of gold from Zimbabwe. It is significant that as late as the beginning of the nineteenth century ivory was universally described as a 'produce of Mozambique' in Surat's customs returns.[3]

E.A. Alpers, however, has argued that the truncation of Kilwa's maritime hinterland to Sofala by the Portuguese forced it to reorient its trade and seek to exploit its own continental hinterland towards the end of the sixteenth century. He quotes some Portuguese sources which seem to suggest that the Yao, the principal long-distance traders in east-central Africa, shifted their trade between Mozambique and Kilwa several times during the seventeenth and eighteenth centuries in response to economic conditions pertaining at those ports. However, Gaspar Bocarro's overland journey from the Zambezi to Kilwa in 1616 provided little evidence for an active long-distance trade except between Kilwa and the Ruvuma. The guides he had taken from the southern end of Lake Nyasa turned back at this point. It was only on the Ruvuma that he first encountered cloth from 'the coast of Melinde'. Eighteenth-century Portuguese sources are fairly circumstantial attempts to explain away fluctuations in the trade of Mozambique by officials who had little access to reliable information from the East African coast north of Cape Delgado since they were expelled by the Omanis at the end of the seventeenth century. Even the French trader, Morice, who does indicate that trade contacts had been forged between Kilwa and Lake Nyasa by the 1770s, specifies that the trade was conducted through a relay system and that no single tribe dominated the whole length of the trade route, and he makes no reference to the Yao.[4]

The cyclical fluctuation in the supply of ivory by the Yao to Mozambique Island can be better explained by the diversion of the ivory trade to the market towns on the Zambezi which were nearer to the sources of ivory. Mozambique Island was preferred by African traders because the Zambezi was often held as a monopoly by the Captain of Mozambique while prices were more competitive at Mozambique Island. As Barreto stated in 1745:

> It is much easier for the [African] traders . . . to bring their ivory to Tete than to carry it to Mozambique, but they avoid coming to Tete in order not to be subjected to the monopoly of the governor of Mozambique.[5]

Trade was subject to a 40 per cent re-export duty on imports from Mozambique Island to the provinces, a measure that was intended to centralise trade at the capital. During the second half of the eighteenth century, however, the import duty on 'velorio' trade beads, a staple in the trade at Mozambique, and on cloth was reduced successively from 20 per cent to 10 per cent by 1793. More important was the reduction in the re-export duty from 40 per cent in the 1760s to 30 per cent in 1787 and 10 per cent in 1793. The combined effect of these two series of measures was a marked increase in the export of ivory from the colony as a whole, and a diversion of the ivory trade from Mozambique Island to the provinces. It is reported that Delagoa Bay, which used to be visited by one boat from Mozambique once in a year or two, received twenty-two ships between 1789 and 1799. Thus, whereas in the 1760s Mozambique Island supplied nearly 75 per cent of the ivory exported by the colony as a whole, by the early 1790s, although the total export of ivory had increased by more than 40 per cent, the share of Mozambique Island had declined to less than 4 per cent (see Table 3.1).

Table 3.1 *The ivory trade of Mozambique, 1754–1817*

Year	Duties (percentage) Import on beads	Re-export	Ivory arriving at Mozambique Is. (arrobas)	Total ivory export from Mozambique (arrobas)	Price (cruzados per arroba)
1754					59
1757					57
1759	20	40		10,766	
1760			6,750	9,484	
1761				8,792	
1762			7,752	10,484	
1763–7					56
1777					56
1781			1,950		
1785			3,750		
1787	15	30			76
1793	10	10		13,000	
1795			375		
1800		40			
1801	20	30		6,000	
1802			4,500		
1809				7,000	105–127
1817				4,000	

Notes: 1 *arroba* = 14.69 kg.   1 *cruzado* = (1777) MT$ 0.27; (1813) MT$ 0.38.
Sources: Alpers (1966), pp. 182–3, 193, 240, 256, 277; Alpers (1975), pp. xiv, 105, 119, 176; Salt, p. 82; Freeman-Grenville (1965), p. 88; Milburn, Vol. 1, p. 60.

The undoubtedly catastrophic decline in the Yao ivory trade to Mozambique Island, therefore, was more than compensated for by an increase in the supply of ivory from other parts of the province and need not imply the total abandonment by the Yao of Mozambique as a whole. The increase in the trade of Mozambique during the second half of the eighteenth century receives further confirmation from the number of Indian traders settled there which increased from about 200 in the 1760s to about 300 in the 1780s. Moreover, whereas only one vessel each from Diu and Daman visited Mozambique in the 1750s, in the 1770s five vessels arrived from Diu alone.[6]

It was, in fact, only at the beginning of the nineteenth century that, in an attempt to recentralise the trade at Mozambique Island and increase the revenue of the colonial state, the ivory trade in the colony as a whole was rendered less economical by the increase in the re-export duties to 40 per cent by 1800 (although it was reduced to 30 per cent the following year), and import duties were at the same time raised to 20 per cent by 1801. Total duties, including custom house charges and pilotage, which Henry Salt estimated at 5 per cent, therefore amounted to a prohibitive 55 per cent in the provinces and 25 per cent at Mozambique Island. This may have had the effect of diverting trade to the capital where Salt found large numbers of Yao traders in 1809, selling slaves as well as ivory. But the increased duties had rendered the whole colony unprofitable to ivory traders. The total export of ivory from Mozambique as a whole had been halved by 1800, and it plunged to a nadir by 1817 when it stood at less than one-third of the quantity exported in the 1790s.

The result was a spectacular upswing in the price of ivory at Mozambique. In an effort to curb the activities of the Indian merchants, who were held responsible for the inflation in prices, and to foster a Portuguese merchant class, the authorities tried to impose a price ceiling at 40 *cruzados* in the early 1780s, but they were forced to double it by the 1790s. The price, which had averaged less than 60 *cruzados* per *arroba* from the 1740s to the 1770s, nearly doubled by 1809. Mozambique was inexorably pricing itself out of the market. The fact that the price of ivory at Surat also doubled between 1802–3 and 1808–9 is a further indication of India's reliance at this time on Mozambique for its supplies of ivory (see Graph 3.1). The destruction of Portuguese shipping in the Anglo-French naval warfare then raging in the Indian Ocean may also have contributed to the rise in ivory prices, but there was no recovery in Mozambique's ivory exports following the cessation of those hostilities. The fact that the price of ivory at Surat declined to its normal level after 1810 shows that new sources of ivory to the north were being opened up as a result.[7]

These suicidal fiscal changes were being effected at a time when Kilwa's hinterland had already extended as far as Lake Nyasa, primarily for the supply of slaves to the French. The direct Bisa trade with Tete on the Zambezi, which had apparently been established by 1793, was gravely threatened by 1798. It is significant that the governor of Sena on the Zambezi himself undertook the expedition to the Kazembe in 1798 to reopen the trade. His first-hand account is therefore likely to be relatively reliable. He commented:

> I now think with reason that the great number of tusks which once went to Mozambique, and which certainly came from these lands, goes at present to Zanzibar, or the neighbourhood . . . because they get more for their ivory.[8]

In 1810 Pereira reported that the subjects of the Kazembe, an important source of ivory near Lake Mweru, had ceased to come to trade at Tete since Lacerda's expedition. The barter price of ivory on the Zambezi had nearly doubled between 1799 and 1810 which, in view of the increased duties, must have become uneconomical.[9]

The genesis of the Indian mercantile class

Whereas the Portuguese became embroiled in Anglo-French naval warfare, Oman remained neutral, and fully utilised its neutrality to augment its shipping by purchasing English and Portuguese prizes from the French, and to capture a considerable portion of the trade in the western Indian Ocean, even threatening to capture the lucrative China trade. It was reported in 1803 that the Omanis, 'in the course of ten years have increased their tonnage from a number of Dows and Dingeys, and two or three old ships, to upwards of fifty fine ships.' Indian vessels flocked to Muscat to acquire its neutral flag when the British were unable to offer protection to them, and one Surat shipowner held 2,000 tons of shipping at Muscat. An additional reason for the Omani success was their greater competitiveness, for it was stated that they could carry freight at a cost of between a half and one-third of what a British ship could.[10]

The commercial boom in the trade was reflected at Zanzibar by the doubling of its revenue between 1804 and 1819 since it and other coastal towns were probably well placed to take advantage of the sharp upswing in the price of ivory in the Indian market. The expanding trade provided the Swahili section of the merchant class with a niche in the entrepôt trade, and as late as the 1840s several Swahili merchants of Mafia, claiming regal Shirazi descent and a relationship with the *Mwinyi Mkuu* of Zanzibar, were conducting trade on a considerable scale along the East African coast. In foreign trade, however, their role was limited. As early as 1775 Morice had remarked that they lacked sufficient capital and large vessels to trade beyond the coastal waters to any great extent. Their commercial interests apparently brought them close to their Omani conquerors and, according to Morice, they 'viewed with indifference Arab occupation which hurt neither their rights nor their interests', although the Dutch slave traders who visited Zanzibar in 1777 recorded considerable divergence of economic interests, especially where the slave trade with Europeans was concerned.[11]

At the beginning of the nineteenth century, however, according to a British naval officer, Captain Smee, the foreign trade was 'chiefly in the hands of the Arabs belonging to Muscat [and] Maculla' and, it should be added, to 'old Arabs' settled along the coast, such as the Mazrui of Mombasa. These Arabs were also able to take advantage of the opportunity not only to tap the ivory resources of the coast to the south as far as Mozambique and to forge trade links with their own hinterland, but also to trade with India and Arabia directly. They owned many dhows and traded on their own account as well as transporting goods as freight. In the 1820s one of them had a capital of MT$25,000, and in 1824 a single dhow carried 556 *fraselas* of ivory and 337 *fraselas* of gum copal to Bombay, and returned with a sizeable consignment of brass wire which was especially important in the trade with the Kamba.[12]

The boom in Omani commerce as a result of Anglo-French warfare, however, was a temporary phenomenon, lasting only between 1798 and 1806. With the coming of peace the Omanis lost their advantage, and there was a desertion of the Arab flag by Indian vessels. By 1817 the English prizes acquired by them during the war had begun to decay. Moreover, many of the Omani merchants were still too wedded to the French slave trade, and they may have devoted their efforts after the end of the war to reactivating the slave trade to the south, even after it had been proscribed by the Moresby Treaty in 1822. Saleh b. Haramil risked the confiscation of his valuable estates by continuing to participate in this highly lucrative smuggling trade, and lost. Others, including Saleh, sought to recompense themselves for the decline in the slave trade by turning their attention to the production of cloves with slave labour which was extremely lucrative before the late 1840s. Many failed to foresee that the foreign slave trade was on a declining curve, and overproduction would soon overtake the profitability of cloves. It was the ivory trade that was poised on a long-term ascending trajectory.[13]

The Indian merchants, on the other hand, were riding on a rising tide of the ivory trade. At the beginning of the nineteenth century the Indian merchant class at Zanzibar was still embryonic. The British naval officer, Lieutenant A. Bissell, writing in 1799 makes hardly any reference to it, though he does mention 'the small trading vessels from Muscat and the Red Sea.' By 1811 there were a number of Indian vessels trading at Zanzibar, but many of the Indian traders, particularly from Surat and Bhownagar in British India, appear to have been seasonal, with limited roots in the East African trade. The relative insignificance of the Indian section of the mercantile class is indicated by the fact that, of the 25,000 crowns which the governor of Zanzibar was asked to raise to repair one of the Sultan's vessels, the Indian traders were called upon to pay only 3,500 crowns. Their commercial activities were still confined to Zanzibar itself, like other foreign traders, and they were apparently not allowed to own land outside Zanzibar town. They complained of 'oppression' and of 'heavy impositions and exactions of the local authority at Zanzibar', and they called on the transient British warships to protect them.[14]

Nevertheless, there was already by 1811 a section of the Indian traders, the 'few adventurers from Cutch and the coast of Scinde', who appear to have been more settled, and they formed the nucleus of the Indian section of the merchant class at Zanzibar which by 1819 numbered 214. They were described as wealthy and were said to have held 'the best part of the trade'. It was to one of these 'Banians', an offshoot of the Indian merchant class at Muscat, that the customs of Zanzibar began to be farmed out as early as 1804. The foundation of this class was being laid on the evolving Indian dominance over both the import and export trade of Zanzibar. Smee estimated in 1811 that nearly 50 per cent of the imports at Zanzibar consisted of 'Surat cloths' from Kutch and Surat which had established their reputation for quality and durability, and yet cost only half as much as their Manchester competitors at that time. Their Indian names, such as *bafta* and *kaniki*, passed into Kiswahili and have remained current, long after being displaced by machine-made textiles. In return the Indians took large quantities of ivory and other commodities.[15]

During the first few decades of the nineteenth century Indian trade with East Africa was dominated by Kutch, and to a lesser extent Gujarat, which explains the cultural dominance of these regions over the Indian merchant class at Zanzibar ever since. Kutch imported twice as much ivory as the British ports of Bombay and Surat, and she supplied as late as 1839 about three times as much cotton goods. The 'Swally' trade, as the trade with East Africa was called, (from *Sawahil*, the coast), came to dominate the foreign trade of Kutch. Whereas in 1818 the trade was mentioned without any superlatives, by 1833 it was described as 'the most valuable branch' in which up to twenty vessels from the main port of Mandvi were involved.[16]

Indian trade with East Africa, however, suffered from a number of structural weaknesses which ultimately led to its subordination and integration into the international capitalist system then dominated by Britain. The first was the recurrence of famines in the somewhat marginal lands of Kutch and Gujarat which were the main areas in commercial contact with East Africa. 'The saying is that a famine comes every ten years', and famines were responsible for the violent fluctuations in the trade figures of Bombay and Surat. They had a direct effect on the production of cotton goods and on purchasing power even for necessities of life, let alone luxuries like ivory. The famine of 1813 is said to have killed nearly half the population of Kutch and forced many others to migrate elsewhere. There was a 75 per cent reduction in the import of ivory into Surat and Bombay in 1813-14 compared to 1809-10 despite a sharp reduction in the price. There was a corresponding increase in the import of bullion, while at Bhownagar foodstuffs replaced ivory as the chief import. Famines of lesser intensity occurred in 1803, 1823-5, 1833-4, etc.[17]

The second structural weakness arose from the political subordination of India to British rule, and from the backwardness of her industries at a time when industrial capitalism was ascendant in Britain. As late as 1813 it was admitted that British manufactured goods had found a limited market among Indians partly because of 'the excellence of their own manufactures'. To foster the growth of the British textile industry, therefore, prohibitive tariffs were imposed on Indian manufactured goods entering Britain, amounting to nearly 80 per cent on calicoes in 1813, while only a nominal duty of 2.5 per cent was imposed on British cotton goods entering India. More important, perhaps, was the ability of competing industrial capitalists in Britain to improve and enlarge their industrial plants to lower the cost of production and thus undercut the Indian textile industry. Indian textiles were displaced not only from their traditional foreign markets but even in India itself. While the export of cotton piece goods to Britain declined by 75 per cent between 1814 and 1835, the import of British cotton goods into India increased more than fiftyfold during the same period. Even where India appeared to continue to export cotton goods, as for example to East Africa, they were increasingly of British manufacture, or manufactured from British yarn. The East India Company proudly proclaimed in 1840:

> This company has in various ways, encouraged and assisted by our great manufacturing ingenuity and skill, succeeded in converting India from a manufacturing country into a country exporting raw materials.[18]

The colonial underdevelopment of India had begun.

Finally, as a result of the increasing affluence of the upper classes in industrialising Britain, an increasing proportion of the imports of ivory into India began to be siphoned off to London. At the beginning of the nineteenth century nearly 80 per cent of the ivory imported into Surat and Bombay, and probably also into Kutch, was consumed within India. Smaller amounts were exported to China, and only 6 per cent was exported to London. However, while the Indian home market remained stagnant, and even declined from an annual average of Rs283,000 during the first two decades of the nineteenth century to Rs225,000 during the next two decades, the total amount of ivory imported on average each year into Bombay increased from Rs357,000 to Rs437,000 during the same period, and nearly tripled by the middle of the nineteenth century.[19] Simultaneously, the re-export of ivory from Bombay to the United Kingdom rose from an annual average of Rs20,000 during the first two decades to Rs311,000 during the next two decades when it exceeded the consumption of the Indian home market. During the middle decades of the century the re-export to London more than doubled, siphoning off nearly two-thirds of the total amount of ivory imported into Bombay (see Appendix A). Bombay had assumed increasingly the role of an intermediary in the ivory trade between East Africa and London. Though this re-export trade brought profit to the merchants involved, the inevitable competition between the Indian and English markets gradually raised the price of ivory above the level which the poorer classes could afford and it may have resulted in the shrinkage of the Indian market.

Thus, both in the imports and exports of East Africa, India increasingly became merely a staging post and a mechanism for the commercial integration of East Africa into the international capitalist system dominated by Britain. Moreover, Bombay's position in the trade was vulnerable since the ridiculous triangular trade between Zanzibar, Bombay and London via the Cape of Good Hope could be short-circuited by direct British trade with East Africa. The specifically Indian trade with East Africa was thus undermined during the first half of the nineteenth century. The Indian merchant class trading with East Africa was in no position to control or influence these wider phenomena by which they were being moulded. The impoverishment of their homeland conditioned them to migration. John Kirk believed that the destruction of Indian cotton manufacturing was the chief cause of increasing Indian migration.[20] Typical of a merchant class, the Indians sought to accommodate themselves to the ascending capitalist mode of production the best way they could, and began to migrate to East Africa to flourish as agents of capitalism there. In fact, the weakening of the specifically Indian trade permitted the class to be weaned from its motherland and to be indigenised in the East African environment. The extent to which they had been indigenised and freed from the narrower, more specifically Indian economic forces made them immune to the vicissitudes of the Indian branch of the trade, and allowed them to come into harmony with economic forces in East Africa.

This nascent merchant class could not have developed to play its full role in the commercial empire if its members had continued to be subjected to the disabilities they suffered as foreign traders at Zanzibar. Moreover, if they were to develop as an entirely foreign merchant class, they would have posed a political threat to the empire. There was, therefore, a mutual desire on the part of the Omani authorities and the Indian merchants to integrate the latter into the commercial life of Zanzibar as an indigenised class. Religious toleration and protection were offered to the Hindus and the Khojas, who were heretics in the eyes of the Ibadhi Omanis. Economic disabilities were gradually lessened. At least by 1828 the Indians had to pay only the 5 per cent import duty. The restriction on Indian trade on the Mrima coast was similarly removed by the convenient and significant mode of their adoption of the Arab flag when going to the mainland. This was the most guarded privilege for local merchants and formed one of the cornerstones of the commercial empire (see p. 121). The acquisition by the firm of Jairam Sewji of control over the customs of Zanzibar soon after 1819, and of the Mrima after 1837, highlights the primacy of the Indian traders in the economic life of Zanzibar. By the 1840s they had done away with the last major disability by beginning to acquire landed property outside Zanzibar city limits. It should be pointed out that they obtained all these concessions long before the appointment of a British Consul to Zanzibar in 1841.[21]

The expansion of foreign trade

While the weakening of the Indian trade had the effect of loosening the apron strings that attached the Indian merchant class at Zanzibar to India, the simultaneous and phenomenal expansion of the East African trade permitted it to grow and to consolidate itself in the commercial empire centred at Zanzibar. The opening up of new sources of ivory north of Cape Delgado and the expansion of the Indian trade at Zanzibar from the beginning of the nineteenth century initially had the limited purpose of making up for the decline in the supply of ivory from Mozambique. By 1815 that demand was being met, as is indicated by the decline in the price of ivory at Bombay to the previous levels (see Graph 3.1 and Appendix B).

From the 1820s, however, a vast new market began to be opened up to meet the demand of the affluent classes in the capitalist West. They had formerly consumed the 'hard' variety of ivory from western Africa for the manufacture of cutlery handles. During the first two decades of the nineteenth century an annual average of about 125 tons of ivory were imported into the United Kingdom to which West Africa contributed more than 70 per cent of the total. In the early 1820s the market suddenly expanded to a new plateau at about 200 tons, and then again in the mid-1830s to 275 tons. Thus within two decades the demand had more than doubled (see Appendix C and Graph 3.2). This peculiar stepped escalation was probably related to the popularisation of new uses of ivory. What is readily apparent from Graph 3.2 is that the traditional supply from West Africa stagnated, and even declined after 1840, and its proportion diminished to a mere 35 per cent, perhaps because the supply could not be expanded, and probably also because the 'hard' variety was not suitable for the manufacture of combs, piano keys and billiard balls.[22]

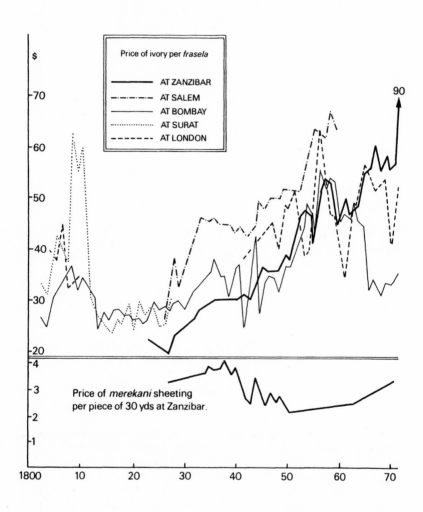

Graph 3.1   Prices of ivory and merekani *1802/3–1873/4*

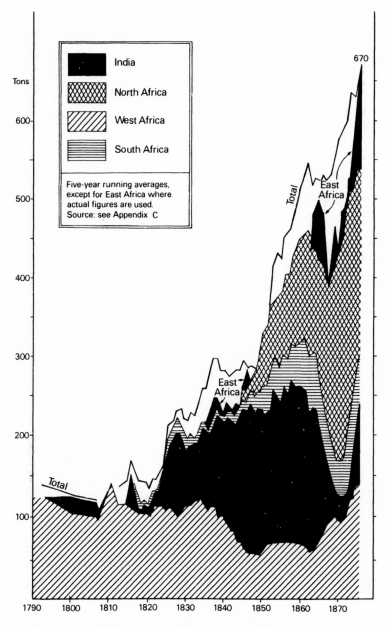

Graph 3.2   Ivory imports into the United Kingdom 1792–1875

Most of the increase during this period was met by the re-export of East African 'soft' ivory from Bombay. The United Kingdom customs records, confirming those of Bombay, show a steep rise in the import of ivory from an annual average of less than 10 tons during the first two decades to 95 tons during the next two. British demand, however, appeared to be insatiable, skyrocketing from an annual average of 280 tons in the 1840s to more than 800 tons in 1875. Bombay increased its share to 160 tons in the 1840s and 1850s, but it could not take fuller advantage of the expanding British market. This was not because the supply from East Africa had reached a ceiling; it continued to rise during the 1850s. The reason seems to lie in the opening up of other virgin fields.

South Africa, which had supplied very small quantities during the first half of the century, expanded its supply to over 50 tons per annum over the next quarter century. A more spectacular development occurred in North Africa where Sudanic ivory, reaching the British market through Egypt and Malta, grew from almost nil before 1850 to an average of nearly 165 tons during the third quarter of the century (see Graph 3.2). These sources may have been able to offer ivory at lower prices, as suggested by the dip in prices during the late 1840s and early 1850s (see Fig. 3.1). The arrest in the re-export of ivory from Bombay, combined with the temporary decline in the price, apparently permitted the Indian home market to claim a larger share of the ivory (see Appendix A).

The phenomenal rise in the English demand for ivory through Bombay had rejuvenated East Africa's trade with India and broadened the arteries without altering the direction of trade as far as East Africa was concerned. There were some attempts to short-circuit the triangular ivory trade by establishing direct British trade with Zanzibar. There is evidence of a Liverpool vessel trading at Zanzibar and Mombasa in 1825, but such were isolated cases. Substantive British trade may have been initiated by India-based English merchants who had been trading for ivory as far as Delagoa Bay. In any case, Robert Norsworthy appears to have been the first English merchant to appreciate the full potential of short-circuiting the ivory trade, and he appears to have gained his knowledge in India. He may have visited the East African coast before his first known visit in 1833, for he had already sent a report on the commercial prospects of the coast to the London firm of Newman, Hunt and Christopher who appointed him their agent at Zanzibar.[23] The English firm embarked in the 1830s on a large-scale expansion of British trade by setting up a vast commercial network involving a resident agent, three brigs picking up cargo at the main ports, and three 'small sharp schooners' collecting merchandise from the smaller ports from Mozambique and Madagascar in the south to Berbera in Somalia, as well as from Lamu and Kilwa in East Africa itself. Although the firm probably contributed a large proportion of the 25 tons of ivory annually imported into the United Kingdom directly from the western Indian Ocean in the mid-1830s, it seems to have overestimated the capacity of the East African market to expand so suddenly. As an acute American merchant observed, they maintained so many schooners 'when their whole trade at the outports would not pay the expense of one vessel.' They also underestimated the vested interests they were injuring by penetrating the entrepôt trade, short-circuiting the Indian trade, and precipitating a damaging competition with other foreign traders which may have contributed to an increase in the price of ivory at Bombay by 33 per cent during the first half of the 1830s. They alienated Jairam Sewji, the farmer of customs, and they complained about a 'monopolist ring' involving Jairam, the American Consul and Seyyid Said which, they claimed, hindered English trade. Moreover, they allegedly suffered from embezzlement and mismanagement by their agent, Norsworthy, and their local Arab partner, Amer b. Said, to whom they had advanced MT$30,000 worth of goods which he was accused of having used to set himself up as a big shipowner and landowner. By 1838 the firm had wound up its East African operations, having incurred a loss of between MT$80,000 and MT$150,000. The first British attempt to short-circuit the ivory trade with Bombay had thus failed.[24]

Of greater significance to the commerce of Zanzibar was the entry of the American traders, especially from the small port of Salem,

Plate 8   Zanzibar harbour, 1886, with the various foreign consulates to the right of the old lighthouse

Massachusetts, which was trying desperately to stave off its demise by pioneering on the frontiers of American foreign trade. The Americans specialised in a few commodities with high proportionate value, hoping to monopolise and control the growth of trade in order to maximise profit. They were introduced to the East African staples almost simultaneously in India, Madagascar and the Mascarenes where they had been previously trading. Madagascar was an important source of hides to supply Salem's rapidly expanding tanning industry, and jerked (sundried) beef for the slave workers of Cuba. N.L. Rogers, one of the pioneers, later claimed that he opened up the trade from information obtained while trading in Mauritius and Bourbon between 1804 and 1816. On the other hand, Jairam Sewji related in the 1850s that his father, 'learning that a vessel manned by whites was at Majunga [in Madagascar]', went over in a *bugalo* to induce the captain to visit Zanzibar. The first recorded American visit to East Africa was that of Captain Johnson in 1823 when he traded at Zanzibar and Mombasa for copal and ivory; small quantities of gum copal began to arrive in Salem the same year. In 1825 a vessel returned from Madagascar with US$14,700 worth of ivory which undoubtedly came from the East African coast.[25]

Meanwhile American traders also began to penetrate the East African market from India where they had also traded. Small quantities of ivory and copal were exported from India in the 1820s to the United States where 'Indian' ivory had acquired a reputation of being finer than 'African', presumably the 'hard' variety from West Africa where Americans had been trading for some time. In 1826 Captain Millet, who had bought ivory the previous year in some northern port, extended his voyage from Mocha to Zanzibar and bought nearly MT$12,000 worth of ivory in East Africa. The following year he came directly to East Africa with a cargo that was nearly one-third cotton goods, unlike his previous cargo which had been entirely specie. Captain Bertram, who was to be one of the most prominent Americans trading with Zanzibar in subsequent decades, arrived in 1831 with gunpowder and US$30,000 in specie, demonstrating confidence in the trade. He reportedly met the Sultan, who was on the point of despatching a large cargo of copal to India, and MT$13,000-worth of the cargo was immediately transferred to the American ship, which returned to Salem with the largest quantity of uncleaned copal from East Africa yet delivered.[26]

As relative newcomers, the Americans were subjected to a series of what they regarded as disabilities that hindered the expansion of their trade. Edmund Roberts, who had obtained information at Bombay about the commercial potential of 'the Arab ports on the east coast of Africa', arrived at Zanzibar during Seyyid Said's first visit to the island in 1828. His cargo consisted of a great variety of textiles, apparently of

Indian origin, as well as gunpowder and arms, which he exchanged not so favourably for copal and other commodities, but not ivory, perhaps because he arrived after the Indian dhows had departed with the tail-end of the monsoon. He was detained for four months while his cargo was being collected and this, he said, contributed to the failure of his voyage. But he particularly complained about the 5 per cent duty on both imports and exports, a MT$100 anchorage fee, a compulsory commission of 2.5 per cent 'for the benefit of Bon Amedy', apparently an official agent for foreign traders, and the restriction on American trade with any but the governor and the collector of customs. Above all, he charged that the Americans were not received on the same footing as the English, presumably traders from India. He claimed that the latter enjoyed favourable treatment under a commercial treaty that was not, however, negotiated until 1839. He also claimed that these privileges were granted after the British government had paid Said 'a large sum of money for the suppression of the slave trade'. No such compensation was paid after the Moresby Treaty of 1822, but Said may have bluffed Roberts to ward off his demands, though eventually he agreed to grant the Americans similar concessions.[27]

Roberts therefore proposed to Said a commercial treaty and asked him to make him a 'bearer of dispatches to my government stating upon what terms American vessels shall be received into Your Highness's ports and in fact, sending a commercial treaty.' Said expressed a general desire for an increase in American trade, and considered extending his own commercial activities to the United States and negotiating a treaty, but he said he did not have a suitable navigator. At that time, however, he was more concerned about the political situation in East Africa, having just returned from an expedition against Mombasa and Pate. He asked Roberts to send him a large number of bombs and mortars, ostensibly for use against his Portuguese enemies to the south, but Mombasa was probably the main consideration. He told Roberts that he was anxious that the British should not know about it, perhaps because they had been pressing him for a peaceful solution to the conflict with Mombasa since they had withdrawn their protectorate in 1826.[28]

By 1832, when American trade had begun to reveal its potential more clearly, Said had himself become anxious to encourage it by sending a message to the American president in connection with the proposed commercial treaty. By then Roberts's scheme was well under way. In January 1832, he received his commission as 'agent for the purpose of examining, in the Indian Ocean, the means of extending the commerce of the United States by commercial arrangements.' He was to be rated as the captain's clerk to keep his mission secret from other powers who might wish to thwart American objectives. According to Roberts, Said readily acceded to the demands that the Americans should be treated on the terms of the 'most favoured nations'. Export duty and all other charges apart from the 5 per cent duty on imports were to be abolished, and there was a provision against price fixing by the Sultan and a government monopoly over foreign trade. The Americans were to trade freely everywhere, except in muskets, powder and ball which could be sold only to the government in Zanzibar, a limitation imposed because of the 'rebellion' in Mombasa; this restriction was lifted after that island was subdued in 1837.[29]

As the first commercial treaty between Zanzibar and a foreign power, it was vague on many questions and did not even consider others which were to cause strains in American relations with the Sultan. The reservation of the Mrima coast in favour of the local traders (see p. 121) was not mentioned, although it was included in subsequent treaties, and the questions of transhipment duties and adjudication of disputes between the Americans and Zanzibar subjects were not raised. Roberts reported that specie was not charged any import duty, but the treaty makes no reference to it. On the other hand, when the limitation on the sale of arms was lifted by Said, the treaty was not amended.[30] Imperfect as it was, the treaty governed American relations with Zanzibar until the end of the century. The Americans could not hope to negotiate a more favourable treaty once competitors from other nations had entered the Zanzibar market, but they also refused to accede to Said's pleas for modifications. They and the Sultan thus resorted to a verbal understanding – often with veiled blackmail on both sides – that, while the wording of the treaty would not be changed, the Americans would refrain from exercising their rights to the full so long as their foreign competitors did the same.

Although American trade undoubtedly benefitted from the regularisation of commercial relations with Zanzibar through the treaty, American traders did not wait for the treaty before rapidly expanding their activities. Between 1827–8 and 1835, when the treaty came into effect, at least thirty-three American merchant vessels are known to have visited East Africa or to have returned with substantial quantities of ivory and copal from the Indian Ocean. But they were still exploratory voyages. The Americans' commercial system of 'annual voyages' and coastwise collection of commodities without a permanently resident agent who could collect and bulk a cargo, meant that a vessel could be detained for several months, as Roberts realised. Captain Hart remarked in 1834 that they had great difficulty in collecting a cargo; 'their plan was to touch upon different parts of the coast, and leave one or two of their crew.' This is confirmed by numerous letters of instruction given to the captains in the 1830s. Captain Smith was asked to stop at Mozambique, Ibo, Zanzibar, Brava, Bombay and Cochin 'to see what can be done there.'[31]

Early American traders also suffered from a lack of acquaintance with local demand, and thus tended to bring large amounts of specie. Captain

Smith was advised to pay a quarter or one-fifth in goods so as to push American merchandise. Hart found an American brig at Zanzibar which had brought goods the previous year which 'did not answer', and thus had brought dollars on the present voyage. Specie, however, was a poor substitute for the right type of merchandise, for its 'profitability' lay merely in its exemption from the 5 per cent import duty. Muskets and gunpowder were restricted before 1837. The Americans had not yet begun to concentrate on their one strong staple, the famous *merekani* unbleached cotton goods. By 1834, however, these began to form about one-third of American cargoes. In 1835, W.S.W. Ruschenberger commented:

> The American cotton manufactures have taken precedence of the English . . . The English endeavour to imitate our fabric by stamping their own with American marks . . . but the people say the strength and wear of the American goods are . . . superior.[32]

By 1859 imports into Zanzibar of American cotton goods were worth nearly two and a half times as much as those of English cottons.[33]

By the mid-1830s, therefore, the Americans had firmly established their trade with Zanzibar on the secure foundations of the supply of *merekani* and the demand for the two most important exports, ivory, which went to supply the comb manufacturers of Connecticut, and copal used in the manufacture of varnish for which a copal-cleaning industry was established in Salem in the mid-1830s. Like their English contemporaries, the Americans were encroaching on certain local vested interests. Roberts's trick of making the commercial treaty retrospective from the date of Congressional approval rather than after the exchange of ratification, as was the normal practice, which forced the custom master to reimburse the Americans export duty charged over a whole year, could not have endeared them initially to the custom master, and Jairam may also have resented the abolition of the export duty. American Consul Waters also challenged Jairam's right to transport charges on goods exported through the custom house, and he also refused to pay transhipment duties which amounted to between MT$12,000 and MT$15,000 during his tenure.[34] Moreover, the Americans were short-circuiting the trade to India which must have affected Indian commercial interests at Zanzibar and Bombay. There is a deep trough in India's trade with East Africa during the 1830s, although this was also partly related to the famine which was then affecting Gujarat (see Appendix A).

However, by this time the Indian merchants had already begun to shift their centre of gravity to Zanzibar and thus to benefit from the expanding middleman's role there. Moreover, American demand for East African commodities was for a new and distant market. A distinction was maintained at Zanzibar in the quality and price of ivory between the more expensive *Bab Kutch* for Indian bangle manufacturers, and *Bab Ulaya* for the North Atlantic market. Simultaneously, the Americans supplied cotton goods at a time when the Indian textile industry was under severe pressure from British cotton goods. They were therefore welcomed as commercial allies both by the Indian merchant class at Zanzibar and by Seyyid Said.[35]

An important factor in this alliance was the credit system that the American traders evolved. Until the mid-1830s most of the trade was apparently conducted on cash terms which often involved the Americans anchoring for several months to make up their cargoes. Shortage of local capital may have hindered the expansion of trade, and the Americans therefore began to advance goods and sometimes cash for four to six months while the local traders contracted to pay back the credit in specified local commodities. The earliest written contract that has come to light dates from 1833 and indicates that an Indian and an Arab merchant jointly undertook to deliver at Majunga in Madagascar in eight to eleven months 3,000 *fraselas* of copal as well as hides and gum arabic. These goods were to be paid for in muskets, other goods and cash. This example did not involve an advance of goods or money, but a pattern was soon established under which short-term loans of merchandise or cash were made on which, until the 1860s, no interest was charged.[36] This system enabled a larger number of Indian and Arab merchants to play the middleman's role in collecting the required commodities from the mainland without needing to invest their own meagre capital, and it permitted the richer ones to expand their commercial activities. The system not only lubricated the commercial organisation, but in this formative period it also permitted the merchant class to accumulate the capital with which to finance long-term caravan trade into the heart of Africa and also the plantation economy on Zanzibar.

While American trade was expanding rapidly, its organisation was still primitive as the traders had no resident agent. They were therefore forced to dispose of their cargoes within a short time and contract for the return cargo under conditions which favoured local merchants. The vessels' arrivals could not be timed exactly to best commercial advantage, and, if there happened to be another vessel in port, the market was flooded with imports, while the local merchants could set their terms of contract knowing how desperate the foreign traders would be. The presence of an English agent in Zanzibar from 1833 had enabled his firm to compete against the Americans more successfully. He could take major decisions on the spot which introduced a certain degree of flexibility, contract ahead of arrival of his vessels to reduce their turnaround time, and take advantage of any opportunities during the off-season to obtain merchandise or frustrate rivals. The next stage in the evolution of the American commercial system in Zanzibar, therefore, involved the establishment of a commission agency by R.P. Waters who had been appointed the first American Consul in 1837. He transacted business both for merchant groups from Salem and for the Bertram-Shepard and the Pingree-West groups, as well as for any other American vessel visiting Zanzibar. But following his visit to the United States in 1840 he became a partner and exclusive agent for the Pingree-West group, and the rival group soon followed suit in appointing their own agent. American trade, therefore, began to be increasingly a complex year-round affair.[37]

The appointment of resident agents enabled the Americans to consolidate their commercial position in Zanzibar. This is best exemplified by the 'partnership' between the custom master and the American Consul. Jairam was a powerful local commercial figure, and all foreign traders and agents had to apply first to him. He would then call the 'native merchants together, make known their offer, then take it upon himself to say through what House the business must be transacted, and there [was] no alternative'. Waters initially agreed to work within the existing system and not to attempt to cut out local merchants from their middleman's share. Although the commercial treaty with the United States placed no restriction on American trade on the Mrima coast, he made no attempt to upset the status quo. He even obliged the local authorities by supplying an affidavit that no foreign trader had ever traded there, which persuaded the American government not to challenge the reservation. In 1840 Waters confessed to doing nine-tenths of his business with the custom master, and the latter reciprocated by supplying Waters's needs first. The English agent Norsworthy was understandably bitter about what he called the 'monopolist ring'; he even implicated the Sultan who had allegedly sent the Governor of Zanzibar, Suleiman b. Hamed, to the Mrima to force local merchants to sell their ivory and copal to Jairam at a price that allowed a large margin of profit.[38]

British Consul Hamerton claimed in 1841 that he had broken the ring, but there is nothing in Waters's voluminous and fairly complete papers to corroborate such a calamitous turn of events. In fact, what broke the ring was the basic contradiction between the American desire to monopolise and control the growth of trade at Zanzibar, and the interest of the merchant class at Zanzibar led by Jairam, and of the Sultan, in its rapid expansion. When Waters became part-owner and exclusive agent of one of the two rival American firms, he unleashed severe competition between them. The following year his firm entered the entrepôt trade with its own schooner in an attempt to cut out the local middlemen as the English firm had done earlier. He alienated Jairam by refusing to pay transhipment duties, and he diversified his clientele and reduced his dependence on Jairam. By 1842 he did less than one-third of his trade with Jairam, while he increased his commercial dealings with at least nineteen Indian and Arab traders and plantation owners, including

Table 3.2 *The value of Waters's contracts with merchants at Zanzibar*

	1839	1840	1841	1842 (MT$)	1843	1844	1845
Jairam Sewji	17,100	44,100	38,600	45,000	13,200	31,700	11,700
Mohammad b. Abd al Kadir		4,400	10,800	8,700	10,400	3,500	10,500
Isa Abd al Rahman			7,600	7,200	8,300	8,300	2,500
Bandali Bhimji			4,500	4,900	3,500	13,700	13,100
Virji, Kanu and Kasu			1,300	10,700			
Topan Tajiani				21,200		30,600	21,800
Ramji							10,000
Others			5,500	17,300	2,100	3,300	800
Total value of contracts	17,100	48,500	68,300	115,000	37,500	91,100	70,400
Number of customers	1	2	14	20	8	8	7

Source: PM Waters' Papers, IV. See also Bennett and Brooks (eds) (1965), pp. 224, 226–8, 356–8.

Topan Tajiani, the second most important Indian merchant in Zanzibar (see Table 3.2).

These measures were tremendously profitable to Waters personally. He is said to have accumulated between US$80,000 and $100,000 during his seven and a half years' stint at Zanzibar, and settled down at Salem as a gentleman farmer, merchant, banker and industrialist. But the American policy of controlled growth failed. Jairam had begun to realise that external demand for African commodities was growing rapidly, and that cut-throat competition between the foreign traders was precisely what was advantageous to the Zanzibar merchants, because it lowered the prices of imports and raised those of exports. The Americans complained bitterly about the custom master's 'hard grasping character', and the way he encouraged all foreign traders to visit Zanzibar.[39]

To curb the damaging competition, the rival Salem firms sought accommodation as early as 1841. In 1846 and 1847 they combined temporarily in sending some vessels under joint ownership and consigned to a single agent. However, the trade was still sufficiently lucrative – and rendered the more so by Salem's monopolistic experiments – to attract other American merchants from Boston, New York and Providence from the mid-1840s onwards. Whereas Salem had almost completely monopolised American trade with Zanzibar before 1848, its share fell to two-thirds by the mid-1850s. The 'intruders' received a warm welcome from the custom master and the Indian merchants at Zanzibar, and they reciprocated by appealing not only to their pockets but also to their hearts, naming one of their ships after the custom master. The Salem merchants tried desperately to strangle the 'interlopers', even if it meant temporary financial losses, but they failed to keep these competitors, as well as European merchants, out of the trade. Salem's attempt to corner the Zanzibar trade had failed.[40]

Because of competition for the staples which rendered them less profitable, the European latecomers tried to diversify their activities. The English firm of Cogan, Henderson and Co., apart from trading in copal and ivory, tried to manufacture coconut and sesame oil and sugar, but its scheme to exploit the guano deposits of Latham Island to the south of Zanzibar was defeated by an unusually high tide which washed off the bird droppings.[41] The German firm of O'Swald & Co. diversified its import trade by importing larger quantities of metal wire and beads, and it specialised in the very profitable export of cowries to West Africa where they were used as currency. Between 1850 and 1878 it shipped 27,000 tons of them. It established its agency in 1849, and by 1857 it had thirteen vessels involved in the trade.[42] The French traders found it difficult to compete in the import trade and were content with the 5 per cent saving in import duty on specie which was their main import item. For export they concentrated on oleaginous grains, particularly sesame, for the manufacture of oil in France.[43]

Plate 9   Ahmed bin Nu'man, Seyyid Said's envoy to the United States, 1840, in the ship Sultana

Plate 10   Landing horses from Sultana, London, 1842

As if to add salt to the wound, Seyyid Said sought to challenge the foreign traders by initiating his own trade to their home grounds. As a sovereign he enjoyed a number of advantages which made him, in the eyes of the foreign traders, an unfair and deadly competitor. He enjoyed exemption from all customs duties, and he could exercise an enormous influence in collecting his cargo within East Africa. In 1840 he sent the *Sultana* to New York, the first excursion into the Atlantic. With their backs to the wall the American merchants fought hard to defeat his schemes. They could count on their country's protectionist tariffs and other port charges which apparently rendered the *Sultana's* venture not so profitable. They also tried to buy him out by offering to relieve him of the 10,000 *fraselas* of sugar which he wished to send to the United States for refining in order to discourage him from mounting another trans-Atlantic venture. But their trump card was the threat to exercise their right to trade on the Mrima Coast according to their commercial treaty which would have opened the floodgates to all other foreign traders under their respective 'most favoured nation' clauses. In vain did Said try to obtain a modification of the treaty. Apparently they ultimately arrived at a modus vivendi by which Said refrained from extending his direct trade to the United States. In return the Americans refrained from challenging the structure of the commercial empire and the interests of the Sultan and the local merchant class.[44]

Said, however, persisted in his commercial ventures to England and France, posing a severe threat to the traders of those nations at Zanzibar. They feared that he would soon monopolise the trade and complained about the heavy internal duty on exports and their exclusion from the Mrima coast whereas Indian merchants, who, they said, were British subjects, traded there freely. But they failed to persuade the Americans to open the gates for them. However, Said's trade allegedly suffered from mismanagement by his own English agent, and his consignments were sometimes so large that they affected his own profitability and that of some of the big Indian merchants who participated in his ventures. Moreover, his commercial expeditions were bound to affect Jairam's customs revenue. The Americans attempted to exploit this contradiction to enlist Jairam to their side, but whether this contributed to the cessation of all of Said's excursions to the West in the 1850s is not clear from available evidence.[45]

The dynamo of merchant accumulation

Throughout the nineteenth century Zanzibar was a beneficiary of extremely favourable barter terms of trade which can be attributed to industrialisation and the development of capitalism in the West. On the one hand, improvements in the method of production of industrial goods, coupled with intense competition among foreign traders at

Zanzibar, led to a marked decline in the price of imported manufactured goods. Richard Burton commented that the price of cloth and beads had declined by half between 1802 and 1856. This is corroborated by some precise data for the price of *merekani* which shows a decline of 47 per cent between the early 1830s and the 1850s, at an average of about 2.5 per cent per annum. This contributed to the decline in the profitability of the import trade of the Americans since cotton goods constituted about 90 per cent of their total imports in the mid-1840s. At the same time, competition for those goods in their home market kept the prices high. The Americans thus had both ends of their import candle burning at the same time. Captain Loarer estimated the profit margin at no more than 7 per cent to 8 per cent, and the Americans themselves often reported no profit at all. The shortage of cotton goods in Salem was ultimately overcome by the building of the Naumkeag Steam Cotton Co. in 1847, with many merchants interested in the Zanzibar trade on its board of directors, and with Waters as its president.[46]

Simultaneously, intense competition for African commodities, in view of the apparently very elastic world demand, had the effect of raising their prices at Zanzibar. The price of gum copal rose from MT$3 in 1823 to MT$8 in 1853, and a further rise was only arrested by the flooding of the market by inferior copal from West Africa and New Zealand. American merchants attempted to keep the price of East African copal high in the United States market by controlling its export from Zanzibar, using the slow manual cleaning process, and seeking to prevent the introduction of potash to clean it chemically at a faster rate. But as M.W. Shepard, one of the most prominent American merchants in the Zanzibar trade, observed in 1847:

> It is evident that the monopoly of copal in this country will prove of great injury to our trade if persisted in . . . Besides, the high price causes large quantities of inferior copal to come into our market, thus circulating impure varnish, and in the end may produce a prejudice against all varnish, so as to throw it out of use.[47]

However, Waters could not resist his capitalist instinct and he eventually introduced potash-cleaning which, coupled with an increase in American duties on unporcessed gums in 1847, dealt a death-blow to Salem's own copal-cleaning industry. Salem, however, had a more limited effect on copal prices since the copal market was controlled by Bombay and London.[48]

In the case of ivory, despite the rapidly increasing supply of ivory from different parts of Africa, the demand tended constantly to outstrip it. As a result, the price of ivory at all the major markets exhibited a steeply rising trend throughout the nineteenth century. At Zanzibar the price rose from about MT$22 per *frasela* in 1823 to MT$89 in 1873, an average annual increase of about 6 per cent. Salem followed the Zanzibar pattern very closely, allowing for transportation costs and a margin of profit which Loarer estimated in 1849 at about 25 per cent. However, the price difference between the two places narrowed from about MT$16 in 1843–4 to MT$10 in 1852–3 (see Graph 3.1). The profitability of the American trade as a whole was thus being squeezed between the declining prices and profitability of its manufactured exports to Zanzibar and the rising prices and narrowing margins on the imports of African commodities. The profit margin was still about 30 per cent in 1846, although the Americans did not consider it 'flattering'.[49]

The declining profitability of American trade at Zanzibar was partly a reflection of the relative success the Sultan and the local merchants had in trapping a disproportionate part of the surplus within East Africa to help in the accumulation of their own capital, but that accumulation was primarily based on the momentous divergence between the price curves of African exports and those of the manufactured imports which constituted a dynamic force for commercial expansion. The apparent inability of the supply of ivory to keep pace with the demand was probably due to the fact that the exploitation of such a primary commodity of the hunt placed a ceiling on the yield per unit area. In many cases the exploitation was vicious, threatening to exterminate the species, or force it to retreat to less accessible parts. This necessitated constant expansion of the

Plate 11   Ivory market at Bagamoyo, 1890s. Smaller tusks were tied in bundles, while larger ones were carried individually by professional porters. Note Arab and Indian merchants in the centre and German officials in the background

103

hinterland to supply the demand for ivory. In the case of Zanzibar the frontiers had extended as far as what is now eastern Zaire by the 1870s. Moreover, tsetse fly prevented the use of beasts of burden in the transport of goods and necessitated their being carried on human shoulders. The consequent increasing cost of transportation thus contributed to the rise in the price of ivory. In 1870 the cost of transportation from Tabora in central Tanzania to the coast amounted to about MT$9 per *frasela*, or about one-sixth of the price at the coast which then stood at MT$58 per *frasela*.[50]

Despite the increasing cost of transportation, however, such was the steep rise in the price of ivory that it did not entirely cancel out the price advantage. At the same time, the price of cotton goods and other manufactures used in the interior to exchange for ivory tended to decline. Thus, whereas the price of *merekani*, for example, declined at an annual rate of 2.5 per cent, the price of ivory rose at about 6 per cent, giving an 8.5 per cent divergence in the barter rate of exchange favourable to East Africa. This brought a windfall of mercantile profit into the hands of the Zanzibar merchant class led by the merchant prince and the custom master, and this helped finance the expansion of the commercial empire.

This merchant class was not ethnically homogeneous. Its Arab and Swahili sections had been involved in the slave trade with the Europeans as well as with Arabia, and some persisted in it to supply slaves to Zanzibar and the Kenya coast. In the late 1840s Ali b. Yusuf b. Ali was 'occupied above all in the slave trade', and sent MT$20,000-worth of merchandise to Kilwa annually. The expanding commerce of Zanzibar, however, provided other profitable niches for them, especially in coastal and caravan trade. Amer b. Said acted as an agent for American and English merchants, allegedly defrauded both to set himself up in commerce with his own dhow and schooner, and had one of the largest houses in town.[51] Muhammad b. Abd al Kadir, apparently the greatest merchant in the 1820s, was still prominent in the late 1840s, specialising in the supply of hides from Lamu and Brava. Said b. Denine was locked in intense competition with the Indian custom master but by 1841 they had made their peace, and he was said to have been involved in the 'monopolist ring' with Jairam, the American Consul and Seyyid Said.[52] Abdullah b. Salim al-Harthi was heavily involved in the coastal trade, making numerous expeditions to the Swahili coast and Mozambique, and advancing goods to more than fifty merchants scattered as far as Madagascar. He also owned a 400-ton Indian-built vessel which traded with Arabia and India. Among those who succeeded in maintaining their foothold in foreign trade were members of the ruling dynasty, especially Seyyid Said himself who conducted an extensive trade in the Indian Ocean using his warships in peacetime, and his son Khalid, the 'perfect Banian', who amassed a fortune from his commerce with India.[53]

Nevertheless, by the middle of the nineteenth century the mercantile class at Zanzibar was predominantly Indian. Historians have hitherto tried to explain the rise of this section to commercial hegemony in terms of race, ascribing business acumen to the Indians as if it were an inherent racial characteristic, and crediting Seyyid Said with foresight in transplanting that class to East Africa to bring about commercial growth. Many have followed closely a contemporary traveller, W.G. Palgrave, who argued:

> Sa'eed knew that, whatever might be the energy and enterprise of his own subjects, their commercial transactions would never attain real importance except by the cooperation and under the lead of Indian merchants . . . [who are] far more skilled in the mysteries of the ledger and the counter than ever Arab was or will be.[54]

Some historians have made the further assumption that the Indians also brought their capital from India, and that their firms were merely branches of the Bombay firms. As we have seen, settlement by Indian merchants in East Africa had preceded the shift of Said's capital to Zanzibar and was due to causes independent of the Sultan, although he may have encouraged it. Moreover, with the exception of Sewji Topan, the farmer of customs, few of the Indian merchants at Zanzibar hailed from an origin of big finance, and apparently none from Bombay, though a number of them, having emerged as big merchants at Zanzibar, did shift their headquarters to Bombay during the second half of the nineteenth century. Many of the Indians in East Africa, in fact, retained a strong tradition of poverty as a cause of their migration, and they include Topan Tajiani, the second most considerable Indian merchant during the nineteenth century. The fact that the short-term American credits played such an important role initially in getting them established in the Zanzibar trade is an indication of the limited capital that the class possessed at the beginning.[55]

The strong tradition of *karkasar* (strict economy) and lack of ostentation, typical of an accumulating capitalist class emerging from rural poverty, permitted Indian mechants to build up their initial capital fairly rapidly. Loarer estimated in the late 1840s that Hari Bhimji, one of the principal Indian merchants at Zanzibar and described as 'very rich and very powerful', whose commercial transactions with only one of the American firms averaged about MT$10,000 a year, spent only about MT$25 per annum on house rent, food and other living expenses. He added that most of the other Indian merchants subsisted on MT$5 at Zanzibar, and MT$2-3 on the mainland.[56] Many of the Indian merchants were men of limited capital who operated largely in the entrepôt trade as general merchants, buying small quantities of cotton goods, muskets, gunpowder and brass wire from foreign traders at Zanzibar, and supplying in exchange cloves, copal and ivory. Some of them owned their own dhows in which they traded with the mainland as far south as Mozambique and Madagascar, and with India. They were therefore able to make good use of the advance of goods by the Americans to accumulate their own capital. However, these credits were for too short a period to finance more than the entrepôt trade, whereas there was a critical need to finance the expansion of trade, especially the long-distance caravan trade into the deep interior.

This need was met by the accumulation of vast quantities of merchant capital in the hands of a resident class, made possible by the tremendous profitability of the Zanzibar trade during the nineteenth century. As early as 1811 the profit rate may have been close to 25 per cent judging from the rate of interest that the English visitors had to pay.[57] A considerable portion of this profit was cornered by Jairam Sewji whose firm farmed the customs of Zanzibar for half a century and dominated the trade of the commercial empire. During its tenure the rent of the customs nearly quadrupled, and it must have been so profitable that the firm was prepared to write off MT\$340,000 of the Sultan's debt in 1871 to retain control over it (see p. 207). Jairam was, of course, heavily involved in the trade with India and had some dhows regularly plying between Zanzibar and Bombay. In 1837 he planned to expand the trade by chartering American vessels to carry goods to Kutch, but the British authorities at

Plate 12   Indian nautch in Zanzibar, c.1860. Note the Indian merchants on the left and the carved door in the background

Bombay discouraged this incursion by foreign shipping into their domain although in the late 1850s a French ship was chartered by the firm to carry cloves to Bombay. By 1839 it was stated that Jairam was making an annual profit of about MT\$100,000 from his various activities. In 1842 the assets of the firm stood at MT\$4 million, and this rose to MT\$5.5 million by 1846. In the mid-1860s 'his profits in Zanzibar alone during the past four or five years were over \$1 million.'[58]

With this capital the firm was able to finance a considerable proportion of mercantile expansion in the commercial empire. By the early 1870s it had MT\$475,000 advanced to Indian traders at Zanzibar and on the mainland. It was also with such capital that the firm gradually shifted its headquarters to Bombay, as did that of Tharia Topan. From Bombay Tharia was to enter the lucrative China trade in the 1860s. Attempts were also made to develop trade with Europe by at least three merchants who either owned or chartered vessels for the trade. Tharia Topan, who owned three large vessels, had MT\$266,000 invested in his 'London business' alone. He seems to have been discouraged from entering the American market directly, much to the relief of American merchants at Zanzibar. His London business, however, proved not so profitable, for he claimed to have lost MT\$100,000 in 1867, and he contemplated withdrawing from it temporarily.[59]

With the accumulation of a substantial amount of merchant capital in the hands of the Indian section of the merchant class at Zanzibar, its credit relations with the foreign traders began to be transformed. As early as the mid-1840s there began a reversal in the flow of credit. Initially Seyyid Said, and later Jairam Sewji, were prepared to offer interest-free loans to American merchants to stimulate trade from which they would benefit. By the late 1840s one of the American firms was conducting its regular trade with a loan of MT\$20,000 from the custom master who had begun to demand interest. This was soon standardised at 9 per cent, and he was prepared to offer up to MT\$50,000 to one of the American firms. The Americans in turn sought to use these loans to induce Jairam to help them collect their smaller debts and to supply information as to the creditworthiness of the merchants they did business with. By the 1860s and early 1870s many of the foreign firms seemed to be working substantially with loans from Indian financiers. One of the French firms owed them about MT\$400,000, and two of the American firms had borrowed nearly MT\$600,000. In addition, the firm of Jairam Sewji had invested MT\$100,000 with the English firm of Fraser & Co. which was involved in the production of sugar in Zanzibar. Thus Indian moneylending capital advanced to foreign firms at Zanzibar amounted to more than a million dollars, of which MT\$665,000 was advanced by the firm of Jairam Sewji alone.[60]

Another avenue of profitable investment of Indian merchant capital was the caravan trade. Few Indian merchants themselves penetrated the interior before the end of the nineteenth century, but their capital penetrated far and deep more than half a century before that. Loarer says that goods were advanced to Arab and Swahili traders at a price which was usually 50 per cent above their real value, and that the predetermined price for African commodities was never less than 40 per cent below the market price. Such a high profitability rate of 90 per cent may be exaggerated, but it may also indicate the high risks of the caravan trade due to famines, wars and desertion. In 1861 in Unyamwezi J.H. Speke met Sirboko, 'a broken-down ivory merchant', who had lost all his property in a fire and was thus afraid to return to the coast. In 1895 the judge in a case between Tippu Tip and Tharia Topan ruled that the profit margin in favour of the latter was great 'but so was the risk'. Many of the Arab and Swahili caravan traders were men of very limited capital, and many of them were therefore converted into mere 'factors' for the Indian financiers. Thus large amounts of Indian merchant capital were tied up in the caravan trade. The customs collector at Pangani had MT$26,000 in outstanding debts in the Pangani valley. Tharia Topan financed Tippu Tip's marathon journey to eastern Zaire to the tune of MT$50,000. By the early 1870s the firm of Jairam Sewji had MT$270,000 invested in loans to 'the Arabs of Unyanyembe in the interior.'[61]

Some of the Indian merchants also began to divert part of their capital to the clove economy during the 'clove mania' of the 1840s when clove prices were still buoyant. They were pursuing the Arabs into one of their last economic niches. The plantation was a favourite avenue for investment by both coastal and caravan traders. Amer b. Said had an estate with 300–400 slaves, and Abdullah b. Salim al Harthi had 1,500 slaves. Loarer commented in the 1840s that many caravan traders, after three or four journeys, acquired enough capital to retire to a life of greater comfort and social prestige on a clove plantation in Zanzibar. As late as 1869 when he left on his twelve years of trading and empire-building in eastern Zaire, Tippu Tip apparently had no plantation of his own. By 1895 he reportedly had seven *shambas* (plantations) and 10,000 slaves.[62]

However, as the price of cloves fell, moneylending capital began to penetrate and undermine the whole landowning class, expropriating them of whatever little profit that still remained, and foreclosing on mortgages when landowners failed to keep up with their repayments. According to C.P. Rigby in 1861, 'probably three-fourths of the immovable property on the islands of Zanzibar and Pemba are either already in the possession of British subjects [Indians] or mortgaged to them.' When he embarked in 1860 on a campaign to emancipate Indian-owned slaves, he blocked further Indian investment in clove production, though moneylending capital continued to squeeze the landowners. By the early 1870s the single firm of Jairam Sewji had nearly MT$285,000 tied up in mortgages and loans to Arab and Swahili landowners in Zanzibar and on the coast.[63]

Finally, Indian merchant capital began to undermine the financial integrity of even the Busaidi state, especially after the death of Seyyid Said. Since no distinction was maintained at Zanzibar between the personal fortune of the Sultan and the state treasury, the whole inheritance, including warships, worth about MT$1.5 million, had to be divided among his numerous male and female children. His successor, Seyyid Majid, therefore had to buy back from his brothers and sisters these apparatuses of state, which he could do only by obtaining advances from the farmer of customs. As a consequence the Sultan's debt rapidly mounted, reaching MT$540,000 by 1871. In fact the Indian farmer of customs began to use this debt to ensure the continuance of the obviously lucrative customs in his own hands. To free himself from this dependence on the Indian firm the new Sultan Barghash tried to repudiate the debt and replace the farmer of customs. However, the British Consul General intervened to prevent the rival firms of Tharia Topan and Bhima from accepting the offer unless the debt was repaid first. A compromise was finally arrived at by which the firm of Jairam Sewji waived MT$340.000 of the debt, leaving a balance of MT$200,000 interest-free, in return for a renewal of the contract for another five years at MT$300,000 per annum.[64] This event clearly demonstrated the chain of dependence of the Sultan on the Indian firm which, in turn, was by the 1860s dependent on the political support of the British.

Conclusion

The phenomenal expansion of Zanzibar's trade, almost fivefold within the first half of the nineteenth century, owed its origin ultimately to industrialisation in the West, and it was inevitable that the economy of the commercial empire would be sucked into the whirlpool of the international capitalist system. Initially the process was indirect as India was converted from East Africa's independent trading partner into a conduit for the exchange of African ivory for English manufactured goods.

The subordination and decline of India in the commercial relations with East Africa enabled the Indian merchant class to be weaned from its motherland so that it could serve international capitalism as a resident merchant class in East Africa. The extremely favourable terms of trade permitted that class to flourish and accumulate huge quantities of merchant capital. However, foreign trade was so profitable that merchant capital was permanently trapped in the sphere of circulation, apart, that is, from a brief incursion into clove production before overproduction rendered it unprofitable and the emancipation of Indian-held slaves made it impossible. In its commercial form it enlarged the scale of commerce and extended the frontiers of the commercial empire to the heart of Africa. In its moneylending form it undermined not only the landowning class but even the Zanzibar state.

But this merchant capitalism was compradorial, thriving on international trade and subordinated to the developing capitalism in the West. Its economic subordination was to be clinched by its political subordination to Britain during the third quarter of the nineteenth century. The re-alienation of the merchant class undermined its integrity, and its decline as an independent force 'expresses the subordination of merchants to industrial capital with the advance of capitalist production.'[65]

Notes

1. Freeman-Grenville (1962b), p. 15; Sheriff (1975a), p. 12; Sheriff (1981), passim, for a fuller discussion of early trade on the East African coast. *Encylopaedia Britannica* (1910), Vol. 15, p. 92; Owen (1856), pp. 65-8. Letters from M.H. Sheriff, a former ivory merchant in Zanzibar, dated 23 February 1965, 19 February and 6 April 1966.
2. Ellis, pp. 46, 50; Burns (1836), p. 56; Freeman-Grenville (ed.) (1962a), p. 25.
3. IOR, P/419/41, Table 2; Sutton (1973), pp. 18-24.
4. Alpers (1975), chs 2 and 3; Freeman-Grenville (ed.) (1962a), pp. 195-8. See pp. 158-9 below.
5. Alpers (1975), p. 56.
6. ibid., pp. 105, 114, 144, 158, 173-4, 209-10; Smith (1969), pp. 171-89.
7. Alpers (1975), pp. 118-19, 174-6; Salt, pp. 32-3; Milburn, Vol. 1, p. 60; IOR, P/419/40. There were similar rises in the price of ivory at the then smaller ivory markets of Bombay and Calcutta. The price of ivory at Mozambique in 1809 (£21.15s to £24 per cwt = 77 to 85 *cruzados* per *arroba*) was already higher than the price at London in 1808 (£22 per cwt = 78 *cruzados* per *arroba*), although at this date London had little influence on the East African ivory trade.
8. Burton (1873), pp. 95, 57.
9. ibid., pp. 130, 168, 200; Cunnison (1961), pp. 65, 67, 69.
10. IOR, P/419/40, 'Muscat'; IOR, P/419/41, nos 49, 52, 54; IOR, P/174/16, nos 60-71; IOR, P/174/8, nos 58-72; Maurizi, p. 30.
11. Freeman-Grenville (ed.) (1962a), p. 198; Albrand, pp. 72-3, 78; Loarer, 'Momfia', ANSOM, OI, 2/10/2.
12. PRO, Adm. 52/3940, Emery's Journal, entries for 20, 30 September, 7 October 1824, 24 January, 28 February, 3, 14 March, 6 June 1825, 27 March 1826; Ross, passim.
13. Gavin (1965), pp. 19-21; IOR, P/174/28.
14. Gray (1962a), p. 98; Freeman-Grenville (ed.) (1962a), p. 198; Smee, pp. 492, 503; IOR, MR, Misc. 586, pp. 164-5; Petition from Lalchund,

et al., 31 March 1811, MA, Diary 380/1811, pp. 4878-9; Nicholls, p. 290; Albrand, p. 73; Loarer, 'Ile de Zanguebar', ANSOM, OI, 5/23/1.

15. Smee, p. 512. He estimated the value of 'Surat cloths' at '12 lacs of rupees', equal to about MT$545,000; and the total value of imports at about £300,000, equal to about MT$1,100,000. Albrand, p. 73; Capen, Vol. 3, p. 299; IOR P/419/60, no. 46; IOR, P/419/39-59. See also Appendix A below; Postans, pp. 171-3.

16. In the late 1830s Kutch imported about 100 tons of ivory worth MT$210,000, and exported MT$275,000-worth of cotton goods. Bombay imported an average of MT$113,000-worth of ivory and exported MT$94,500-worth of cotton goods. Postans, pp. 169-73. See also Appendix A below. MacMurdo, p. 218; *Gazeteer of the Bombay Presidency*, Vol. 5, pp. 117-19; Leech, pp. 44-6; Burns (1836), p. 27.

17. *Gazeteer of the Bombay Presidency*, Vol. 5, pp. 17-18, 107-8, 296; IOR, P/419/49, no. 2; IOR, P/419/51, no. 2; IOR, P/419/51-4, Trade of Bhownagar. See Appendix A below. Extract from the Proceedings of the Government in the Political Department, 28 October 1830, NAI, 26/11/1830-PC-5; Bombay to Court of Directors, 8 November 1831; same to same, 9 January 1833, ibid., 2/1833, p. 16; same to same, 10 December 1833, ibid., 37/1833, nos 1-6.

18. Dutt, Vol. 1, pp. 185-8, 214-6; Dutt, Vol. 2, pp. 79-80; Chaudhuri, pp. 3, 26-7, 34; Bhatia, p. 16; Postans, p. 171.

19. Bombay custom records (IOR P/419) give only the value of imports and exports. It is not clear if 'official' values were used as in the case of the United Kingdom until 1854, since the volumes give no explanation about the compilation of these statistics.

20. Kirk's Administrative Report, Zanzibar, 1870, PRO, FOCP, 1936.

21. See pp. 126-7, 220-1. Nicholls, p. 290, attributes the improvement in the position of the Indians to the British Consul, but they were well established by 1841.

22. Maris to Shepard, 12 September 1851, PM, Shepard Papers, 36. When 'hard' ivory, presumably from eastern Zaire, began to reach Zanzibar in the 1840s, American traders tried desperately to avoid taking it. Bennett and Brooks (eds) (1965), pp. 410-11; *Encyclopaedia Britannica* (1910), Vol. 15, p. 92, (1970), Vol. 12, pp. 806-7.

23. Extract from a letter to Crocker, 1 June 1823, MA, 22/1823, pp. 29-43; Emery's Journal, 23 September 1825, PRO, Adm. 52/3940; Norsworthy to Newman, Hunt and Christopher, 27 June 1834, PRO, FO 84/425.

24. Bennett and Brooks (eds) (1965), pp. 190-1, 195-6, 199, 202-3, 206-7, 221; Petition of R.N. Hunt, 5 December 1837, MA68/1837, pp. 51-5; Hunt to Cogan, 10 October 1838, PRO, FO 84/425; Norsworthy to Richmond, 12 September 1841, PRO, FO 54/4; Hart, 'A visit to Zanzibar in HMS Imogene', NAI, 8/5/1834-PC-40. The published version in *BR*, Vol. 24, pp. 274-83 suppresses certain critical passages.

25. Putnam, Vol. 4, p. 31; Northway, p. 130; Bennett and Brooks (eds) (1965), p. xxvi; Osgood, p. 54; Emmerton to Howard, 5 December 1823, HSBA, Emmerton Papers, IV; Impost Books for the *Fawn*, 6 January 1824, BHS, Lefavour Ms. 16,977; Tagnery, pp. 65-8.

26. IOR P/419/54-5, Exports of Ivory from Bombay; EI, SCHR, Outward

cargo of the *Ann*, 4 March 1826; EI, SCHR, Outward Manifest of the *Black Warrior*, 1 December 1830; EI, SCHR, Entry to merchandise, 3 April 1832; EI, SCHR, Invoice of merchandise from Zanzibar and Mocha, 1 January 1827; EI, SCHR, Shipped at Mombasa and Lamu, 1 January 1828; EI, SCHR, at Brava, Lamu and Mocha, 10 November 1828, PM, Shepard Papers, 1; Bennett and Brooks (eds) (1965), pp. 148-51; Northway, pp. 149-50; Paine, pp. 443-4; Putnam, Vol. 1, p. 52.

27. Roberts to Woodbury, 19 December 1828, Roberts to Said, 27 January 1828, LC, Roberts' Papers, I, V.

28. Roberts to Woodbury, 26 December 1828, LC, Roberts Papers, I, V.

29. Bennett (1959), pp. 244-5; Livingstone to Roberts, 27 January 1832, NAW, Special Missions, M77/152, p. 73; Jackson to Senate, 30 May 1834, LC, Roberts Papers, VI; Roberts (1837), pp. 361-2; Ruschenberger, Vol. 1, pp. 151-4; Said to Waters, 13 June 1837, PM, Waters Papers, X; Bennett and Brooks (eds) (1965), p. 220.

30. Bennett and Brooks (eds) (1965), p. 163.

31. See Appendix C. Hart, pp. 37-8; Owners of the *Cherokee* to W.B. Smith, 4 April 1836, PM, Shepard Papers, 3.

32. Ruschenberger, Vol. 1, pp. 65-6; BHS, Journal of the *Monmouth*, 8, 11 and 29 November 1831; Hart, p. 40.

33. Russell, p. 344.

34. Northway, pp. 373-4; Bennett and Brooks (eds) (1965), pp. 162, 216-18.

35. Loarer, 'Dents d'éléphant', ANSOM, OI, 5/23/3.

36. Contract between Amesa Wantan [Khamis b. Uthman] and Javaroh [Javershah Nathu] with J. Emmerton, 4/3/1833, HSBA, Emmerton Papers, VI, containing their signatures in Arabic and Gujarati. Numerous contracts in PM, Waters Papers, IV; Wadya to Waters, 18 March 1842, Jelly to Waters, 20 May 1845, 24 October 1845, PM, Waters Papers, II, V, VI.

37. Bennett and Brooks (eds) (1965), pp. 211, 236-7; West to Waters, 27 January 1841, PM, Waters Papers, III; Hamerton to Bombay, 13 July 1841, Waters's statement, 2 July 1841, Norsworthy to Hamerton, n.d. [1841], PRO, FO 54/4.

38. Bennett and Brooks (eds) (1965), pp. 240, also 225, 223; Waters's affidavit, 27 May 1839, MAE, CCZ, Vol. I, p. 268; Norsworthy to Richmond, n.d. [1841], PRO, FO 54/4.

39. Bennett and Brooks (eds) (1965), pp. 224, 251, 340; Ward to Pingree, 24 February 1846, EI, Ward's Official Correspondence, pp. 10-14; Northway. pp. 272-3.

40. Bennett and Brooks (eds) (1965), pp. 232, 243-4, 251-2, 340, 486; Consular Returns, 1848-55, NAW, T100/1-3; J. Waters to R. Waters, 31 August 1844, PM, Waters Papers, IX; Shepard to Fabens, 15 September 1844, Webb to Fabens, 8 January 1846, Outward invoices of the *Eliza*, 7 September 1846, 19 October 1847, PM Fabens Papers, II, IV; Greene to Bertram, 10 June 1852, PM, Shepard Papers, 37.

41. Loarer, 'Ile de Zanguebar', 'Commerce des Anglais', ANSOM, OI, 5/23/2; Guillain, Vol. 2, pp. 4, 368-9.

42. O'Swald, pp. 10, 22; Guillain, Vol. 3, p. 198; Bennett and Brooks (eds) (1965), pp. 437, 440, 444, 452; Burton (1872), Vol. 1, pp. 207-9.

43. Broquant to MAE, 30 December 1841, MAE, CCZ, Vol. 1, pp. 96-7;

Extract of a report by Captain Charles Larue of the *Georges Curior* of Bordeaux, 17 July 1845, ANSOM, OI, 15/65; Bennett and Brooks (eds) (1965), pp. 251, 348.

44. Eilts, pp. 253, 271; Bennett and Brooks (eds) (1965), pp. 360, 389–90, 398; Ward to Shepard, 20 December 1847, EI, Ward's Letter Book, 1848–9; Hamerton to Bombay, 3 March 1842, NAI, 29/6/1842–SC–80/82.

45. Hunt to Aberdeen, 25 July 1845, PRO, FO 54/8; Said to Hunt, 10 March 1845, PRO, FO 54/10; same to same, 19 March 1847, PRO, FO 54/11; Maris to Shepard, 18 and 25 May 1849, PM, Shepard Papers, 31; Loarer, 'Ile de Zanguebar', ANSOM, OI, 5/23/2; Cochet to MAE, 19 January 1857, MAE, CCZ Vol. II, pp. 104–6; de Belligny to MAE, 7 October 1850, MAE, CCZ, Vol. I, p. 479; Rabaud, p. 158; Burton (1872), Vol. 1, pp. 319–20; Bennett and Brooks (eds) (1965), p.365.

46. Loarer, 'Pavillon Nord Américain', ANSOM, OI, 5/23/2; Webb to Shepard, 25 May 1844, PM, Shepard Papers, 47; Burton (1860), Vol. 1, p. 4; Zevin, pp. 680–2; Anon., p. 191; Northway, pp. 130, 373. See Graph 3.1 for prices.

47. Shepard to Fabens, 7 January 1847, 29 March 1845, Bertram to Fabens, 29 January 1848, PM, Fabens Papers, IV; Bertram to Fabens, 16 August 1845, 31 March 1846, Webb to Shepard, 25 May 1844, PM, Shepard Papers, 43; J. Waters to R. Waters, 5 May 1844, PM, Waters Papers, IX.

48. Fabens to Shepard, 29 August 1844, PM, Shepard Papers, 43; Bennett and Brooks (eds) (1965), pp.500–1.

49. Bennett and Brooks (eds) (1965), pp. 229–30, 389; Ward to Fabens, 9 May 1846, Shepard to Fabens, 31 March 1846, 5 April 1848, PM, Fabens Papers, IV; R. Waters to J. Waters, 16 December 1844, PM, Waters Papers, IX.

50. Calculated from Stanley (1872), pp. 52–4. He estimated the cost of transporting ten loads (about 20 *fraselas*) from the coast to Tabora at MT$185 or £124 per ton. This was paid by the American explorer; local traders probably paid less. Wrigley, p. 75, estimated the cost for the 1890s between Buganda and Mombasa at £130 per ton. Beachey (1967), p. 275, gives the cost at £50 per ton from Ujiji to the coast, but he does not give his sources or indicate the year to which it applied. See Graph 3.1 for ivory prices.

51. Loarer, 'Ile de Zanguebar', ANSOM, OI, 5/23/2; Isaacs, Vol. 2, pp. 294–5; Ruschenberger, Vol. 1, pp. 51–2, Petition of R.N. Hunt, 5 December 1837, MA, 68/1837, pp. 51–5; Native Agent at Muscat to the Persian Secretary, 13 May 1838, MA, 65/1838–9, pp. 196–8. Armere b. Syed to J. Rogers and Bros., 18 April 1835, N.L. Rogers to Armere b. Syed, 22 August 1835, Waters to Said, 21 and 26 October 1837, PM, Waters Papers, VII.

52. Guillain, Vol. 3, pp. 388–9; Loarer, 'Ile de Zanguebar', ANSOM, OI, 5/23/2; Waters's Notes, 11 November 1842, PM, Waters Papers, IV; Hamerton to Bombay, 6 September 1841, NAI, 5/4/1842–SC–8/10; Bennett (1959), p. 254.

53. Loarer, 'Ile de Zanguebar', ANSOM, OI, 5/23/2; Rigby to Bombay, 12 September 1859, NAI, 23/12/1859–SC–11/12; Rigby to Bombay, 4 July 1860, MA, 12584/13, p. 33; Guillain, Vol. 2, p. 228, Vol. 3, p. 267;

Forbes to Palmerston, 18 September 1839, PRO, FO 54/3; Fabens to Shepard, 28 October 1848, PM, Fabens Papers, IV.

54. Palgrave, Vol. 2, pp. 369-70; Coupland (1938), p. 301, (1939), pp. 4-5; Ingham, pp, 19, 73, 80; Nicholls, pp. 209, 212, 217.

55. By 1839 there were already 900 Indians settled in Zanzibar, including many of the most important merchants. Cogan's Memo, 5 December 1839, PRO, FO, 54/3; Morris, p. 9. Topan Tajiani, head of the second most important merchant house in Zanzibar, originated from Lakhpat, Kutch, from a modest background of oil milling. Topan, Vol. 1, pp. 2, 17-9, Vol. 3, p. 95.

56. Loarer, 'Ile de Zanguebar', ANSOM, OI, 5/23/2; Fabens' Account Books, under Hari Bhimji & Co., PM, Fabens Papers.

57. Smee and Hardy, IOR, MR, Misc. 586.

58. Melville to Bombay, 19 December 1837, Bombay to Government of India, 15 January 1838, MA, 9/1838, pp. 114-19; Rigby to Bombay, 1 December 1859, NAI, 16/3/1860-FC-10/15; Bennett and Brooks (eds) (1965), p. 222; Hamerton to Bombay, 22 December 1842, MA, 55/1843; Broquant to MAE, 14 February 1846, MAE, CCZ, Vol. I. He says Jairam had '30 million in a Bombay bank', probably French francs which the French Consuls normally used in their correspondence. At MT\$1 = 5.50 francs, this gives a figure of MT\$5.5 million in 1846, a more realistic figure in view of the 1842 figure; Nicholls, p. 217; Ropes to Bertram, 23 October 1866, EI, Ropes Emmerton Papers, BBI.

59. Bennett and Brooks (eds), (1965), pp. 252, 451; Jeyram Shivjee to Bombay, 5 November 1853, MA, 91/1853, pp. 163-8; Topan, Vol. 1, pp. 2, 24-6, 51-2, Vol. 12, pp. 401, 429-52. The firm of Jairam Sewji was originally a branch of the firm with headquarters in Mandvi, Kutch, but the connection had apparently been severed by the early 1840s. Hamerton to Bombay, 22 December 1842, MA, 55/1843; Rigby to Secretary of State for India, 1 May 1860, PRO, FO 54/17. He shows an outflow of MT\$300,000 to India in bullion in 1859 but no inflow, except from Europe. Rigby to Bombay, 1 December 1859, NAI, 16/3/1860-FC-10/15; Rigby to Coghlan, 15 October 1860, MA, 56/1861, pp. 207-13; Jablonski to MAE, 13 December 1867, MAE, CCZ, Vol. III, pp. 69-80; Ropes to Bertram, 6 June, 21 August, 18, 24 September 1866, 9 June 1867, Hathorne to Bertram, 26 November 1867, Webb to Bertram, 10 January, 21 December 1868, 25 March, 27 September 1869, EI, Ropes Emmerton Papers BBI; Webb to Ropes, 12 November 1867, 10 January, 3 March 1869, PM, Ropes Papers; Webb to State Department, 10 March 1869, NAW, T100/5.

60. McMullan to Fabens, 24 September 1848, PM, Fabens Papers, IV; Ward's receipt, 6 November 1848, Ward to Bertram, 3 February 1849, EI, Ward's Letter Book, 1848-9; Ward to Webb, 14 June 1849, PM, Shepard Papers, 47; Mansfield to Marcy, 31 January 1856, NAW, T 100/3; Bennett and Brooks (eds) (1965), p. 486; Jablonski to MAE, 7 November 1863, MAE, CCZ, Vol. II, pp. 324-43; Webb to Bertram, 27 March 1867, 26 January 1868, Ropes to Bertram, 21 August 1866, EI, Ropes Emmerton Papers, BBI; Kirk to FO, 22 May 1872, PRO, FO 84/1357; Kirk to Bombay, 24 November 1871, PRO, FO 84/1344; Frere's 'Memorandum on "Banyans" in East Africa', 31 March 1873, PRO, FO 84/1391.

61. Loarer, 'Ile de Zanguebar', ANSOM, OI, 5/23/2; Speke (1863), pp. 101-2; Bennett and Brooks (eds) (1965), p. 532; Ropes to Bertram, 5 July 1867, EI, Ropes Emmerton Papers, BBI; Burton (1872), Vol. 1, p. 331; Tippu Tip, pp. 59-61, paras 37-40; Topan, Vol. 7, pp. 232-7, 252-7; Brode, pp. 26, 47-8; Frere's 'Memorandum on "Banyans" in East Africa', 31 March 1873, PRO, FO 84/1391; *Zanzibar Gazette*, 136/1, 187/5-7 (1895).

62. Loarer, 'Ile de Zanguebar', ANSOM, OI, 5/23/2; Tippu Tip, p. 59, para. 39; Mackenzie, p. 93.

63. Petition of R.N. Hunt, 5 December 1837, MA, 68/1837, pp. 51-5; Rigby to Bombay, 4 April 1859, IOR, L/P & S/5/140; Rigby to Bombay, 21 March 1860, NAI, 5/1860-Pol. Pt. A-289; Rigby to Bombay, 14 September 1860, MA, 159/1860, pp. 267-73; Rigby to Bombay, 12 July 1861, IOR, L/P & S/9/38, pp. 195-7; Derche to MAE, 2 May 1860, MAE CCZ, Vol. II, pp. 199-213; Frere's 'Memorandum on "Banyans" in East Africa', 31 March 1873, PRO 84/1391; Nicholls, p. 347. See pp. 205-6.

64. Hajee Khuleel b. Hoosein to Persian Secretary, 2 October 1858, MA, 148/1858, pp. 141-3; Coghlan to Bombay, 4 December 1860, MA, 12584/13, pp. 56-86; Kirk to Bombay, 24, 28 August 1871, MA, 143/1871.

65. Marx, Vol. 3, p. 329. For political subordination of the Indian merchants, see ch. 6 below.

Four

The Structure
of the Commercial Empire

The central position of Zanzibar island, the direct sovereignty exercised over it by the Sultan of Muscat, certain administrative and fiscal steps taken by this prince, the more extensive production and consumption at this locality than at any other on the coast which enables it to receive and furnish an entire cargo; finally the facility of its port and the great security which strangers find there have made it the pivot of commerce.[1]

Perhaps there could not have been a more succinct summary of the pristine position of Zanzibar in the commercial economy of East Africa during the nineteenth century than in the quotation given above. The economy was based on two definable sectors, production on the offshore islands themselves, and the transit trade. The two sectors, however, were not isolated from each other, and the former was increasingly subordinated to the latter as the century progressed. Each sector threw up its own dominant class which collaborated as well as competed with the other, increasingly under the overall hegemony of international capitalism.

On the islands of Unguja and Pemba there had developed slave-based production of cloves, coconuts and sugar, largely for export. Between 1859 and 1870-1 available data indicate that products originating from the islands contributed an average of 22 per cent of the total value of exports of Zanzibar (see Table 4.1). Since the slave system depended on the slave trade, which was largely financed by merchant capital; most of the cloves were exported by the merchants; and, finally, large parts of the clove plantations were increasingly mortgaged to moneylenders, this meant that the ruling class in Zanzibar, predominantly Omani landowners during the first half of the nineteenth century, was gradually being subordinated economically to the merchant class.

The rest of the exports of Zanzibar during these years originated from a vast hinterland on the African mainland which extended far beyond

116

Plate 13   Zanzibar crowded with dhows. In the foreground a view of the inner court of the Old Fort

Table 4.1 *Value of cloves and coconuts in the total exports of Zanzibar, 1859–1864/5*

Year	Cloves	Coconuts	Total	Total exports	Cloves and coconuts as percentage of total exports
		(MT$ '000s)			
1859	264	96	360	2,084	17
1861/2	202	102	271	1,277	21
1862/3	332	143	475	2,319	20
1863/4	206	350	556	2,479	22
1864/5	469	157	626	2,208	28
Average	295	170	465	1,999	22

Sources: Calculated from the tables in Rigby to Secretary of State for India, 1 May 1860, PRO, FO 54/17; Playfair to Bombay, 1 May 1864, 10R, L/P&S/9/41, pp. 297–322; Playfair to FO, 1 January 1865, *PP*, 52/1865, pp. 174–80; Ropes to State Department, 31 December 1865, NAW, T100/5.

Zanzibar's actual sovereignty. Its entrepôt role developed partly from geographical factors which were, however, activated by economic and political factors during the eighteenth and nineteenth centuries. Zanzibar is located within the belt of reliable monsoons that controlled shipping in the Indian Ocean before the age of steam. In fact, the island is at the southern end of the monsoon system with at least 80 per cent reliability, and is therefore ideally located to serve as the entrepôt for the coast to the south. As the French trader Morice noted in the 1770s, Indian vessels preferred to unload their cargoes at Zanzibar, and traders from Pate in the north and Kilwa in the south went there to trade. Communication between the two extremes was conditioned by the monsoons, and it was therefore interrupted during certain seasons. Since the East African coast is at the periphery of the monsoon system, it experiences longer intervening seasons of variable winds strongly influenced by land and sea breezes which can be used by coastal vessels to 'steal' from one port to another, and to ply between the mainland and the offshore islands almost throughout the year. These winds were therefore admirably suited to the entrepôt activities of Zanzibar.[2]

Within this belt, however, the choice of Zanzibar specifically as the seat of the Omani commercial empire was determined more by historical and political considerations. Both Mombasa and Zanzibar have sheltered harbours and careening facilities in the adjoining creeks. In addition,

Plate 14   Dhow careening facilities in the Zanzibar creek

118

taking account of the pre-industrial technology prevailing during the eighteenth century, Mombasa had the almost-impregnable Fort Jesus that had withstood the Omani seige for three years at the end of the seventeenth century. In fact it was chosen by the Omanis as the seat of their first governorship after the expulsion of the Portuguese from the East African coast. However, the change in dynasties in Oman in the middle of the eighteenth century had led to the secession of the Mazrui governors of Mombasa who proceeded to establish their own independent state.[3]

The Busaidi dynasty was therefore left to develop Zanzibar as its seat, and as early as 1744 it had established a governorship and what was described as a 'ridiculous little fort' there.[4] This choice was later to prove fortunate, for Zanzibar lay opposite the richest part of the hinterland during the nineteenth century. The development of Zanzibar's control over that part of the coast, however, did not arise merely from geographical factors; it was carefully cultivated during the nineteenth century through political and administrative means to give Zanzibar a monopoly over the trade of the Mrima coast which was reserved for local traders, and to enable the Zanzibar state to appropriate a sizeable revenue through a differential taxation system.

Control over the coast implied indirect control over production in a vast and expanding hinterland. Within the coastal belt economic activities were characterised either by slave-based production of food and oleaginous grains, especially along the coast of Kenya, or the 'mining' of gum copal along the coast of Tanzania.[5] The commercial exploitation of the interior required the development of the caravan system and long-term credit. The trade from this vast hinterland constituted more than three-quarters of the trade of Zanzibar by the 1860s.

The entrepôt

In an incisive discussion of the fiscal administration of the Zanzibar state C. Guillain argued that:

> In a state completely deprived of manufacturing industries there is no fear of foreign competition, and consequently, no necessity for imposition [of taxes] on their entry into the country. It appears, moreover, that to burden indigenous export commodities with duties merely has the effect of making their sale difficult, i.e. to diminish the general richness of the country and the well-being of its inhabitants. It is therefore evident that in the Arab states of Africa the customs are no more than an instrument of revenue for the sovereign.[6]

This quotation brings out clearly the fundamentally *commercial* character of the state whose economic policies where based on the twin pillars of commercial monopoly and an attempt to corner as much as possible of the surplus in the sphere of circulation through customs duties. In its

119

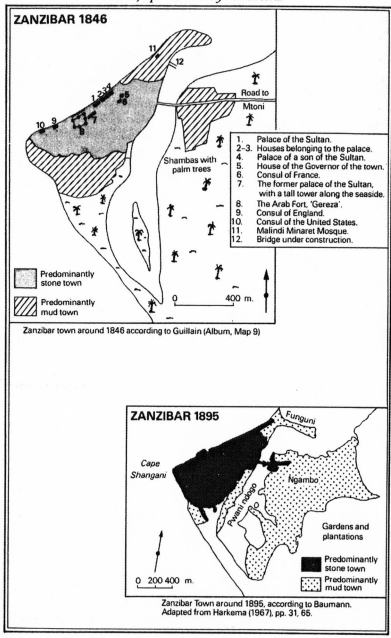

ZANZIBAR 1846

Road to Mtoni

1. Palace of the Sultan.
2-3. Houses belonging to the palace.
4. Palace of a son of the Sultan.
5. House of the Governor of the town.
6. Consul of France.
7. The former palace of the Sultan, with a tall tower along the seaside.
8. The Arab Fort, 'Gereza'.
9. Consul of England.
10. Consul of the United States.
11. Malindi Minaret Mosque.
12. Bridge under construction.

Shambas with palm trees

Predominantly stone town

Predominantly mud town

0   400 m.

Zanzibar town around 1846 according to Guillain (Album, Map 9)

ZANZIBAR 1895

Funguni

Cape Shangani

Pwani ndogo

Ngambo

Gardens and plantations

Predominantly stone town

Predominantly mud town

0   200 400 m.

Zanzibar Town around 1895, according to Baumann.
Adapted from Harkema (1967), pp. 31, 65.

Map 4.1   Zanzibar: the entrepôt, 1846 and 1895

relation with the hinterland the commercial empire evolved an economic policy that sought to centralise as much of the foreign trade through Zanzibar as possible. By making a distinction between that part of the coast perennially linked with Zanzibar, and the peripheral areas to the north and the south which are only seasonally so linked, and which had greater potential for independent contact with overseas markets, the geographical factor furthered that policy. The peripheral areas used the facilities of the entrepôt especially when trading across Zanzibar into the opposite economic region, such as the import of Indian textiles to Kilwa through Zanzibar, or the export of slaves from Kilwa to the coast of Kenya and the north. On the other hand, the dominance that Zanzibar exercised over the Mrima coast geographically was reinforced politically by excluding foreign traders from this part of the coast by creating the 'Mrima monopoly'.

The Mrima formed a direct economic dependency of Zanzibar. It was an area, in the words of Seyyid Said, 'from whence Zanzibar receives the greater part of the revenue', and was the richest source of ivory and copal. It was studded with many small ports, most of them open roadsteads, with limited individual markets. This region was declared an economic reserve for Zanzibar and the local traders as regards ivory and copal. It was not Seyyid Said's personal monopoly, as is often alleged, though his own trade, as well as that of his family and some of the prominent Arabs, was exempted from the heavy internal duties. The reservation guaranteed the local traders an intermediary role between the Africans from the interior and the foreign traders at Zanzibar. The Zanzibar authorities may well have had in mind the disruptive effects of the French trade at Kilwa in the 1770s, and were determined to prevent the diminution of Zanzibar's vital hinterland.[7]

This monopoly probably long preceded Seyyid Said. Guillain believed that trade with the coast was open to all until 1837 when the Arab merchant Said b. Denine was granted a monopoly of the Mrima trade in return for a certain fixed sum. He argued that this explained why the Mrima monopoly was not specified in the American treaty of 1833, whereas it was stipulated in the English treaty of 1839 and all subsequent ones. However, as early as 1804 Captain Dallons had complained that the French were excluded from trading on the mainland; obviously not at Kilwa, where they continued to trade, but from the coast opposite Zanzibar. The Americans themselves admitted that they had never traded on that part of the coast, though they refused to revise the treaty, and they often used the omission to blackmail Seyyid Said to obtain concessions.[8]

The precise extent of the monopoly has been unclear. Mrima in the parlance of the islanders is the mainland opposite; more narrowly, it refers to that part of the coast where the Mrima dialect is spoken.

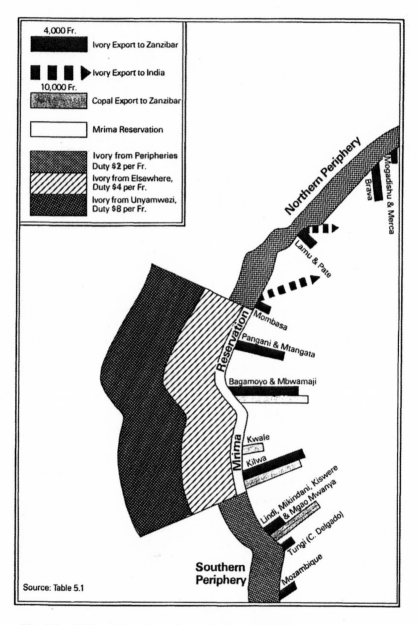

Legend:

- 4,000 Fr. — Ivory Export to Zanzibar
- Ivory Export to India
- 10,000 Fr. — Copal Export to Zanzibar
- Mrima Reservation
- Ivory from Peripheries, Duty $2 per Fr.
- Ivory from Elsewhere, Duty $4 per Fr.
- Ivory from Unyamwezi, Duty $8 per Fr.

Map 4.2a   Differential taxation and centralisation of trade, 1848

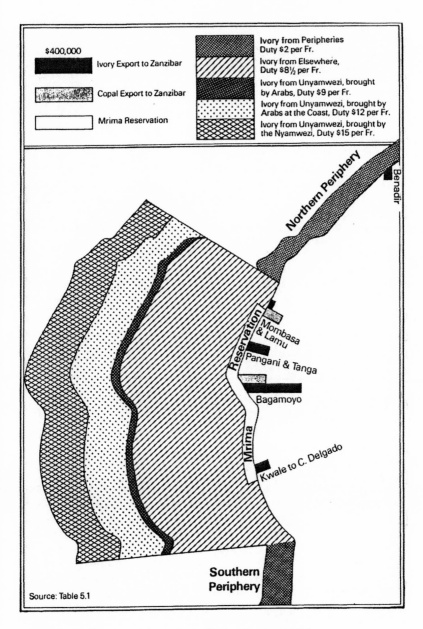

Map 4.2b   Differential taxation and centralisation of trade, 1872–3

C. Sacleux placed the boundaries at Vanga and Rufiji, and H.E. Lambert and W.H. Whiteley shifted them north, to between Gasi and Saadani. A clear territorial definition of the monopoly, however, was set down in Article X of the English treaty which delimited the reservation as that from 'Tangate to the port of Quiloa', i.e. between Mtangata near Tanga and Kilwa. Almost identical articles were included in all subsequent commercial treaties.[9]

This monopoly, however, was confined to the two commodities of ivory and copal which constituted 36 per cent of the exports of Zanzibar between 1859 and 1864–5 (see Table 4.2). The precise quantities of these commodities from different parts of the coast are not available, but according to figures given by the usually reliable Captain Loarer in the late 1840s, more than 60 per cent of all the ivory exported to Zanzibar from the whole coast between Mogadishu and Mozambique originated from the Mrima coast, although some of the ivory from the peripheral areas bypassed Zanzibar and was exported directly overseas. In the case of copal the proportion originating from the Mrima coast was even larger (see Map 4.2).[10]

Table 4.2 *Value of ivory and copal in the total exports of Zanzibar, 1859–1864/5*

Year	Ivory	Copal (MT$ '000s)	Total	Total exports	Ivory and copal percentage total exports
1859	697	187	884	2,158	41
1861/2	310	104	414	1,277	32
1862/3	253	160	413	1,949	21
1863/4	930	163	1,093	2,479	44
1864/5	740	105	845	2,208	38
Average	586	144	730	2,014	36

Sources: As Table 4.1.

Having thus created a monopoly over ivory and copal from the Mrima coast in favour of local traders, the Zanzibar state proceeded to construct a fiscal structure designed to squeeze the maximum amount of surplus out of the trade passing through. The peripheral areas, which had greater potential for independent commercial relations with overseas markets, and where political control was often also weak, had to be treated with circumspection since too heavy a duty might have led to diversion of trade to beyond the boundaries of the commercial empire or, worse, to political rebellion. Thus these areas were offered substantial duty reductions to induce them to channel at least part of their foreign trade through the entrepôt. The Mrima, on the other hand, was ruthlessly squeezed.[11]

By the late 1840s, gum copal coming from the coast north of Mbwamaji and south of Lindi paid MT$3/8 per *frasela*. This amounted to about 7 per cent duty when the price of copal was about MT$5 per *frasela*; and the duty remained the same until the 1860s when the price had risen to MT$8, so that the duty rate in fact declined to 5 per cent. On the other hand, copal coming from the Mrima coast between Mbwamaji and Lindi, from where more than 95 per cent of the copal originated, paid a duty in kind of 20 per cent, so that the value of the duty collected rose in line with the rise in the price of copal.

The pattern of duties on ivory was even more intricate and instructive. Ivory coming from the peripheral areas north of Lamu and south of Kilwa was charged MT$2 per *frasela* in the late 1840s when the price at Zanzibar was about MT$35. This amounted to less than 6 per cent duty; and the rate for these regions remained unchanged until the 1860s when the price had risen to more than MT$45, thus reducing the duty rate to less than 5 per cent. As a result of the low duties, more than a quarter of the ivory from Mombasa and about half of that from Lamu, as well as sizeable quantities from the Benadir and the southern periphery as far as Mozambique, continued to be channelled through Zanzibar in the 1840s.

Ivory coming from the Mrima coast, on the other hand, was ruthlessly exploited not only for the benefit of the revenue of the Zanzibar state, but also in an effort to stimulate the coastal Arabs to penetrate the interior in order to displace their Nyamwezi rivals. In the 1840s ivory other than that from Unyamwezi coming from the Mrima coast between Mombasa and the Rufiji was charged at the basic rate of MT$4 per *frasela*, which was double the rate charged on ivory from the peripheral areas. However, ivory from Unyamwezi was charged MT$8 per *frasela*, and all attempts at evading these duties by diverting ivory to other ports were defeated by charging the same rate along the whole coast from Mombasa to Cape Delgado. By 1864, although the price of ivory had increased by only about 30 per cent, the basic rate of duty had more than doubled to MT$8.50, and Kilwa was brought firmly within this inner region. In addition, however, fiscal policy had been modified to favour coastal Arab penetration of the interior, and to exploit ivory brought by the Nyamwezi traders to the maximum. Thus, whereas Arab traders bringing ivory from Unyamwezi paid only MT$9 duty per *frasela*, Arab merchants buying ivory on the coast paid MT$12; and Nyamwezi traders who brought ivory to the coast paid the maximum rate of MT$15, which then amounted to more than 30 per cent duty. The lower rate paid by Arab caravan traders indicates the powerful influence that this section of the merchant class was able to exert in the political economy of Zanzibar by the 1860s (see Map 4.2).[12]

This system of fiscal administration had evolved during the first half of the nineteenth century, and was made possible by the centralisation of the customs administration in the hands of the most prominent Indian mercantile firm of Jairam Sewji. Along certain parts of the coast the Omanis had encountered at the time of conquest a tax structure that was variable in character, and these taxes were often paid in the form of a 'present' in return for protection and permission to trade. By the late eighteenth and early nineteenth centuries these payments had begun to approximate to customs duties. In the peripheral areas of the southern Tanzanian and Benadir coasts these practices were allowed to persist long after their inhabitants had recognized the suzerainty, often nominal, of the Omani ruler, in return for a certain fixed sum transmitted to the Omani authorities.[13]

For those parts of the coast which came under more direct Omani rule, the customs administration at the beginning of the nineteenth century was still extremely fragmented, according to Dallons in 1804, apparently to prevent the governors from becoming 'too well established' and independent of the Omani metropole. Thus the revenue of Kilwa and Mafia was farmed out to the governor of Kilwa for MT\$6,000, and in turn by 1811 he had sublet it for MT\$12,000–MT\$20,000 to an Arab merchant called Abdullah, who was also the governor of Mafia. Zanzibar was then farmed out to 'a Banyan or an Arab whose rich estates in Muscat guarantee his fidelity to the Prince'; and the mainland opposite was rented out to another person with similar sureties. As late as 1837, when the customs of Zanzibar had already come under the control of Jairam Sewji, the Mrima was farmed out to the Arab merchant, Said b. Denine, which earned him about MT\$10,000. Until the late 1840s Pate was still being farmed out to a party of local inhabitants; and Pemba continued to be let separately to Said b. Muhammad b. Nasir for MT\$12,000 in the late 1840s.[14]

It appears that the customs of Zanzibar fell into the hands of the firm of Sewji Topan some time after 1819 when the previous Ethiopian governor and farmer of customs, Yakut, died. In 1842 the firm claimed that they had been farming the customs for twenty-four years, and in 1827–8 the American merchant and future negotiator of the treaty with the United States, Edmund Roberts, had commercial transactions with 'Sewar, Banyan Collector of Customs'.[15] According to Loarer, the Sultan consolidated the customs of the mainland coast in 1822, and this fell into the hands of Sewji Topan's son, Jairam, soon after 1837 when he bought out Said b. Denine. Mombasa also appears to have fallen into his lap soon after its conquest in 1837. By the late 1840s the revenues of Mafia and Lindi had also fallen under the control of that firm, although they continued to be sublet to their respective governors, Abubakr b. Abdullah and Muhammed b. Issa. Thus by the mid-century the firm had 'the power to collect all the duties established by a regulation of the Imam on the commerce of the whole coast from Cape Delgado to Mogadishu'. It continued to control the customs continuously, with one five-year inter-ruption, until the 1880s.[16]

Because of the distance of the East African coast from the seat of Omani power before it was shifted to Zanzibar, and because the commercial empire had developed before a governing bureaucracy had evolved, the Omani had resorted to the practice of farming the revenue, a practice well-established in Muslim lands as well as in Europe until the eighteenth century. This practice characterised the whole life of the commercial empire, with the farm coming up for auction every five years. It was only in 1886 that Seyyid Barghash replaced it with a government department, in a desperate attempt to transform the commercial empire into a political one, and to stave off, unsuccessfully, its dismemberment.[17]

The standardisation and centralisation of the customs administration seems to have served well as an 'instrument of revenue for the sovereign'. During the first decade of the nineteenth century, the total annual revenue from the East African dominions amounted to MT\$40,000. By 1819 it had doubled, and it stood at MT\$84,000, according to John Kirk, when it passed into the hands of Sewji Topan. By the late 1840s it had doubled again, and by the 1860s annual revenue was MT\$310,000.[18] This phenomenal, nearly sevenfold growth of the revenue between 1804 and 1865 partly reflects the enormous expansion of the trade of Zanzibar as the boundaries of the commercial empire were extended to include the whole eastern half of middle Africa and beyond. It also partly reflects the steep rise in the price of some of the major export commodities, especially ivory and gum copal. This marked growth occurred despite the fact that the revenue from the export of slaves was lost within this period after the slave trade to the south and to the north were made illegal in 1822 and 1845 respectively.

The revenue had also grown so enormously despite the various 'most-favoured-nation' commercial treaties that the Zanzibar state had signed with the United State and several European powers from 1833 onwards. These treaties had suppressed all export duties and had reduced all dues to a single import duty of 5 per cent *ad valorem* on all goods other than specie, which entered duty free. As Table 4.3 shows, between 1859 and 1864/5, annual imports other than specie averaged about MT\$1,300,000. At the rate of 5 per cent, the annual duty on merchandise imports, therefore, averaged only MT\$65,000. This was only 31 per cent of the value of the farm of customs which was MT\$206,000 in the early 1860s. The fact that these commercial treaties failed to hinder the growth of state revenue arose out of the mechanism whereby the *elastic internal* customs adminis-tration was kept beyond the purview of the *frozen external* system of customs duties. This, in fact, therefore permitted the charging of export duties indirectly to exploit the trade fully for the benefit of the sovereign and the farmer of customs.

Table 4.3   *Import duties as a proportion of total revenue, 1859–1864/5*

Year	Total imports	Specie	Merchandise (MT$ '000s)	Calculated import duty	Value of customs	Import duty as percentage of customs
1859	2,453	750	1,703	85	206	41
1861/2	1,168	322	846	42	206	21
1862/3	1,607	378	1,229	61	206	29
1863/4	1,399	271	1,128	56	206	27
1864/5	1,807	215	1,592	80	206	34
Average	1,687	387	1,300	65	206	31

Sources: As Table 4.1.

Economic dependence

By the middle of the nineteenth century the commercial empire was economically vibrant but structurally fragile. Its economy was essentially commercial. Both the productive sector, producing cloves and other agricultural commodities, and the transit trade sector were primarily dependent on international trade. During the century the trade of Zanzibar continued to expand very rapidly. Its prosperity was based, on the one hand, on the highly profitable transit trade which enjoyed very favourable terms of trade as a result of the diverging price curves of ivory exports and imports of manufactured goods. At the same time the slave sector had been transformed from one based on the export of slave labour to one that depended on the export of agricultural goods produced by slave labour, which tended to stabilise the sector.

Both sectors, however, were almost entirely dependent on international trade and on market forces over which Zanzibar could not exercise decisive control. The economy had developed reliance on a few commodities and their specialised markets, as well as on limited sources of supply for its imports. Textiles constituted nearly 40 per cent of total imports by 1859, supplied almost entirely by the United States and India in equal proportions. Ivory accounted for nearly one-third of the total exports, and went largely to India and the United States. These two countries accounted for nearly two-thirds of the total imports and exports of Zanzibar. Thus, any event affecting the major staples or markets was bound to have a considerable destabilising effect on the economy of Zanzibar. By the mid-century, however, that economy had become more broadly integrated into the international economic system, and this introduced greater resilience, permitting Zanzibar to search for alternative markets and sources to tide it over the crises.

128

Zanzibar's internal trade with the African coast and the adjacent islands buttressed its entrepôt role, providing much of its exports and consuming much of its imports, leaving a very profitable residue in the hands of the merchant class. In the 1860s the internal trade constituted about two-fifths of the total value of the commerce of Zanzibar (see Table 4.4). What is notable is the fact that the trade relied so heavily on only a few staples. In 1859 a single commodity (ivory) constituted more than half of the total value of imports, and five staples (textiles, beads, muskets, metal wire, and gunpowder) accounted for 90 per cent of the total value of exports.

The external trade of Zanzibar, which constituted the remaining three-fifths of its total commerce (see Table 4.5), was largely a mirror image of the internal trade, modified only by the absorption of most of the slaves within East Africa, and the production of cloves and coconuts on the islands of Zanzibar and Pemba for export. In the case of external trade as well, there was a heavy reliance on a limited range of staples, though to a lesser extent. In 1859 the most important export commodity (ivory) constituted about one-third of total exports, and the five most important import commodities (textiles, bullion, beads, muskets, and gunpowder) accounted for about four-fifths of total imports.

Ivory was the most important local product to enter the trade. In 1859 about 250 tons were imported from the African mainland, worth more than half the total value of imports from that region; at the same time 220 tons were re-exported, worth one-third of the total value of exports to foreign countries. Most of the ivory was exported to the United States and India in almost equal proportions, although by then a considerable proportion of the ivory sent to India was subsequently re-exported from Bombay to England. In addition, about 20 per cent of the ivory went directly from Zanzibar to Europe in 1859.

Gum copal was the other important commodity imported from the African coast entirely for re-export. It was 'mined' in the coastal belt on the mainland, gum from Zanzibar being of an inferior quality. It normally constituted the third most important export from Zanzibar, more than half going to the United States, although with the dislocation of the American market during the Civil War larger quantities went to Germany and India.

As has been shown earlier (see Chapter 2) slaves had ceased to be an important export at Zanzibar with the transformation of the slave sector. They nevertheless remained the second most important import from the mainland in terms of value. Moreover, since a large proportion of commercial agriculture on the islands and in the coastal belt depended on slave labour, its importance to the economy of the commercial empire was far-reaching. The most important of these commodities was cloves which formed the second most important export in terms of value. It was

Table 4.4 *Internal trade of Zanzibar by commodities, 1859–1864/5*

(a) Imports from the East African coast and adjacent islands

Commodities	Quantity	1859		1861/2–1864/5 average	
		Value (MT$)	Percentage	Value (MT$)	Percentage
Ivory	16,000 Fr	880,000	51	443,370	34
Slaves	19,000	260,000	15	150,000	12
Gum copal	25,000 Fr	150,000	9	152,000	12
Cowries	25,000 Jz	150,000	9	42,000	3
Food grains	226,000 Jz	94,000	6	124,941	10
Hides	4,000 Sc	80,000	5	29,000	2
Sesame	4,000 Jz	24,000	1	107,000	8
Orchella	–	–	–	62,500	5
Cloves				88,000	7
Total internal trade		1,725,500	100	1,292,377	100
Total trade		4,089,855	100	2,788,119	100
Internal trade as percentage of total			42		46

(b) Exports to the East African coast and adjacent islands

Commodities	Quantity	1859		1861/2–1864/5 average	
		Value (MT$)	Percentage	Value (MT$)	Percentage
Textiles		900,450	69	673,226	67
Beads		115,000	9	24,250	2
Metal wire		60,500	5	52,410	5
Muskets	20,000	66,500	5	18,000	2
Gunpowder	10,000 Bbl	50,000	4	19,385	2
Bullion				106,250	11
Total internal trade		1,307,750	100	1,006,555	100
Total trade		3,391,500	100	2,984,759	100
Internal trade as percentage of total			39		34

Notes: Fr – frasela.; Jz – jizla = 22 Fr.; Bbl – barrels.; Sc – scores.
Sources: Rigby to Secretary of State of India, 1 May 1860, PRO, FO 54/17; Playfair to Bombay, 1 May 1864, MA, 54/1864, pp. 16–33; Playfair to FO, 1 January 1865, PRO, FO 54/22; Seward to Bombay, [1865], MA, 73/1865.

131

Table 4.5 *External trade of Zanzibar by commodities, 1859–1864/5*

(a) Exports

Commodities	Quantity	1859 Value (MT$)	Percentage	1861/2–1864/5 average Value (MT$)	Percentage
Ivory	13,960 Fr	696,668	33	558,141	28
Cloves	138,860 Fr	264,418	13	300,706	15
Gum copal	25,025 Fr	176,542	8	133,048	7
Cowries	22,900 Jz	244,360	12	57,743	3
Hides	4,750 Sc	121,390	6	61,798	3
Coconuts		95,527	5	168,837	9
Sesame	24,000 Jz	98,800	5	147,031	7
Orchilla	–		–	62,421	3
Bullion		370,000	18	237,200	12
Total external trade		2,083,750	100	1,978,204	100
Total trade		3,391,500	100	2,984,759	100
External trade as percentage of total			61		66

(b) Imports

| Commodities | Quantity | 1859 | | 1861/2–1864/5 average | |
		Value (MT$)	Percentage	Value (MT$)	Percentage
Textiles		936,324	40	832,874	56
Beads		103,930	4	64,990	4
Metal wire		34,440	1	67,336	4
Muskets	22,780	89,490	4	11,750	1
Gunpowder	11,912 Bbl	42,151	2	20,518	1
Bullion		750,000	32	296,639	20
Total external trade		2,364,355	100	1,495,742	100
Total trade		4,089,855	100	2,788,119	100
External trade as percentage of total			58		54

Sources: As Table 4.4.

133

then still primarily the produce of Zanzibar. During the first half of the 1860s an average of about MT$88,000-worth of cloves were imported from Pemba, but this was less than a third of the total value of cloves exported from Zanzibar. It was only after the hurricane of 1872 that Pemba overtook Zanzibar as the larger clove producer.

The trade of Zanzibar was constantly expanding, and not only in the traditional staples. New commodities were entering the trade during the 1860s to meet growing demand for them in the industrialising West. Coconuts have been a constant feature of the coastal landscape, and there was a regular trade in coconut products between the islands and the mainland, and with the old trading partners in Arabia and India. However, to meet the rapidly expanding demand for vegetable oil in France and Germany, coconut products and oleaginous grains began to be exported in ever-increasing quantities. Export of coconut products to France rose from MT$96,000 in 1859 to about MT$169,000 annually during the early 1860s. Large quantities of sesame began to be produced along the northern coast of Kenya for export, rising from about MT$100,000 in 1859 to an annual average of MT$150,000 in the 1860s. More than half of this went to France and about one-third to Germany. Another industrial crop was orchilla weed which was used in the dyeing process. It was imported from the northern coast of Kenya and Somalia, and exported primarily to France and Germany, with the remainder going to India and Britain.

Cowries were essentially a windfall commodity which entered the market briefly in the late 1850s. To meet a shortage of cowrie shell currency in West Africa, the enterprising German firms tried to cash in by transporting huge quantities from East to West Africa. In 1859 about 3,500 tons of cowries worth MT$150,000 were imported from the African mainland, and the re-export of a similar quantity was valued at MT$244,000, which may give an indication of the profit that accrued to the merchants at Zanzibar. Although the trade persisted for some time, the market was quickly flooded.[19] The value of cowries exported declined drastically to an average of under MT$60,000 during the 1860s.

Apart from relying on a few staples in its import and export trade, Zanzibar depended on only a handful of trading partners who dominated certain branches of trade (see Table 4.6). By 1859 India accounted for more than one-third, followed by the United States which accounted for more than a quarter of the trade of Zanzibar. These two countries, moreover, dominated the major branches of trade, supplying 90 per cent of the cotton goods and absorbing as much ivory, in almost equal proportions. The American Civil War during the first half of the 1860s, and its repercussions on the Indian market, therefore had major unsettling effects on Zanzibar.

Table 4.6 *External trade of Zanzibar by countries, 1859–1864/5*

Imports	1859 Value (MT$)	Percentage	1861/2–1864/5 average Value (MT$)	Percentage
USA	568,795	23	99,725	7
British India	448,230	18	687,765	47
Kutch	260,424	11	98,586	7
France	516,451	21	151,465	10
Germany	455,701	19	238,107	16
Britain	–	–	102,391	7
Arabia	79,231	3	69,298	5
Total imports	2,453,000	100	1,473,278	100
Exports				
USA	534,100	25	165,535	9
British India	467,500	22	603,939	34
Kutch	313,400	15	280,035	16
France	247,500	11	221,911	13
Germany	161,000	7	221,790	13
Britain	25,050	1	126,716	7
Arabia	105,200	5	111,687	6
West Africa	230,000	11	8,750	1
Total exports	2,158,000	100	1,759,708	100

Sources: As for Tables 4.1.

The Civil War deprived the New England cotton industry of its raw materials, and the subsequent econonic changes destroyed its major economic advantages.[20] The distant events had an immediate effect on total American exports to Zanzibar. The Civil War caused a steep rise in the price of American cottons which were soon priced out of the market. American textiles imported into Zanzibar declined from about 6,000 to 7,000 bales before the war to 50 bales in 1864–5. But the war had delivered a more permanent blow to American dominance in the textile trade. By 1873 American traders had to admit that American cottons were 'almost played out here'. With the American source of cottons suddenly blocked and English cottons not yet fully accepted, consumption of other staples of the caravan trade, beads and brass wire, greatly increased.[21]

The Civil War also had a more general disruptive effect on the American economy, and thus on American trade with Zanzibar. As luxuries, ivory and gum copal were among the first to be affected, and by 1862 their prices in the United States were very low. The American export of ivory from Zanzibar in 1861–2 was reduced to almost nil, while India's share rose to over 60 per cent. The American share of gum copal exports declined to less than 10 per cent, while larger quantities went to Germany and India. The withdrawal of the Americans from the ivory market had a significant influence on ivory prices at Zanzibar. They declined from about MT$55 per *frasela* in 1857 to MT$44 in 1864. There was a partial recovery in American exports in 1863–4, probably mostly for re-export to London, but it was not until after the war that the pre-war figures were attained again.[22]

During these difficult times, the Americans did their best to persevere in the trade and maintain their good name. They overcame the threat to their shipping from Confederate raiders by using the neutral English flag. They attempted to continue in the trade by importing English cottons into Zanzibar themselves.[23] The finest stroke, however, was their success in manipulating local currency problems in East Africa to their immediate advantage. The French and the Germans had hitherto been the greatest importers of specie. With the interruption in the American supply of textiles, however, the Germans realised the advantage of importing English cottons. The Maria Theresa dollars, so essential in the local coastal trade, therefore, became scarce. The shortage of currency at Zanzibar was affecting traditional cash remittances to India.[24]

Towards the end of 1863, therefore, the American Consul took a step that seemed to offer a solution not only to the local currency problem but also to that faced by American traders. He pointed out to the Sultan that although the Americans were unable to import cotton goods, the demand for African goods remained high in the United States. This was forcing American traders to burden themselves with debts at high rates of interest. Therefore, recognition of American gold coins at par with the Maria Theresa dollar would permit the flow of much-needed coins to Zanzibar. What he did not mention was that he was asking for the acceptance of American coins at a premium of about 2 per cent. Added to the fact that specie was not subject to the 5 per cent import duty, it was soon to emerge as a convenient short-term import substitute for the Americans. In fact even German merchants and the Sultan himself took the opportunity of importing American gold coins which soon flooded the market and became the principal local currency.[25]

However, Bombay refused to recognise this artificial over-valuation of American coins at Zanzibar, and the remittances to India therefore suffered a proportionate loss. Within a year Indian merchants were clamouring against Sultan Majid's proclamation recognising American coins. Early in 1865 the Sultan attempted to revoke the proclamation but the Americans were able to hold him to his word. It was not until 1868 that British Consul Kirk was able to negotiate in a meeting with prominent Indian merchants who included Dewji Jamal and Lakha Kanji a new arrangement whereby only the Maria Theresa dollar was recognised, and the rest of the coins were allowed to find their own market value.[26]

Despite these efforts, however, the Americans had great difficulty overcoming the depression in their trade with Zanzibar. And such was the significance of American trade in the economy of Zanzibar that its collapse during the war caused a precipitous decline in the total trade of Zanzibar, from over MT$4 million in 1859 to less than MT$2.5 million in 1861–2 (see Table 4.5).

Nevertheless, by the 1860s, the structure of the commercial empire had assumed its most mature form. Its foundations rested on production on the offshore islands and the coastal belt, and on the transit trade from the vast African hinterland. The former had developed as the mainstay of the ruling landowning class and was therefore hardly taxed, except for the duty on Pemba cloves to discourage overproduction. The transit trade, on the other hand, was considered fair game and was subject to differential taxation as regards different parts of the coast and commodities to squeeze out the maximum amount of revenue without diverting the trade from the entrepôt. To further underwrite the primacy of Zanzibar, the richest section of the coast, the Mrima, was declared reserved for local traders. Such centralisation of trade required an integrated fiscal structure which evolved under the custom master who acquired control of almost the whole coast by the late 1830s.

The commercial economy that had developed by mid-century was therefore prosperous, and it yielded a handsome revenue to the Busaidi state. But it was dependent on international trade. Specifically, it was dependent on a few staples, which gave it the character of a monoculture. It also tended to rely on a few markets, so that developments in these markets – over which Zanzibar could exercise no influence – had major consequences for its economy. To that extent the economy was also fragile. Nevertheless, by the middle of the nineteenth century the commercial empire had been integrated into the international economic system so that Zanzibar could explore other opportunities and markets within that system.

The capital: planter town or commercial centre?

The structure of the commercial empire was reflected in its capital city. The settlement on the triangular Shangani peninsula had originated as a fishing village, and it became the seat of the Shirazi Queen Fatuma towards the end of the seventeenth century. She had maintained friendly relations with the Portuguese and was exiled for a while to Oman when her allies were driven out in 1698. As late as 1811, however, the town still consisted mainly of huts, although it also had 'a good number of stone buildings in it belonging to the Arabs and merchants'. Even by 1842, according to Burton, it still had only five storehouses of the 'humblest description', and the eastern part of the peninsula was a coconut plantation. It grew rapidly and by 1835 it had an estimated population of 10,000 to 12,000.[27]

Although population estimates of the town during the nineteenth century are not very reliable, Table 4.7 gives at least an indication of the rapid growth of the metropolis. This is supported by the few maps of the city for the period that are extant (see Map 4.1).

Table 4.7   *The population of Zanzibar town, 1835–1910*

Year	Population	Source
1835	10–12,000	Ruschenberger, Vol. 1, p. 46.
1846	20–25,000	Guillain, Vol. 2, p. 80.
c. 1850	50,000	Osgood, p. 45.
1857	25–45,000	Burton (1872), Vol. 1, p. 81.
1860	25–30,000	Quaas, in Harkema (1967), p. 42.
1860	60,000	Rigby, in Russell, p. 328.
1865	40,000	von der Decken, in Harkema (1967), p. 42.
1866	40–50,000	Jablonski, in ibid.
1869	70,000	Kirk to Bombay, 2 May 1870, PRO, FO 84/1325.
1876	80–100,000	Christie (1876), p. 418.
1885	80,000	Schmidt and Luders, in Harkema (1967), p. 42.
1895	60,000	Baumann, in ibid.
1910	35,262	Police Census, Min. of Communication, Zanzibar

Until recently scholars assumed that Zanzibar was a typical trade city which flourished on external trade. R. Menon was the first to address the question of the fundamental character of the city. He argues that urban growth there was not the result of wealth accumulated by merchants who appear to have invested little in social infrastructure and building. This, he says, is clear from the limited urban development in the period before 1835 when Zanzibar was essentially a maritime trading town. He asserts that:

> urban development on a large scale and the erection of substantial stone buildings occurred only with the transition to a plantation economy which took place after 1835. From this time on Zanzibar was slowly, if incompletely, transformed into a plantation town.[28]

Menon's critique of the 'trade thesis' is partly based on the theoretical consideration that it speaks only of the sphere of circulation and does not deal with the more important question of production. He argues that there is a relationship between urbanism as a way of life, the city as a built form, and the dominant mode of production. He says that the trade thesis ignores the organisation of production that enabled trade to take place, and also the process of material reproduction of the town and the townspeople from one year to the next.[29]

Plate 15   Sokokuu fruit market under the walls of the Old Fort, c.1885

As regards the second aspect, that of production of subsistence for the townspeople, Menon correctly directs our attention to the parasitic relationship between town and country, and shows that it was always the indigenous inhabitants, and later imported slaves, who engaged in the material production that kept the town going.[30] We do not have much direct evidence of the production of commodities by the indigenous peasants for sale in the town, but after the conversion of the tribute in labour to a payment in kind by 1811, and to an annual poll tax of MT$2 per person by 1834,[31] their participation in the production and supply of subsistence to the town can be assumed. As the slave economy developed, and since clove picking is so seasonal, the plantation owners tried to shift much of the reproduction costs of the slaves onto the shoulders of the slaves themselves. They were each given a plot of land and allowed two days of the week free to work on it and dispose of the surplus in the town market on Fridays.[32] The Sokokuu produce market under the walls of the Old Fort was a bustling place as Giraud's sketch so effectively portrays, and there were subsidiary markets at Malindi and Mnazi Mmoja.[33] In addition, the plantations took care of the reproduction of the big landowners, who retired to a life of prestige and luxury in the town to be near the Sultan's court.

Menon, however, does recognise the difficulty in the case of Zanzibar as regards the first aspect that he feels the trade thesis has ignored, i.e. the organisation of production, since most of the commodities that Zanzibar merchants traded were produced not in Zanzibar but by societies on the African mainland.[34] As shown above, an average of 78 per cent of the merchandise passing through the entrepôt during the 1860s originated on the mainland.[35] This included gum copal dug up along the coast, ivory that was hunted for all over the interior as far as eastern Zaire and slaves, captured particularly in the southern hinterland around Lake Nyasa. These commodities were produced by societies at different levels of social development, from tribal to fully developed class and monarchical societies. They were not fully integrated into the Zanzibari social formation; only their foreign trade, which constituted only a small proportion of their total production, transited through Zanzibar.

On the other hand, this transit trade provided profit to a large merchant class resident on Zanzibar, not only American, European and Indian traders, but also Arabs involved in the entrepôt trade. Commerce also provided a substantial proportion of the revenue of the Busaidi state, since clove production by the ruling landowning class was not taxed.[36] This consideration could not but affect fundamentally the urban development of Zanzibar. Menon argues that the most significant growth of the city occurred between 1835 and 1890 at a time when the slave mode of production was spreading on the island. This, however, was also the period of an even more rapid development of Zanzibar's trade – the value of the customs rent rose from MT\$84,000 in 1819 to MT\$310,000 in the 1860s[37] – whereas the slave mode stagnated with overproduction from the 1840s.

Menon also argues that merchants tend to invest their profits to expand the sphere of circulation, rather than spending them on social infrastructure and construction.[38] This is certainly true, particularly in the accumulation phase; but the merchant class was becoming indigenised, and, even if its members did not build large palatial houses on the seafront, their modest homes – and some not so modest – as well as the bazaars, proliferated during the period and became the locus of town life. And beyond the bazaars lay the expanding wattle-and-mud huts, both on the peninsula and increasingly across the creek in Ngambo, whose function in the city cannot be explained in terms of the urbanised and locally unproductive landowners hanging around the court, but only by the role their occupants played in the commercial economy of Zanzibar, as will be shown below.

Menon makes the curious statement that the Omanis were never 'true merchant capitalists', a suggestion that cannot be sustained. The Omanis came to Zanzibar initially as merchants, and, while many of the later immigrants from the 1830s went into plantation agriculture, a large number retained one foot in the foreign trade to Arabia and India and in the entrepôt trade, and a new field was opening up for many in the caravan

Plate 16   View of Zanzibar town, c.1885. The Old Fort in the foreground, Beit al Hukm and the old lighthouse behind it

Plate 17   Forodhani − Zanzibar sea-front. From left to right: the Grand Hotel Afrique Centrale; the Sultan's ice factory; Beit al Sahel Palace; and the old lighthouse destroyed in the British bombardment of 1896

141

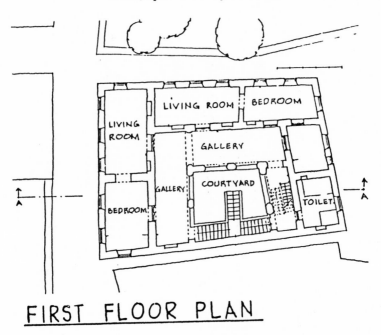

FIRST FLOOR PLAN

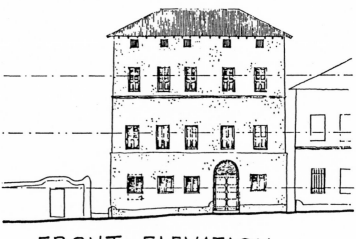

FRONT ELEVATION

Plate 18   Arab house in Zanzibar

142

Plate 19   Zanzibar architecture: verandah around the inner courtyard

Plate 20   The carved Zanzibar door

Plate 21   Horse racing on the Mnazi Mmoja, Zanzibar, c.1846

Plate 22   An Indian shop in Zanzibar, c.1860

trade which provided the capital for many of their plantations, as in the case of Tippu Tip.[39] There were about 300 Omanis in Zanzibar in the 1770s and about 1,000 by 1819, and the figure jumped to 5,000 by the 1840s.[40] A number of them settled around the Old Fort, the more privileged preferring sites on the seafront to catch the breeze. The district centred on the palace complex consisting of the Beit al Sahel, which was built by Seyyid Said in 1843, and the Beit al Hukm which had a tall lighthouse in front of it (see Map 4.2).

A typical Arab house was a modest whitewashed square building with small windows on the outer walls, and an open courtyard in the middle to permit ventilation and light to penetrate the rooms. The courtyard was lined with verandahs where the occupants spent much of their time, ensuring privacy for the womenfolk. The courtyard was a functional area; in the pungent words of Burton, a 'dirty yard, paved or unpaved, usually encumbered with piles of wood or hides, stored for sale, and tenanted by poultry, dogs, donkeys and lingering slaves.'[41] The entrance was adorned by the beautiful carved Zanzibar door which portrayed the status of the owner. The front room generally served as a reception area, the *baraza*, but the other rooms on the ground floor, which had little privacy or ventilation from the narrow lanes, were used as slave quarters or for the storage of merchandise. American visitors during the 1840s, who witnessed active construction of a 'large number of very tenantable houses' occupied by the Arabs and Indians, said some of them were three or four storeys high, although the majority had only two storeys.[42]

The homes of the merchants in the bazaar area behind the seafront were generally plain and functional, small and, in early days, lacking an internal courtyard or carved doors. Albrand enumerated 214 Indians in 1819, and in 1835 Ruschenberger described their shops as mere 'holes, raised a foot or two above the street.'[43] By the 1840s, when the 'Banians' numbered 400 to 700, the wealthier merchants, of whom there were about 40, were building 'large and commodious residences'.[44] Judging from Baron von der Decken's sketch of an Indian 'nautch' in Zanzibar, some even had carved doors by the 1860s (see illustration on p. 106). The living quarters moved to the upper floors, and some of the houses had verandahs built along the outer walls; while the rooms behind the shop on the ground floor served as store-rooms. By 1860 whole new quarters were being established in the city that were largely inhabited by them, with some degree of concentration by the different castes and sects around their communal and religious establishments. The Indian population of the city had grown fifteenfold by the 1870s when it numbered nearly 3,000 (see Table 4.8).

The Indians, who tended to be associated with trade, were not a homogeneous merchant class, and were in the process of transition from seasonal merchants into an indigenised community. The most prominent

146

section of the merchant class during the first half of the nineteenth century were the Hindus (Bhatias and Vanias) who were concentrated in the wholesale business; one of them, Jairam Sewji, controlled the customs for half a century. However, even among them, there were 77 artisans out of a total of 314 adult males, practising as goldsmiths, blacksmiths, carpenters, tailors and barbers, and many of the remainder were small shopkeepers, pawnbrokers and moneylenders. According to Guillain and Burton, the 'Banians' were birds of passage rather than colonists. Because of caste restrictions they could not bring their families to reproduce themselves in East Africa. There was not a single Hindu woman on the island as late as 1857, and scandals were often caused by their cohabitation with slave girls. Oral evidence, however, speaks of Ibji Sewji, the custom master's brother, who brought his wife amidst much fanfare, and the Hindus eventually became stabilised as a resident community.[45]

Muslim Indians, on the other hand, facing no such religious restrictions, began to settle earlier. By the 1840s the 165 Khoja households had 26 married women. By the 1870s there were nearly 700 females in a population of over 2,000 Khojas organised in 500 households. A similar pattern applied to the smaller Bohora community which numbered about 300, and there were 250 Sunni Muslims (see Table 4.8). Christie says that by the mid-1870s most of the Khojas were locally born and permanent settlers. Their houses, excepting those belonging to some half-dozen wealthy wholesale merchants, were two storeys high, arranged in narrow streets converging towards the market place and the custom house. The frontage of the shop, being the most valuable part, was very narrow, 12 to 14 feet wide. At night even the shop was converted into sleeping quarters. Outside business was conducted by the husband while the retail shop was run by the wife. By the 1870s the poorer Khojas had begun to spread into Ngambo across the creek and lived in a very unhealthy condition with high infant mortality.[46] It is clear that the Muslim communities had become stabilised and were reproducing themselves in East Africa, although new immigrants continued to come from India. This holds important implications for investment in their living quarters as well as commercial establishments.

Perhaps the strongest confirmation of the predominantly commercial character of the developing city comes from the growth of the working-class quarter. Menon has made an important contribution in tracing the development of the so-called 'native quarter' and the class that inhabited it, but he has misinterpreted its significance. He claims that the establishment of Ngambo across the creek 'coincided roughly with the period when the slave mode of production was at its peak'.[47] From Guillain's map it is clear that in 1846 wattle-and-mud huts predominated in the Malindi quarter in the north, and to the south of Cape Shangani on the peninsula itself (see Map 4.1). Even as late as the mid-1870s there were

147

Table 4.8 *The Indian population of Zanzibar, 1819–74*

Year	Community	No. of houses	Males	Females	Children	Total	Source
1819	Khojas	165				214	Albrand, p. 73
1840	Muslims			26			Kirk, 1870[a]
1844						6–700	Burton (1872), Vol. 1, p. 356
1845	Banians					400	Pickering, p. 260
1846						500	Guillain, Vol. 1, p. 80
c. 1850	Banians	80				5–700	Osgood, p. 45
1870	Hindus	535		700		200	Kirk, 1870[a]
	Khojas	40	75	65	110	2,100	ibid.
	Bohoras	520	850	650	725	250	ibid.
1874	Khojas		109	78	131	2,225	Prideaux, in
	Bohoras		15	10	16	318	Harkema, p. 52
	Memons					41	

Note: [a] Kirk's Administrative Report for Zanzibar, 1870, PRO, FO 84/1344.

148

still many huts interspersed with stone houses in the centre of the city. In 1857 Burton described this 'native town' on the peninsula as:

> a filthy labyrinth . . . The meanest hovels are of palm-matting . . . thatched with cajan or grass, and with or without walls of wattle-and-daub . . . The better abodes are enlarged boxes of stone, mostly surrounded by deep, projecting eaves, forming a kind of verandah on poles and shading benches of masonry or tamed earth where articles are exposed for sale.[48]

Already in the mid-1840s huts had begun to sprout across the Darajani bridge in Ngambo, although in 1857 when Burton visited the city the area was still largely covered by bush and plantations. The substantive development of Ngambo thus appears to have occurred sometime thereafter, for by the time his book on Zanzibar was published in 1872 he was informed that the area around the creek had all been built up 'of late years'.[49] By 1895 the 'mud town' was largely confined to Funguni in the north and the southern and eastern extremities of the peninsula. On the other hand, it had grown enormously in Ngambo which then consisted of fifteen major *mitaa* (wards) and several minor ones (see Map 4.1).[50]

The 'native quarter', both on the peninsula before the 1860s and in Ngambo thereafter, was inhabited by the emerging working class. Menon argues that this consisted of free Swahili as well as slaves, although he says it had become extremely difficult to make a distinction between them.[51] In fact there is little evidence of the existence of free workers in a social formation dominated by the slave mode of production. Apart from poor Hadhrami Arabs who had worked as porters in the early part of the nineteenth century, and perhaps the Malgash who inhabited the tip of Funguni in the late 1850s and had a quarter of their own in Ngambo in the 1870s, the working class – according to Christie, who had a very intimate knowledge of the city during the 1870s – consisted largely of slaves. They included in the first place domestic slaves in the households of the landowning class, who were 'out of all proportion to the amount of work done', but they lived in their owners' houses in the stone town on the peninsula.[52]

Christie is fairly emphatic about the inhabitants of Ngambo who he says were largely slaves owned by Hadhrami Arabs, Comorians and other slaves (a curious case of slave-owning slaves or freed slaves). Owners of a small number of slaves tended to live with their slaves, while the larger owners may have lived in the stone town. Christie enumerates several categories of these slaves who were all connected with the commercial economy of Zanzibar. There were about 1,000 domestic slaves who worked for American, European and Indian households. In addition, there were 10,000 to 15,000 day-labourers who presented themselves at the custom house or business houses to clean gum copal or

Plate 23   Hamali porters in Zanzibar. Long poles were used to carry heavy loads before hand carts were introduced

orchilla weed and prepare copra. Both these groups were paid by their employers, but they had to share their wages with their owners. There was also a small segment of professional porters (*hamalis*) who performed heavy tasks on contract under Hadhrami supervision, and wages were paid to the owners who then shared with their slaves. They kept all the proceeds when they worked overtime or when they were not required by their masters for contract labour. They considered themselves 'superior to the country slaves and ordinary labourers'. There was also a class of artisans who had a much stronger position vis-à-vis their owners, and an arrangement had to be worked out as to the proportion of their earnings that went to their masters. Fishermen, some of whom were free Swahili, formed another distinct group.[53]

The servile working class was thus variegated, but what is clear is that, apart from the unproductive domestic slaves in landowning households who lived in the stone town, the class was largely connected with the commercial economy of the entrepôt and was involved in cleaning, preparing and transporting commodities. Zanzibar city was thus much more than an abode of the politically dominant landowners; it was not merely a larger version of nineteenth-century Malindi town on the coast of Kenya, which comes closest to Menon's conception of a plantation town.[54] To characterise Zanzibar as a plantation town is to refuse to go beyond the seafront into the labyrinth of the bazaar and the 'native quarter'; it is·to close one's eyes to the vast commercial activity which was the *raison d'être* of not only East African coastal cities but of many cities in the pre-industrial epoch.

Notes

1. Guillain, Vol. 3, pp. 302–3.
2. See Map 1.2 and p. 43 above. See also Prins (1965), p. 303; Johnson (1945), p. 452; Christie (1876), p. 11; Harkema (1976), pp. 82, 84; Guillain, Vol. 3, pp. 357–8, 370; Loarer, ANSOM, OI, 5/23/2, Pt 2; Burton (1872), Vol. 1, p. 73–4.
3. Hoyle, pp. 14–17; Datoo (1975), pp. 43–7; Harkema (1967), pp. 130–1; Berg (1971), chs 1 and 2; Spear, chs 3 and 4. The Mazrui history of Mombasa passes over the less glorious periods in silence, but Mombasa does appear to have been occupied in 1754, 1775 and 1784. See also Freeman-Grenville (ed.) (1962a), pp. 193, 213–19; Freeman-Grenville (1975), p. 128; Alpers (1966), p. 155.
4. Strandes, p. 275.
5. Burton (1860), Vol. 2, pp. 403–8; Guillain, Vol. 3, pp. 319–21.
6. Guillain, Vol. 3, p. 386.
7. Said to Palmerston, 2 June 1839, MA, 54/1839, p. 149. Loarer, 'Quiloa Quevindja', ANSOM, OI, 2/10/2, B and C.
8. Guillain, Vol. 3, pp. 388–9; Freeman-Grenville (ed.) (1962a), p. 200; Bennett and Brooks (eds) (1965), pp. 239, 347, 353–5, 359–60.
9. Sacleux, p. 591; Whiteley (1969), map; Whiteley (1956), p. 3; Lambert, pp. 7–9; Hamerton (1855), pp. 25–60; Coupland (1938), p. 481; Bennett and Brooks (eds) (1965), pp. 353–8; Desfosses to MAE, 19 November 1844, MAE, CCZ, I; Loarer, 'Ports au sud de Zanguebar', ANSOM, OI, 2/10/2, B, under 'Quiloa'.
10. Loarer, 'Lois et coutumes de douane', 'Ivoire', ANSOM, OI, 2/10/2, A–D; Guillain, Vol. 3, pp. 310–11, 392. Loarer's figures for the total import of ivory into Zanzibar in 1848 amount to between 16,100 and 19,200 *fraselas*; Guillain says 'native traders' gave him a figure of 17,000 to 18,000 *fraselas*; there is also a table of exports of ivory in 1848 which gives a total of 18,700 *fraselas*. All these estimates originate from the same source, the French expedition. They appear to be exaggerated. An American memorandum of the early 1850s gives more precise figures for exports to the United States and Europe, though it seems to be greatly underestimating exports to India. These figures may be compared with Rigby's in 1859:

Sources	To US	To Europe	To India	Total exports
Loarer (1848)	6,000	3,700	9,000	18,700
American:				
1852–3	3,393	1,102	1,100	5,975
1853–4	3,416	1,260	250	4,926
Rigby (1859)	6,500	460	7,000	13,960

Loarer's estimates may, therefore, have to be halved, although his proportions for the different parts of the coast may be taken as a guide. The other sources in the table above are: 'Memo of Exports from 14/5/1852', NAW, RG 84, Z:C–3, Misc. Rec. Bk., 1852–6; Rigby to Secretary of State, 1 May 1860, PRO, FO 54/17.

11. Duty rates in the early 1860s in Hines to Seward, 25 October 1864, in Bennett and Brooks (eds) (1965), pp. 531–2; Playfair to Bombay, 1 May 1864, IOR, L/P&S/9/41. Figures on ivory and copal exports to Zanzibar for 1872–3 are contained in Prideaux's 'Administrative Report for the years 1873 and 1874', quoted in W.T. Brown (1971b), p. 32.

12. ibid.

13. Loarer, 'M'gao M'kindany', 'Meurka', ANSOM, OI, 2/10/2, A; Loarer, 'Lois et coutumes de douane', ANSOM, OI, 2/10/2 A–D.

14. Freeman-Grenville (ed.) (1962a), pp. 198, 200, 205, 211; Guillain, Vol. 3, pp. 386, 388–90.

15. Hamerton to Bombay, 22 August 1842, MA, 55/1843; 'Mohamed b. Sef, governor of Zanzibar, Sewar, Banyan Collector of Customs, in a/c with Edm. Roberts, 10/1827–1/1828', LC, Roberts Papers, V. This is the earliest reference to Sewji Topan as the custom master. Hitherto historians had held, following John Kirk, that the firm of Wat Bhima (Aulad or sons of Bhima?) were the first to farm the customs of Zanzibar in 1833. See Kirk's Administrative Report, 1870, 18 July 1870, PRO, FO 84/1344; Mangat (1969), pp. 3, 4n, 15; Gray (1962a), p. 143. The representative of the firm in 1870 was said to have been fifth in descent from the founder of the Zanzibar firm. It is possible that the firm may have controlled the customs for brief periods before 1833, but contemporary evidence for 1827–8 is unmistakable, and from the mid-1830s that firm seems definitely to have been in control according to American records. Hamerton says in 1842 that Sewji Topan had farmed the customs for twenty-four years, i.e. since 1819. Hamerton to Bombay, 22 December 1842, MA, 55/1843. See also Kuhlmann to MAE, 27 March 1852, MAE, CCZ, Vol. 2, pp. 27–34; Guillain, Vol. 3, p. 372.

16. Guillain, Vol. 3, pp. 388–90; Loarer, ANSOM, OI, 5/23/2.

17. *Encyclopaedia Britannica* (1910), Vol. 10, p. 180; Mangat (1969), p. 18.

18. Freeman-Grenville (ed.) (1962a), p. 198; Theal, Vol. 9, p. 13; Albrand, p. 78; Kirk's Administrative Report, 1870, 18 July 1870, PRO, FO 84/1344; Loarer, 'Lois et coutumes de douanes', ANSOM, OI, 2/10/2, A–D; Playfair to FO, 28 June 1865, PRO, FO 84/1245.

19. For the impact on the West African market, see Hopkins, pp. 149–50.

20. Speke (1862), pp. 139–40; Stanley (1872), pp. 52–4. As late as 1871 Stanley felt he needed to take nearly two and a half times as much *merekani* in value as the next most important type, *kaniki*. Zevin, pp. 680–2; Bennet (1961a), p. 32; Bennett (1963), p. 32.

21. Webb to State Dept, 30 September 1873, NAW, T100/6; Goodhue to Seward, 1 July 1865, NAW, T100/4; Bennett and Brooks (eds) (1965), pp. 521–2, 536, 538–9; Webb to Ropes, 9 May 1873, PM, Ropes Papers.

22. Bennett and Brooks (eds) (1965), p. 521; see Fig. 3.1; Mansfield to Marcy, 1 January 1857, NAW, T100/3; Invoice of ivory on *Col. James Scott*, 26 April

1864, PM, West Papers, 3; Maris to Goodhue and Ropes, 3 June 1864, PM, Ropes Papers; PRO, Cust. 5/73.

23. Bennett and Brooks (eds) (1965), pp. 523–5, 534; Webb to Ropes, 1 November 1866, PM, Ropes Papers; 'Extract from the Administration Report of the Political Agent at Zanzibar', *TBGS*, Vol. 18 (1865), p. 82; Bennett (1961a), p. 54.

24. In 1859 specie exports to India exceeded those of ivory. In the 1860s this was reversed. Jablonski to MAE, 26 March 1864, MAE, CCZ, Vol. 2, pp. 365–7; same to same, 31 December 1867, MAE, CCZ, Vol. 3, pp. 69–80.

25. Hines to Majid, 29 December 1863, NAW, RG 84/Z:C–3, Misc. Rec. Bk. 1860–71; Bennett and Brooks (eds) (1965), p. 524; Playfair to Bombay, 21 June 1864, MA 54/1864, pp. 93–100.

26. Playfair to Bombay, 15 March 1865, Frazer & Co. to Bombay, 5 November 1866, Seward to Bombay, 8 June 1867, NAI, 10/1868-Pol. A–497/9; Kirk to Bombay, 12 April 1868, PRO, FO 84/1292; Colomb, p. 388.

27. Gray (1962a), pp. 83, 102; Freeman-Grenville (1965), p. 104n; Burton (1872), Vol. 1, pp. 82–3, 103.

28. Menon, p. v.

29. ibid., p. 17.

30. ibid., p. 18.

31. See pp. 57–9 above.

32. Christie (1871), p. 34; Christie (1876), pp. 318–20.

33. Burton (1872), Vol. 1, p. 92.

34. Menon, p. 17.

35. See p. 116 above.

36. See p. 53–4 above.

37. See p. 127 above.

38. Menon, pp. 9–11.

39. See p. 104 above.

40. Freeman-Grenville (ed.) (1965), p. 79; Albrand, p. 72; Osgood, p. 45; Burton (1872), Vol. 1, pp. 368–78.

41. Burton (1872), Vol. 1, p. 85.

42. Browne, p. 332; Osgood, pp. 29–30.

43. Albrand, p. 73; Ruschenberger, Vol. 1, p. 35.

44. Pickering, p. 260; Osgood, p. 45; Guillain, Vol. 3, p. 372; Browne, p. 332.

45. Prideaux, in Harkema (1967), pp. 50–1; Guillain, Vol. 3. p. 372; Burton (1872), Vol. 329; Christie (1876), pp. 344–7. An oral communication from Roshan Alloo, a Zanzibar merchant, mentions the case of Ibji Sewji's wife but Christie does not speak of any being present as late as the mid-1870s.

46. Christie (1876), p. 336.

47. Menon, p. 41.

48. Burton (1872), Vol. 1, pp. 96–7.

49. ibid.

50. Menon, p. 43.

51. ibid., p. 45.

52. Pickering, p. 19; Burton (1872), Vol. 1, p. 82; Christie (1871), p. 36;

Christie (1876), p. 333. Menon, p. 47, says that slave-owners were reluctant to have slaves live with them because of the rising cost of reproducing them, and therefore pushed them to live in Ngambo. It is difficult to conceive of domestic slaves who did not live in the owners' houses. On the other hand, landowners who were getting impoverished may have begun to hire out slaves to other employers, and they joined the class of working slaves rather than remaining as domestic slaves. See below.

53. Christie (1871), pp. 37–41; Pickering, p. 189.
54. Martin (1973), passim.

Five

The Hinterland
of Zanzibar

The economy of Zanzibar, as we saw in Chapter 4, depended for three-quarters of its value on commodities coming from a vast hinterland that extended halfway through middle Africa by the third quarter of the nineteenth century. While we cannot here attempt a comprehensive exposition of the development of commodity production and trade throughout this region, it is necessary to define the extent of the hinterland of Zanzibar, and some of the factors and processes by which this area was commercially integrated with the coast and, through it, with the international economic system.

In the euphoria over what T.O. Ranger termed the 'discovery of African initiative' during the 1960s, African history was made to make a full swing from the pre-existing 'external initiative' interpretation of the colonial school. As regards the development of long-distance trade routes between the interior and the coast, E.A. Alpers went so far as to assert that they were established 'exclusively through African initiative'. He himself examined the role played by Cisi ironsmiths among the Yao who may have pioneered the linkage between the regional trading network which had developed in the interior for the distribution of iron hoes, with that which had developed behind Kilwa, with the initiative naturally coming from the interior.[1] A.D. Roberts proposed a more neutral theory which associated the development of regional trade in commodities of immediate usefulness in the subsistence economies of the interior with the fact that the raw materials, such as iron and usable salt, are fairly localised and scarce, and sometimes required specialised technology to exploit them.[2] It is possible to postulate from this a series of such regional trading networks that could at various times and places be linked under different stimuli. Such an expanded network could have permitted the infiltration of specific exotic objects, as well as information about the demand for certain commodities, over long distances through a sort of relay system. Such a stage may have preceded the development of single trading parties venturing across the whole length of the route.

A more fruitful approach, however, has been through an examination of the internal dynamics of these societies and, specifically, the development of surplus production and exchange of some of the vital commodities, and the emergence of embryonic merchant classes in some of the societies. K. Jackson and J. Lamphear, for example, added a whole new dimension when they argued that population pressure forced the Kamba to disperse from their well-watered hills into drier plains prone to famines. This conditioned them to increasing dependence on hunting and trade in ever-widening territory which eventually brought them in touch with the coast. Their participation in hunting and trade appears to have given birth to a nascent merchant class. In the case of Unyamwezi, A.C. Unomah traces the development from within the African society of a merchant class that shared common interests and collaborated with the coastal traders in expanding the sphere of commodity production and circulation, and the closer integration of the interior into the international economic system through Zanzibar (see p. 181).[3]

Roberts, however, had recognised that the primary commodity which precipitated the forging of trade links between the coast and the interior was ivory, which had no commercial value previously in the Nyamwezi economic system and, we may add, slaves, who existed in some societies but were rarely a commodity for exchange. The external demand for these commodities, therefore, cannot be ignored in considering the process of commercial assimilation of the interior. This demand, first felt at the coast, impelled Swahili and Arab traders to expand the immediate hinterland of the various coastal cities and, in places, to penetrate deep into the interior. They were backed by the Omani state which at times encouraged their commercial enterprise with lower taxes; by the Indian financiers who provided long-term credit facilities; and by the extremely favourable terms of trade which African commodities, particularly ivory, enjoyed throughout the first three-quarters of the nineteenth century.

Perhaps the issue of historical significance is not so much who blazed the trail; there is evidence to show a great degree of interpenetration of different groups' hinterlands and, at different times and places, of coastal or interior traders cutting across to the source of the commodities in demand. More important is the social transformation that African societies began to undergo, and the process of their integration into the commercial empire.

The hinterland of Zanzibar can be divided into three sectors based on their relation to the entrepôt and the differential taxation system that was evolved to centralise the foreign trade and exploit it to maximum advantage. As Table 5.1 shows, the core was the hinterland behind the Mrima coast which produced more than two-fifths of the ivory and gum copal in

Table 5.1 Imports into Zanzibar from the African coast, 1848–1873/4

| | 1848 | | | | 1872/73 | | | | 1872/3–73/4 | |
| | Ivory | | Copal | | Ivory | | Copal | | Average total value | |
	Volume (fraselas)	Percent-age	Volume (fraselas)	Percent-age	Value (MT$ '000s)	Percent-age	Value (MT$ '000s)	Percent-age	MT$ '000s	Percent-age
Northern hinterland										
Benadir	2,500	13			21	3			133	13
Lamu and Mombasa	2,000	10			7	1	1	–	20	2
Total		23				4				15
The core: Mrima										
Pangani and Tanga	3,350	17			140	21			151	14
Bagamoyo	4,500	23	12,500	42	400	61	200	96	453	43
Total		40		42		82		96		57
Southern hinterland										
Kilwa	4,375	22	8,750	29						
Kiswere to Tungi	1,910	10	8,650	29						
Total		32		58	79	12	8	4	225	21
Other ports	850	4							77	7
Total	19,535	99	29,900	100	657	100	209	100	1,058	100

Sources: Loarer, 'Ivoire', 'Gomme copal', ANSOM, OI, 5/23/3; Loarer, 'Ports au Sud et au Nord de Zanguebar', ANSOM, OI, 2/10/2; Brown, p. 32, and Harkema (1967), p. 71, based on Prideaux's 'Administrative Report for the years 1873 and 1874', Zanzibar Blue Books, 1875–80.

157

the late 1840s; by the early 1870s nearly three-fifths of the total value of African imports into Zanzibar, and more than 90 per cent of ivory and copal originated from the same coast. The northern periphery exercised its option of more direct trade with India and Arabia to a greater degree before the middle of the nineteenth century but, as the century wore on, and although there was no increase in the duty charged, there was a decline in the importance of ivory as the Kenya coast turned increasingly to agricultural production based on slave labour for export. The southern periphery lost that option, particularly after the collapse of the French slave trade, and it was gradually incorporated into the core as regards taxation. However, in terms of the hinterland and the trade routes, and even in terms of major commodities – slaves remaining the leading export of the southern coast – it remained a distinct sector (see Map 4.2).

The southern hinterland

The peripheral area to the south, extending from Kilwa to Tungi Bay near Cape Delgado, enjoyed varying degrees of political and economic independence. As far as the climatic factor was concerned, the ports along this coast enjoyed the freedom of direct external contacts to the south-east, to Mozambique, Madagascar, the Comoros and the Mascarenes. Kilwa made the most of this facility during the eighteenth century in establishing a prosperous trade in slaves to the French islands. However, this region was at a distinct disadvantage in its economic relations with the northern rim of the Indian Ocean. The trading season between the north-east monsoon and the first sailing with the south-west monsoon in April/May was too short, and this necessitated the 'wintering' of the dhows until the second sailing in August. As we have seen, Indian vessels preferred to go only as far south as Zanzibar, and yet the trade with the north for the necessary imports was crucial to Kilwa's southern trade.

In the 1770s Kilwa apparently controlled the adjoining Mgao coast as far south as Mikindani and, though an Omani governor was appointed at Kilwa after its conquest, the indigenous ruler was left to control the mainland section of the kingdom, an authority which he continued to exercise as late as 1811. Captain Loarer, admittedly in context of the perennial French search for a foothold on the coast, described this as a 'neutral territory, not belonging to the Portuguese and attached only nominally to the authority of Seyyid Said' to obtain his protection, but retaining considerable independence. There were no Omani governors or customs officials at Tungi, Mikindani, Mgao Mwanya or Kiswere.[4] Political relationship thus appears to have been in the nature of an Omani overlordship and indirect rule which characterised the commercial empire even in Zanzibar. As each part of the coast came under Omani rule, some form of accommodation was sought with the pre-existing ruling factions to facilitate commercial exploitation with the minimum of administrative expenditure or organisation. Part of the inducement on this part of the coast was the low duty charged on ivory and other commodities.

Within the coastal belt there appears to have been considerable development of agricultural production based on slave labour by the late 1840s. Large quantities of millet and sesame were exported to Zanzibar and Arabia, and the region also produced nearly half the total amount of copal from the coast. All these commodities were collected by short-distance caravans, organised by coastal Swahili traders as well as by the Makonde and Ngindo traders and producers. They extended five to six days' journey from the ports and operated throughout the year. In addition, 'large quantities of cowries' were collected on the coast south of Mnazi, and there was an important shipbuilding industry, using the excellent *mzimbaty* and *mvule* wood, at Mzimbaty and Mikindani, to supply dhows to merchants from Zanzibar.[5]

Many of the ports along this coast were also termini of long-distance caravan routes specialising in ivory and slaves. During the second half of the eighteenth century it seems that trade was conducted through a sort of relay system rather than through trading expeditions that travelled along the whole length of a route. Speaking of slaves reaching Kilwa in the 1770s, the French trader, Morice remarked that 'they come from quite a long way, of 200 leagues or thereabouts. I speak of their slaves for they change masters on the way.'[6] At that time the trade routes appear to have been dominated by different ethnic groups in the interior who were anxious to preserve their monopoly over the trade. Morice noted that 'the Africans do not allow those on this side of the river to go and trade on the far side.'[7]

While the Africans from the interior undoubtedly dominated long-distance trade at this time, there is indication of coastal penetration even at this early date. This may have involved Africans who had settled on the coast returning 'to their former homes up-country: there [to] buy ivory and slaves', according to the 'History of Sudi'.[8] But, according to Morice, they also included Swahili and even Arab traders. The 'Moors [Swahilis],' he remarked, 'can go everywhere. The Arabs who go there dress like Moors, and in this disguise they go as far as the sweet [water] sea.'[9]

By the 1770s it seems that the southern hinterland, as a result primarily of demand for slaves from the French and the Arabs, had extended beyond Lake Nyasa. Referring to the above-mentioned 'sweet sea', Morice said he believed it to be 'a great lake known by the name of Zultan or as Zemba'. Elsewhere, he estimates that it was:

> a month's march from the sea doing seven or eight miles a day. This fresh water sea has a rise and fall of eight feet. It takes two days to cross it in a boat rowed by six oarsmen. There are some islands more or less in the middle of it where boats wishing to cross it can put in.[10]

From the details of this description there is little doubt that the lake described is none other than Lake Nyasa. The route lay through the country of the 'Dzibys' (Zimba?) and the 'Mounjous' (Yao). Morice goes on to say that beyond the lake lay 'a huge country which has been crossed by the natives of the country who, after two months travelling, found the ocean and saw ships there manned by Europeans'. It has been argued that, in view of the known relation of the Yao with Mozambique, Morice may be referring to a circular route ending at Mozambique. It is more tempting to link this allusion to the contact between Kazembe and the coast of Angola through Mwata Yamvo, although the link was probably tenuous at this time.[11]

The development of these trade routes extending into the hinterland of Mozambique led to a diversion of trade to Kilwa. The Portuguese perennially complained that the Swahili traders inundated the interior of their possessions with 'contraband' merchandise as far as Tete and Sena on the Zambezi, especially with Indian textiles, *kaniki*, guns, gunpowder and glass beads, and were diverting ivory from their termini on the Zambezi, to Kilwa. In 1810 Pereira reported that the subjects of the Kazembe had ceased to come to trade at Tete. The war between the Kazembe and the Bisa may have caused the disruption, but the movement was probably accelerated by the inept Portuguese fiscal policies which made the ivory trade in Mozambique uneconomical.[12]

The description of the extent of the hinterland of Kilwa given by Captain Hardy in 1811, though vague, seems to correspond with that given by Morice in 1775. Trade routes from the southern Tanzanian ports extended through the countries of the Ngindo, the Matumbi and the Yao to the 'Black Mountains', forty-five days' march into the interior. These may well be the mountains skirting the eastern shore of Lake Nyasa. The lake itself is not mentioned, but the reference to two islands in a river is reminiscent of Morice's description.[13]

By the middle of the nineteenth century there were regular trade routes between the coastal termini at Kilwa, Lindi, Mikindani and Ibo in northern Mozambique, on the one hand, and the shores of Lake Nyasa, on the other. Some of the routes led to the northern end of the lake, and the German traveller, Albrecht Roscher, who was lost in the interior, had reached the northern end of the lake in the company of an Arab caravan in 1859. In 1866 David Livingstone, after leaving Mikindani, followed the Ruvuma to Mataka's, the head village of a Yao chief. The most important nodal point, however, was the southern end of the lake where dhows were maintained to cross the lake to the west bank. According to John Kirk in 1858, it was here that the Swahili traders took over the slaves from other traders coming from the west. From here the trade routes extended to Kazembe and Katanga as far as Lake Mweru and Lake Bangweulu in the north-west. Coastal traders were also encroaching on the hinterland of Mozambique, penetrating southwards through Tete, which was stocked with commodities brought by 'Arab caravans from Zanzibar', as far as Victoria Falls. As late as 1860 C.P. Rigby reported that goods were 'taken from Zanzibar hundreds of miles through the African continent to the Portuguese settlements on the Zambezi and sold cheaper than if imported by sea at Mozambique or Quillemane'. Livingstone even found Arabs in Linyati in the present-day Caprivi Strip of Namibia.[14]

Kilwa was the most important commercial centre along the southern coast. Until the end of the eighteenth century this was located at Kilwa Kisiwani of medieval fame, but by 1812 it had withered, and was described as 'a petty village', although Loarer says it was a place of great commerce until 1830. Its decline may partly have been due to the rise of its rivals on the mainland, termini of the trade routes from the interior where, as Morice had reported, much of the direct trade was transacted. There is some evidence that a change had occurred in the navigability of the waters around Kilwa. It seems that the southern passage, which was navigable as late as 1812, as well as the straits to the west of the island, had been silting up, and the anchorage can now be reached only through the northern passage. According to Richard Burton the shift occurred in about 1830 when the people of Kisiwani migrated to the mainland because harbours with deep roadsteads such as Kisiwani were vulnerable

Plate 24   A slave caravan approaching the coast

161

to British anti-slavery patrols. The traders preferred harbours with shallow roadsteads such as Kilwa Kivinje on the mainland. But the British anti-slavery crusade in East African waters had hardly begun by that time. The 'Ancient History of Kilwa Kisiwani' attributes the shift to rivalry and a split within the ruling dynasty of Kilwa.[15]

The most probable explanation for the decline of Kilwa Kisiwani was the decline of its major artery of trade to the south after the suppression of the French slave trade. Some time after 1809 Kilwa was included within the Mrima 'monopoly' whereby foreign traders were debarred from trading there for ivory and copal. However, care was taken not to provoke the diversion of trade to other ports outside the commercial empire. Since Kilwa was the major terminus of the trade routes from the Lake Nyasa region as well as a minor terminus of the Unyamwezi route, customs authorities at Kilwa maintained a differential rate of internal duties on ivory according to origin. The Yao, Makua, Ngindo and Bisa traders who could divert their trade were charged the same low duty of MT\$2 per *frasela* in the late 1840s that was applicable to the southern peripheral region. Ivory from Unyamwezi, on the other hand, apparently attempting to avoid the higher rates farther north, was charged the same duty as was applied to the Mrima ports at MT\$8 per *frasela*. There was less likelihood of diversion of the low-priced bulky coastal commodities such as copal and grains, and they paid 20 per cent and 15 per cent respectively, the same rate as for the rest of the Mrima[16]

With Kilwa Kisiwani thus reduced to an outport of Zanzibar, the double transhipment from the mainland termini to Kilwa Kisiwani and then again to Zanzibar made less economic sense. Kisiwani thus began to give way to Kivinje. Kivinje was in existence from at least the 1770s since it is marked on Morice's map, but as late as 1811 it was still insignificant, and even in 1824 it was described as only 'a significant village'. However by 1819 it was already important enough to have an Omani governor. In 1844 J.L. Krapf described it as:

> the most important town on the coast between Mozambique and Zanzibar, with twelve to fifteen thousand inhabitants, the centre of the trade of those regions, and the confluence, as it were, of the two streams of wealth flowing from north and south.[17]

Loarer stated in 1849 that the town contained only thirty stone houses which had only recently been constructed, and nearly 2,000 mud huts built by the Makonde, the Ngindo, the Nyasa, the Yao and the Swahili, which is a graphic demonstration of class differentiation in the coastal towns.[18]

By then Kilwa was the centre for the annual export of 6,000 *fraselas* of gum copal and 5,000 *jizla* (about 1,000 tons) of millet, products of the coastal belt. It was visited annually by forty large caravans from the country of the Maravi, the Yao, the Nyasa and the Nyamwezi, bringing 4,000 to 4,500 *fraselas* of ivory, 150 to 200 *fraselas* of rhino horns, 10,000 *fraselas* of tobacco, and 'worked iron, products of the industry of the Maravi'. Kilwa thus accounted for nearly one-third of the total ivory exported from the East African coast in the 1840s. There appears to have been a substantial decline in the export of ivory from Kilwa by the 1890s when it contributed only 4 per cent of the ivory tusks exported from the coast of Tanganyika. Kilwa, however, was the premier slave port of the East African coast, with nearly 90 per cent of the slaves originating from it, although, according to Loarer, the slave trade accounted for only 25 per cent of the value of the trade of Kilwa in the 1840s. By then between 10,000 and 12,000 slaves were annually exported from Kilwa, and although this is said to have declined to between 8,000 and 10,000 in 1848, it had risen to nearly 19,000 by the 1860s.[19]

Some of the smaller ports of the southern Tanzanian coast were also termini of long-distance as well as short-distance trade routes by the 1840s. Four to five large caravans, composed of 400 to 500 men, of whom two-thirds were slaves, arrived every year at Lindi from the country of the Yao, the Nyasa and even from Unyamwezi, but Loarer added that the best ivory from these areas was normally sent to Kilwa and Pangani which were richer commercial centres. Tungi and Lindi exported annually 1,400 to 2,100 *fraselas* of ivory. Before 1830 a number of these ports had flourished on the slave trade, but by the late 1840s some, like Mikindani, had declined. Lindi exported 1,000 to 1,200 slaves a year, and all the caravans going to Tungi were accompanied by 'a large number of slaves'.[20]

By the 1840s, the foreign trade of this coast was largely controlled by Zanzibar. Twenty dhows from Zanzibar, which visited Tungi annually as part of their trade extending as far south as Madagascar, handled most of the trade of that port, although the port was also visited by six vessels from the Comoros trading between Madagascar and Mozambique, and by four Indian vessels. Many of these traders, Indian as well as Arab, only resided at these ports seasonally, going to Mozambique or Zanzibar during the other seasons, except at Lindi where some were settled. Some of the Indian and other merchants had substantial investments in this trade. In 1850 British warships destroyed what they thought to be 'barracoons' near Cape Delgado which were allegedly capable of holding 5,000 slaves, though not a single slave was found. One of the Indian merchants, Laxmidas Kalianji, said to have been a cousin of the custom master at Zanzibar, allegedly suffered a loss of MT$50,000, and about the same value of the muskets, powder, brass wire and piece goods belonging to many native merchants was also destroyed.[21] Although the latter category in this case included the Arabs from Zanzibar, they also comprised resident merchants who retained a considerable share of the trade.

Some, especially at Mgao Mwanya, possessed a fairly large number of small boats employed in the very active entrepôt trade between Tungi and Kiswere, and two or three large dhows employed in long-distance voyages. The principal and richest merchants at Tungi and Mnazi were of Arab origin, and the one at Kiswere was a Swahili originating from Lamu who traded with Zanzibar and the Mgao coast. The latter spoke a little French, harking back to the French slave-trade connection.[22]

The most successful local merchant was probably the ruler of Lindi. Under Ibrahim b. Issa b. Salim al-Barwani, Lindi enjoyed almost complete independence, and Ibrahim 'never regarded himself as a vassal of the Imam'. Lindi had prospered on the slave trade to the south, and Ibrahim had imposed dues even on dhows which merely sailed within sight of the port. After the Moresby Treaty of 1822 the slave trade to the south declined and was a trickle by 1830; this made Lindi more dependent on the trade to the north where the demand for ivory, copal and slaves was growing. After the death of Ibrahim in 1833 or 1834, Seyyid Said began to exercise a degree of sovereignty over Lindi, confirming the successor, Muhammad b. Issa, and imposing a customs establishment on behalf of the custom master at Zanzibar to collect duty on trade with places other than Zanzibar. This, however, apparently did not prevent Muhammad from chasing all his rivals, Indian as well as Arabs, from Lindi.[23]

These merchants and rulers, not only Arab or Swahili, but also – in the case of Mikindani and Mgao Mwanya, at least – Makonde and Ngindo, owned extensive plantations of millet and sesame worked by slaves. They formed the local ruling class along the southern coast under the general, sometimes tenuous suzerainty of Zanzibar. They ruled over the 'unpropertied' Swahili of the coast, and the Makonde and Ngindo of the immediate hinterland which, in places, was said to extend up to ten days' journey, or about 120 miles. As far as the region further into the interior was concerned, they exercised a powerful control over the trade passing through their region from which they appropriated their middleman's profits. These were substantial. In the case of ivory, Loarer suggests a profit rate of 25 per cent to 44 per cent, and even higher rates for copal in the smaller ports.[24]

The northern hinterland

The peripheral areas of the north reproduce the patterns of economic relations, taxation and political dependence of the southern areas, but the specific historical conditions facing them during the first half of the nineteenth century were different. The most important factor was the region's ability to have direct external commercial relations with Arabia and India. These branches of trade, unlike the southern area's trade with the Mascarenes, continued to grow in importance throughout the nineteenth century. Since the ports along this coast were convenient export centres *en route*, much of the trade with the north was probably conducted directly. Only those commodities which were in demand at Zanzibar from American and European traders used the facilities of the entrepôt, unless the foreign traders made their own arrangements to collect them at those ports. On the other hand, the hinterlands of many of these ports were constricted by the *nyika*, and agricultural development was restricted to a narrow coastal belt. However, economic forces in the nineteenth century were powerful enough to link them with the hinterland deeper in the interior beyond the *nyika*.

The Benadir ports of the southern Somali coast formed the region furthest to the north that channelled some of its trade through Zanzibar. Lee V. Cassanelli argues that long-distance trade here was segmented, that inland commerce remained largely in Somali hands until the 1890s, and that even in the interior no one Somali group monopolised the whole of the caravan trade. This trade may have been of long standing, but in response to the steeply rising demand for ivory and hides for the American market, there was an expansion of the hinterland during the nineteenth century. By 1811 Lugh on the Juba was sending 'immense quantities' of slaves and ivory to Brava. By the second half of the century Somali traders had penetrated to Samburu and Rendille country around Lake Turkana, and by the end of the century ivory from as far away as Bunyoro was finding an outlet at Brava. However, the main part of the hinterland appears to have been the southern extension of the Harar highlands and the sources of the Juba and Shebelle rivers in southern Ethiopia. These areas provided 'most of the ivory and aromatic woods, myrrh and gum involved in the long-distance caravan trade'. By the late 1840s more than 2,000 *fraselas* of ivory were finding an outlet at the Benadir, part of which was exported directly to India. Long-distance trade was in fact becoming so important that it had apparently begun to undermine the pre-existing social formation. This may have provoked the Bardera *jihad* in which the reformers attempted to impose an 'ivory prohibition'. However, powerful interests had been enmeshed in the trade, and the Sultan of Geledi took up their cause to defeat the reformers and reopen the trade routes by 1847.[25]

Although a considerable part of the foreign trade of the Benadir was direct with Arabia and India, a portion of it was channelled through Zanzibar to supply American and European traders there with 1,000 to 1,200 scores of hides, ivory, sesame, and orchilla weed. According to Prideaux, in 1873 and 1874 Somali products contributed an average of one-eighth of the imports to Zanzibar from the African mainland. According to a French Consul, it was this commercial link with Zanzibar which made the Benadir recognise the suzerainty of Zanzibar, but this authority was 'seasonal' and tenuous. The ports retained considerable

165

independence under a republican constitution which grouped Somali confederacies in the hinterland with merchant interests at the ports. From 1837, following the capture of Mombasa, Seyyid Said attempted to impose his political representative and customs officials to exact the 5 per cent import duty and the MT\$2 export duty on ivory. In the 1860s these duties yielded about MT\$200 from Brava, MT\$500 to MT\$2,000 from Mogadishu and MT\$3,000 to MT\$5,000 from Merka, about one-third of which went to the Somali chiefs in the hinterland. These figures may be a reflection not so much of the relative commercial importance of the three ports as Zanzibar's relative political control. Rivalry between them had permitted Seyyid Majid of Zanzibar to maintain a contingent of soldiers at Merka.[26]

The coast of Kenya formed a fragmented region which was less peripheral to the commercial empire, as evidenced by the persistent effort on the part of the ruler of Zanzibar to subjugate it politically during the first half of the nineteenth century. Located within the region of reliable monsoon, it not only had the potential for an independent economic base but even threatened to rival Zanzibar. The struggle along this part of the coast during the second half of the eighteenth century and the first half of the nineteenth century is therefore strongly reminiscent of that at Kilwa in the late eighteenth century. However, once conquered, it made little economic sense to channel its trade with Arabia and India entirely through Zanzibar. It was therefore not included within the Mrima reservation. Nevertheless, it was an important source of ivory and other commodities, and Zanzibar's political control permitted the levying of a higher rate of duty there than the ones levied on either the Benadir or on the southern periphery.

The economy of the coast had a dual character, consisting of foreign trade and a strongly agricultural base in the narrow coastal belt, strengthened in the 1850s by the decline in the price of slaves (see p. 70). Lamu is situated at the southern mouth of a network of waterways. These, with the help of a very active coastal traffic, drained a large basin of commodities in demand. Lamu developed as the entrepôt for the archipelago itself, for Pate, Siu and for the small villages on the mainland opposite the archipelago which were markets for the Oromo (Galla). Moreover, Lamu was situated closer than any other place in the archipelago to 'the principal indigenous market' at Kao which was near the mouth of the River Tana. The Tana was not only settled by the agricultural Pokomo and by the Oromo, but was also a corridor of trade of great length leading to the highlands of Kenya. Both the Oromo and the Dahalo were said to bring their ivory to points along the river. The famous Kamba trader Kivui was attempting to open a new trade route to the Tana when he was killed in 1843.[27]

The hinterland of Mombasa was severely constrained by the *nyika* wilderness, the most sparsely populated belt in Kenya, at least thirty miles wide, sharply separating the narrow coastal belt from the highlands of the interior. Mombasa had owed its medieval prosperity not to the exploitation of its own continental hinterland but to its convenient location for the Indian dhows and to its maritime hinterland that extended as far as Sofala. During the eighteenth century, however, a more positive relationship began to develop between the merchants of Mombasa and the Mijikenda, then expanding from their forest enclosures in the coastal range of hills into the drier plains where their economy was supplemented by hunting and trade. According to Thomas Spear, the Mijikenda held the key to Mombasa's commercial relations with the interior. The Digo were the first to open up the rich Pangani valley region across the Umba plains to the northern Mrima ports of Wasin and Tanga which, according to Hardy, traded only with the people of Mombasa. The Giriama further north had meanwhile begun to penetrate more directly into Kamba country and Kilimanjaro with small caravans as early as 1800. However, the Mijikenda probably derived more of their wealth from their middleman's position between the coast and the interior, allowing coastal traders to pass through their territories only in the 1830s, and as late as the mid-century allowing only one Kamba caravan leader, Kivui, through to Mombasa.[28]

During the eighteenth century Mombasa had developed political and military alliances that were based on a triangle of economic relationships between the Mazrui, the Swahili tribal confederacies of Mombasa, and the Mijikenda who, according to F.J. Berg, 'looked upon certain leaders of the Swahili tribes of Mombasa as their intermediaries with the outer world'.[29] The inclusion of the representative of the Mijikenda in the delegation to seek Omani aid in overthrowing the Portuguese in 1729–30 is an eloquent testimony to the growing relations between Mombasa and the Mijikenda. In 1746 the latter offered refuge to the Mazrui leader who reciprocated by granting commercial and other privileges to Mijikenda trading with Mombasa. Mijikenda visiting Mombasa on public business were entertained and maintained by the ruler of Mombasa. Though relations with them were not uniformly smooth, it was reported in 1825 that, in a conflict with the Oromo, 'the inhabitants of Mombasa will take up the Wanika's [i.e. Mijikenda] cause as they are duty-bound to do'.[30]

In this triangle of relationships mutual interdependence and the value of cooperation was well recognised though none flinched from taking full advantage of its strategic position. The Mijikenda brought a large amount of gum copal from their own territory almost throughout the year, though the peak periods coincided with the monsoon trading seasons between December and April, and again in August and September. They were freely allowed to enter the island and were a regular feature of the island's population. However, the Mijikenda kept a tight control over the inhabitants of Mombasa when they began to penetrate the Mijikenda country to Kwa Jomvu where a fair was annually held in August. At the fair, trade had to be conducted through interpreters who bought goods first on their own account and then sold them to the Swahili. Commercial transactions conducted in the Mijikenda territory were, moreover, subject to heavy tolls so that coastal traders seldom cleared 5 per cent in the transactions. The latter may well have resented their dependence, but they were probably well placed, by their control over the imports, to make up for any losses. During nearly three years of British occupation of Mombasa between 1824 and 1826 there were only two conflicts, one of which was over the harbouring of runaway slaves by the Mijikenda. Neither conflict was allowed to disrupt their relations.[31]

The dynamic of commercial expansion during the nineteenth century, however, did not lie with the Mijikenda middlemen, but at the two extremes of the long-distance trade route that was to develop; at the coastal end as a result of the steeply rising demand for ivory, and inland among the Kamba who were then undergoing a transformation in their economy and society. The convergence of these two forces in the early part of the nineteenth century was probably primarily responsible for the vaulting of the *nyika* wilderness that opened up a vast hinterland for Mombasa.

The transformation of Kamba society has been impressively analysed by Jackson using oral traditions, and by Lamphear using documentary evidence. They argue that the Kamba, after a period of confinement in the Mbooni hills where they had developed advanced agriculture, were forced by population pressure to begin to expand into Kitui during the second half of the eighteenth century. However, they were migrating into lower and drier areas, prone to periodic famines. It was probably part of their adjustment to the ecological factor that they increasingly turned to pastoralism, hunting and trade to supplement their agricultural economy. From this developed regional trading in foodstuffs which provided an essential support for the later long-distance trade in ivory and other commodities. With increasing insecurity of trade, especially outside the home area, there also developed an organisation to provide protection and leadership in which the young warriors and hunters played a more prominent role. They provided a framework of commercial contacts between widely dispersed Kamba settlements through which information could be communicated over a large area. Famines, leading to dispersion and settlement, may have contributed to the building of this framework. It is this framework, in which the Mijikenda may have provided the connecting link with the coast initially, which apparently facilitated the infiltration of knowledge of the rising demand for ivory at the coast. This knowledge spurred further Kamba penetration into areas rich in ivory around Mount Kenya, Lake Baringo, and as far north as the Samburu country near Lake Turkana. Already in 1811 coastal sources described the Kamba as inhabiting territory ten days' journey from Mombasa, and by 1826 they were specifically stated to be trading at Kwa Jomvu in Mijikenda territory. Krapf suggests that there were already Kamba settlements in Mijikenda country by the 1820s, though the famous one near Rabai was established only after the great famine of 1836.[32]

Jackson had added a whole new dimension to the discussion of nineteenth-century Kamba trade which previously had assumed tribal homogeneity. He shows that a stratification factor operated, and that the ivory traders constituted 'a small economic class' of powerful or prominent men (*mundu munene*). They did accumulate wealth to some extent in cattle, but Jackson was struck by the lack of emphasis in oral traditions on such accumulation, and the greater emphasis placed on personal following and clients. It appears that the traditional egalitarian constitution of the Kamba may have encouraged a rapid redistribution of wealth in trade goods and a translation of the class's economic primacy into social and political prestige to camouflage the transformation that the Kamba were undergoing. This also helped protect the traders' position and enabled them to utilise the existing social organisation and ideology to recruit their personnel. Nevertheless 'the traders of the period of the long-distance exchange in ivory were a nascent class'; their prosperity was based on a finite resource from hunting which began to be exhausted from the middle of the nineteenth century. It was reported that Kamba hunting parties made it a practice to kill every animal in a herd they came across, and the extinction of elephants in their hunting regions was thus very rapid. They therefore became increasingly dependent on their middleman's position as they expanded their commercial activities well beyond their home grounds. There they met stiff competition from their coastal rivals who were driven into the interior by the rising demand for ivory and its rising price, an expansion of the trading frontier that was financed by accumulated merchant capital at the coast. Coastal traders, who may have offered a better price, were eagerly sought by the people around Mount Kenya by the 1870s to drive the Kamba from their territories. It is worth noting that Kivui met his death at the hands of a party of Mount Kenya people. The decline in the Kamba share of the trade reduced the flow of commodities that had underwritten the economic and social position of the nascent Kamba merchant class. They were thus faced with the only alternative of settling down in their homeland like the Gogo, charging a toll on the caravans in transit, and supplying them with the necessary provisions produced to some extent by slave labour. Contrary to Jackson's conclusion, the Kamba were not reverting to an economy and organisation like that prevalent before the 1800s; they were the exhausted shell, sucked dry of their economic vitality by international trade and thrown by the wayside.[33]

With the loss of momentum by the Kamba, coastal traders began to penetrate the interior. They may have initially preferred to cross the *nyika* further south where water and provisions could more easily be obtained along the foothills of the Usambara-Pare chain to Taveta, and where the risks of Maasai and Oromo raids were minimal. In the second half of the 1840s a caravan of over a hundred people from Vanga was the first to penetrate along this route to the Kamba and Kikuyu countries, returning with 90 to 95 *fraselas* of ivory. By 1856, a large trading party of about two hundred Arabs, Swahili and slaves, under Muhammad b. Ahmed, was able to go from Mombasa directly to Kitui from where it dispersed to trade in the Kamba and Kikuyu countries. By the late 1860s such coastal traders had largely captured the trade, and were extending their activities as far as Lake Turkana and Marsabit in the north, and the Gulf of Kavirondo in the west.[34]

The expansion of Mombasa's own continental hinterland threatened to provide the Mazrui with an independent economic base outside of Zanzibar's commercial empire, and even to challenge the latter's primacy. Located to the north of Zanzibar, Mombasa could cultivate more direct commercial relations with Arabia and India. A large quantity of maize was exported directly to Arabia. A Mombasan merchant claimed in 1835 to have been trading in ivory and copal in Bombay for the previous twenty-two years. In Lieutenant J.B. Emery's journal there are numerous references to the loading of dhows for India. At least one of these belonged to an Indian, but the trade was still dominated by the Arab and Swahili merchants of Mombasa. When direct trade began to be increasingly difficult as a result of Seyyid Said's blockade of Mombasa, these merchants attempted to charter Indian vessels under English colours, and even to transfer the ownership of their own vessels to Indian merchants at Bombay to maintain contact with India.[35] Moreover, they sought to secure and expand their economic base by active maritime commercial activities which stretched as far south as southern Tanzania and Mozambique to procure their supplies of slaves and ivory. They attempted to monopolise the trade of the northern Mrima coast to tap the Pangani valley, encroaching into Zanzibar's primary hinterland. Finally, they sought to control the Lamu region by allying themselves with the Swahili merchants of Pate and other towns in the archipelago.[36]

Despite Mombasa's commercial vitality, however, its economy was fragile. The profitability of its foreign trade, despite its own agricultural production, left it dependent on grain imports from Pemba whose capture by the Busaidi, T. Boteler believed, facilitated its subjugation. Secondly, even though the trade with the interior was expanding, it was apparently not doing so fast enough, perhaps as a result of the tight Mijikenda control, the harsh *nyika*, and factors internal to Kamba social transformation. Boteler commented in the 1820s that MT\$60,000-worth of goods would overstock the market for six to eight months.[37] Finally, Mombasa's trade with the northern Mrima ports was curbed when they were conquered by the Busaidi in 1825, and her incursions into the Lamu archipelago were energetically resisted. In vain did the Mazrui seek internal and external allies; the British Protectorate (1824–6) offered a temporary respite, but the threat to call in the French if the British withdrew had little effect on British policy in the Indian Ocean in which Seyyid Said occupied a more strategic position.

These pressures exerted on Mombasa seem to have imposed severe strains on the alliance between the Mazrui, the rival Swahili confederacies of Mombasa and the Mijikenda which was the basis of Mombasa's political independence. Its collapse facilitated the subjugation of Mombasa by Seyyid Said in 1837. He set out to reconstruct this alliance to provide cheap administration and to keep up the flow of goods. He set up a triumvirate consisting of a representative from each of the two Swahili confederacies and an Arab. They were granted MT\$800 in lieu of their right to import goods free of duty, though this amount was successively reduced as he felt more secure. He also excluded Mombasa from the Mrima reservation, which was defined for the first time in the Treaty of Commerce concluded with the British in 1839, in order to permit Mombasa to expand its overseas trade, though few of the American and European traders seem to have bothered to trade there. Until the late 1840s Mombasa's commercial orientation was still northwards, despite Seyyid Said's efforts to channel it through Zanzibar. According to Loarer, 2,500 to 3,000 *fraselas* of ivory were exported directly to India by Indian merchants visiting Mombasa, and only about 1,000 *fraselas* were directed to Zanzibar.[38] After the mid-century, however, the commerce of Mombasa entered a period of crisis. As ivory resources in its own hinterland began to be exhausted there was a marked decline in the export of ivory from Mombasa (see Table 5.2). There was also a re-orientation of Mombasa's foreign trade towards Zanzibar as it became more fully integrated into the commercial empire by 1872 (see Table 5.3).

Table 5.2 *Exports of ivory from Mombasa, 1849–87*

	Volume (fraselas)
1849	2,500–3,000
1872	1,250
1873/4	720
1883	700
1887	500

Sources: Loarer, 'Mombas', ANSOM, OI, 2/10/2D; Guillain, Vol. 3, pp. 266–7; Berg (1971), p. 277; Spear, ch. 4; Harkema (1967), p. 68.

Table 5.3   *Mombasa's foreign trade, 1872*

	Zanzibar	India
	Volume (fraselas)	
Exports		
Ivory	927	323
Copal	3,294	480
	Value (MT$)	
Imports	15,000	13,318

Source: Harkema (1967), p. 68.

The core of the commercial empire

The core of the commercial empire encompassed the central region of eastern Africa directly facing Zanzibar. It was bordered to the east by the Mrima coast, and was traversed by two sets of long-distance trade routes penetrating deep into the African interior as far as Uganda in the north-east, eastern Zaire in the west, and northern Zambia in the south-west. By the 1870s, more than half of Zanzibar's total imports from the African coast came through the Mrima ports (see Table 5.1).

The first set of trade routes ran along the Pangani valley which penetrated deep into the *nyika* as far as Kilimanjaro and Mount Meru. The routes may have been of considerable antiquity. By the early eighteenth century, H.C. Baxter asserts, Arabs were settled 25 miles up the Pangani and, although he does not indicate his sources, such a modest penetration is not improbable. A number of villages at the foothills of the Usambaras formed natural trading centres between the contrasting eco-logical zones of the mountains and the plains, and they may have begun to be strung together by long-distance caravan routes. By 1811 these routes appear to have extended as far as Kilimanjaro, near the head-waters of a river where 'it became thick with woods and bushes, which prevents its source from being known to the *traders*' (my emphasis), an indication of commercial penetration. Hardy places 'Gazitae' around the headwaters, and this could be identified with Johann Rebmann's 'Kaptei', a section of the Iloikop (agricultural Maasai) who are placed north of Kilimanjaro.[39]

These routes were not initiated by what Lamphear alleges to have been a 'commercially-oriented kingdom' of the Kilindi in the Usambara mountains which, he says, was motivated by trade in expanding towards the coast. Hardy refers to the Shambaa as sedentary agriculturists who came to exchange their produce, including ivory and slaves, at the 'very large town' of 'Kezoungo', probably Kwasunga near Korogwe, but not as long-distance traders. Steven Feierman has now convincingly shown that

172

the political economy of the Shambaa kingdom was based on tribute exacted from agriculturists, and that the kingdom, in fact, expanded towards the populated areas of northern and eastern Usambara and the Bondei hills rather than the sparsely populated *nyika* where the trade routes ran.[40]

The routes were, in fact, initiated by the plains and coastal people, responding to the specific demands of their economy or of international trade impinging upon them. Feierman argues that oral traditions of the Kamba in the Pangani valley and in the hinterland of the Mrima ports suggest that they were the pioneers from the early eighteenth century. It is difficult to link this initiative with any known changes in the demand for ivory at the coast at that time, and it may not have been commercially significant. From the beginning of the nineteenth century a definite stimulus for forging commercial links with the interior has been identified in the rapidly expanding demand for ivory which must have pushed coastal traders into the interior. Hardy's informants about the trade routes in 1811 were probably coastal traders, and their itineraries are more detailed for the coastward section. According to Loarer in 1849, the plains people attempted to prevent coastal traders from penetrating too deep into the interior in an effort to preserve their own middleman's role between the coast and the interior. These included the Digo and, more importantly, the Zigula whose ecology favoured trading and hunting to supplement their economy. The famine of 1836 apparently launched them into a life of trading and expansion at the expense of the Shambaa kingdom.[41]

Trade along the valley, in fact, appears to have undermined the political economy of the mountain kingdom since it provided guns and commercial wealth to the plains people. There was a 'hidden shift in the balance of power within Shambaai itself' according to Feierman. A section of the Kilindi ruling class, realising that power now depended on trade, had created a commercial centre at Mazinde in the plains along the caravan route. Coupled with the internal contradiction between the Kilindi ruling class and the exploited Bondei subjects who rose in a mighty revolt to throw off the Kilindi yoke, the trade factor contributed to the disintegration of the feudal kingdom.[42]

Towards the middle of the nineteenth century, therefore, the political economy of the Shambaa kingdom had begun to change 'from one based primarily on tribute and territorial control to one based primarily on trade'. A diarchy had developed over the northern Mrima ports of Pangani and Tanga which recognised the coexistence of the Shambaa kingdom and the Omani commercial empire. The *diwanis* of those places were said to have been Kimweri's appointees, and they had to pay a nominal tribute every two or three years to the ruler of the Shambaa kingdom, but they had to be confirmed by the Sultan of Zanzibar. The

Shambaa, however, were not allowed to trade directly with Zanzibar, and Krapf earned the hatred of the coastal traders for trying to cut them out of their middleman's role at the coast and establish direct contact between the Shambaa kingdom and the foreign traders at Zanzibar.[43]

The Pangani corridor was the outlet for commodities from Kilimanjaro and other adjoining territories. The trade routes led in the first instance to Arusha which served as an inland trade centre. From there, later, traffic developed through the Serengeti to the Gulf of Kavirondo. Initially it was difficult to continue the route to Buganda via Busoga, allegedly because of Buganda's traditional fear of approaches from the east, although later the Kabaka favoured a more direct trade connection with the coast through Maasailand. According to Loarer, the corridor also provided an outlet for the Nyamwezi traders. By the late 1840s, 3,200 to 3,500 *fraselas* of ivory were brought annually to Pangani and Mtangata, not so much by the large seasonal caravans as by small trading parties throughout the year. Most of the ivory was sent to Zanzibar, as well as about 2,500 tons of millet produced by the Zigula and coastal settlers using slave labour.[44]

The central trade routes terminating between Saadani and Mbwamaji, and especially at Bagamoyo, constituted perhaps the most important single set of trade routes for Zanzibar. It will be recalled that the *nyika*, which runs closely behind the coastal belt in Kenya, is more

Plate 25   Bagamoyo, c.1887

174

broken and recedes further into the interior in Tanzania. This implies a progressive enlargement of the potential immediate hinterland extending as far as the broken chain of mountains from the Usambara and Nguru mountains to Uluguru and the eastern arm of the southern highlands of Tanzania. Within this maritime region a series of trading networks centred round the coastal towns probably developed during the eighteenth century when there seems to have been a recrudescence of urban development along the coast. By 1811 there were about ten such towns between Pangani and Mbwamaji alone. When the demand for commodities procurable from this hinterland developed, a number of short-distance trade routes were forged as far as the mountain chain. Saadani appears to have been ringed by the Doe who were described as cannibalistic both in contemporary documentary sources as well as in the traditions written down at the end of the nineteenth century. According to Hardy, coastal traders had to fight their way to the Zigula country where 'a large trade' was carried on in ivory, slaves and cattle in exchange for Indian cotton goods and metals.[45]

Further south a constant exchange was maintained with the 'Mrima tribes' to exchange grain for Indian cloth. The Zaramo are mentioned for the first time in 1811 as inhabiting the country about seven days' march into the interior. Little is said about their commercial relations with the coast, but one of the trade routes, extending from the unnamed port near the mouth of the Ruvu, which was probably Bagamoyo, must have passed through their country. Hardy obtained two itineraries from two brothers who had traded along these routes. One of them died at Zanzibar while Hardy was still there, and it is probable that they were coastal traders; moreover, their itineraries are more detailed in the coastward section as far as the chain of mountains.[46]

On the other hand, as we have seen, Roberts has suggested that a series of regional trading networks developed in the interior as a result of unequal distribution of commodities vital to a subsistence economy, such as iron and salt. Under specific stimuli these networks might have been linked up to provide a large lacework of linkages along which information about demand for specific commodities as well as exotic goods might have filtered over long distances, relayed from one network to another. Roberts goes further to suggest that this regional system permitted the accumulation of commodities such as ivory as a by-product, and produced, as it were, the capital to finance long-distance trade. It is possible that the chinaware reported to have reached Buganda during the eighteenth century may have filtered through such a network. However, it was the rapidly rising demand for ivory at the coast from about 1800 that made it economic for firm trade routes to be established across the waterless bushland of Ugogo and over long distances.[47]

By 1811 it appears that two trade routes of great depth were already in existence from this part of the coast. One of them extended in a south-westerly direction through Ukutu, and then along the Ruaha into Uhehe. This seems to correspond to the route leading to Isanga in eastern Ukimbu which J.H. Speke labelled as the 'old caravan route to Ujiji' on his map. This route did not seem to have to contend with any overwhelming natural obstacles since it skirted Usagara along the pass formed by the Ruaha, and it also avoided Ugogo, which suffered so much from drought and scarcities. The route appears to be more detailed for Ukutu in which a place-name is given on an average for every two and one-third days' journey, while the stations beyond are placed an average of twelve days apart. It seems that the regional trading network in the coastal region was linked with that to the west of Usagara by a migration, as suggested by Aylward Shorter, from Usagara to Ukimbu, or by an infiltration of conus-shells which were used as chiefly emblems.[48] Once the increased demand for ivory began to be felt along the coast from about 1800, that knowledge spread rapidly throughout the interior. By 1825 coastal traders, led by the Indian Musa 'Mzuri', had themselves already penetrated as far as Isanga and Isenga. According to Richard Burton, these centres:

> were the great terminal of the Arab trade before it extended throughout Unyamwezi in 1830–35. . . . At Usanga and its adjoining district, in those early days of exploration, the Arabs and the coast merchants met the caravans from Unyamwezi bringing with them the slaves and ivory collected from the interior countries.[49]

In 1831 Lief b. Said travelled from Isanga/Isenga to Itumba, Ugunda, Usagusi, and even as far as Lake Tanganyika across which, he says, there was 'a great trade in ivory . . . and slaves' with the Guha on the western bank.[50]

The second route ran directly west and, according to Hardy, it was called the 'Condohee' branch by the Nyamwezi, probably a reference to the Nkondoa branch of the Wami river which forms a gap in the chain of mountains and which the modern railway follows west of Kilosa. The region beyond is stated to be inhabited by the 'Man na Wau' tribe, perhaps another corruption of Nyamwezi, as far as two lakes called Wangarah and Zawarah, about twenty-eight days apart. In the latter there was said to be 'a high rocky hill with a few trees on it'. This may well be a reference to Ukerewe island which was conspicuous enough to give its name to Lake Victoria in the early missionary accounts at the coast. The other lake referred to may be Lake Tanganyika.[51]

It is likely that this route, which had to traverse Ugogo, was pioneered by Nyamwezi traders from the interior, perhaps during the first decade of the nineteenth century. Nyamwezi slaves had begun to appear at the coast, and a number of them were emancipated from a slaver captured in

Plate 26   An ivory caravan approaching Morogoro, c.1887

1810. The above-mentioned trader, Lief b. Said, was apparently a second-generation Muslim Nyamwezi settled at Zanzibar by the 1830s, judging by his father's Muslim name. However, despite these references to Nyamwezi slaves, Smee and Hardy suggest that they traded primarily in ivory.[52] Oral traditions recorded in the 1960s seem to remember only the more illustrious successors of the real pioneers. Mpalangombe and Ngogomi, unsuccessful claimants to the Usagusi chiefship, are remembered as pioneering the trade, but their adventure can be dated only to *c.* 1830. Sumbwa traditions speak of Kafuku as 'a great merchant, and a . . . caravan leader' who, when traversing Ugogo with 'some thousands of followers', got embroiled in a skirmish and was killed. In 1857 Burton dated the incident to 'about one generation ago', therefore probably not before 1830. By then, judging from Kafuku's 'thousands of followers', Nyamwezi trade was already well developed. Coastal penetration along this route did not take place until *c.* 1825 when Saif b. Said al-Muamari pioneered it. The disruption of the southern route by the Sangu forced coastal traders to the Ugogo route in the 1840s, and thereafter both Nyamwezi and coastal traders used that route on which the former predominated even as late as the 1850s.[53]

The co-existence of Nyamwezi and coastal trade between the interior and the coast was bound to lead to the establishment of a coastal presence in the interior as well as to stimulate the emergence of a merchant class

Plate 27   Porters of the interior. Top: Rear – Mganga (medicine man), porter, Kirangozi (guide); Front – Mwinyi Kidogo, mother and child. Middle: Ivory porter, cloth porter and woman in Usagara. Bottom: Ivory porter in Unyamwezi

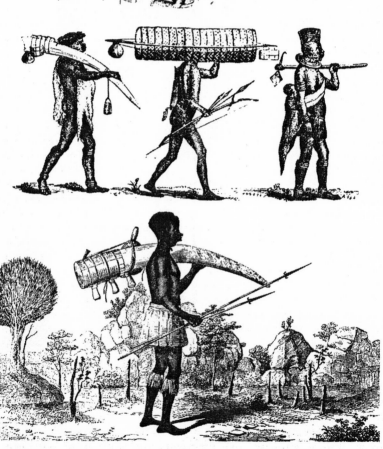

178

from within the social formation in the interior previously characterised by communal and, in some cases, by feudal modes of production. Competition between these two sections of the merchant class spawned by international trade was inevitable but, as both were increasingly integrated into a single commercial system in which neither could hope for a complete monopoly over the whole length of the trade route, collaboration was also an important aspect of the history of relations between them.

As a result, perhaps, of the competition, pioneering coastal traders were attracted initially to chiefdoms which had not hitherto played a significant role in long-distance trade. To them they offered an outlet for their ivory, and sometimes military support. In return they were given protection and even commercial concessions. Msene was very hospitable to the Arabs who, a few years previously, had helped beat off a large plundering party of the Watuta. When the chief of Upuge failed to offer protection to the coastal traders, they were invited by Ifundikira, the chief of Unyanyembe, to move to his chiefdom where he did not even demand a present from them, although he normally received one. He apparently agreed not to impose a tax on the Arab transit trade, and offered his daughters to prominent coastal trades to seal the new relationship.[54]

These centres formed important nodes in the development of the coastal system of trade in Unyamwezi. Hawking from village to village may have proved cumbersome for the whole caravan. Depots were therefore established at the chiefly centres while agents dispersed in all directions to exchange their goods for ivory. The need for more permanent centres where caravans could rest and provision themselves was felt particularly when coastal traders expanded beyond Unyamwezi. Kazeh (near present-day Tabora) developed as a commercial centre for the coastal traders where trade routes branched to the north-west, west and south-west. Nyamwezi porters, arriving from the coast at the beginning of the rainy season in August or September, disbanded to return to their agricultural pursuits, and recruitment of others at this time was difficult. Delay at Kazeh was therefore inevitable, and a commercial centre with storehouses, etc., a necessity. It was founded in the early 1850s when the coastal traders, led by Musa 'Mzuri' and Thnay b. Amer al-Harthi, were invited by Ifundikira into Unyanyembe. By 1858 there were about ten *tembes* (oblong Nyamwezi-type houses) with attached garden plots, storerooms and outhouses for slaves, and the town included several itinerant artisans, such as gunsmiths, carpenters and masons. The Arabs lived 'comfortably, and even splendidly'. Thnay b. Amer, whose health forbade him to travel, emerged as a 'general agent', having built 'a village containing his store-house and his depots of cloths and beads, slaves and ivory'. Burton estimated that the number of Arabs at the settlement rarely exceeded twenty-five, and during the trading season it fell as low as three or four.[55] The Arabs generally planted foodstuffs for their own consumption at Kazeh and other stations where they stopped for more than a season, but at Kazeh the Arabs by 1861 appeared 'more like great farmers, with huge stalls of cattle attached to their houses'. Some, like Salim b. Saif, were abandoning trade to engage in agriculture, employing a large number of slaves in the cultivation of cassava, wheat and other grains for sale to the passing caravans. By the early 1870s Kazeh had visibly grown westwards, containing over 50 *tembes* and *bomas* (residential enclosures), and Livingstone estimated a population of about 80 male Arabs and about 1,500 dependants. The permanence of Arab settlement is perhaps best indicated by the example of Amran b. Masud who had spent more than $3,000 on his house, the 'Bahrain', whose door and rafters were 'a marvel of carving work'.[56]

Coastal presence in the interior, however, was only one side of the coin; the other was the emergence of an indigenous merchant class in the interior. In the traditional political economy of Unyamwezi, dominated by a communal mode of production, the position of the *mtemi* (chief) was originally derived from his social function of leadership in clearing the bush and establishing agriculture, but a distinct exploiting and ruling class had not emerged. The demand for ivory created a new source of wealth over which the chiefs attempted to assert their rights, demanding

Plate 28   Arab traders visiting Livingstone and Stanley at Kwihara, 1871, in front of a typical tembe

one of the tusks from each elephant hunted in their territories. However, it was the sub-chiefs and headmen who were responsible for the collection of the ivory tax as well as the *hongo*, the toll exacted by the chiefs throughout the interior from passing caravans. This new wealth appears to have enabled many of the headmen to usurp the chiefships. R.G. Abrahams has recorded a series of such usurpations around the middle of the nineteenth century as a result of which the principle of succession simultaneously changed from a matrilineal to a patrilineal system. The role of the new chiefs, however, was not merely a passive one of revenue collection; many of them are recorded in both documentary sources and oral traditions as playing a more active role in organising hunting and trading caravans to the coast. Unomah argues that, unlike in Buganda or Bunyoro where a royal monopoly was established, in Unyamwezi even the chief's right to one of the tusks could not always be enforced, and a 'policy of laissez faire was practised'. This allowed 'commoners' as well as royal princes and 'medical experts' to participate in the trade. All of these people, therefore, formed part of the *vbandevba*, or what Unomah calls 'a new agrico-commercial bourgeoisie', since almost all of the *vbandevba* were also great cattleowners and farmers, in many cases using slaves, imported especially from the Maniema country in eastern Zaire, to produce foodstuffs for sale to the passing caravans.[57]

Cooperation between the *vbandevba* and their coastal counterparts was so strong in some of the Nyamwezi chiefdoms, such as Unyanyembe, that Unomah considers both as constituting parts of the same bourgeoisie, despite their different origins. Commercial competition between them, he argues, never led to open hostilities in Unyanyembe, and the struggle of Mnywasele in the early 1860s was with all merchants, Arab as well as Nyamwezi, who were growing too powerful, and who ultimately defeated him. Nevertheless, contradictions between the Nyamwezi traders in general and the coastal traders did exist, and they sharpened as the economic position of the former weakened. As shown above, internal duties at the coast discriminated against Nyamwezi traders. Moreover, as the century wore on, the accumulation of merchant capital at the coast permitted the fitting out of larger and better-financed caravans for trading into the interior. By the early 1870s, a single Indian firm at Zanzibar had advanced MT$270,000 to 'the Arabs of Unyanyembe'.[58] Secondly, Unyamwezi was becoming progressively exhausted of ivory. In 1858 Burton noted that 'the elephant roams in herds throughout the country . . . the animal is far from becoming scarce'. But elephant mortality was very heavy. In the early 1860s an average of 24,000 tusks of ivory weighing more than 5 lbs each were being exported from Zanzibar annually, apart from an unknown quantity of 'scrivello' or tusks weighing less than 5 lbs. By 1871 H.M. Stanley had to march far to the south-west of Kazeh before he saw 'a small herd of wild elephants', and little

Nyamwezi ivory came to the market by 1872. The net result of these changes was a decline in the commercial position of the Nyamwezi traders. Whereas in Burton's time a majority of the caravans travelling to the coast were Nyamwezi, by the early 1870s V.L. Cameron met only two Nyamwezi caravans among the many he encountered on the way.[59]

The Nyamwezi were forced to adjust to the changing situation in three main ways. Some turned to agricultural production more wholeheartedly to supply the caravans which still had to pass through their territory en route to the new frontiers, and to charge *hongo* for additional revenue, thereby playing a rôle similar to that of the Gogo and the Kamba at a comparable period of their history. The more energetic pushed on to the frontier themselves to carve out their empire, in Ukimbu under Nyungu ya Mawe, in Usagara, or in Katanga under Msiri. For a very large number, however, porterage was the only alternative way of earning a cash income to satisfy their desire for imports which had developed into social necessities. Initially this activity may have been confined to the long dry season. With greater distances to be covered between the coast and Katanga, and the lucrativeness of the ivory trade, porterage wages rose from MT$6 to MT$9 in the early days to MT$20 by the 1870s. Porterage was therefore no longer only a part of the total economic life, but became a full-time activity for many of the professional *pagazi* in gangs employed by Arab and Nyamwezi traders in eastern Zaire and elsewhere. This implied a diversion of labour of massive proportions from productive activities such as agriculture in their home country. Stanley was perhaps only partly exaggerating when he described the Nyamwezi in their native country as a dying race. In the 1890s, it was estimated that 80,000 to 100,000 porters travelled between the coast and Kazeh every year, and they constituted about one-third of the male population of Unyamwezi. The Nyamwezi had become a nation of porters, and their country a labour reserve, a foretaste of the colonial situation.[60]

It is in this light that we should see the repeated conflicts between Nyamwezi chiefs like Mirambo and Nyungu ya Mawe, and the coastal traders. Each sought to restrict the activities of the coastal traders and the wealth they derived from trade in or through Unyamwezi. They realised that the fragmented political structure of Unyamwezi enabled coastal traders to play one chiefdom off against another to expand their own share and freedom in trade. They therefore sought a solution in the enlargement of scale of their political organisation.[61] However, the alliance between the coastal traders and the *vbandevba*, especially in Unyanyembe, had become a powerful force. While the coastal traders, typical of a merchant class, wavered between confrontation and accommodation, and their militancy often backfired, their opponents, as deeply immersed in international trade, could not hope to eliminate their rivals so long as they wished to prosper by the same trade. They did not wish to disengage from international trade but only to establish monopoly control over the ivory resources of the interior. They thus hoped to bargain from a position of greater strength with the Zanzibar state which controlled the coastal termini and charged a higher duty on Nyamwezi caravans. Despite the conflicts, therefore, the trade, though periodically disrupted, was never entirely stopped. The Nyamwezi were unable to apply the ultimate sanction, which would have cut their own throats equally with those of the coastal traders; the Nyamwezi merchant class were unable to destroy their twin brothers.

The moving frontier

Tabora had developed as an inland emporium from which diverged three sets of trade routes to the frontiers of the commercial empire. One set of trade routes led to the north to Lake Victoria near Mwanza. This was followed by Speke in 1858 and on it, according to Emin Pasha, coastal ivory and slave traders were still active in 1890.[62] The second led into the interlacustrine region proper, via Karagwe to Buganda and the north. In this region coastal traders stood on an equal footing with their Nyamwezi competitors. They were both moving into a region with a highly centralised system of government and a jealous control by the rulers over foreign trade, which was often confined to the capital. Considerable proportions of the commodities in demand were acquired by the rulers through the tribute system or from raids, so that trade was often more directly with the rulers. They coveted foreign trade partly for prestige reasons, but also for economic and later, perhaps, for military reasons. They 'greatly encouraged, by gifts and attention, the Arab merchants to trade' at their capitals, and stories of individuals who had been showered with 'wealth in ivory and a harem containing from 200 to 300 women' were current when Burton visited Kazeh in 1858.[63]

Coastal traders appear to have pioneered the route into Karagwe in the early 1840s, and Musa 'Mzuri' soon had the opportunity to establish very cordial relations with its ruler. In about 1855, when Rumanika, the ruler of Karagwe, was besieged by his rebel brother Rugero, Musa persuaded Suna, the Kabaka of Buganda, 'by a large bribe of ivory . . . to raise the siege by throwing a strong force into the field'.[64] Karagwe's importance, however, lay not so much in its own resources as in its role as a highway to the kingdoms further north. Rumanika proudly described himself as their gatekeeper to the south and maintained good relations with all of them even when they were fighting among themselves. Karagwe appeared to J.A. Grant to offer none of the commodities in demand, neither ivory nor slaves, nor salt, copper or iron. Nevertheless, it was strategically located not only for the exchange of commodities of long-distance trade with the coast, but also of those in the regional trading networks. Thus, salt from the south, iron wire from Rwanda, ivory from the north, slaves in both directions, and goods from the coast passed through Karagwe in what would appear to have been a brisk trade. Regular communication was maintained with Buganda through the Arab depot at Kitangole on the Karagwe border with Buganda, and later at Kafuro.[65]

The route to Buganda may have been pioneered by coastal traders around the middle of the nineteenth century. In 1876 Emin Pasha met Ahmed b. Ibrahim who claimed to have been the first Arab in Buganda. He claimed to have gone there three times during the reign of Suna (d. 1856), the first time being in *c.* 1844. However, Ahmed does not appear to be very reliable, and there is no firm evidence of any Zanzibari trader in Buganda before Thnay b. Amer in 1852, who was soon followed by the Baluchi Isa b. Husain and the 'Arab half-caste' Salim. Burton commented in 1858 that the 'distance has hitherto prevented more than half a dozen caravans travelling to Kibuga', the capital of Buganda.[66]

Because of the density of human population, elephants were already rare in Buganda in 1858 except in Buddu. The Kabaka thus obtained ivory and slaves from Busoga and Bunyoro either by plunder, trade or as a return present for cloth, brass and beads which he sent to the neighbouring rulers. The Kabaka was thus determined to prevent direct contact between coastal traders and the territories beyond his which would have deprived him of his middleman's share in the trade. He was also determined to prevent the Banyoro from acquiring arms and ammunition. To break this monopolistic hold, a new route was developed with the help of Haya traders through 'Kiswere' by which ivory found its way south from Bunyoro and apparently from the region as far north as the northern border of present-day Uganda. In 1861 this was still a new route, and Grant saw that the Banyoro rarely killed elephants, and then with 'the rudest uncertain methods'. It was not until about 1877 that two coastal traders, Said b. Saif and Fundi Hassan, could outflank Buganda and penetrate to Bunyoro. By 1890 coastal traders constituted a force in northern Uganda sufficiently strong to need to be subdued by Sir Frederick Lugard when the British came to partition the area. Here they had at last reached the watershed that divided Zanzibar's hinterland from that of Khartoum, and they began to meet competition from Egyptian traders penetrating up the Nile.[67]

The poverty in ivory of Karagwe and Buganda, combined with the impediment placed on the free movement of trade into Rwanda, and into Bunyoro and Busoga by the Kabaka, probably restricted the total volume of trade with the interlacustrine region. Early attempts to open a trade route to Busoga through Buganda were frustrated by the Kabaka; and, although he later favoured a more direct route to the coast eastwards across Maasailand, the route never became important. Some fortunes were made, but participants in this northern branch of the trade appear to have been few. R.W. Beachey believes that Bunyoro's great ivory reserves were still intact at the end of the century.[68]

The El Dorado of the Zanzibari traders by the 1850s had shifted to eastern Zaire. Commercial contacts with Lake Tanganyika may have been of some time depth. A. Wilson has attempted to link this trade with the expansion of the Luba Lomami empire towards Lake Tanganyika at the beginning of the nineteenth century, but there is no conclusive evidence of this trade across Lake Tanganyika to the east coast before the early 1830s. Lief b. Said's itinerary speaks of 'a great trade in ivory . . . and slaves' across the lake with a people on the west bank called the 'Yoah'. These were probably the Guha who, as Wilson shows, traded extensively on the lake as far south as Marungu as well as at Ujiji. They also traded with the Maniema and, as subject people of the Luba Lomami empire, they provided an important link with the regional trading system extending over a large part of eastern Zaire. Although this was new as a direction of trade for the empire, it was not the first commercial contact with the east coast. The Bisa had apparently already linked up with the empire by a more southerly route, perhaps terminating at Kilwa or on the Zambezi.[69]

The first reference to Ujiji in particular occurs in the early 1840s, but Burton asserts that until the late 1850s a permanent coastal settlement

Plate 29   Ujiji, 1871. Note the rectangular Swahili-type houses and the round African huts

had not yet evolved on Lake Tanganyika, and that it was visited by 'flying caravans' of coastal traders from Tabora during the fair season. Burton had in mind the young Omani Said b. Majid al-Muamari whose porters, half-loaded with a valuable store of ivory, marched 'like mad men' back to Tabora where he had his establishment. Said had a dhow on the lake to trade at the 'ivory and slave mart of Uvira' at its northern extremity. Ownership of a dhow, however, was already a portent of a more regular link.[70]

It appears that by the 1850s others had already begun to establish permanent bases, especially on Kasenge island, for trade to the west of the lake which, according to Burton, because of its dangers, 'the thriving merchants have hitherto abandoned . . . to debtors and desperate men'. The death that Hamid b. Sulayyam and his slaves, as well as Salim b. Habib, met trading in Uruwa emphasised the dangers, but this did not deter people like Tippu Tip who led his first trading venture on his own to Uruwa at about this time.[71]

Coastal penetration to the west of Lake Tanganyika was two-pronged. The south-western prong focused on the lands of the Kazembe and Katanga which were approached either by land from Tabora, or more directly from the east coast, passing to the south of Lake Tanganyika, or from Ujiji across the lake to its southern end at Marungu. C. Pickering makes the earliest reference to the latter in the early 1840s, calling it 'Malungo'. Burton describes it as 'one of the most important divisions of the lands [west of] the Tanganyika' and, although it was considered dangerous, it was often visited by Arab merchants. Muhammad b. Saleh al Nabhani claimed that his father was the first to open the trade to Kazembe, perhaps in the 1830s.[72] A.C.P. Gamitto came across two 'Moors' at the court of the Kazembe in 1831, and he added that 'the nations of the eastern part of Africa which frequent Cazembe are the Bisa and the Impoanes, the name given to the Arabs of the Zanzibar coast'.[73] They began to be most active in the early 1840s, Ian Cunnison suggests, when Bisa trade declined following the conquest and devastation of their country by the Bemba in the early 1830s. One of these Arabs was Muhammad b. Saleh himself who, in 1841–2 by Burton's reckoning, led a party of 200 slaves by the Marungu route. On their way back they became embroiled in a clash with Nsama Chipioka of Itabwa to the east of Lake Mweru. The plundered remnant of the caravan retreated to Kazembe where they were well received and given large rice *shambas*. They were unable to leave the country, they alleged, because they could not find porters to carry their accumulated store of ivory and copper, or perhaps because the route was still blocked by Chipioka. Burton, however, reported that 'the more acute Arabs' suspect that they were unable to face their creditors.[74]

The 1841–2 incident spawned a major centre of Zanzibari commercial activities at Kazembe's court. These radiated throughout a large area of middle Africa that at times extended as far as the Angolan coast. The Hungarian officer Ladislaus met some Arabs in the early 1850s at Quinhamo, which was probably on the Kasai north of Dilolo. This may be the same group, with three 'Moors' accompanied by a caravan of forty porters, that brought ivory and slaves to Benguela in 1852. They stated that 'having got into the interior and barterd away in succession all the goods which they had provided . . . they found it difficult to retrace their steps'. They mentioned, moreover, that they had left one of their companions at Kazembe to guard their ivory. The 'Moors' included 'Abdel' and 'Nassolo' who may be identified with Abdel Al and Nasir b. Salim al-Harthi who were part of the 1841–2 expedition. Moreover, their itinerary through Marungu seems to coincide with that of the 1841–2 expedition. They were encouraged by Major Coimbra's men, whom they met in Katanga, to proceed to Angola where they were commissioned to carry a despatch to Mozambique which they delivered in 1854.[75]

This was by no means an isolated incident. In 1853 Livingstone met a party of Arabs from Zanzibar led by Said b. Habib al Afifi among the Makololo at Linyati, in the present-day Caprivi Strip in Namibia. When he returned from Luanda with glowing reports of commercial prospects in Angola, Sekeletu immediately made arrangements with Said to conduct a fresh party with a load of ivory to Luanda. In 1860 Said claimed that he had visited Luanda three times. Ibn Habib is mentioned among the participants in the 1841–2 expedition, and he said in 1860 that he had left Zanzibar about sixteen years earlier. In 1853 his father had left Zanzibar in search of his son with whom he eventually settled down at Kazembe where Said had married a daughter of an African chief.[76]

This westward extension, however, including Said's Makololo expedition, did not prove profitable, and the Zanzibaris appear to have abandoned it to the Portuguese traders who had penetrated to Katanga, and to the Garanganza under Msiri who had established themselves there probably in the late 1850s. The Zanzibaris retained their base at Kazembe for penetration into Katanga for ivory, and especially copper, which played such an important role in the trade of the interior.[77] They also gradually consolidated their commercial hold over south-eastern Zaire and north-eastern Zambia. Said b. Habib had a house at Pweto at the northern end of Lake Mweru, and traded extensively between Katanga, Chikumbi, the big trading centre south-east of Kazembe, and Lake Tanganyika on which he had at least three large canoes. Muhammad b. Saleh was still at Kazembe, and his son, with a number of Nyamwezi, was residing at Kabakwa to the north of Lake Mweru. Said b. Umar lived at a village near Kazembe and traded as far as the Chambeshi and Chikumbi. On the Chambeshi Livingstone met a party of Zanzibar traders who had come to trade for ivory with the Bemba and in Marungu.[78]

Most of these traders depended for their trade between Katanga and the coast on the route over which Itabwa occupied a strategic position. It was situated close to Mweru wa Ntipa, a major source of ivory and a convenient base to tap the ivory resources in Bemba country. Itabwa, in the late 1860s, was still dominated by the same Chipioka who had dispersed Muhammad b. Saleh's caravan nearly twenty-five years earlier. He was determined to exploit his strategic position to the full by refusing to give the customary return present of ivory for cloth, and by driving a hard bargain. With the arrival in 1867 of Tippu Tip at the head of a large, well-armed caravan of 700 people, however, the balance of forces shifted significantly in favour of the Zanzibari traders. The immediate cause of the conflict was alleged to have been Chipioka's attempt to ambush the traders. Tippu Tip forced Chipioka to agree to his own peace terms and obtained, either as booty or in trade, 1,950 *fraselas* of ivory and 700 *fraselas* of copper. Moreover, he established a more permanent political as well as a commercial base in the country with a significant role in the political affairs of the region. With the defeat of this 'Napoleon of these countries', as Livingstone termed Chipioka, at the hands of Zanzibari guns, anxiety spread rapidly through the region, creating a panic among the people, who often refused to trade and deserted their villages. Chipioka himself retaliated by cutting up all Zanzibari traders in the area. One large peaceful caravan under Said b. Ali al-Hinawy and Hamis wa Mtoa was badly mauled, and between twenty-five and sixty Swahili were killed.[79]

It appears that by this time, while some areas rich in ivory still remained, ivory was becoming scarce in Kazembe's country, either because the elephants were being killed or driven off after thirty years of exploitation, or because of the decreasing ability of the Kazembe to deliver ivory as he gradually lost control over parts of his dominions such as Katanga. In seven months Muhammad b. Gharib was able to buy only three tusks and, according to Livingstone, 'it is not want of will that prevents ivory being produced'. The Kazembe, moreover, was becoming pathetically indebted to Muhammad. Zanzibari traders thus began to raise eyes to newer frontiers to the north. Said b. Habib had already extended his operations to Uruwa and had collected over 200 tusks. Muhammad b. Gharib began to buy copper and slaves to exchange for ivory further north. In the early 1870s Tippu Tip led his large caravan to Uruwa, Utetela, and finally Maniema, which was to become the centre of his 'empire-building' activities in the era of the Scramble.[80]

In thus pushing to the north they were to meet an almost contemporaneous drive from Ujiji to Uruwa and Maniema. According to Stanley the first Arabs returned from Maniema only in about 1867. It was a genuine 'frontier' region where ivory tusks were allegedly used as door posts; but that was not necessarily an advantage. The merchants were

Plate 30   Tippu Tip, Arab trader of the Congo

189

used to trading in areas where incentives for commerce had preceded them. In this frontier region they were forced to build up their own infrastructure for the exploitation of the ivory resources. They had to rely on their own slaves or a permanent gang of Nyamwezi porters for their transportation; they often had to indulge in hunting for ivory themselves. The commodities in demand differed, and sometime incentives for trade were lacking. They found that the people suspected their desire for ivory to be a mere subterfuge to plunder them, which was perhaps sometimes the case. A proliferation of small, weak chiefdoms sucked them into deep involvement in local politics. And yet this was, at this time, the richest untapped ivory source, and prices were ridiculously low.[81] Zanzibari activities were centred at Nyangwe and Kasongo where many traders settled. Nyangwe was described as 'one of the greatest market places in Africa'; 'all roads', it was said, 'led to Nyangwe'. The hinterland expanded rapidly to the north into Kivu, and down the Lualaba as far as Stanley Falls where traders had a post, while at Isangi at the confluence of the Lualaba and the Lomami a mosque was built. They expanded south-wards to link up with their fellow Zanzibaris from Kazembe.[82]

By 1873 Zanzibari traders had stretched the canvas of Zanzibar's hinterland to its furthest: the watershed between the west-flowing and east-flowing channels of trade then stood halfway down the continent. Eastern Zaire was then yielding such a rich harvest of ivory that 'the old beaten tracks of Karagwah, Uganda, Ufipa and Marungu, have been comparatively deserted'. 'The limitation of exhaustive exploitation', as R.C. Harkema has aptly termed it, had driven Zanzibari traders from one virgin field to another, exhausting them successively, and leaving them ravaged. But by spilling over into the western basin, they were overstretching the canvas. With the penetration of the Belgians up the Congo, this frontier region, pioneered by the Zanzibaris, was gradually sucked into a new commercial and political domain oriented to the west.[83]

Where the flag did not follow trade

By the early 1870s, the boundaries of the commercial empire extended from Tungi Bay near Cape Delgado, passing to the south of Lake Nyasa, as far as Linyati in the Caprivi Strip in Namibia. From there it extended northwards through Katanga and down the Lomami to its confluence with the Lualaba. The boundary then extended to the northern end of Lake Tanganyika, and northwards again to include much of Uganda and Kenya, terminating at the Benadir of Somalia (see Map 5.1). In drawing these bold lines on the map, however, it should be realised that they did not encircle a closed commercial area. The hinterland was highly frag-mentary, and extensive areas had no, or only irregular trade connections with Zanzibar. Secondly, it must be remembered that East Africa was

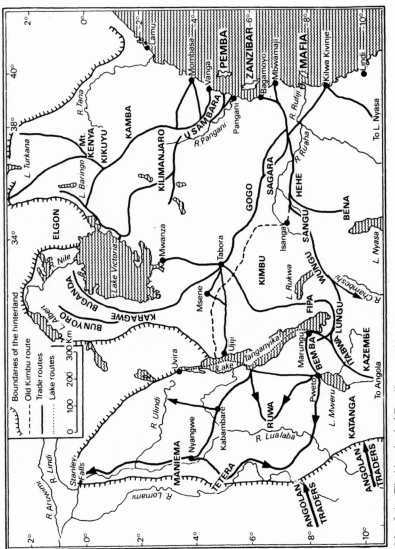

Map 5.1   The hinterland of Zanzibar, c. 1873

then still in the age of human porterage, and this imposed severe limitations on the quality and quantity of commodities that could enter the channels of trade. Only those commodities that could withstand the high and constantly increasing cost of transportation (see p. 113, n. 50) could be carried along the whole length of the caravan trade routes (although many other items of significance to local and regional trade, such as iron hoes, salt and foodstuffs, were carried along different sections of these routes). Thirdly, the hinterland of Zanzibar was not developing in isolation, but in an era of commercial expansion into the interior of Africa from many directions. The position was therefore competitive, and at the peripheries there were frequent cases of interpenetration and encroachments. In the south the development of the hinterland of Zanzibar from the eighteenth century was often at the expense of the Portuguese in Mozambique. In the north, the rival Zanzibari and Khartoumer commercial drives appear to have reached northern Uganda almost simultaneously. In the west, as we have seen, the frontier region in eastern Zaire, pioneered by the Zanzibaris, was to fall like a ripe apple into the laps of the Belgians.

The commercial empire suffered not only from external encroachments, but also from internal weak links. By the 1870s the valuable ivory fields formed a broad arc extending from Bunyoro, passing into eastern Zaire, as far as north-eastern Zambia, at least 500 to 700 miles from the coast as the crow flies. The favourable terms that ivory enjoyed at the coast, and the cheapness of ivory in the frontier regions, enabled the commodity to withstand the high cost of transportation. However, it had to be transported through a wide belt of territory which was once the central ivory region itself. By the 1870s, this area had, for the most part, been hunted out of cheap ivory, and its occupants, who had at one time flourished by long-distance trade, were thus deprived of a lucrative share in the trade. The coastal traders were utterly dependent on a couple of slender lifelines to hold together the rambling commercial empire. These lifelines should not be viewed as purposively constructed trade routes, let alone roads. They were merely zones through which caravans passed seasonally and the paths constantly shifted according to natural or human circumstances. The caravans had to pass through the exhausted belt, and yet they still needed essential provisions from the impoverished peoples; thus the tension between the traders and the peoples along the routes.

One of these was the main trunk road through Unyamwezi to Tabora, with branches to Uganda, to Ujiji and eastern Zaire, and to northern Zambia and Katanga via Ufipa. Tabora was therefore a crucial node in the network of trade routes of almost the whole interior. The community of coastal traders which grew up there was a typical product of the commercial empire. It consisted of adventurers who had left the coast

192

individually to seek or repair their fortunes in the interior, and they carried with them a strong sense of individual freedom. They neither sought nor wished for the protection of the authority at Zanzibar in the initial stages of their establishment: the Harthi, who had been accused of complicity in Barghash's rebellion in 1859 were, in fact, political refugees from Zanzibar.[84] The community, moreover, was seasonal. While there was a core of permanent settlers, often those too old for distant travelling, there was a larger group who seasonally departed for, or sent their agents to, distant frontiers. In 1858, as we have seen, the community used to shrink from twenty-five to as few as three. The community was therefore generally weak and often at the mercy of the polities in the interior. Typical of a merchant class dependent on peace for the continuation of trade, its members developed pacifist tendencies. In 1869 Seyyid Majid had strongly disapproved of Tippu Tip's riding roughshod over Itabwa, and 'all caravans leaving for the interior were thenceforth strictly enjoined to avoid all warfare with the native tribes'. In 1870 the Tabora Arabs deprecated Tippu Tip's high-handed action in Ugala, refusing him hospitality, a grave matter for an Arab, until he had agreed to release the prisoners for whom they were prepared to pay a ransom in ivory. Stanley's exasperation at their 'timidity', and Alison Smith's characterisation of them as 'contemptible' betray a gross misunderstanding of the historical context.[85]

However, as a merchant class, they were not without distinct class interests which they would struggle to defend and extend, in combination with their local allies when possible. Ifundikira's successor, Mnywa Sele, was fearful of the increasing influence of the merchant class, Nyamwezi as well as coastal, which he saw as detrimental to the political prerogatives of the *ntemi*. He first moved against the coastal traders to prove that they 'were living on sufferance only in [his] country' by imposing new taxes on all merchandise entering Unyanyembe. He then confronted the indigenous *vbandevba*, and executed Ifundikira's wife and her brother. But the target was apparently Karunde, Ifundikira's daughter and wife of Tippu Tip's father, who represented *vbandevba* interests. According to Unomah, Mnywa Sele is seen in Nyamwezi traditions as a 'destroyer of commerce, destroyer of country', a very telling comment on the political economy of new Unyanyembe and the convergence of economic interests between the indigenous and coastal traders. A combination of these merchants dislodged Mnywa Sele who carried on guerrilla warfare for five years (1860–5). He attempted to blockade Unyanyembe by cutting off the routes to Karagwe, the west, and the coast. The commerce of Unyanyembe was disrupted, many coastal traders 'were absolutely ruined', and some, like Thnay b. Amer, were killed in the skirmishes. But the war also hurt the Gogo who depended on the caravans for their revenue. Mnywa Sele was in fact killed by one of the Gogo chiefs.[86]

The struggle was revived by Mirambo, who realised that the presence of coastal merchants in Unyanyembe tilted the balance of power in favour of that chiefdom. At one stage he demanded that the coastal traders shift their allegiance and centre of trade to Urambo, but without success. They feared the absolute control Mirambo wished to exercise over the whole of Unyamwezi and the trade passing through it. According to Unomah, he then attempted to mobilise the Nyamwezi against the coastal merchants, but the *vbandevba*, led by the ruler of Unyanyembe, demurred. The coastal merchants, however, were by no means united; some, like Said b. Salim, tried to make their peace with Mirambo. Tippu Tip attempted to reconcile the warring parties, but without success. The war, which began in 1871, therefore, was not one between the Arabs and the Nyamwezi, but between a coalition of mercantile forces in Unyanyembe, *vbandevba* as well as coastal, against Mirambo who was himself one of the new breed of trader chiefs, who had the sympathy, though not active support, of a section of the coastal community. The war was to drag on until Mirambo's death in 1888, and during this time commerce was badly disrupted, with a measurable effect on the price of ivory at Zanzibar.[87] The coastal traders attempted to keep the trade flowing by building dhows on Lake Victoria, or by trying to revive the ancient route to the coast through Usangu and along the Ruaha. The latter attempt, led by Amran Masud, misfired and many Arabs were killed in 1873. The economic blockade had repercussions well beyond Unyamwezi, and the Sultan of Zanzibar sent 3,000 soldiers, and the Kabaka allegedly 17,000, to fight against Mirambo. Such was the community of economic interest in the commercial empire by the 1870s.[88]

However, these interests lacked the essential political and military infrastructures to sustain them. In this commercial empire, the flag had not followed trade in consolidating its hold on the country and its resources. The military power of the Zanzibari traders in the interior still consisted of the moving band of armed traders and their porters and slaves, ranging from 6 to 200 men, growing into larger but temporary alliances of up to 1,000 men in unsafe areas. As Burton put it, the coastal traders were 'too strong to yield without fighting but . . . not strong enough to fight with success'.[89] At the inland emporia where coastal traders settled, some form of political community arose among them which was more akin to a republic in which the most respected was recognised as a leader, but not a ruler. In later times, in the 1860s, he began to be referred to as the *liwali*, governor. Cameron reported that the Sultan of Zanzibar had confirmed Said b. Salim al-Lamki as the *liwali* of Tabora, probably in recognition of the role that Said was already playing. But he was not a representative of the Zanzibar state in the interior: the Sultan had little power over him, and provided little support, except briefly during the Mirambo crisis. Livingstone, in fact, described Said as 'merely a trade agent of certain Banyans of Zanzibar'. On the other hand, the ruler of Unyanyembe, representing *vbandevba* interests, seems to have had an effective say in his selection. During the Mirambo crisis, Said b. Salim was chased out because he was considered pro-Mirambo, and Isike, the ruler of Unyanyembe, objected to the election of Tippu Tip to the post for the same reason. Unomah further mentions 'the self-made *Liwali* Abdullah b. Nasib (Kisesa)' who was a close ally of Isike. More than anything else, the *liwali* represented the mercantile alliance that had developed during the nineteenth century between the coastal traders and the merchant classes in the interior. A scattering of these *liwalis* around the commercial empire, therefore, could hardly have provided a political framework to hold the empire together on the eve of the Scramble.[90]

Notes

1. Alpers (1967), p. 13; (1969), pp. 43-4.
2. Roberts (1970), pp. 43-9.
3. K. Jackson; J. Lamphear; A.C. Unomah.
4. Nicholls, pp. 34-5; Loarer, 'Ports au Sud de Zanguebar', ANSOM, OI, 2/10/2, A and B.
5. Loarer, 'Ports au Sud de Zanguebar', ANSOM, OI, 2/10/2, A and B.
6. Freeman-Grenville (1965), pp. 119-20.
7. ibid., pp. 137, 106.
8. Freeman-Grenville (ed.) (1962a), p. 231.
9. Freeman-Grenville (1965), pp. 106, 109, 137.
10. ibid., 76, 106, 137. Elswhere Morice says that the river was 12 or 15 leagues wide, i.e., 36 to 45 miles. The lake in fact varies in width between 10 and 50 miles. It is subject to seasonal variations in level of about 4 feet, with greater variations occurring in cycles of about eleven years. *Encyclopaedia Britannica* (1962), Vol. 15, p. 665.
11. Freeman-Grenville (1965), p. 76. Morice seems to have underestimated the distance from the coast, or rather the pace. In 1616 Bocarro took fifty-three days from Tete to Kilwa, a linear distance of 650 miles, and his unencumbered servants returned the same way in twenty-five days, an average of 12 to 26 miles per day respectively. Mondevit, pp. 348-9; Cunnison (1966), p. 226.
12. Burton (1873), p. 95.
13. Hardy's Journal, pp. 194-5, IOR, MR. Misc. 586.
14. Harkema (1964), passim; Rigby to Secretary of State, 1 May 1860, PRO, FO 54/17.
15. Freeman-Grenville (ed.) (1962a), pp. 203, 210, 224-5; Harkema (1964),

pp. 44–5; Harkema (1967), p. 131; *Encyclopaedia Britannica* (1962), Vol. 13, p. 381; Loarer, 'Quiloa', ANSOM, OI, 2/10/2.

16. Freeman-Grenville (ed.) (1962a), p. 203; Nicholls, p. 36. See p. 125.
17. Krapf, pp. 344, 423; Freeman-Grenville (ed.) (1962a), pp. 109, 202, 206; Owen (1833), Vol. 2, p. 3; Albrand, pp. 78–80.
18. Loarer, 'Quiloa', ANSOM, OI, 2/10/2.
19. ibid; Krapf, p. 344; Harkema (1967), p. 70; see Table 5.1; Nicholls, p. 374.
20. Loarer, 'Ports au Sud de Zanguebar', ANSOM, OI, 2/10/2, A and B.
21. ibid; Hamerton to Wyvill, 8 May and 14 June 1850, Bunce to Wyvill, 27 May 1850, Wyvill to Hamerton, 8 June 1850, Commander of the *Castor* to Hamerton, 8 June 1850, Description of the Slave Dow for condemnation, 8 June 1850, Bunce to Hamerton, 11 June 1850, Hamerton to Malet, 11 June 1850, PRO, FO 84/815; NAI, 20/12/1850-PC-31.
22. Loarer, 'Ports au Sud de Zanguebar', ANSOM, OI, 2/10/2, A and B.
23. ibid.
24. ibid.
25. Cassanelli, ch. 4; Smee, pp. 509–10; Loarer, 'Ports au Nord de Zanguebar', ANSOM, OI, 2/10/2D.
26. Guillain, Vol. 3, p. 307; Harkema (1967), p. 71; Cassanelli, ch. 4; Alpers (1983), pp. 445–8.
27. Krapf, p. 245.
28. Spear, ch. 5.
29. Berg (1973), pp. 127–9.
30. Cashmore, p. 164; Lieutenant Emery's Journal, entry for 9 October 1824, PRO, Adm. 52/3940; Owen (1833), Vol. 2, p. 154.
31. Lieutenant Emery's Journal, entries for 9 October 1824, 12 July 1825, PRO, Adm. 52/3940.
32. Jackson (1972), pp. 219–43, 262; Lamphear, pp. 79–83; Sheriff (1975b), passim; Low, p. 314; Krapf, p. 117; Hardy's Journal, p. 187, IOR, MR, Misc. 586; Lieutenant Emery's Journal, entry for 6 July 1826, PRO, Adm. 52/3940. The Kamba were known as the 'Maremungao' along the coast in the early nineteenth century.
33. Jackson (1972), p. 263; Dundas (1913), p. 505; Lamphear, pp. 80, 92, 99.
34. Jackson (1972), pp. 264–5; Guillain, Vol. 3, pp. 289–97; Krapf, p. 195; Burton (1872), Vol. 2, pp.62–7; Christie (1876), pp. 184, 191, 197. Christie quotes Plowden (1868) who said that Enarea in southern Ethiopia was frequented by traders from Zanzibar, though Christie believed there was no direct trade. Wakefield (1870) and New (1873) held that Samburu was the limit of coastal caravans by 1870. Abir, pp. 136–7, believes that Zanzibari caravans did not reach the northern shores of Lake Turkana until about 1890.
35. Petition from Nakhoda Mussood b. Tulloh, 8 December 1835, Agha Mohamed Rahim Shirazee to Chief Secretary, 23 January 1836, NAI, 27/6/1836-PC-4; Master Attendant to Superintendent, Indian Navy, 16 March 1837, MA, 68/1837, pp. 20–3; Lieutenant Emery's Journal, entries for 15, 20 September 1824, 21 March 1825, 6 April 1826, PRO, Adm. 52/3940.

36. Lieutenant Emery's Journal, entries for 15, 25 September 1824, 14 March, 5, 6 April, 29 May and 17 September 1825, 5 May and 13 June 1826, PRO, Adm. 52/3940.
37. Boteler, Vol. 2, pp. 1–2.
38. Loarer, 'Mombas', ANSOM, OI, 2/10/2D; Loarer, 'Ivoire', ANSOM, OI, 5/23/3; Guillain, Vol. 3, pp. 266–7; Lamphear, pp. 87, 97–8.
39. Baxter, p. 21; Hardy's Journal, pp. 188–9, IOR, MR, Misc. 586; Stahl, p. 12. See also map in Wakefield and in Cooley (1845).
40. Lamphear, pp. 93–4; Hardy's Journal, pp. 188–9, IOR, MR, Misc. 586; Feierman, pp. 120–4.
41. Feierman, pp. 125–8, 137–41. Loarer, 'Pangany', ANSOM, OI, 2/10/2D.
42. Feierman, p. 144 and ch. 6.
43. ibid., pp. 120, 139; Krapf, pp. 369, 382–3, 396, 416–17.
44. Loarer, 'Pangany', ANSOM, OI, 2/10/2D; Harkema (1964), p. 7; Cooley (1852), pp. 55, 79. Grant mentioned that Juma b. Mbwana led a small caravan in 1852 across Maasailand to Mwanza, and then across the lake to the mouth of the Kagera; but after the middle of the 1850s, according to Burton, this route was 'no longer practicable' because of the Maasai. Grant (1864), pp. 257–8; Burton (1860), Vol. 2, p. 228; Holmes, p. 482.
45. Hardy's Journal, pp. 188–91, Smee, entry for 7 April 1811, IOR, MR, Misc. 586; Freeman-Grenville (ed.) (1962a), p. 238.
46. Hardy's Journal, pp. 178–82, IOR, MR, Misc. 586.
47. Roberts (1970), pp. 43, 45–8, 51–2, 65, 68; Oliver, p. 153; Tosh, p. 111.
48. Hardy's Journal, pp. 178–82, IOR, MR, Misc. 586; Speke (1863), map; Shorter (1968a), p. 367; Shorter (1968b), pp. 100, 105–6. Hardy's Journal gives the itinerary with 'towns' and 'tribes', many of which cannot be identified reliably:

'Towns'	No. of days from coast	'Tribe'
Mas du ras su	3	Macote [Kutu?]
Changogo	5	"
Toon doon guah	7	"
Laturne	10	"
Ganger	14	"
Luerra	20	"
Who Luaha [Ruaha]	32	Whohah [Hehe?]
Gugu	45	"

49. Burton (1859), p. 300; Burton (1860), Vol. 2, pp. 223–4.
50. MacQueen (1845), pp. 371–3; Cooley (1845), pp. 206–7; Cooley (1852), pp. 53–60. There may be a typographical error in the name of the trader, whose first name may have been Saif, although Burton (1860), Vol. 2, p. 56, suggests Khalaf. However, the trader is described as a Nyamwezi settled at Zanzibar who was said to have been 40 years old in 1845. Cooley

gives an itinerary of 'an aged Arab merchant of Zanzibar', Muhammad b. Nasur, which extended as far as Buha, about four days from the lake.

51. Hardy's Journal, pp. 178-81, IOR, MR, Misc. 586.See also Cooley (1845), map.
52. Smee, p. 510; IOR, MR, Misc. 586, doc. 5, 'List of different tribes composing the cargo of slaves taken by Sir Edward Hughes Indiaman'.
53. Roberts (1970), p. 49; Burton (1860), Vol. 1, pp. 263, 307, 341; Burton (1872), Vol. 2, p. 292; St. John (1970), p. 214.
54. Burton (1860), Vol. 1, pp. 327, 396; Speke (1863), pp. 76-8; Bennett (1973), pp. 214-15; Roberts (1970), p. 50; Tippu Tip, pp. 39, 65; Unomah, p. 78.
55. Burton (1860), Vol. 1, pp. 324-9, Vol. 2, p. 370; Livingstone (1874), Vol. 1, p. 183; Speke (1863), p. 91. Bennett (1961b), p. 4, quotes Becker in 1881 to the effect that the Arab colony had been founded seventy years previously. Even if the date were correct, it does not necessarily mean that the colony was at Kazeh.
56. Burton (1860), Vol. 1, pp. 270, 376; Burton (1872), Vol. 2, p.297; Livingstone (1874), Vol. 1, pp. 64, 68-9, 182, 222; Speke (1864), p. 371; Stanley (1872), map opp. p. 259, pp. 264, 271, 549; Cameron, Vol. 1, pp. 150, 164. Cameron puts the number of coastal traders at an auction at 150. Roberts (1970), p. 69; Shorter, n.d.
57. Abrahams (1967), pp. 38-9; Unomah, pp. 86-96, 104-16, 120-1; Burton (1860), Vol. 2, pp. 31-2; Roberts (1970), pp. 48-9.
58. Unomah, pp. 101, 115-16. See pp. 108, 125, above.
59. Burton (1860), Vol. 2, pp. 297-8; Stanley (1872), p. 358; Livingstone (1874), Vol. 2, p. 182; Cameron, Vol. 1, pp. 57-76, 80-1, 85, 111, 124, 139, 145; 'Memo', PM, Ropes Papers and Brown Papers. Harkema (1967), p. 70, gives an average of 15,000 tusks exported from German East Africa in the early 1890s.
60. Stanley (1872), pp. 324, 540-2; Burton (1860), Vol. 2, pp. 258-60; Cameron, Vol. 1, pp. 373-4. An Arab in Maniema employed as many as 600 permanent porters; Roberts (1970), pp. 56-7, 68-9; Unomah, pp. 98-9; Harkema (1964), p. 5; Harkema (1967), p. 80.
61. Bennett (1971), ch. 3; Bennett (1973), pp. 214-15.
62. Harkema (1964), p. 6.
63. Burton (1860), Vol. 2, pp. 183-4, 193, 195-6; Speke (1863), pp. 242, 276; Tosh, pp. 111, 113.
64. Burton (1860), Vol. 2, pp. 183, 224; Grant (1864), p. 186.
65. Grant (1864), pp. 144, 158-9, 193; Speke (1863), pp. 201, 211, 233, 262, 265; Burton (1860), Vol. 2, p. 177.
66. Gray (1947), pp. 80-97; Gray (1961), pp. 8-10; Schweinfurth, p. 113; Burton (1860), Vol. 1, pp. 392-3, Vol. 2, p. 193; Stanley (1874), Vol. 1, p. 453; Stanley (1961), p. 117. Ahmed first claimed to have reached Buganda in AH 1270/AD 1854, and then revised it to AH 1260/AD 1844. Burton describes Hamid b. Ibrahim al Amri whom he met in 1857 as 'a bilious subject twenty-four or twenty-five years old'. In 1844 he would have been eleven or twelve years old; and Ahmed told Stanley in 1876 that he had been in Africa for about eighteen years, which would place his arrival in 1858. His earlier date of 1854 seems more likely.

67. Burton (1860), Vol. 2, pp. 186, 196–8; Schweinfurth, pp. 67, 115, 117; Grant (1864), p. 281; Speke (1863), pp. 238, 242, 482–3, 557; Speke (1864), p. 259; Harkema (1964), p. 6.

68. Stanley (1878), Vol. 1, p. 455; Stanley (1961), p. 117; Burton (1860), Vol. 2, pp. 215–16; Speke (1863), pp. 187–8; Beachey (1967), p. 283.

69. Roberts (1970), pp. 49–50, quoting Tippu Tip, mentions that an Arab expedition crossed the lake in 1820 to visit the Luba kingdom; and Stuhlmann says that the first Arab reached the lake in 1825. MacQueen (1845), p. 373; Wilson, p. 111.

70. Cooley (1852), p. 60; Pickering, p. 203; Burton (1860), Vol. 1, p. 323, Vol. 2, pp. 84, 97, 116; Speke (1864), p. 241; Stanley (1872), pp. 269, 410. By 1871, Said was described as one of 'the great magnates' of Ujiji, and his son maintained an establishment at Kazeh. See also Bennett (1973), pp. 219–21.

71. Burton (1860), Vol. 2, pp. 86, 147–9; Burton (1872), Vol. 2, pp. 300–1; Speke (1862), pp. 140–1; Speke (1864), pp. 205, 229–30, 241; Livingstone (1874), Vol. 1, p. 335, Vol. 2, p. 9; Tippu Tip, pp. 39–41. Alison Smith seems to think the trip marked 'a revival of Arab enterprise' (Tippu Tip, p. 9), since she could not believe that Burton's harsh characterisation of the Arabs involved could apply to the famous man. But Tippu Tip was then still a humble merchant, led only a few people, and could not compete with his fellow merchants for the larger tusks.

72. Pickering, p. 196; Burton (1860), Vol. 2, pp. 149–51; Livingstone (1874), Vol. 1, p. 277.

73. Cunnison (1966), p. 228; Livingstone (1874), pp. 224, 246. Muhammad b. Saleh claimed he was present at Kazembe in 1831 when Monteiro was there. 'Impoane' is probably a rendition of the Swahili word 'pwani' which means coast.

74. Cunnison (1966), p. 228n; Cooley (1854), pp. 269–70. There are two versions of the incident, obtained probably from the same source, Amer b. Said al Shaksi, whom Burton met in 1858 at Unyanyembe, and whom Tippu Tip met in about 1863/4 in Ulungu. Burton (1860), Vol. 2, pp. 151–2; Tippu Tip, pp. 47, 55. He was 'rescued' in 1867 by Livingstone to whom he declared he had lived with four Kazembes. Livingstone (1874), pp. 247–8, 276, 287, 297. He finally departed for Ujiji where he became 'the practical head' of the coastal community. Cameron stated that he had not been east of Ujiji since 1842. Cameron, Vol. 1, pp. 241–2.

75. MacQueen (1856), pp. 128–30; MacQueen (1860), pp. 136–53; Cooley (1852), pp. 286–91; Cooley (1855), pp. 75–6; Livingstone (1857), p. 217n; Burton (1860), pp. 151–2; *Proceedings of the Royal Geographical Society*, Vol. 3, p. 363. Said b. Habib may well have been part of this expedition. He informed Livingstone that Porto went only as far as Cutongo and gave the despatch to Ben Chombo to deliver to Mozambique.

76. Livingstone (1857), pp. 223, 501; Said b. Habeeb, pp. 146–8; MA, 59/1860, pp. 57–64; Burton (1859), p. 257n; Burton (1860), Vol. 2, pp. 151–2; Rigby to FO, 5 October 1861, PRO FO 84/1146, pp. 338–9.

77. Livingstone's comment in *Proceedings of the Royal Geographical Society*, Vol. 1, p. 249; Cooley (1852), pp. 266–7; Cunnison, pp. 229–30; Tippu Tip, pp. 11, 87–9; Livingstone (1874), Vol. 2, p. 176; Smith (1963), pp. 264–5.

78. Livingstone (1874), Vol. 1, pp. 187, 216, 241, 273, 282-3, 297, 321-2, Vol. 2, pp. 3, 8; Livingstone to Seward, 1 February 1867, PRO, FO 84/1292; Churchill to FO, 5 October 1867, PRO, FO 84/1279.
79. Tippu Tip, pp. 11, 49-55; Roberts (1967), pp. 244, 249-53; Livingstone (1874), Vol. 1, pp. 210, 218-20, 231, 260, 330.
80. Livingstone (1874), Vol. 1, pp. 265, 296, 298-9, Vol. 2, p. 35; Tippu Tip, pp. 12-13.
81. Stanley (1872), pp. 460-1; Burton (1860), Vol. 2, pp. 148-9; Cameron, Vol. 1, pp. 299, 364-5, 373-4; Livingstone (1874), Vol. 2, pp. 25, 118, 144.
82. Harkema (1964), pp. 5-6; Livingstone (1874), Vol. 2, pp. 66-7, 72, 188; Cameron, Vol. 2, p. 9. Livingstone mentions Zanzibari expansion north to the Lindi river, and to the confluence of the Lomami and the Lualaba near the 'Kisingite' (Swahili for 'threshold'), or cataract.
83. Cameron, Vol. 2, pp. 25-6, 51-4, 56-8; Stanley (1872), p. 460; Harkema (1964), pp. 5-6.
84. Heanley, p. 108; Rowley, p. 216; Burton (1860), Vol. 1, p. 329; Bennett (1961b), p. 13; Bennett (1973), pp. 216-18.
85. Roberts (1967), p. 253; Stanley (1872), p. 180; A. Smith's introduction to Tippu Tip, p. 17 and pp. 73-5.
86. Unomah, pp. 153-70; Speke (1863), pp. 72, 76-8; Speke to Rumanika [3/3/1862], in *Proceedings of the Royal Geographical Society*, Vol. 7, p. 232. Tippu Tip, p. 41; Bennett (1961b), pp. 9-10.
87. Unomah, pp. 247-71; Cameron, Vol. 1, pp. 150-1; Bennett (1963), pp. 3, 86, 89; Livingstone (1874), Vol. 2, pp. 90, 166; Stanley (1878), Vol. 1, p. 492. Stanley refers, with some exaggeration, to Mirambo's 'doubling of the price of ivory'.
88. Holmes, pp. 488-9, 491; Livingstone (1874), Vol. 2, pp. 88, 97, 194; Stanley (1872), p. 266; Cameron, Vol. 1, p. 164; Shorter, n.d.; Bennett (1971), ch. 3.
89. Burton (1860), Vol. 1, p. 327; Harkema (1964), pp. 2-3.
90. Bennett (1961b), p. 11; Bennett (1963), pp. 76-80; Unomah, p. 269.

Six

The Empire Undermined

The vast hinterland of Zanzibar was structurally weak but, although it suffered repeatedly from conflicts in the interior, it did not break apart until European colonial powers intervened in the 1880s to partition it among themselves. Economically the commercial empire was fragile, as was demonstrated by the American Civil War, but it was also resilient. The empire had been integrated more generally into the international economic system so that it could absorb economic shocks and diversify its markets and the commodities it could offer for export. However, throughout the nineteenth century various constraints had been imposed on it. Because of its economic dependence on international trade these gradually restricted its ability to respond to economic shocks. The commercial treaties with the various Western powers had tied the hands of Zanzibar to the maximum of 5 per cent duty on imports without obtaining reciprocal privileges for Zanzibar, and the 'most favoured nation' clause did not prevent the United States from clamping a 40 per cent import duty on Zanzibar cloves. Even the 'Mrima reservation' introduced in the treaties with the European powers was legally inoperative since it was not included in the treaty with the United States, and the Americans were able to use the threat of trading directly on the mainland to blackmail Seyyid Said into suspending his plans for direct trade with the United States. Finally, the treaties granted foreign powers 'extra-territorial rights' not only over their own nationals and over disputes between foreign nationals, but also over Zanzibar subjects in the employ of these nationals.[1]

More crucially, however, the commercial empire was becoming politically subverted by British imperialism. British influence over the Busaidi dynasty, of course, went back to the end of the eighteenth century when the special unequal relationship developed between the Omani state and the British in India, who were determined to maintain their dominance over the trade of the Persian Gulf. The various slave trade treaties provided a convenient path for the penetration of British influence and power into East Africa under a humanitarian guise, and were a prelude to British supremacy at Zanzibar. The emergence of the Indians as the

201

most powerful local merchant class provided Britain with a second way of exerting its influence on the policies of the commercial empire under the excuse that they were British subjects. These provided the various ideological justifications for the exercise of British supremacy in the western Indian Ocean. When the balance of economic power shifted within the Omani state from the Arabian heartland to its colony in East Africa, the British representative was forced to follow Seyyid Said to Zanzibar. By the time of Seyyid Said's death in 1856, the British had become convinced that the old state was no longer capable of sustaining effective control over both parts of the kingdom, and that a partition would permit the richer African half to develop its potential more fully as well as enable the British to exert a more effective control over the divided parts. The first chapter of the partition of the commercial empire was thus being finalised long before 1884.

The subordination of the Indian merchant class

The Indian merchants had been indigenised and granted the privileges enjoyed by other native traders to permit them to develop the full potential of the commercial empire and ensure thair loyalty to Zanzibar. Most of them had migrated from the peripheral British 'Protected States' in India with little hope of British protection in East Africa. They had built up their economic power and obtained the removal of economic disabilities without British support and long before the arrival of the first British Consul in 1841. The 700 Indians already settled in East Africa by then viewed British protection as only liable to impose restrictions on their trade. They shared with the rest of the population their economic fortunes and sentiments, and exhibited a 'violent feeling' against British interference in the affairs of Zanzibar.[2]

Atkins Hamerton had been appointed in the dual capacity of British Consul and Political Agent of the Bombay government. The interests of the Foreign Office at this time were largely confined to maintaining the status quo in East Africa, which meant denying the French a base there, and to its own anti-slavery crusade which had shown little flicker since the Moresby Treaty of 1822 prohibiting slave trade with the European colonies to the south. The Bombay government, on the other hand, had appointed its agent to keep an eye on the sensitive Persian Gulf but had little interest in Zanzibar. Jt attempted to dissuade Seyyid Said from diverting all his attention to his African dominions, but in vain. When in *c.* 1840 the Sultan shifted his capital to Zanzibar, where Hamerton reluctantly had to follow him, the Indian government even asked to be 'relieved from all care for British interests at Zanzibar' in 1842, but this proved to be premature.[3]

At Zanzibar, therefore, Hamerton found himself in a milieu in which British interests were marginal, and with little leverage to influence the local political scene. The people influential with the merchant prince were merchants: the Indian custom master who stood at the head of the most powerful merchant class; the American Consul who represented the most important foreign merchant group; and the local Arab and Swahili traders and landowners closely associated with these two groups. Direct British trade with Zanzibar was erratic and generally small at that time, and whatever leverage it produced was monopolised by Robert Cogan, who had negotiated the 1839 British commercial treaty with Zanzibar and was a personal rival of Hamerton. Sir Reginald Coupland even argued that Hamerton, an ex-army and political officer, lacked sympathy for British merchants, and failed to support or encourage British mercantile interests either out of spite for Cogan, or from his desire to maintain cordial relations with the Sultan.[4] To overcome this feeling of impotence and isolation in the diplomatic wilderness, Hamerton set out to build up a base that would make him an 'arbiter' in the affairs of Zanzibar. The economically powerful Indian merchant class provided one of the leverages.

Upon his arrival Hamerton found the Indian merchant class was indigenised to such an extent that all business disputes and bankruptcy cases were handled by the Omani governor of Zanzibar, Seyyid Sulaiman b. Hamed. Although Hamerton claimed to have succeeded in asserting his authority over Indian bankruptcy cases, as late at 1847 the case of a prominent Indian merchant was settled without the least reference to him. The Indians denied that they were British subjects since a majority hailed from the 'Protected State' of Kutch. According to Hamerton, Seyyid Said called together the principal merchants and asked them to sign a declaration drawn up by the Indian custom master, Jairam Sewji, that they were Zanzibar subjects. Hamerton asserts that many refused because they had their families and properties in British India. This assertion, however, is not corroborated by contemporary American and other records. On the contrary, as late as 1856, Hamerton's rival movement to get Indians, not naturally British, to place themselves under his jurisdiction, had won only twelve adherents according to the British agent at Muscat.[5]

Seyyid Said also sought to deny Hamerton's claims by appealing to his superiors. He wrote to the Secretary of State for Foreign Affairs, Lord Aberdeen, asking whether Indians who were born in Zanzibar or had resided there for a long time, who had local wives and children, and possessed estates and slaves were British subjects. Aberdeen replied categorically that 'no natives of India, excepting the natives of those portions of India which form part of the dominion of the British Crown are entitled . . . to British Consular protection.' The Treaty of Alliance between the East India Company and the Rao of Kutch had not placed Kutch under the English Crown since the Company specifically engaged to 'exercise no authority over the domestic concerns of the Rao.' Seyyid Said had been assured by the negotiator of the British treaty with Zanzibar that its provisions were not applicable to Kutchis, and Hamerton himself had admitted in 1841 that not all the Indians at Zanzibar were British subjects.[6]

Recognition of the distinction in terms of their exact legal status among the Indians, however, would have deprived Hamerton of control over the wealthiest and most influential section which included the custom master and the most prominent merchants. He therefore tried to gloss over the precise composition of the Indian community. In two dispatches he spoke of Indians as British subjects, 'inhabitants of Bombay, Surat and other places in India', and omitting any reference to Kutch from where the majority came. Bombay, however, was not interested, and it had already asked to be relieved of involvement in Zanzibar.[7]

Hamerton therefore turned to the only weapon that remained to put teeth into his threats against the recalcitrant Indians. He could count on the rabidly anti-slavery sentiments of the Foreign Office and the British Navy. Soon after his arrival he had reported that all the 700 Indians settled in East Africa were slave dealers, and that the custom master received duty on each slave landed at Zanzibar. Without a military force under his command, however, Hamerton was obliged to apply to Seyyid Said to issue a proclamation forbidding his subjects from buying or selling slaves to British Indians. His main target, the Kutchis, however, escaped his ill-aimed blow. He reported with regret to the Bombay government that the measure would ruin British Indians and drive them out of the trade to the benefit of the Kutchis. On the other hand, the measure placed many British Indian subjects, to whom Arab plantations had been mortgaged, at the mercy of the landowners now that the Indians could not use slave labour to recover the value of their mortgages. Though the Advocate General of India suggested that the concerned Indians were entitled to compensation 'after the example of our West Indian and other slave colonies', they were too ignorant of their rights to demand compensation. The episode unsettled the market, making capital scarce and preventing the arrangement of further mortgages. An American merchant reported in 1846 that there was then more fear of bankruptcies than formerly.[8]

The visit of the British warships, *Castor* and *Dee*, in 1850 provided Hamerton with a second opportunity, but this time he ignored the legal distinction. He had collected information on Indian commercial establishments near the southern border of the Zanzibar dominions, and he applied pressure on Seyyid Said to grant British warships permission 'to enter bays, ports, creeks, rivers' in the region within his dominions in their anti-slavery crusade. In May they discovered at Massani and Kionga around Cape Delgado what they described as 'barracoons' capable of containing 5,000 slaves, and a dhow with 'that peculiar odour'. But they found no slaves despite the fact that May and June were among the most active months for local distribution of slaves; the 'barracoons' were in fact full of goods owned by some of the most prominent Indians. Both places were put to the torch; and four Indians were arrested and taken to Zanzibar.[9]

The most prominent was Lakhmidas Kalianji, said to be a cousin of Ebji Sewji, the custom master's brother and a militant opponent of British claims. He was said to have suffered a loss of at least MT$50,000, and about the same value of muskets, gunpowder, brass wire and piece goods belonging to many native merchants were also destroyed. Hamerton admitted that he 'totally failed in being able to procure anything like satisfactory proof such as would be required in an English court of law as to who were the real proprietors', but this did not prevent him from imprisoning the Indians in Zanzibar for over a month without trial, and then deporting them to India. The condemnation proceedings of the alleged slave dhow and 'barracoons' were held at Cape Town where the accused could not be present, as was usual in such cases before an Admiralty Court was established at Zanzibar in 1867. The British Consul had at last succeeded in violently shaking the Indians' self-confidence. Some of the wealthiest, according to American traders, decided to close down their businesses and go away, because they no longer enjoyed security for their trade and property at Zanzibar. A great depression in the commerce was still in evidence nine months later, with the Americans unable to dispose of MT$150,000 worth of goods.[10]

This is not to argue that the Indians did not participate in the slave sector of the economy. The slave trade was so integral a part of the whole commercial organisation that Sir Bartle Frere was led to admit that it was 'nearly impossible' for any one involved in East African trade 'to feel sure that no part of his commercial transactions is connected directly or indirectly with the slave trade.'[11] By 1861 three-quarters of the immovable property on Zanzibar was said to be either already in the possession of the Indians or mortgaged to them, and the value of landed property was estimated in terms of the number of slaves. Indians played a crucial role in financing the caravan trade which would imply an inevitable involvement in the slave economy not only by the Indians but also by American and European merchants who supplied the imports and took ivory and copal, as well as cloves, sugar and sesame from slave-worked plantations.[12]

The campaign was intensified under Hamerton's successor as British Consul, Christopher Palmer Rigby, who ignored the wider indirect entanglement of the Western traders but concentrated his attention entirely on Indian involvement, regardless of their exact legal status. Early in 1859 he commenced emancipating domestic slaves owned by

Indians. They were fined MT$10 for each slave freed and were forced to give a plot of land for their sustenance; some were imprisoned, publicly flogged in cases of allegation of cruelty, and then deported. Mohammed Wazir, who was born in Zanzibar as was his father, and whose grandfather had come from the Comoros, had his twenty slaves emancipated in 1860 and was deported. Kanu Manji, a prominent merchant who had traded on a large scale with the Americans since the 1840s, had several plantations by 1860. His long business career came to an abrupt end with the emancipation of his seventy-nine slaves and his deportation. By September 1860 Rigby had emancipated 5,606 slaves belonging to 'natives of India, whether British subjects, or nationals of the protected states.'[13]

Rigby's successors, though hardly 'soft' on the slave question, were more conscious of legal considerations and the consequences of their actions. The emancipation of slaves on Indian plantations had the effect of greatly reducing the value of all landed property, for it was taken as a prelude to a general emancipation, and no one would advance money on the security of any landed property. One estate worth MT$30,000 a few years previously could not fetch MT$8,000 in 1862. The next three British consuls, therefore, adopted a more cautious approach, seeking to define precisely British jurisdiction over the Indians. It was soon realised, by no less a person than Henry Adrian Churchill, British Consul, 1865–70, who was much closer to Rigby's way of thinking, that the British Consul had no right to deprive the Kutchis of their slaves. The only legal approach was to ask 'the natives of the Protected States' upon their arrival whether they desired to place themselves under British protection or under the jurisdiction of the Sultan of Zanzibar. Thus the 'Rules and Regulations' of 1867 were framed under which only nine Kutchis had registered themselves at the British Consulate by 1869.[14]

The issue, however, was not merely legal but political. John Kirk was later to comment that 'while the natives of Kutch established in Zanzibar were under our sole protection and jurisdiction we held the most wealthy and enterprising among the mercantile community and our influence was in all matters paramount.' On the other hand, with the return to legality in 1867, Sultan Majid 'confidently looked forward to the time when British influence would be reduced to an equality with that of France and other foreign powers.'[15] It was this diminution of British influence that had pinched Churchill, who set about to reverse the trend by trying rather ingenuously to challenge the legal distinction. He argued that though the Kutchis had forfeited British protection in Zanzibar by failing to register at the British Consulate, they were nevertheless under British jurisdiction as were all other British subjects, i.e., with responsibilities but without rights.[16]

Although Bombay was not impressed by the argument, a change had begun to come over the Indian government, which had previously considered the anti-slavery campaign a 'troublesome irrelevancy'. It had begun to resolve to interfere 'with a high hand, and authoritatively, to put down slave dealing when carried on by the subjects of a Native State'. The approach, however, was to be legal. It was argued that since Kutchis were not British subjects, they could be put on the footing of quasi-British subjects in matters in which the British government was concerned, such as slave dealing. Bombay therefore suggested that 'if it is expedient' to interfere in the question, it could only be done by an understanding with the Rao of Kutch 'in virtue of which his subjects will be legally, as well as morally liable to our jurisdiction, and in turn, entitled to our protection as well as compensation.' In April 1869 the Rao was induced to issue a proclamation to the effect that 'the claims and disputes of [Kutchis] who permanently reside in, or frequent for the purpose of trade, the ports of Muscat and all other places in Africa, Arabia and the Persian Gulf . . . should be settled by the British government in the same way as if it were its own subjects.' When Majid questioned the Rao's authority over the Kutchis in East Africa, particularly those born and bred there, Kirk threatened 'to bring matters to a crisis by asserting at once the full powers given me under the Rao's proclamation . . . that besides [Majid] would stand in open antagonism to the will of H.E. the Governor of Bombay.'[17]

Majid's climbdown marked the final surrender by the Zanzibar authorities in the struggle which had stretched over nearly three decades for control over a powerful merchant class which continued to enjoy the extraordinary privileges granted them as local traders. Hegemony over this class permitted British consuls to exercise a powerful influence on the financial administration of the Omani state. As early as 1862, at Consul Pelly's 'dictation', the custom master had refused to advance a loan to the Sultan, and he made sure that no other Indian merchant would do it either. He also dictated the rate of payment of the customs rent to the Sultan. In 1871 Kirk decisively intervened to frustrate Sultan Barghash's attempt to displace the firm of Jairam Sewji which had held the contract for half a century. His intervention was occasioned by the rumour that Barghash wished to repudiate the huge debt owed to the custom master, although Kirk admitted that the debt had been deliberately built up as a way of forcing the Sultan to renew the contract with the same firm. Although the contract was then worth MT$450,000 to MT$500,000, Kirk forced a compromise by which MT$340,000 of the debt was waived while the rent of the customs was allowed to remain at the same level of MT$300,000 per annum. Barghash was the net loser by at least MT$410,000 over the five-year period. Even Bombay was led to protest at this uncalled-for interference.[18]

The transformation of the Indians from an indigenised merchant class to an entrenched alien body through which a foreign power could go for the economic jugular of the Omani state alienated the Indians and exacerbated the natural strains between the different classes in society, such as those between the indebted landowners and the moneylenders. In 1870 Barghash retaliated by issuing a proclamation trying to restrict their movements and rescind their privileges. In reaction to the increasing transfer of land to Indian moneylenders, Barghash tried to confine them to the city of Zanzibar, but the British Consul protested against this move as contrary to the commercial treaty with Britain. In 1871 Barghash hesitated before allowing the custom master to fit out a military expedition to Unyamwezi in case that opened up a way to major Indian encroachment into the interior, one of the last niches for Arab traders.[19] The Indo-Arab economic alliance, which had formed one of the bedrocks of the commercial empire under Seyyid Said, had begun to crumble, and the economic integrity of the empire had thus been subverted.

The dismemberment of the Omani kingdom

Majid's climbdown on the question of British control over the Indian merchant class was not surprising. It was a natural consequence of a long history of Busaidi subordination to British power that dated back to the end of the eighteenth century, but it began to adopt a more ominous form during the last years of Seyyid Said's rule. As the kingdom, particularly the African half of it, developed and was integrated into the world capitalist system, Western powers, and particularly Britain, began to exercise increasing influence over the affairs of the Sultanate. As early as the 1840s French and American observers had begun to comment on Said's subservience to the British. Captain de Kerdudal, a French naval officer, described him in 1843 as no more than an English governor who feared Britain would absorb all his possessions. In 1851 American Consul Ward reported a general impression among the Arabs at Zanzibar that when Said died, the English 'will decide who shall be the new Sultan and that the country will come under the protection of England.'[20]

Said's increasing dependence on the British may have resulted from his realisation that the tribal/dynastic structures of Oman were no longer adequate in holding the far-flung empire together. Added to this was the fact that during his reign the economic centre of gravity had shifted decisively from the metropole to the East African colony, symbolised by the transfer of his capital from Muscat to Zanzibar. This was reminicent of the earlier shift within Oman from the interior to the mercantile coast during the eighteenth century. Oman had then undergone a social revolution as a result of which the more secular mercantile forces had achieved prominence in the political economy of the kingdom, although the tribal *shaikhs* and the *ulema* had still retained enough influence to ensure that their consent in the election of the ruler remained necessary. But after the Napoleonic Wars Muscat had stagnated and part of the merchant class had migrated with the merchant prince to the lush and prosperous colony. In Oman this weakened the influence of the merchant class and the control that the Busaidi dynasty exercised over the heartland. Throughout the 1830s Said was constantly recalled from Zanzibar to put down rebellions in Oman. After the 1840s, much to the consternation of British Indian authorities who were concerned about peace in the Persian Gulf, Said frankly began to neglect Oman. He increasingly relied on the British to uphold his position, a reversal of the roles the British had in mind. Between 1840 and his death in 1856, he spent very little time in Oman.[21]

Meanwhile, the Omani ruling class in Zanzibar had become indigenised and economically diversified as it moved into the slave plantation economy and the caravan trade. The change was graphically portrayed by the octogenarian former governor of Zanzibar, Sulaiman b. Hamed, who witnessed the transformation of the Arabs from those who had worked with their own hands to those who came to rely almost entirely on slave labour. The distance between the two halves of the kingdom gradually increased as the practice grew of dividing inheritance between the Oman-based and Zanzibar-based sections of Arab clans and families according to their residence. Already by the time of Princess Salme, one of the daughters of Seyyid Said who later eloped with a German trader in 1866, this social distance had begun to be expressed in attitudes. Born and bred in Zanzibar, she said:

> Few of us cared much about going to Oman, as the proud Omani ladies rather regarded Zanzibar women as uncivilised creatures . . . all the members of our family born in Oman thought themselves much better and of higher rank than any of their African relations. In their opinion we were somewhat like negroes . . . and our speaking any other language but Arabic [i.e. Kiswahili] was the greatest proof of barbarity in their eyes.[22]

Cognisant of the growing economic and political distance between the two halves of his kingdom, Said began to toy with the idea of dividing it as early as 1844. He wrote to Lord Aberdeen:

> After us we constitute and appoint our son Said Khalid to be ruler over all our possessions in Africa . . . and in like manner we appoint our son Said Thuweenee to be ruler over all our possessions in Oman.[23]

In a covering letter Hamerton explained that Said's object was 'to ascertain whether he may look to Her Majesty's Government to guarantee' the partition. Said sought that guarantee because he had disinherited his eldest and most popular son, Hilal, against whom he did not think Khalid could hold his position. Hamerton questioned 'the soundness of the Imaum's policy in sub-dividing his empire', but the British government at the time was not prepared to get entangled in a succession dispute, and apparently sent no reply.[24]

Whatever may have been his wishes, Said probably realised that under Omani law and custom he had no right to partition his kingdom. 'According to the prevailing ideas of learned men,' wrote the British Political Resident in the Persian Gulf, 'no potentate can legally partition his dominion' or public property inherited from his ancestors. G.P. Badger, a member of the Zanzibar-Muscat Commission, pointed out that such a division 'would have been absolutely null and void since not a single instance is adducible, from the preceding annals of the principality, of an Imam or Seyyid disposing of his territories by will or otherwise.'[25] Moreover, the only will that Said left behind referred solely to his personal property. Rigby's explanation that it did not deal with the critical question of succession because he had already settled it during his lifetime does not hold much water.[26]

According to Ibadhi ideology the Imam had to be elected by the elite of the society, which comprised – after the social transformationof the eighteenth century – prominent merchants, tribal *shaikhs* and the *ulema*, and he had to be confirmed by the common people. Even after the spiritual position of the Imam had been displaced by the temporal powers of the Sultan, the formality of election remained, and it was quoted by both sides in the succession dispute that followed Said's death. Long before then it had been accepted that the successor would come from within the ruling dynasty, although primogeniture was not a recognised principle. Ultimately, as some of the contestants cynically put it, 'might, coupled with election by the tribes, is the only right.'[27]

Said's death at sea in 1856 on his way back from Oman set the stage for testing that might. The kingdom was then under the governorship of his three eldest sons: Thuwaini at Muscat, Majid at Zanzibar and Turki at Sohar. There was an attempt to settle the succession dispute amicably with the dispatch in 1857 of an envoy, Muhammad b. Salim. According to Thuwaini, Majid agreed to pay him a tribute of MT$40,000 and recognised that Zanzibar was to be subordinate to Muscat. He also asserted that Sohar was subsidiary to Muscat since its governor received a monthly stipend from the revenue of Muscat. According to Rigby, representing Majid's position, the envoy had been sent to request Majid to assist the Muscat treasury as the revenue of Zanzibar exceeded that of Muscat; Majid agreed to remit MT$40,000 annually as free gift on the express stipulation that Thuwaini would refrain from hostilities against Turki and would pay the latter MT$10,000 of the subsidy.[28]

In 1844 the British government had been unwilling to get involved in guaranteeing succession as Said had desired, and as late as 1859 Bombay wished to remain neutral in the dispute. What it could not be neutral about was any disturbance of the peace in the Persian Gulf, a matter of vital concern to British Indian interests. Thus when Thuwaini fitted out an expedition against Majid, Bombay sent its Resident in the Persian

Gulf to Muscat to dissuade, and ultimately to prevent, him from resorting to violence, and to address any claims he had to British arbitration. When he decided to proceed to Zanzibar anyway, Bombay sent a warship to intercept him.[29] The British had thus intervened to prevent the resolution of the succession dispute in the traditional Omani way, the first, though not the last, time in Omani-Zanzibari history, which made Britain the virtual kingmaker. Thuwaini was forced to submit to arbitration by the Governor General of India.

The British representatives in the Persian Gulf were generally in favour of maintaining the status quo, and thus the formal unity of the Omani empire. This position went unchallenged because of the absence of a British Consul from Zanzibar since Hamerton's death in 1857. With the appointment of Rigby in his place a year later, despite a warning against compromising Britain's neutrality in the dispute, he began to formulate a position that was decidedly in favour of Majid, and therefore of the partition of the kingdom through British intervention. Soon after Thuwaini's expedition was turned back in early 1859 he wrote a strong recommendation for Majid, who 'shows himself on every occasion very partial to Europeans . . . and is earnestly desirous of acting up to his treaty engagements to prevent the export of slaves from his dominions': all the qualities of a British protégé. To strengthen his argument with the British government Rigby attempted to revive the old French bogey. He suggested that Thuwaini had demanded from Majid the cession of Mombasa which he allegedly wanted to make over to the French, although there is no confirmation for this, and it is perhaps too transparent to require serious refutation.[30]

Locally Rigby proceeded to intervene directly in the dispute, first by taking an active role in organising resistance against Thuwaini's expedition. When an Omani envoy arrived to try to settle the dispute with Majid without involving the British, Rigby told him that the question now had to be settled under 'proper guarantee'. He went on to argue that Said had the right to divide his kingdom, adducing some historical precedents which, as Badger noted, did not exist. He also told the envoy that he hoped Majid 'would never pay a farthing' as subsidy to Thuwaini.[31]

Rigby then moved to eliminate local opposition to Majid and British influence in Zanzibar, represented by Majid's younger brother Barghash and the Harthi clan. Barghash's position was frankly nationalist: 'My brother Majid's wish is to give the country to the English . . . We, however, will not give our country either to the English or to the French or the Americans, or to anyone else; but if we sell it, we shall do so only at the cost of our blood and war to the death.'[32] The Harthi were one of the oldest Omani clans in Zanzibar and owned a considerable amount of landed property. Rigby alleged that they wished to embroil the sons of Said in conflict among themselves in the hope of displacing the Busaidi dynasty altogether. He therefore tried to divide the clan and, in his own words, 'almost daily urged His Highness to seize the chiefs of this tribe and to arrest Barghash', and deport them all to Muscat.[33]

As a result of Rigby's intervention and support, Majid finally arrested all the leading Harthi *shaikhs* and compelled Barghash to dismiss his retainers. Barghash was also ordered to leave Zanzibar, but at the last moment he slipped into the interior of the island to raise his standard of revolt. Majid marched against him, but the British mailed fist had to come out of the velvet glove to crush the revolt. Rigby called on a visiting British warship to land troops and attack Barghash's stronghold. It was Rigby who personally arrested the Omani prince and sent him into exile in Bombay.[34]

In London the question was raised as to whether Rigby had not taken sides in a civil war, and his conduct was justified only on the excuse that the disturbances 'had already led to the murder of one British subject and to the wounding of another and threatened the immediate destruction of British property and the prospective annihilation of British trade.'[35] The excuse could not have been more transparent; the reality of British power in Zanzibar and the Busaidi dynasty's dependence on Britain had never been so explicit.

The interception of Thuwaini's expedition and the suppression of Barghash's revolt had at last made the British arbiters in the affairs of the Omani kingdom. Moreover, both their actions and the emerging perception of how their interests in the Persian Gulf and East Africa could best be served under the prevailing conditions began to determine their ultimate decision on the question of succession which they had forced Thuwaini to submit to their own arbitration. In presenting the matter to the Indian government, Bombay raised the question whether Said had the right to divide his kingdom; but it also raised the political question from its perspective:

> Zanzibar is a thriving and rising port destined apparently to become the commercial emporium of East Africa and to exert a very great influence over its future progress . . . The British government . . . cannot be indifferent to the power of a friendly and comparatively civilised native power on the East Coast of Africa, a power which has shown a most laudable desire to discourage the slave trade and to promote the development of legitimate commerce.

Rigby's influence on Bombay's thinking is unmistakable. On the other hand:

> Muscat is a place of limited commercial capabilities but its geographical position, the superiority of the race by which it is inhabited and the occupation by its ruler of Bunder Abbas, Kishn and other places in the Persian Gulf give it a certain political importance . . . It

cannot be forgotten that the influence of Muscat in the Persian Gulf has been uniformly exercised in the furtherance of objects which the British government has at heart, viz. the suppression of piracy and of the slave trade and the maintenance of maritime peace. It would have been a grievous mistake to allow Syud Thooenee to exhaust his resources in an attempt to annex Zanzibar to his dominions.[36]

A year later Bombay phrased the question that would have to be dealt with by the investigating commission in the classical form of British utilitarian political theory:

Whether it is necessary that actual rights should be recognised, [whether] peace and tranquillity may not be effectually secured by inducing the antagonist parties to make mutual concession . . . whether judicious compromise will not be of more real benefit to the interests of all concerned . . . than any rigid adherence to pretensions based on exact rights.[37]

In other words, the commission would have to ascertain not only what was 'right' but also what was 'expedient'. The meaning of these words was underlined in an additional set of instructions issued to the commissioner, Brigadier W.M. Coghlan. He was told to:

estimate fairly the value of the rival claims to the sovereignty of Zanzibar and its dependencies, and to suggest such an adjustment . . . as may be satisfactory to both parties, most conducive to the general welfare of the people and tribes hitherto subject to the Imaumship of Muscat, and withal, best calculated to maintain peace and to *ensure the furtherance of our just interests in Oman and along the Eastern Coast of Africa dependent on Zanzibar.*[38] (author's italics)

By the time Coghlan was commissioned, the deck had clearly been stacked, which led him to inquire whether 'the claims of Seyyid Thowenee to the sovereignty of Zanzibar, and to the annual payment of tribute by his brother [were] points definitely disposed of' by the Indian government.[39]

Coghlan was accompanied by an accomplished Arabist, G.P. Badger, who studied in depth and eventually translated Salil Ibn Razik's *History of the Imams and Seyyids of Oman.*[40] They considered first the question of Said's right to divide his kingdom, and concluded that, as Majid himself was obliged to admit, 'the sovereignty of Oman had hitherto depended on election, the principal tribes generally choosing the candidate who was either most beloved by them or who possessed the greatest power to enforce his pretensions.'[41] In fact both contenders based their claim on election, but by whom? Thuwaini argued that according to Omani custom he was elected by the Omani people to the rulership of the parent state, and he thus became the lawful ruler of all of Said's kingdom. Majid, on the other hand, argued that he was elected by 'my brothers and family and all the people from Tink [Tungi near Cape Delgado] to Marbat' on

213

the southern coast of Oman. He did not even claim any sovereignty in Oman proper, and did not dispute Thuwaini's right over it. Omani emigrants to the East African dependencies had never previously elected an Omani ruler, although as members of Omani clans they could be said to have participated indirectly through their tribal *shaikhs*.[42] Clearly, therefore, Majid's claim was a departure from tradition, and was nothing less than an act of secession. It was not the first time in Omani history: the Mazrui of Mombasa had seceded in the eighteenth century, but the British had not prevented Said from ultimately reasserting his sovereignty in 1837.[43]

On the grounds of right alone, therefore, there was only one verdict that Coghlan could reach, and this was to declare in favour of Thuwaini's sovereignty over Muscat and Zanzibar jointly. But he performed a sudden volte-face at the end of his report, and argued – there is no evidence that this was Majid's argument, although it does appear to be based on Rigby's lengthy memorandum urging partition on grounds of both history and expediency – that, during Said's reign of over half a century, conditions of the two parts had radically changed, particularly after the transfer of the seat of government to Zanzibar. A large number of Omanis had settled in Zanzibar and the African mainland, and those possessions were actually more extensive and valuable than the Arabian territories, Zanzibar's revenue exceeding that of Muscat by 77,000 crowns.

> Such being the altered condition and circumstances of the African dependencies, it seems consonant with reason and justice . . . that the people of those countries should have a voice in the election of the sovereign . . . Regarded from one point of view, that act may be characterised as *a national revolution*.[44]

Coghlan therefore concluded that, on grounds of right alone, 'Syud Majid's claim to the sovereignty of Zanzibar and its African dependencies are superior to any which can be adduced in favour of Syud Thooenee.'[45] This is a considerable stretching of the argument from enfranchisement of the Zanzibar Arabs in the election of the joint ruler of Muscat and Zanzibar, to support for secession by Majid, and that justified on grounds of 'right'.

While there is evidence for growing socio-economic and even political distance between Oman and Zanzibar, Coghlan produced little evidence to support such an important thesis of a national revolution. In 1840 M. Guillain had reported that even the Swahili people 'range themselves, without hesitation, on the side of a claimant chosen by Oman', which he found surprising since Zanzibar was by then the seat of government and controlled the navy. It is true that by the late 1850s the people of Zanzibar had begun to resent the annual incursions by the so-called Northern Arabs who had been cut off from more lucrative trade and were not averse to general lawlessness, kidnapping and smuggling of slaves after the slave trade to the north was made illegal. But whether this was a national revolution or merely an act of secession by a prince ultimately depends on whether he was able to mobilise popular support to make his pretensions stick, or whether he had to rely on external support to keep him on the throne. Rigby reports that when Majid was threatened by Thuwaini's expedition, 20,000 Arabs, Baluchis, Makranis, Comorians, Swahilis and even Africans from the mainland poured into Zanzibar to support his cause. But this is hardly substantial evidence of a national cause. A number of these groups were part of the Sultan's mercenary army; and Majid expended a large part of his fortune and guns among other groups to win their allegiance. Even among the Arabs, as Rigby admitted, Thuwaini had 'many secret supporters', including Barghash and a number of his sisters, as well as the large and influential Harthi clan.[46]

But the British case did not rest merely on the contrived considerations of 'right'. Coghlan went on to reinforce it with arguments 'on the score of expediency'. Rigby's memorandum played a decisive role in this respect. He had argued that the connection between Oman and Zanzibar was detrimental to the interests of the two territories. Arab government was personal, and the presence of the ruler was essential to the orderly administration of a state. He quoted Hamerton's report to show that even Said had difficulty governing both parts of the Omani kingdom. 'His absence from Oman destroyed his influence with the tribes and nearly caused him the loss of all his Arabian possessions.' Zanzibar, he argued, was destined to be the chief centre of commerce and civilisation between Port Natal and Cape Guardafui and the centre of a vast kingdom extending deep into the African interior. If it were treated as a dependency of Oman and suffered from neglect or feeble rule, the empire would disintegrate, the slave trade treaties would be disregarded, foreign powers would establish a foothold on the African coast, and all hope of progress would be destroyed. On the other hand, the separation of Zanzibar from Muscat would deal a great blow to the slave trade.[47]

Coghlan further argued that, if Thuwaini had persisted in his expedition, a civil war would have broken out in Oman and, as John Elphinstone, Governor of Bombay, put it, 'in grasping the shadows of sovereignty in Zanzibar, Seyyid Thuwaini would have lost the substance in Muscat.' There was indeed a plan for his rival Turki to move against Muscat if Thuwaini moved against Zanzibar, and Majid had sent to Sohar money, two large iron guns and ammunition.[48]

Coghlan concluded his report by remarking that:

> Fortunately, the expediency on which [my conclusions] are based, and which alone would hardly suffice to justify the severance of that state from the parent state of Muscat, is adequately supported and confirmed by the arguments founded on right.[49]

He therefore went on to make recommendations which formed part of the Canning Award:

1. That Seyyid Majid shall be confirmed in the independent sovereignty over Zanzibar and its African dominions.
2. That, as regards the succession to that sovereignty, neither the ruler of Muscat nor the tribes of Oman shall have any right whatever to interfere; that the sovereign of Zanzibar, in conjunction with the people, shall be left absolutely free to make whatever arrangements they may deem expedient for appointing future successors to Seyyid Majid.
3. That, in consideration of these concessions, Seyyid Majid shall be bound to remit to Seyyid Thwain the stipulated yearly subsidy of 40,000 crowns; and further to liquidate all the arrears due on that account since the payment was suspended.
4. That this subsidy of 40,000 crowns per annum shall be a primary and permanent charge on the resources of the Zanzibar state, payable by the sovereign of that state to the ruling sovereign of Muscat and Oman.[50]

As Thuwaini bitterly commented, 'the man who is given a bone can only suck it . . . but he who is given flesh eats it; I am the elder brother and I have a bone in Muscat. Majid has the flesh.'[51]

Coghlan's recommendations were based on political considerations rather than on Arab constitutional practice. The maintenance of Said's kingdom had been the basic plank of British policy in the western Indian Ocean throughout the first half of the nineteenth century. Muscat was the base on which rested British influence in the Persian Gulf. Similarly Zanzibar constituted the nucleus of future commercial expansion in Africa. The award was therefore designed to meet the requirements of British policy under the changed circumstances of the mid-nineteenth century, and in the light of the exposed inadequacies of Omani political structure. If it was a revolution, it was one that established not the independence of Zanzibar but the paramountcy of Britain over both Zanzibar and Oman. Hereafter, every Sultan of Zanzibar had to be approved by the British Consul.

Increasing British dominance in the affairs of the Omani kingdom had undoubtedly aroused French concern, but British colonial historians, relying almost exclusively on Rigby's obviously partisan accounts, have tended to exaggerate the French role and objectives. When the French warship *Cordelière* arrived in Zanzibar soon after Thuwaini's expedition had been turned back, Commodore de Langle and the French Consul protested strongly that the British had no right to interfere in the dispute, and they tried to reconcile Majid and Barghash, and even to mediate between Majid and Thuwaini. When the Zanzibar harbour was suddenly crowded with four British and two French warships, de Langle agreed that the succession dispute was 'not affairs for ships of war to interfere with', and he undertook mutually to reduce them to one small vessel for each side. On 4 June 1859, Napoleon III wrote to Majid offering condolence on his father's death and congratulating him on his succession. In any case, contrary to Rigby's accusations, the Coghlan Commission found no evidence for any French conspiracy with Thuwaini to unseat Majid.[52]

However, when the British expressed concern about a missionary institution being constructed in Zanzibar by the Bishop of Réunion, alleging it to be a 'large barrack', the French decided to bury the ghost of British fears by offering to enter into a formal engagement to respect the independence of Zanzibar. Their main interest was in Madagascar and the Comoro Islands. On the other hand, having established their paramountcy at Zanzibar and Oman, the British could not, and at this time did not wish to, ask for more than the recognition of the new status quo. On 10 March 1862, therefore, the two powers signed the Anglo-French Declaration:

> Her Majesty the Queen of the United Kingdom of Great Britain and Ireland and His Majesty the Emperor of the French, taking into consideration the importance of maintaining the independence of His Highness the Sultan of Muscat and His Highness the Sultan of Zanzibar, have thought it right to engage reciprocally to respect the independence of these Sovereigns.[53]

This was the final act in the dismemberment of the Omani kingdom: it had now been given international recognition. The formal independence of Zanzibar had been recognised without diminishing the immense power of the British consuls at Zanzibar. The first phase of the colonial partition of the commercial empire had thus been played out.

The nationalist reaction: accession of Barghash

There was an inevitable reaction to the assertion of British paramountcy in both Oman and Zanzibar, and a desire to reunite the kingdom that had been torn asunder by Canning's knife. The amputation of the richer colony had deprived Oman of an important source of revenue and weakened the mercantile ruling class at Muscat. Ignored economically as the Busaidi dynasty turned its attention to East Africa and relied on Indian financiers and merchants, militarily as it rested its power on Baluchi and Hadhrami mercenaries in place of the former tribal levies, and politically as it depended increasingly on the British government to buttress its authority in place of the tribal and popular consensus, many Omanis supported the Mutawwa movement to reknit the country on a new basis. But the clock of history could not be turned back. The preceding history of Omani involvement in international trade and politically with the

British had created powerful compradorial constituencies. In Oman they were weakened by the seccession of Zanzibar and were repeatedly challenged by the fundamentalists, leading to a period of economic stagnation and political instability. In the more secular mercantile atmosphere of Zanzibar, on the other hand, they were more entrenched.

What did threaten the stability of these constituencies in Zanzibar were not so much the religious revivalists but the British, who were undermining their economic well-being by unleashing the anti-slavery campaign, and subverting their political integrity by asserting British supremacy. The Omani revivalists and the Zanzibari nationalists briefly came together in a common cause against the British, during Barghash's rebellion in 1859, and with his accession in 1870. But apart from the inherent instability of this alliance of convenience, the combination provoked stiff British reaction. For it was seen in the context of a much wider Muslim response to Western pressures in the Near East. Hence the British determination not to allow it to gain a foothold whether at Zanzibar or Oman, although the method in the case of the former appeared in the guise of a humanitarian crusade against the slave trade.

The Mutawwa movement was led by religious fundamentalists who ignored existing tribal alignments and sought to produce religious and political solidarity among the mass of the tribesmen by emphasising the fundamental tenets of the Ibadhi sect. They attempted to revive the Imamate which Seyyid Said had renounced in favour of the more secular concept of the Sultanate. In 1868 Thuwaini's son Salim was overthrown by Azzan b. Qais, who belonged to another branch of the Busaidi dynasty. He was thoroughly committed to the movement, adopted the title of Imam, and tried to exclude British influence from Muscat.[54]

The movement first appeared in Zanzibar in 1859 when one of its joint leaders, Saleh b. Ali Al Harthi, who owned large sugar and clove plantations, participated in Barghash's rebellion.[55] When Majid died in 1870 its local adherents first contemplated an interregnum to give Azzan time to come from Muscat, but they ultimately made a pact with Barghash, who shared their distaste for British domination if not in full measure their religious zeal. Rigby, as we have seen, had played a direct role in crushing his rebellion and had sent him into exile in Bombay. When he was allowed to return in 1861, he was forced to live in seclusion. Although he caused no trouble, he must have chafed at Majid's submissiveness to the British Consul, but he seems to have kept these feelings to himself. In 1868 John Kirk, who had known him for some time, wrote that 'Barghash is now a very intelligent liberal man, outspoken and quick, but a man of energy and very well disposed towards us.'[56]

When it became clear on 7 October 1870 that Majid was dying, British Consul Churchill moved quickly to demonstrate his kingmaking powers.

He invited Barghash to the consulate where he offered him British support in return for concessions on a new treaty to limit the slave trade which the Foreign Office had proposed. That a foreign power should thus intervene and impose conditions on succession even before Majid had breathed his last must have been galling to the prince. But, according to Kirk, Barghash said he knew well that the future was in the hands of the British Consulate, and he assured Churchill that, should he succeed in his candidature, he would do all in his power to obtain the requested treaty 'and even more'. Churchill cheerfully wrote to Bombay the day after Majid's death that 'the decided attitude of this Agency with regard to the succession of Seyyid Barghash has closed the mouths of many who were inclined to reject his candidature . . . while the Prince was made to understand that he himself had no chance if Her Majesty's Government were against him'.[57]

The proconsul had exceeded his brief, for he had committed his government without even consulting his superiors. The Governor of Bombay did not object to the assertion of British power in Zanzibar so much as to the choice of the candidate. Majid's old ally, Turki, who was equally subservient to the British, was then in exile in Bombay while Oman was in the hands of Azzan. Bombay argued that Turki could establish his claim to the throne 'on the ground of seniority', although that was not an accepted principle of Omani constitutional practice. It considered Churchill's action in lending his support so actively to Barghash to have been 'injudicious and precipitate'.[58]

In fact Churchill regretted his action long before hie received the rebuke from Bombay. Whatever may have been Barghash's motive in giving the alleged undertaking, he did not wish to see himself as a British-appointed Sultan. When Churchill sent Kirk to him a day after his formal recognition as Sultan to discuss the slave trade treaty, which was likely to prove extremely unpopular with his subjects, Barghash denied having made any such pledge. He added: 'even if the matter referred to at the time were in my hands, I would not have promised you its fulfilment before calling together the great men of the state from all parts of the country and taking their advice, and was this possible when my brother Majid was still alive?'[59] Barghash was reiterating an important Omani constitutional principle that the Sultan was not some absolute 'oriental despot', a concept sometimes fixed in Western minds and applied indiscriminately to all Eastern potentates, but *primus inter pares* among a collection of tribal *shaikhs*. This had been brought out by the Zanzibar-Muscat Commission but without registering on the mind of the British Consul; and it was brought out again during the subsequent negotiations on the new slave trade treaty.

But the imperious Churchill had no time for such constitutional niceties. He immediately drafted a dispatch to Bombay:

His Excellency the Governor will judge from this how little the new Sultan can be relied upon and how desirable it would be to unseat him on the first pretext. Seyyid Turki . . . could dispute the right of succession: but he should come here, if at all, with English influence to back him. I am now firmly convinced that nothing short of force will induce the present fanatical party in power to fulfil the concessions made by Seyyid Majid with reference to the Slave Trade, and I venture to submit that the sooner strong measures are adopted with them, the better.[60]

Churchill attributed Barghash's change of attitude to the Mutawwa faction which had become influential with the accession of the new Sultan. Its leaders set about reforming the state and reducing British influence. They purged several *shaikhs*; some were degraded, others imprisoned, and the properties of many were confiscated. They tried to clean up the judicial system, which, even by British accounts, was thoroughly corrupt under Majid. They annulled judicial decisions taken by Majid and his *kadhis* wherever they departed from Ibadhi law, and appointed new *kadhis*. Most seriously for the British, the Sultan issued a proclamation which sought to eject Indians from the plantations and prohibit them from trading outside the precinct of Zanzibar city. The last measure may have been directed as much against the British, who had established their suzerainty over the Indians, as against the merchant and moneylending class to which the Arab landowning class had become heavily indebted. The proclamation contravened the treaty of commerce between Zanzibar and Britain which allowed British subjects freedom to trade, purchase, sell or hire land or houses in the dominions of the Sultan. The British consul was instructed by London to inform Barghash that 'such an infraction of the treaty will not be tolerated.' The proclamation was never enforced.[61]

Relations with the British deteriorated rapidly over the next couple of months. In November Churchill took Majid's former *wazir*, Sulaiman b. Ali, under consular protection and sent him off to Bombay. Sulaiman had taken the field against Barghash in 1859 and had fostered friendly relations with the British under Majid. As such, he felt his life might be in danger. The sovereign of Zanzibar must have been furious at such an intervention between him and his subject, although the British justified it under the extra-territorial clause of the treaty, having taken him into consular employ. Barghash in turn, while accepting the treaties and conventions signed by his predecessors, refused to recognise any measures Majid had taken to restrict the slave trade unilaterally, and bluntly rejected consideration of any new treaty, remarking that 'the one actually in existence, and the trouble resulting therefrom is quite enough for us and more than enough.' Churchill retorted that Barghash's predecessors had 'never complained of the weight of England's friendship', and asked if his government was to conclude that 'the presence of a British agent at Zanzibar can lead to no further good results?' Nerves were so frayed on both sides that Barghash turned to Germany for protection, but that country was still too preoccupied with events in Europe to think of adventures in Africa.[62]

British influence at Zanzibar had never been at so low an ebb since the early 1840s when Said had found the then newly appointed British Consul Hamerton unbearable. The strained relations were not merely due to personal differences between Barghash and Churchill. Kirk, who was to emerge later as an astute conciliator, expressed himself equally strongly when he wrote that 'the old traditions of Zanzibar are rudely disturbed by a prince who for his own ends has attached himself to an ultra-fanatic party. If they had their way, we should all be banished the kingdom.' And in 1871 Barghash told Kirk in quite strong terms that 'this Sultanate neither belongs to foreigners nor did I get it from their hands. It was left to us by our fathers and grandfathers and I came to it by the will of the people.'[63] But Barghash may have particularly resented the imperious character of Churchill, who was then quite sick and was in fact forced to leave Zanzibar within two months. Churchill may have reacted bitterly at his miscalculation of Barghash and the rebuff he had received, realising that his time was running out. In any case, a change of tactics by his successor, Kirk, had the effect of freezing the conflict over the new treaty until he could receive instructions from London. Barghash's attitude changed dramatically and he quietly abandoned the restrictions on Indians operating outside Zanzibar city. By March 1871 Kirk could write that the Sultan had become 'much more tractable and pleasant to deal with in business matters than the last', although he suspected his motives.[64]

The change in Barghash's attitude may have been related to his relations with the Mutawwa faction's reunificationist and fundamentalist aspirations. Early in 1871 he received letters from Mutawwa supporters in Oman which questioned his independence. 'If you bind yourself to follow the *Imam* [Azzan], he will continue the kingdom to you; but, if you deny him, he will take it from you. Your wealth cannot protect you from him, nor your people save you.' Such a threat to his sovereignty may have aroused self-interest in Barghash, who sent these letters to Kirk. The British Consul tried to fan these flames by suggesting that the Imam's claim to dispose of Zanzibar 'will soon be followed by more substantial demands.'[65] Soon thereafter Azzan was driven out of Muscat by Turki, and Barghash began to free himself from Mutawwa influence. A new modus vivendi began to develop between Kirk and the Sultan as the latter tried to consolidate his position.

Plate 31   Seyyid Barghash bin Said, Ruler of Zanzibar, 1870–88, with his advisers. Tharia Topan, Indian merchant and custom master, stands behind him

The slave trade under attack

The British demand for a new slave trade treaty, the rejection of which by Barghash had led to strained relations with the British Consul, grew out of a claim that the old policy of restricting the trade had failed. This policy had been based on the Moresby Treaty of 1822, which forbade the export of slaves to the south of Cape Delgado; and on the Hamerton Treaty of 1845, which made illegal the export of slaves to the north of Lamu. These treaties permitted British warships to capture slave dhows found beyond these limits, but they left the trade within the Sultan's African dominions between Lamu and Tungi undisturbed. In 1850 Said had given permission to British warships to 'enter bays, creeks and rivers' south of Kilwa to destroy alleged 'barracoons', etc. (see pp. 204–5). And finally, in 1864, Majid issued a proclamation forbidding all slave trade during the monsoon season from 1 January to 1 May when the 'Northern Arabs' were most active, to prevent them from exporting slaves to Arabia. These measures were apparently effective: Hamerton believed in 1850 that the volume of the foreign slave trade had been cut down by as much as 80 per cent.[66]

Though some of the subjects' revenues as well as those of the Sultan himself were affected by these measures, it is remarkable that all these concessions relating to the export of slaves to areas outside East Africa were granted with little resistance on the part of the Sultans, although they often exaggerated the financial losses as a way of obtaining return favours from the British and deterring them from making further demands (see p. 47). It is clear that, with the transformation of the slave sector from one that had thrived on the export of slaves to one that exported slave-produced commodities, the Zanzibar authorities were decreasingly interested in the moribund foreign slave trade. They did not wish to defy the British so long as the supply of slaves to their plantations on Zanzibar, Pemba and the Kenya coast was not affected. On the other hand, all attempts to restrict the local slave trade were resolutely resisted even by the pliant Majid. As early as 1861, the British had proposed an additional article to the treaty to prohibit coastwise trade in slaves between the Sultan's ports, including Zanzibar, because it was argued that 'so long as this coast traffic is permitted to continue, it will be impossible for the Sultan's officers or the commanders of British cruisers to prevent slaves from being exported from the Zanzibar territory.' Majid's blunt reply was that it was 'too much to expect that I should agree to a measure which must certainly prove my ruin.' British Consul Playfair agreed that the measure 'must inevitably cause the downfall of his House.'[67] Churchill was instructed to raise the issue again, but Majid's death left Barghash to say no.

But what was the basis for the claim that the policy of restriction had failed? In fact it rested primarily on a failure to grasp the full significance of the transformation of the slave sector. The Select Committee of the House of Commons which had been set up in 1871 began its report by exposing its mental fixation, or ignorance, by saying that 'the slave trade in negroes from the East Coast of Africa is now almost entirely confined to a trade between the dominions of Zanzibar on the one hand, and the coast of Arabia and Persia and the island of Madagascar on the other hand, the principal and by far the largest portion of the traffic going in the former direction.' It went on to allege that between 1867 and 1869, 116 dhows were captured carrying 2,645 slaves 'while dhows carrying 37,000 slaves must have evaded capture, making the captures about 6.6%.'[68] It is not clear how that figure of 37,000 was arrived at.

Table 6.1 *Slave captures, 1868–70*

Year	No. of dhows captured	No. of slaves freed	Average no. of slaves per dhow
1868	66	1,097	17
1869	32	1,117	35
1870	11	958	87
Total	109	3,172	
Average	36	1,057	29

Source: Lloyd, p. 278.

The committee, however, never stopped to consider whether there was enough shipping to carry that many slaves. Between 1868 and 1870, 109 dhows were captured carrying an average number of slaves which rose from 17 to 87 as the threat of capture grew and the trade became more specialised (see Table 6.1). Admittedly a large number of dhows destroyed in earlier years carried no slaves, but it is also true that by 1870 only 3 per cent of the dhows carried any slaves. In that year Commodore Heath laid a wide-spun web to search every dhow that passed by, stationing warships all along the south Arabian coast, near Socotra and down the African coast. About 400 dhows were boarded, but only 11 were found carrying slaves. Even at the highest average of 87 slaves, but with only 3 per cent of the dhows carrying slaves, it would have required a total fleet of more than 5,000 dhows to carry the nearly 13,000 slaves a year claimed by the Select Committee to have been sent to Arabia. Such a fleet did not exist.[69]

Table 6.1 also reveals a remarkable stability in the number of slaves captured during these three years of most active anti-slavery activities, averaging just over 1,000 slaves per annum. In view of Heath's confidence in the effectiveness of his blockade in 1870, it is quite likely that the number of slaves exported to Arabia by the 1860s was much closer to this

Plate 32   Slave dhow chasing in the Indian Ocean

Plate 33   Slaves captured by H.M.S. London, 1870s

Table 6.2 *The East African slave trade, 1811–73*

| Year | Exports from Kilwa | | | Imports into Zanzibar | | |
	To Zanzibar	Elsewhere	Total	From elsewhere	Total	Value (MT$)
1811					8,000[a]	
1819	13,000[b]					
1822					8,000[c]	
1833					6,500[d]	
1841					9,000[e]	
1844			15,000[f]			
1846			9,000[g]		13,000[g]	
1847			7,000[h]			
1850			11,000[i]			
Mid-1850s					14,000[j]	
1859	15,000[k]			4,000[k]	19,000[k]	260,000[k]
1860/1					19,000[l]	
1861/2					14,000[l]	120,000[l]
1862/3	13,000[m]	5,500[m]	18,500[m]		12,000[l]	100,000[l]
1863/4	14,000[m]	3,500[m]	17,500[m]		14,000[n]	140,000[n]
1864/5	13,821[m]	3,000[m]	16,821[m]		15,000[o]	150,000[o]
1865/6	18,344[m]	4,000[m]	22,344[m]		13,534[p]	150,000[p]
1866/7	17,538[m]	4,500[m]	22,038[m]	1,018[q]	20,576[q]	
1867/8	9,350[s]	3,000[r]	12,350[s]			270,000[t]
1868/9	11,944[s]	3,000[r]	14,944[s]			
1869/70		3,000[r]			17,500[u]	
1870/1		3,000[r]				
1871/2	14,392[v]			3,000[v]	17,392[v]	
1872/3	14,721[w]			408[w]	15,129[w]	
Average	14,210	3,611	17,785	2,129	15,928	170,000

Table 6.3 *Redistribution of slaves in East Africa, 1866/7–1872/3*

Year	Retained in Zanzibar	Pemba	Mrima	Mombasa	Malindi	Lamu	Total
1866/7	11,753[q]	2,389[q]	338[q]	841[q]	217[q]	5,038[q]	8,823[q]
1867/8							7,819[r]
1868/9						1,100[y]	7,855[r]
1869/70							5,009[r]
1870/1		1,060[r]	151[r]	624[r]		2,637[r]	4,472[r]
1871/2				1,600[z]		7,792[z]	8,462[v]
1872/3		3,097[x]	547[x]		5,737[x]		9,381[x]
Average		2,182	345	1,094		5,522	7,403

Notes and Sources for Table 6.2 and 6.3

a. Smee, in Burton (1872), Vol. 2, pp. 492–3, 512, says 6,000–10,000 were exported from Zanzibar. The mean figure has been adopted.
b. Albrand, quoted in Alpers (1975), p. 235, says he was sceptical of the figure in view of the 'miserable' condition of Kilwa.
c. Moresby to Bombay, 23 September 1822, MA, 20/1822, pp. 254–7; Nicholls, p. 207n.
d. Ruschenberger, Vol. 1, p. 140, says 6,000–7,000 slaves were imported into Zanzibar.
e. Hamerton to Bombay, 13 July 1841, MA, 78/1841–2, pp. 218–23, says 8,000–10,000 slaves were annually imported into Zanzibar. The strong urge to successively exaggerate appears clearly in Hamerton who says that the average in 1842 was 15,000; that it ranged between 11,000 and 15,000; and in 1844 says that the average over the previous ten years was 20,000. Hamerton to Bombay, 2 January 1842, PRO, FO 54/5; Hamerton to FO, 21 May 1842, PRO, FO 84/425; same to same, 2 January 1844, PRO, FO 84/540.
f. Krapf, quoted in Martin and Ryan (1977), pp. 74, 87 n. 13.
g. Loarer, 'Esclaves', ANSOM, OI, 5/23/5, gives a range of between 12,000 and 14,000 for the period before 1847; 8,000–10,000 exported from Kilwa and 1,000–1,200 from Lindi. See Nicholls, pp. 207, 374. American Consul Ward gives a figure of 15,000.
h. Krapf, quoted in Alpers (1975), p. 250, was told in Mombasa that about 7,000 Yaos were sold in Kilwa in 1847.
i. Krapf (1860), p. 423, says 10,000–12,000 passed yearly through Kilwa. This seems to be a more sober published estimate than the unpublished one in note f above.
j. Burton (1860), Vol. 2, p. 377, quoting Hamerton who gave an average of 14,000 and a range of between 9,000 and 20,000. Burton (1872), Vol. 1, pp. 464–5, gives an average of 14,000–15,000.
k. Rigby to Secretary of State for India, 1 May 1860, PRO, FO 54/17; Russell, p. 333.
l. Playfair to Bombay, 1 May 1864, MA, 54/1864, pp. 16–33; *PP*, 1865/33, p. 176.
m. Churchill to Bombay, 4 March 1868, PRO, FO 84/1922; quoted in Burton (1872), Vol. 1, p. 347.
n. Playfair to FO, 1 January 1865, PRO, FO 54/22.
o. Seward to Bombay, [1865], MA, 73/1866, pp. 7–25; *PP*, 1867/67, pp. 284, 288; Ropes to Seward, 31 December 1865, NAW, T100/5, gives the value at $240,000.
p. Seward to Bombay, 20 September 1866, PRO, FO 84/1279, says the import duty on slaves amounted to MT$33,834. Churchill to Bombay, 4 March 1868, PRO, FO 84/1292, gives the duty per slave as MT$2.50. The number of slaves is calculated accordingly from these figures.
q. Seward to FO [3/1862], PRO, FO 84/1279, gives 19,588 slaves imported from Kilwa in 1866/7, while Churchill gives 17,538 as exported from Kilwa to Zanzibar. The difference may be accounted for by a portion of the 4,500 said to have been exported from Kilwa to other places or may be due to a clerical error.
r. Kirk to FO, 27 June 1871, PRO, FO 84/1344. The total re-export from Zanzibar for 1866/7 is given as 10,181, but Seward gives the raw data from which the breakdown has been worked out, and the total amounts to 8,823 which has been accepted. Kirk also adds that the total re-exports do not include direct exports to Lamu and other northern ports, on which a duty of MT$4 was paid, and estimated by the Custom Master at 3,000 p.a. He also estimates contraband traffic at no less than 3,000 p.a. But only six months earlier the Custom Master had assured him that few slaves were smuggled out without his knowledge. Kirk to FO, 1 February 1870, PRO, FO 84/1325.
s. Kirk to FO, 1 February 1870, PRO, FO 84/1325. 'Report from the Select Committee on Slave Trade', 4 August 1871, pp. vii, 78, quoted in Martin and Ryan, p. 74. Colomb, p. 34, is probably giving figures for 1868/9 when he says that 12,000 were exported to Zanzibar and 3,000 elsewhere.
t. 'Administrative Report of the Zanzibar Agency, 1870', *PP*, Vol. 91, p. 268.
u. Burton (1860), Vol. 2, p. 377.
v. Kirk to FO, 25 January 1872, PRO, FO 84/1357.
w. Cummings to Admiralty, 10 January 1873, PRO, FOCP, 4207, p. 226.
x. Kirk to FO, 13 January 1873, *PP*, 1874/62, ST8(1874), p. 7.
y. Colomb, p. 455.
z. Berg (1971), p. 341.

average than the wild estimates of the Select Committee. American Consul Ropes estimated the value of slave exports to Arabia in 1864–5 at MT\$10,000 which, at the average price of between MT\$8.50 and MT\$10 used by contemporary British consuls in their trade reports, would seem to confirm such an average.[70] Curiously neither the Select Committee nor most later historians have recognised the significance of these statistics. They were looking for a monster and failed to notice the mouse; they overlooked the fundamental transformation of the slave sector.

The real giant they refused to see was the internal consumption of slave labour within East Africa. Apart from some scattered statistics for the first half of the nineteenth century, some very precise figures are available from custom house records at Zanzibar and Kilwa from the 1860s which expose the real character of the slave sector of the economy at that time. They consist of customs returns for the export of slaves from Kilwa to Zanzibar and elsewhere for seven consecutive years from 1862–3 to 1868–9. We also have a record of the total number of slaves imported into Zanzibar from Kilwa and elsewhere throughout the 1860s, and a breakdown of the distribution of slaves from Zanzibar for some of the years. This is the most reliable set of statistics for the 'internal' slave trade before 1873 when it was still legal. Obviously such figures cannot show the number of slaves smuggled to Arabia, mostly from the northern ports which are covered by the statistics; they also do not take into account slaves imported duty-free by members of the ruling dynasty for their plantations on Zanzibar, Pemba and the Kenya coast, estimated by a British Consul at about 3,500, which has to be added to the customs totals. Finally, they do not include slaves from ports other than Kilwa, which was the main port, who did not pass through Zanzibar, the main slave entrepôt, but the numbers must have been small.[71]

An analysis of Table 6.2 shows that an annual average of about 17,800 slaves were exported from Kilwa. Of these about 14,200 went to Zanzibar and 3,600 elsewhere. In addition, Zanzibar received an annual average of about 2,100 slaves from other points along the African coast. The total number of slaves reaching Zanzibar during this period amounted to about 15,900 each year. If we add to this figure the 3,600 annually exported from Kilwa to points other than Zanzibar, and the 3,500 imported duty-free by members of the ruling dynasty, we arrive at a grand total of 23,000 per annum.

Reliable statistics for the distribution of the slaves from Zanzibar are available only from the mid-1860s although they are more scattered, and the averages are therefore based on fewer observations in some places. We do have figures for total re-export of slaves from Zanzibar for seven consecutive years, giving an annual average of about 7,400 (see Table 6.3). Of these about 2,200 went annually to Pemba, 1,100 to Mombasa,

Takaungu and Malindi, and 5,500 to Lamu from where a number were undoubtedly smuggled to the Benadir coast where there was an expansion of agriculture during this period, and even to Arabia. Kirk suggests that annually 3,000 went to the Benadir; but a sizeable number was also retained in the Lamu region where there was also an increase in production of sesame for export to France and Germany (see p. 71).[72] To the total re-export from Zanzibar must be added the 3,600 annually exported directly from Kilwa to these ports, and perhaps a small portion of the slaves transported duty-free by members of the ruling dynasty who had plantations in Pemba and Malindi as well.[73] This gives an annual total of somewhat more than 11,000 going north of Zanzibar. On the other hand, deducting average re-exports from total imports into Zanzibar, it is possible to calculate the annual number of slaves retained at about 8,500, to which should be added those imported by the Busaidi, giving an annual total of about 12,000 retained in Zanzibar (see Tables 6.3 and 6.4).

Table 6.4   *The East African slave trade in the 1860s: summary*

Average import of slaves into Zanzibar	15,900
Average export of slaves from Kilwa to places other than Zanzibar	3,600
Import of slaves duty-free by the Busaidi	3,500
Total East African slave trade	23,000
Average number of slaves retained in Zanzibar	8,500
Import of duty-free slaves by the Busaidi	3,500
Total retained in Zanzibar	12,000
Total number of slaves re-exported from Zanzibar	7,400
Direct export of slaves from Kilwa	3,600
Total exported to ports north of Zanzibar	11,000
Redistribution of slaves from Zanzibar to:	
Pemba	2,200
Lamu	5,500
Mombasa, Takaungu and Malindi	1,100
Mrima (Tanga, Pangani)	350
Total	9,150

Note: The different totals do not always coincide with each other because the data for different years are sometimes derived from different sources, and they vary in frequency of observations, and therefore of reliability. This summary is intended to give only an approximate picture of the trade.

The question that remains is whether Zanzibar could have absorbed the number of slaves given in Tables 6.2, 6.3 and 6.4, or whether many of them were later smuggled out to Arabia. Apart from agricultural labour to produce annually about 300,000 *fraselas* of cloves[74] as well as coconuts and sugar, it must be remembered that there was an open end to the slave bag of Zanzibar. Some of the slaves passed progressively out of agricultural labour to supervisory, trading or domestic roles in the city, and even to freedom. The British consular doctor, James Christie, who had considerable experience of conditions at Zanzibar and was the author of an incisive article on slavery there in the 1870s, describes a sizeable class of 'wazalia' born in slavery who occupied a much higher position in the slave population. Burton gives a similar picture of members of this class who were often entrusted with responsible jobs, such as agents in caravans going into the interior, and were sometimes manumitted as an act of piety. Seyyid Said manumitted all his domestic slaves on his death. Christie believed that in 1870 there were as many free or freed Africans as the indigenous people of Zanzibar, including the more than 5,000 freed by Rigby from Indian ownership. With prosperity, some slaves were absorbed on the smaller agricultural plots of the Hadimu and Tumbatu people of Zanzibar, or into the force of nearly 1,000 domestic servants of Indian and European residents of the city. Others formed part of the 10,000 to 15,000-strong class of day labourers, porters and artisans in the city employed by American, European and Indian merchants to clean orchilla weed and gum copal, prepare copra and transport goods; these shared their pay with their masters.[75]

In 1870 Kirk worked out what he called the 'normal' demand for slaves and the 'exceptional' demand to replace those who had died during the 1869–70 cholera epidemic. Elsewhere he had taken an average mortality of 10 per cent for the slave population, which seems to be quite reasonable.[76] But if that were applied to his estimate of 'normal' demand it would give the slave population of Zanzibar at 20,000 which is far too low for that time. F. Albrand and E. Burgess had given a figure of 15,000 to 17,000 slaves in Zanzibar in 1819–39. With the 'clove mania' of the 1840s, the number of slaves must have increased steeply. The American trader, Horace B. Putnam, put it at over 60,000 in 1847 and Kirk himself at 70,000 in 1870.[77] Such a population by this time was therefore capable of absorbing a large proportion of the slaves annually retained in Zanzibar, although a certain number of them were undoubtedly smuggled north.

It is not clear why this aspect of the slave sector was systematically underplayed by many who had a very intimate knowledge of the situation, such as Rigby and Kirk. It may be that recognition of this vast internal dimension of the trade would have reduced their ability to interfere legally in the internal trade of the Zanzibar dominions; or it might have exposed the hypocrisy of fulminating against the slave trade while continuing the trade in slave-produced commodities such as cloves, sesame and copal. Whatever may have been the reason, the British conjured up visions of massive torrents of slaves flowing to Arabia, and unleashed the British navy on Arab shipping.

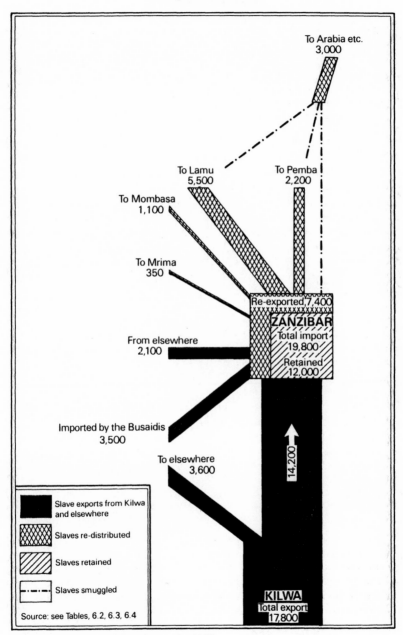

Map 6.1   The East African slave trade, 1860s

The mental make-up of the British navy can be gauged from what W.G. Devereux, one of the most experienced, and the most honest, of the 'slave catchers' in the Indian Ocean, said:

> We are not to be over particular in the reading of antiquated slave treaties, but are to pass with the mythical coach-and-four through their many wide provisos . . . to carry out our little piratical intentions, and do the John Bull to our heart's content at the expense of 'Jack Arab'.[78]

Under the British system of granting bounty money, £5 for each slave or £4 per ton for vessels with only a few or no slaves, the captors had a pecuniary interest in their 'crusade':

> Fortunately within the last few years captains have been appointed to this little squadron whose private fortunes have needed a little repair; at all events, not deterred them from making a little more prize money.[79]

Moreover, there were no mixed commissions, or before 1867 a Vice-Admiralty Court closer than Aden, Bombay, Mauritius or Cape Town where the accused, if they knew their rights, could defend themselves. Even if these distant courts were to pronounce against the captors, dhow owners were often satisfied with compensation that amounted to only one-third of the tonnage money the warships received for such dhows.[80] In the words of Devereux:

> every detained vessel appears to be unfit to proceed [to the port of adjudication], is formally surveyed, formally reported unfit, and very informally scuttled or burnt . . . The captain of the ship is judge, jury and executor.[81]

Without defence witnesses, adjudication proceedings were equally simple and informal.

Under such a 'system of indiscriminate and careless destruction of dhows,' said Devereux, 'I am sure that many a legal trader is unjustly captured':

> I should be sorry to put on paper what I know . . . The name of the British sailor is sadly compromised by acts which can come under no other name than piracy. I believe many a man has been hanged for doing far less.[82]

Between 1861 and 1863, out of forty-three dhows captured, thirty-eight were not carrying slaves. Even some of those that had a slave cargo were captured within the then legal area between Lamu and Kilwa. British Consul Pelly believed that, of a dozen captures by Devereux in 1861, only one was engaged in illegal traffic.[83] A dhow with a valuable cargo of spices and rice, and with four Africans who spoke Arabic, was destroyed, but it

232

flew the Turkish flag, and the Turkish authorities were able to extract a compensation of £5,771 at Mauritius,[84] although this was an exception.

In 1868 and 1869, ninety-eight dhows were destroyed, but how many were guilty? The *Star* destroyed fourteen dhows at Brave and ten at Merka at a time when it was impossible for any dhow to reach Arabia. Very few slaves were taken from them, and of these many were domestic slaves; thirty-six were free men who were later returned to Zanzibar from Bombay. But all the dhows were condemned at Aden. The *Daphne*, the sister ship of the *Star*, had visited these dhows at Merka only a short time previously and had found all free of suspicion, except one which was destroyed. The owners of two of them, a sister of the Sultan of Zanzibar and a British Indian subject, were able to obtain compensation because of their positions, but the Foreign Office refused to order a review of the rest of the cases.[85]

In 1869 the *Nymphe* captured sixteen dhows to the south of Zanzibar which were as usual destroyed, being unfit to be brought to Zanzibar where a Vice-Admiralty Court had finally been established at the end of 1867. Kirk gave decisions in favour of the British captors for ten dhows, and against them in the case of two. He ordered a compensation of £5,539 which was enough to unnerve the commander of the *Nymphe*, Captain Meara. On the pretext that he must proceed to Seychelles while the cases for the remaining vessels were still pending, he obtained their papers and went to Aden where he got them all condemned. In the case of at least three of them Kirk could see no proof that they were engaged in the slave trade. The Foreign Office admitted that bounties could not be awarded for them; but there was no talk of compensation.[86]

The British warships, moreover, were accused of, and Devereux confessed about, indiscriminate looting of Arab property in these dhows:

> by the vast heap [of booty] collected I should think that hundreds of Arabs have been divested of their finery . . . This irregular manner of looting is disgraceful.[87]

The destruction of Arab lives and property naturally enraged the local population, and led Barghash to resist any new treaty to restrict the slave trade. It also threatened the Church Missionary Society station near Mombasa and even the life of the British Consul at Zanzibar.[88]

The threat to Zanzibar's coasting trade was even more grave. Several hundred dhows were destroyed during the decade. W.H. Wylde, the head of the Slave Trade Department at the Foreign Office, pointed out correctly that 'the system on which our naval officers are now acting . . . would not be tolerated for a month by any European power.'[89] But the commercial empire was unable to protest or effectively protect its shipping. That protection was sought from the French 'tricolore' from as early as 1863, and the French looked forward to the day when their flag would fly over the whole coasting trade of East Africa.[90]

Plate 34   Zanzibar town and harbour after the hurricane, 1872

This hope was frustrated only by the destruction of most of the remaining dhows still under the Zanzibar flag in the hurricane of 1872. Although Zanzibar is outside the normal track of tropical cyclones, a freak hurricane swept across the island and touched the southern tip of Pemba and the mainland near Bagamoyo. Zanzibar harbour must have been full of dhows at this time just prior to their departure with the south-west monsoon. Almost all the vessels were destroyed: 150 Arab and Indian dhows were sunk or wrecked, many of them full of cargo, valued at about MT$600,000. All but one European vessel were wrecked. And the whole of the Sultan's navy went down save one ship which had just previously left for Mombasa; Kirk estimated his losses at MT$400,000. Almost all the huts and many of the stone houses in the city were destroyed or damaged.[91]

But the destruction of Zanzibar's agriculture was even more devastating. 'Not one third of the coconut and clove trees are left standing,' Kirk wrote; on some plantations less than 2 per cent of the trees survived, and he estimated that on the great majority only 15 per cent withstood the force of the hurricane. As new trees would not begin to bear fruit for seven to eight years, the loss was incalculable. American and French observers reported a year later that clove production had declined from about 300,000 *fraselas* to 70,000 *fraselas*.[92] Pemba was barely touched, and the wholesale destruction of the Zanzibar plantations was to give an

234

impetus to clove-growing in the sister island which thereafter emerged as the major producer. The landowning class in Zanzibar was economically ruined and demoralised. Coming so soon after the cholera epidemic of 1869–70 that had wiped out nearly one-third of the population of Zanzibar, including entire establishments of slaves, and the war of 1860–5 in Unyamwezi which had interrupted the ivory trade (see p. 193), the effect of the hurricane was intensified: the landowners did not have the energy or the economic wherewithal to start replanting their plantations, although Barghash used all his energy to persuade and even force them to do just that.[93] This was the moment chosen by the British to abolish all trade in slaves.

'I have come to dictate'

The British demand for the total suppression of the slave trade can be seen, in one sense, as the culmination of their crusade during the 1860s. R.J. Gavin, however, argues that the popular campaign had been at a low ebb in England since 1862. Part of the reason was the greater distance, compared with the Atlantic trade, of the East African slave trade from the perception of the English public and their ignorance of it, except through the reports of the popular hero David Livingstone. Gavin suggests that the revitalised campaign against the slave trade in the early 1870s should instead be seen within the larger geopolitical and strategic framework of the sharpening conflict shaping up in the Muslim world, under the impact of European ideas and economic penetration, between the westernising Khedivate of Egypt and the Sultanate at Istanbul, which developed as a centre of Muslim reaction. Muslim revivalism, in its specific manifestation in Muscat and Zanzibar with the Mutawwa movement, threatened the maritime frontiers of British India. It undermined the policy which had been traditional since the 1820s in Bombay; this had been based on alliances with the emergent commercially progressive forces to maintain British influence without formal control. The whole system was cemented by treaties with the chiefs of the Persian Gulf and Zanzibar, and propped up at one corner by the British anti-slavery crusade.[94]

The task of formulating a new policy under the changed circumstances was transferred to London and to a committee representing the Foreign Office, the India Office, the Colonial Office, and the Admiralty, which was directly involved in the suppression of the slave trade. The committee proposed relieving Zanzibar of the obligation to pay the subsidy to Muscat in return for additional facilities for the suppression of the slave trade; limited slave trade to satisfy Zanzibar's own needs was to be allowed but was to be gradually reduced to nil, because immediate suppression, it was feared, would lead to a revolution. Secondly, the subsidy to Muscat was to be paid jointly by the India Office and the Foreign

Office to buttress Turki who would thus be completely in the hands of the British Indian government. Finally, British influence at Zanzibar was to be enhanced by increasing the consular establishment and encouraging British trade by the inauguration of a subsidised mail steamer service to Zanzibar.[95]

The new policy received its first rebuff at Zanzibar when Barghash refused to discuss the new treaty, but the matter was taken up by the representative of the Indian expansionist school, Sir Bartle Frere, former governor of Bombay and now a member of the Indian Council, who set about whipping up public agitation on the slave trade to achieve British political aims at Zanzibar and Muscat. In 1872 the British government announced its intention to seek the total abolition of the slave trade by sea. To demonstrate the importance and power of the special mission it organised to negotiate a new slave-trade suppression treaty, it appointed Frere to lead it, and he was accompanied to Zanzibar by four warships.[96]

The British case was based essentially on the argument that the policy of restriction of the slave trade had failed. The draft treaty which Frere carried therefore proposed the entire cessation of the export of slaves by sea even within the Sultan's dominions, the closing of all slave markets, and the prohibition of possession of slaves by Indians even when they originated from the 'Protected States'. As an inducement to the Sultan, the British undertook to relieve him of the obligation to pay the subsidy to Muscat, and to protect him against any antagonism that might be provoked by his compliance with British demands.[97] This would thus render him totally dependent on British power.

Barghash based his case largely on the economic and financial consequences of the proposed treaty, coming as it did only shortly after cholera had decimated the slave population of Zanzibar, and the hurricane had devastated the clove and coconut plantations and destroyed the shipping. He and his advisers pleaded for a grace period, or even for 2,000 to 3,000 slaves a year to meet Zanzibar's minimum needs; and they referred to the threat of rebellion. 'A spear is held at each of my eyes,' said Barghash. 'With which shall I choose to be pierced?' His council of *shaikhs* was unanimous in refusing 'to commit suicide'. Frere tried to apply the financial screw by suggesting that Zanzibar would have to pay the subsidy, and that Britain would insist on the same concession on gum copal and ivory from the mainland as had been granted to the French by Majid. But Barghash stood his ground.[98]

Much has been made in British accounts of the events to suggest that the villain in Frere's failure to secure the treaty was the French Consul in Zanzibar. Charles de Vienne had returned to Zanzibar to find the negotiations deadlocked, and Frere alleged that de Vienne had directly encouraged Barghash's resistance. France, however, aimed at a solution leading to effective measures against the slave trade without interfering with Zanzibar's independence, to which she was committed under the 1862 treaty. De Vienne was not alone in suspecting that the British anti-slavery campaign was a calculated device to assert greater control over Zanzibar; the Bishop of Réunion and the Americans at Zanzibar held similar views. The bishop wrote to the French Foreign Ministry that 'the road followed leads most clearly to the taking possession of Zanzibar rather than to the abolition of slavery.' De Vienne therefore withheld total support from the Frere mission until he knew whether the British planned to use force; but he counselled the Sultan against going to Paris to seek French protection. That Barghash was driven to such extremity as to consider protection from another European power – as he had done in 1870 when threatened by Churchill – only highlights the fears he entertained about Zanzibar's independence.[99]

On 13 February 1873, a frustrated Frere wrote to London that the 'wishes of England and a large majority of the civilised nations of the world . . . have been thwarted and treated with marked disrespect.' He left Zanzibar in a huff and proposed a programme of action that would stop the slave trade without the explicit sanction of a treaty. He proposed that the right to transport slaves within the Sultan's dominions sanctioned by the 1845 treaty should be withdrawn and that an embargo should be placed on all Zanzibar custom houses to prevent the passage of slaves. He sent a letter to the British naval commander at Zanzibar ordering him to ignore former instructions and to seize all vessels carrying slaves unless they were domestics accompanying their owners, who must be subjects of the Sultan permanently resident in his dominions. British law officers had no hesitation in declaring that these actions were contrary to the 1845 treaty, infringed the Sultan's independence as guaranteed in the 1862 treaty, and would therefore 'amount to an act of war'. It was argued that, if force was to be used, why should it not be used to obtain the treaty.[100]

The question that the British cabinet faced was whether to reverse Frere's illegal action or to endorse the fait accompli. On 14 May it decided to go to war with Barghash if he refused to sign the treaty, and cabled Kirk to:

> Inform the Sultan that HMG require him to conclude the Treaty as presented to him by Sir Bartle Frere . . . You will state to the Sultan that, if the Treaty . . . is not accepted and signed by him before the arrival of Admiral Cummings, who is ordered to proceed at once to Zanzibar, the British naval force will proceed to blockade the island of Zanzibar.[101]

When Barghash tried to argue that treaties had never been concluded in this way, Kirk bared the teeth of British imperialism: '*I have not come to discuss but to dictate*' (my emphasis). The die of British hegemony had been cast. The Sultan reportedly contemplated escaping to the mainland and continuing the fight from there; there were rumours that he might abandon the throne. He also proposed to go to London to argue his case, but Kirk told him he would not be permitted to leave the island. On 5 June Barghash capitulated. He signed the treaty which provided for a complete abolition of the slave trade, the closing of all slave markets, the protection of all liberated slaves, and the prohibition of Indians from possessing slaves. When the Sultan's proclamation was posted, 'a large crowd assembled at the Custom House and read it, not without emotion',[102] but they submitted, knowing that it was not the voice of the Sultan but the dictate of the paramount power. That was the political significance of the 1873 treaty, and it made manifest the shifting political sands on which the commercial empire had been built.

Notes

1. Coupland (1938), pp. 368-9, 385-6, 423-4, 481-2, 487; Hamerton to Bombay, 3 March 1842, NAI, 29/6/1842-SC-80/82; Bennett and Brooks (eds) (1965), pp. 353-7, 359-60, 381-8, 398; Said to US President, 11 March 1847, Ward to State Dept, 15 June 1848, NAW, T100/2; Said to Ward, 12 March 1847, PRO, FO 54/11; State Dept to Ward, 7 October 1847, NAW, RG 84/Z-C.8.2(i), Instructions, 1834-60. 'Extra-territorial rights' were liable to be abused as they were most noticeably when Churchill took Majid's former *wazir* under British protection in 1870. See p. 220. Coupland (1939), pp. 91-2.
2. Hamerton to Bombay, 13 July 1841, PRO, FO 54/5.
3. Board of Directors to Governor General of India, 29 March 1842, NAI, Indian despatches from the Select Committee; Coupland (1938), pp. 471, 492.
4. Coupland (1938), pp. 488-92.
5. Hamerton to Bombay, 25 October 1849, MA, 94/1850, pp. 41-4; same to same, 28 September 1841, PRO, FO 54/4; Hamerton to Secret Committee, 9 February 1842, PRO, FO 54/5; Kirk's Administrative Report for Zanzibar, 1870, PRO, FO 84/1344; Heskeal to Persian Secretary, 22 February 1856, MA, 93/1856, pp. 43-4; Bennett and Brooks (eds) (1965), pp. 376-8.
6. Said to Cogan, 28 September 1845; Said to FO, AH 27/9/1261, PRO FO 54/7; 'Treaty of Alliance', 4 December 1819, PRO, FOCP, 2314. Hamerton to Bombay, 13 July 1841, MA, 78/1841-2, pp. 218-23.
7. Hamerton to Bombay, 28 September 1841, PRO, FO 54/4; Hamerton to Secret Committee, 9 April 1842, PRO, FO 54/5; Kirk's Administrative Report for Zanzibar, 1870, PRO, FO 84/1344.
8. Hamerton to Bombay, 13 July 1841, PRO, FO 54/5; same to same, 13 July

1841, MA, 78/1841-2, pp. 218-23; same to same, 9 December 1847, Report from the Advocate General, 2 April 1844, NAI, 8/6/1844-SC-24/7; Bennett and Brooks (eds) (1965), pp. 350, 376-8.

9. Hamerton to Wyvill, 8 May 1850, Wyvill to Hamerton, 1 May and 8 June 1850, Commander of the *Castor* to Hamerton, 8 June 1850, Bunce to Hamerton, 11 June 1850, PRO, FO 84/815; Hamerton to Bombay, 5 August 1850, NAI, 20/12/1850-PC-31.

10. Hamerton to Wyvill, 14 June 1850, Hamerton to Bombay, 29 August 1851, Advocate General to Bombay, 13 October 1851, MA, 65/1851, pp. 128-34, 143. His opinion was that there was no legal basis for Hamerton's action. Bennett and Brooks (eds) (1965), pp. 465-6, 474-5, 481.

11. Frere's 'Memo. regarding Banians', 31 March 1873, PRO, FO 84/1391.

12. Rigby to Bombay, 12 July 1861, IOR, L/P&S/9/38, pp. 195-7; Pelly to Bombay, MA, 47/1862, pp. 391-404; Bennett and Brooks (eds) (1965), p. 466.

13. Rigby to Bombay, 1 February 1860, MA, 158/1860, pp. 251-77; Churchill to Bombay, 7 August 1867, pp. 2-33; Various contracts in PM, Waters Papers, IV; Fabens' Ledger, 1844-9, PM, Fabens Papers; Rigby to Bombay, 11 February and 4 September 1860, MA, 159/1860, pp. 219-53, 263-73; NAI: 5/1860-PolA-291; Russell, pp. 86, 95.

14. Churchill to Bombay, 14 August 1868, PRO, FO 84/1292; Playfair's memo., 18 November 1865, PRO, FO 54/22; 'Rules and Regulations', 28 February 1867, PRO, FO 84/1279.

15. Kirk to Bombay, 29 April 1869, MA, 154/1869, pp. 20-6; same to same, 16 August 1869, MA, 152/1869, pp. 65-73.

16. Churchill to Majid, 10 and 16 December 1867, MA, 135/1868, pp. 38-9.

17. Seton-Kerr to Bombay, 6 November 1868, Temple to Bombay, 22 April 1868, Bombay to Foreign Secretary of India, 31 March 1868, Proclamation of the Rao of Kutch, 24 April 1869, PRO, FOCP, 2314.

18. Pelly to Bombay, 10 March 1862, MA, 23/1862, pp. 277-86; Kirk to Bombay, 24 and 28 August 1871, 10 April 1872, PRO, FO 84/1344.

19. Churchill to Bombay, 25 February 1869, PRO, FO 84/1307, same to same, 17 November 1870, PRO, FOCP, 1936, pp. 3-4; same to same, 25 March 1871, PRO, FO 84/1344.

20. Nicholls, p. 182; Bennett and Brooks (eds) (1965), p. 482; Guillain, Vol. 2, p. 234; Leigh, pp. 288-9.

21. See pp. 18-24, above; Nicholls, p. 249. On further disintegration of the mercantile edifice and on Ibadhi revivalism after the partition of the kingdom, see Kelly (1968), pp. 550-3; Kumar, pp. 32-3, 44-50.

22. Ruete, p. 96; Gray (1962a), ch. 1, p. 24, ch. 2, p. 31.

23. Said to Aberdeen, 23 July 1844, PRO, FO 54/6. Coghlan, who headed the Zanzibar-Muscat Commission, said that in his opinion Said 'had nothing more in view than to allot subordinate governorships to one or more of his sons under the paramount sovereignty of Oman.' But Said seems to be fairly explicit about the partition. Coghlan to Bombay, 4 December 1860, MA, 12584/13. Khalid died in 1854, and his place was taken by Majid. Nicholls, p. 250.

24. Hamerton to FO, 31 July 1844, PRO, FO 54/6; Kumar, p. 29.

25. Political Resident, Persian Gulf to Bombay, 11 April 1859, MA, 121/1859, pp. 321–22, 375–93. Badger, in Salil, p. xcviii.

26. Syed Saeed's will, dated AH 26/9/1266–AD 6 August 1850, Rigby to Bombay, 17 February 1859, MA, 121/1859, pp. 103–114, 395–401; Coghlan to Bombay, 4 December 1860, MA 12584/13, pp. 56–86, no. 20.

27. Coupland (1939), p. 27; Badger, in Salil, p. xcvii. See p. 18 above.

28. Majid to Coghlan, [October 1860], MA, 12584/13, pp. 116–24; Felix Jones to Bombay, 27 December 1859, NAI, 9/3/1860–FC–21/22; Cruttenden to Rigby, 22 September 1859, NAI, 28/12/1859–PC–7/8; Rigby to Bombay, 17 February 1859, MA, 121/1859, pp. 103–114; same to same, 1 December 1859, NAI, 16/3/1860–PC–10/15.

29. Bombay to Government of India, 3 February 1859, Bombay to Resident, Persian Gulf, 7 January 1859, NAI, 25/2/1859–PC–47/8; Rigby to Bombay, 4 April 1859, NAI, 17/6/1859–PC–5.

30. Rigby to Bombay, 17 February 1859, MA, 121/1859, pp. 103–14; same to same, 18 June 1859, NAI, 29/7/1859–PC–32A/C.

31. Rigby to Bombay, 19 April 1859, NAI, 17/6/1859–PC–10; Russell, p. 80.

32. Coghlan to Bombay, 4 December 1860, MA, 12584/13, no. 52.

33. Rigby to Bombay, 4 April 1859, NAI, 17/6/1859–PC–5; same to same, 18 June 1859, NAI 29/7/1859–PC–32A/C; Suleyman b. Himud to Syud Soweynee, 24 October 1859, NAI, 9/3/1860–FC–21/2.

34. Ruete, ch. 26, for an account of Princess Salme's involvement and viewpoint. Russell, ch. 7, for Rigby's account. Coupland (1939), pp. 23–5.

35. Coupland (1939), pp. 17, 23–6. Bennett (1978), pp. 60–5, makes a spirited defence of Majid as 'one of the most talented rulers of Zanzibar', who manipulated the British to support his claims. This is pseudo-nationalist mythology of African historiography of the early 1960s rather than an analysis of the realities of power at Zanzibar in the 1860s.

36. Bombay to Government of India, 28 February 1859, MA, 121/1859, pp. 75–82.

37. Resolution of the Honourable Board, 16 April 1860, MA, 97/1860, p. 15.

38. Kelley (1968), p. 543. My emphasis.

39. Coghlan to Bombay, 3 April 1860, MA, 96/1860, p. 263.

40. Published by the Hakluyt Society in 1871.

41. Coupland (1939), p. 27.

42. Majid to Coghlan, October 1860, Coghlan to Bombay, 4 December 1860, MA, 12584/13, pp. 116–24.

43. See p. 24–30 above.

44. Coghlan to Bombay, 4 December 1860, MA, 12584/13, nos. 28–9. My emphasis.

45. ibid., no. 39.

46. Rigby to Bombay, 17 February 1859, MA, 121/1859, pp. 103–14; same to same, 4 April 1859, NAI, 17/6/1859–PC–5; Russell, p. 78. Ruete, ch 26.

47. Coghlan to Bombay, 4 December 1860, MA, 13584/13.

48. Heskeal to Political Resident, Persian Gulf, 18 May 1859, MA, 121/1859, pp. 349–50; Rigby to Bombay, 1 December 1859, NAI, 16/3/1860–FC–10/15.

49. Coghlan to Bombay, 4 December 1860, MA, 12584/13.

50. Canning to Seyuds Thooenee and Majid, 2 April 1861, MA, 12584/13, pp. 76, 137–8; Coupland (1939), p. 30.
51. Cruttenden to Bombay, 24 September 1859, MA, 121/1859, pp. 471–87.
52. Coghlan to Bombay, 4 July and 4 December 1860, MA, 12584/13; Coupland (1939), pp. 21–2; Gray (n.d.), ch. 1, p. 11.
53. Quoted in Coupland (1939), pp. 35–6.
54. Gavin (1962), pp. 124–5.
55. ibid., p. 126; Acting Political Agent, Muscat to Bombay, 14 November 1868, MA, 156/1869, pp. 89–92.
56. Gray (n.d.), ch. 4, p. 4; Playfair to Bombay, 18 April 1865, PRO, FO 84/1245. However, in 1869 Kirk had raised the alarm about Barghash's identification with 'the fanatics who cause trouble in Oman, and are sending their commissioner to Zanzibar.' Kirk to Bombay, 26 April 1869, MA, 156/1869, pp. 142–4.
57. Coupland (1939), p. 88.
58. Gray (n.d.), ch. 5, p. 2.
59. Coupland (1939), p. 89.
60. ibid.
61. ibid., pp. 91, 99; Gray (n.d.), ch. 5; Gavin (1962), p. 126; de Vienne to MAE, 20 October 1871, MAE, CCZ, Vol. III, pp. 282–3.
62. Coupland (1939), pp. 91–5.
63. Kirk to Vivian, 12 December 1870, PRO, FO 84/1325; Bennett (1978), p. 94.
64. Coupland (1939), pp. 97–8.
65. Kirk to Bombay, 30 January 1871, Kirk to Barghash, 27 November 1871, PRO, FO 84/1344.
66. Pelly to Bombay, 8 March 1862, PRO, FO 84/1179, which suggests that Majid had undertaken to restrict the trade from 1862, but the proclamation was issued in 1864. Majid's proclamation, 1 January 1864, PRO, FO 84/1224. Coupland (1939), pp. 153, 155, 158–9.
67. Coupland (1939), pp. 156–7.
68. Sulivan, pp. 444–5.
69. Austen (1977), pp. 15–16, has objected to these averages, preferring a figure of between 50 and 200 slaves in the more publicised captures, although he admits he is not sure how representative such cargoes were. The average varied in different sectors of the trade and under different conditions. Over the short distance from Kilwa to Zanzibar when the trade was legal in 1868–9, the average for 81 dhows was 147 slaves; but the 551 dhows conducting the re-export trade from Zanzibar to the Kenya coast carried an average of 64 slaves between 1866–7 and 1870–1, according to reliable statistics supplied to the British Consul by the Custom Master. Kirk to FO, 1 February 1870, PRO, FO 84/1325; same to same, 27 June 1871, PRO, FO 84/1344. After all slave trade by sea had been made illegal, the 219 dhows captured between 1873 and 1881 carried an average of only 13 slaves. 'Memo. respecting the change of policy in suppression of slave trade in Zanzibar', 13 November 1882, PRO, FO 84/1694. A comprehensive quantitative study of over 600 slave captures after 1873 found that 71 per cent of the dhows carried less than 10 slaves and only 9 per cent carried more

than 50 slaves, with a mean of 15 slaves for the whole sample; Glassman (1977), p. 9. The average range given in the table, therefore, is much closer to the vast majority of captures during this period.

70. Ropes to State Department, 31 December 1865, NAW, T100/5. Playfair used an average of between $8.50 and $10 for 1861–2 to 1863–4; Playfair to Bombay, 1 May 1864, MA, 54/1864, pp. 16–33; Playfair to FO, 1 January 1865, PRO, FO 54/22. Austen (1977), pp. 12–13, and Table III A and B, estimates a total export to the north at between 7,000 and 8,000, made up as follows: 1,000 kidnapped by the 'Northern Arabs' from Zanzibar; half or more of those going legally to Pemba and Lamu because he says they could not have been absorbed there (overlook the expanding agriculture in Lamu and the Benadir coast); and all the slaves shipped from Kilwa who did not go to Zanzibar. However, when he comes to consider the question from the import side in the north, he can arrive at a figure of only 4,100 to 5,400, on equally arbitrary lines.

71. Cooper (1977), p. 115.

72. Sulivan, p. 440.

73. Cooper (1977), p. 90.

74. Webb to State Department, 30 September 1873, NAW, T100/6, says 4,500 tons (288,000 *fraselas*). Guillois to MAE, 10 December 1873, MAE, CCZ, Vol. III, pp. 344–9, puts the figure at 300,000 to 400,000 *fraselas*.

75. Christie (1871), pp. 31–64; Burton (1860), Vol. 2, pp. 369–70; Burton (1872), Vol. 1, p. 463; Will of Syed Saeed b. Sultan, AH 26/9/1266, MA, 121/1859, pp. 395–401; Devereux, p. 369.

76. Kirk's table was as follows:

	Normal	Exceptional	Total
Zanzibar	2,000	4,000	6,000
Pemba	1,000	2,000	3,000
Mombasa/Malindi	600	1,000	1,600
Lamu	500	500	1,000
Benadir			3,000
Transferred to Arabia			6,792
Mortality in dhows and immediately on landing			2,000
	4,100	7,500	23,392

The precise figure given for Arabia is not an indication of its accuracy but merely reflects the balance left over after juggling with the figures. Kirk himself admitted that he placed little reliance on these figures. See Sulivan, p. 440. On slave attrition Hamerton in 1844 had given a figure of 22–30 per cent for mortality, desertion or re-export, so that the whole workforce had to be renewed every four years. Hamerton to FO, 2 January 1844, PRO, FO 84/540. On the other hand in 1883 Miles suggests 8–12 per cent. Martin and Ryan, p. 80.

77. Albrand, p. 73; Burgess, pp. 118–21; Bennett and Brooks (eds) (1965), p. 400; Martin and Ryan, p. 77.

78. Devereux, pp. 57, 339.

79. ibid., p. 114. Also Playfair to FO, 1 June 1864, PRO, FO 84/1124.
80. Pelly to Bombay, 30 October 1861, MA, 47/1862, pp. 36–40; Devereux, p. 71; Colomb, p. 194.
81. Devereux, pp. 74, 262–3.
82. ibid., p. 412.
83. Lloyd, pp. 248–9; Rigby to Bombay, 4 October 1861, IOR, L/P&S/9/38; Derche to MAE, 23 April 1861, MAE, PZ, Vol. II, pp. 290–302; Bennett and Brooks (eds) (1965), pp. 518–19; Pelly to Oldfield, 22 November 1861, Krapf to Pelly, 10 April 1862 enclosure in Pelly to Bombay, 22 April 1862, MA, 47/1862, pp. 48–61, 102–9; Russell to Bombay, 29 January 1869, NAI, 11/1869-PolA-217.
84. Rigby to FO, 10 March 1862, PRO, FO 54/19; Playfair to Bombay, 23 May 1863, PRO, FO 84/1204.
85. Russell to Bombay, 29 January 1869, NAI, 11/1969-PolA-217; Kirk to FO, 3 and 4 May 1869, PRO, FO 84/1307; same to same, 2 and 6 May 1870, FO to Churchill, 18 November 1870, PRO, FO 84/1325; Kirk to FO, 25 March, 17 July 1871, FO to Kirk, 23 August 1871, PRO, FO 84/1344.
86. Seward to FO, 3 May 1867, Churchill to FO, 30 November 1867, PRO, FO 84/1279; FO to Consul, 10 October 1867, NAI, 5/1868-PolA-31. Seward had raised an objection whether a mixed commission would not be more appropriate, but it was summarily dismissed. Kirk to FO, 16 April and 8 August 1869, IOR, L/P&S/9/48; same to same 18 July 1869, MA, 152/1869, pp. 113–14; same to same, 22 May 1869, PRO, FO 84/1307; same to same, 16 December, 2 and 3 May, 8 June, 28 December 1870, PRO, FO 84/1325; same to same, 28 March 1871, FO to Kirk 7 October 1871, PRO, FO 84/1344.
87. Devereux, pp. 128–9, 80–2, 391–2; Skinner to Bombay, 7 May 1869, NAI, 9/1869-PolA-27/8.
88. Playfair to FO, 1 June 1864, PRO, FO 84/1224; Pelly to Bombay, 10 January 1862, pp. 203–10, 387–97.
89. Wylde's minute, 1 July 1869, PRO, FO 84/1307; Bennett (1963), p. 34.
90. Playfair to FO, 20 September 1863, PRO, FO 84/1204; Playfair to Jablonski, September 1863, MA, 60/1863, pp. 159–62; Jablonski to MAE, 27 September 1863, MAE, CCZ, Vol. II, pp. 311–15; same to same, 11 May 1863, MAE, CCZ, Vol. III, pp. 279–82; Kirk to FO, 23 April 1867, PRO, FO 84/1307; Kirk to Bombay, 8 April 1870, PRO, FO 84/1325.
91. Webb to Ropes, 20 April 1873, PM, Ropes Papers; Bertram to MAE, 16 April 1872, MAE, CCZ, Vol. III, pp. 304–7; Kirk to Bombay, 22 April 1872, PRO, FO 84/1357.
92. Webb to State Department, 30 September 1873, NAW, T100/6, says the crop declined from 4,500 tons (288,000 *fraselas*) to 600 tons (38,000 *fraselas*); Guillois to MAE, 10 December 1873, MAE, CCZ, Vol. III, pp. 344–9, says it declined from 300,000–400,000 to 50,000–60,000 *fraselas*.
93. Kirk to Bombay, 1 January 1870, MA, 144/1870, pp. 95–8; same to same, 2 May 1870, PRO, FO 84/1325.
94. Gavin (1962), pp. 127–30, 133, 139, 147.
95. ibid., pp. 133–4; Coupland (1939), pp. 165–70.
96. Gavin (1962), pp. 140–4; Coupland (1939), p. 185.

97. Coupland (1939), pp. 182-3, 187.
98. ibid., pp. 186-91, 198.
99. Bennett (1966), pp. 109-21; Coupland (1939), p. 184, 195-7, for the British version. Gavin (1962), p. 145.
100. Coupland (1939), pp. 191, 199-200; Gavin (1962), p. 145.
101. Gavin (1962), p. 146; Coupland (1939), p. 207.
102. Coupland (1939), pp. 209-13; Gavin (1962), p. 146.

Conclusion

The subordination of the Omani commercial empire to British over-rule, which culminated in the partition of the Omani kingdom and the imposition of the 1873 treaty, and eventually in the partition of the African section of the empire between European colonial powers and the declaration of a British Protectorate over Zanzibar in 1890, was part of a long process that was economic as well as political. The social transformation in Oman during the eighteenth century, as a result of increased Omani participation in Indian Ocean trade, had given rise to a mercantile dynasty and state that by their very nature became increasingly dependent on international trade and on the dominant power in the western Indian Ocean. Omani expansion to East Africa was occurring at a time when Britain was consolidating its hold over India, which was a major market for Omani trade, and over the Persian Gulf, which the Busaidi dynasty had considered to be its natural preserve. It was also occurring at a time when Britain was going through a historic revolution from which it was to emerge as the foremost capitalist power. This involved the subordination of merchant capital to serve the needs of the emerging capitalist mode of production on a world scale. The commercial empire that was developing during the nineteenth century, therefore, was growing in the shadow of this epic process, a process that entailed its assimilation into the world system of trade and, in the long run, the subjugation of the Omani state to hegemonic British influence.

During this process a major impetus was given to economic expansion at the periphery of the world system. The suppression of the European slave trade, which was part of the genesis of capitalism,[1] was to give encouragement to the transformation of the slave sector in East Africa. The loss of the market for slaves in the French sugar colonies in the Mascarenes and in the Americas had encouraged Arab slave traders to divert that labour to the clove plantations on Zanzibar when clove prices were extremely attractive, and later to the grain plantations on the East African coast. A large proportion of the slave-produced commodities fed into the world system of trade to supply not only the culinary and alimentary needs of Asia, but, more importantly, also the expanding industrial needs of the West for raw materials such as vegetable oils.

Simultaneously, the affluence of the emerging *nouveaux riches* in the capitalist West suddenly expanded the demand for luxuries such as ivory to manufacture piano keys and billiard balls, and gum copal for the production of varnishes for their carriages and furniture. The demand for these commodities grew so rapidly that throughout the nineteenth century it constantly seemed to outstrip supply, resulting in a steep rise in their prices. On the other hand, the price of manufactured commodities supplied in return by the industrialising West declined as the development of the productive forces reduced their production costs. East Africa was thus a beneficiary of extremely favourable terms of trade as a result of the diverging price curves. This helped finance enormous commercial expansion. By the end of the third quarter of the century the boundaries of the empire enclosed much of eastern Africa as far as present-day eastern Zaire.

The windfall of profit enabled the mercantile state at Zanzibar to increase its revenue enormously, helped by the evolution of an elaborate fiscal structure to corner as much of the surplus in the hands of the merchant prince through the customs organisation as possible. But the major beneficiaries were the various merchant classes that participated in the trade of the commercial empire. In the African interior, commerce facilitated the emergence of merchant classes that accumulated wealth and began to wield increasing influence in the political economies of the social formations there. Coastal traders who had penetrated the interior in pursuit of ivory and slaves occasionally settled down, like their indigenous counterparts, as resident traders and agriculturists to supply passing caravans, but the passion of many was to accumulate enough wealth to retire to a life of comfort and social prestige as plantation owners in Zanzibar. The foreign traders, European and American, were only transiently located at Zanzibar, and their accumulation occurred primarily in their home countries where some of their wealth eventually found its way into capitalist industries, such as the textile mill in Salem, and in banking.

The premier merchant class at Zanzibar, however, was largely Indian. It naturally dominated the northern branch of trade with India which was pre-eminent during the firist quarter of the nineteenth century. With the establishment of Western traders at Zanzibar during the second quarter, it came to handle much of the trade at the entrepôt as well, and to finance the caravan trade into the interior. And it capped its eminence with the acquisition of control over the customs organisation of Zanzibar and the East African coast. While a number of Indian merchants were seduced to divert part of their merchant wealth to agriculture during the 'clove mania' of the 1840s, subsequent overproduction and collapse of clove prices confirmed the class in its vocation, particularly since commerce was the most lucrative activity. The halting of the economic indigenisation of the Indian merchant class was to be confirmed by the political determination of the British consuls to consolidate their hold over this pivotal class in order to exercise their influence over the economy and state of Zanzibar. As British subjects they could not continue to engage in the use of slave labour on the clove plantations.

Merchant capital was thus largely locked up in the sphere of circulation. At the periphery of the world capitalist system it performed the signal function of encouraging production of commodities without directly participating in the production process itself, whether by offering attractive prices for the commodities, or by financing long-distance caravans deep into the heart of Africa. But it is not merchant capital that determines which commodities shall be produced; it is merely a conveyor belt that transmits the respective demands and presides over the exchange between the producing and consuming ends of the circuit. In the specific situation of East Africa during the nineteenth century it was the emerging capitalist mode that called the tune, and the demand was primarily for commodities of the hunt, particularly ivory, but also for slaves to produce cloves and grains at the coast, and for gum copal which was 'mined' in the coastal belt. The initial impetus given by the capitalist mode thus tended to divert labour (sometimes through direct export of that labour as slaves) from the productive sectors such as subsistence agriculture to hunting, porterage and trade, thereby developing, and in some instances overdeveloping, the more backward and secondary sectors of the economies of the African interior. In some cases the process of underdevelopment of these areas can be traced to this period, such as in Unyamwezi and Ukambani. At the coast the external impact tended to encourage the development of the dependent slave mode of production to supply cloves and grains to the industrialising West as well as to Asia. Thus, merchant capital during the nineteenth century, while facilitating the expansion of commodity production, was itself incapable of overseeing the transition to a higher mode. At best it can be credited with pulverising the precapitalist social formations and preparing them for their absorption into the colonial systems later in the century.

Apart from engrossing commercial profit in the sphere of circulation at the coast, merchant capital, in its moneylending form, also began to penetrate the plantation sector to capture much of whatever remained of the surplus. By draining off the surplus from the productive sector it was enervating it and economically undermining the ruling landowning class that organised production. It even subverted the Zanzibar state, which became heavily indebted to the Indian farmer of customs, particularly after the death of Seyyid Said.

Merchant capital, by its nature, is economically dependent on the dominant classes in production, and it cannot therefore be an independent political force. The Omani mercantile state had been subverted from the beginning of the nineteenth century as it acted as a junior partner to British power, particularly in the Persian Gulf. That process of subordination continued, though not so perceptibly, throughout Seyyid Said's reign as he made one concession after another to the British, especially on the question of the slave trade. It was not always realised that the ultimate suppression of the slave trade in East Africa - a delayed reflex - was nevertheless part of the logic of the maturation of the capitalist mode of production.[2] Zanzibar's subordination, however, assumed an ominous form with the death of Seyyid Said. This provided the British with a broad opportunity to intervene more directly to dismember his empire and subordinate the two halves separately to British paramountcy. The buttressing of the pliant rebel prince Majid at Zanzibar, the overt role played by the British consuls in the choice of his successors, and the imposition of the treaty abolishing the slave trade were proofs, if any were needed, that the commercial empire, which was never economically autonomous, could no longer pretend to be politically independent.

Notes

1. Marx, Vol. 1, ch. 24; Williams, passim.
2. Sakkarai, pp. 4–6.

Appendices

Appendix A Bombay trade with East Africa, 1801/2–1869/70

Year	Imports				Exports Value (Rs '000s)		Total imports	Ivory trade		
	Ivory	Copal	Cloves	Total	Cotton goods	Total		Re-export to London	Home market[1]	Total exports
1801/2	227	1		300				67		
1802/3	264	10		282	158	184	334		235	
1803/4	201	1	4	320	88	114	464	8	437	
1804/5	256	10	3	300	134	179	346	10	285	
1805/6			3	326	269	301	376	45	290	
1806/7				439		267				
1807/8	228	41		375	190	295	354	4	318	
1808/9	310	18	3	488	188	297	451	11	445	
1809/10	327	2	6	433	162	277	429	10	364	
1810/11	234	9		382	140	213	380		334	
1811/12	231	12		307	99	164	303	6	216	
1812/13	154	12		227	68	120	334		222	

249

Appendix A—*continued*

Year	Imports				Exports Value (Rs '000s)		Ivory trade			
	Ivory	Copal	Cloves	Total	Cotton goods	Total	Total imports	Re-export to London	Home market[1]	Total exports
1813/14	82	3		332	112	150	191		169	
1814/15	137	11		219	169	260	244	15	142	
1815/16	264	28		445	174	275	408	4	340	
1816/17	291	33		459	201	295	422	34	354	
1817/18	104	31		462	91	136	193		127	
1818/19	115	35		317	82	97	334		282	
1819/20	205	20		445	144	223	368		223	
1820/21	310	27		668	210	358	491	66	310	485
1821/22	157	27		428	171	323	237	96	95	148
1822/23	153	34		397	140	345	262	47	216	351
1823/24	190	30	11	264	162	231	407	77	164	444
1824/25	303	47	1	466	201	337	511	273	151	596
1825/26	245	54		378	208	360	374	428	151	549
1826/27	318	31		441	325	460	499	306	314	610
1827/28	207	26	15	314	227	364	457	177	230	470
1828/29	199	5	8	407	212	354	306	109	136	420
1829/30	160	10		386	222	381	226	201	183	423
1830/31	228	70		390	121	305	396	233	154	633
1831/32	201	54	2	313	110	252	376	406	192	423
1832/33	204	78	1	352	157	256	357	143	203	455
1833/34	175	97		323	209	283	483	453	163	641

1834/35	255	104	13	482	182	318	493	464	226	718
1835/36	258	234	23	559	193	375	483	424	300	894
1836/37	270	50	10	350	390	618	566	361	238	684
1837/38	438	72	63	635	347	645	672	590	301	981
1838/39	273	63	48	471	168	327	567	317	303	709
1839/40	183	32	5	255	202	402	457	371	303	752
1840/41	259	51	56	429	398	653	607	611	475	1,119
1841/42	342	1	77	577	268	490	620	450	522	948
1842/43	320	69	77	541	153	335	518	424	410	888
1843/44	546	3	204	1,002	386	769	728	435	288	890
1844/45	505	34	183	1,022	515	887	700	572	247	854
1845/46	599	119	131	1,021	391	819	769	380	302	732
1846/47	578	88	291	992	468	830	969	670	338	1,021
1847/48	610	100	223	1,180	243	749	1,004	332	345	764
1848/49	679	27	448	1,529	467	999	940	647	365	1,103
1849/50	576	69	317	1,413	537	1,176	914			789
1850/51	683	70	248	1,459	270	742	916	417	427	817
1851/52	801	41	409	1,768	395	823	1,119	866	372	1,299
1852/53	740	68	739	2,012	196	930	955	510	257	831
1853/54	783	78	604	1,938	752	1,403	991	768		799
1854/55	744	111	828	2,305	506	926	1,048	641		664
1855/56	627	113	667	2,047	580	995	901	782		807
1856/57	1,165	79	499	2,018	855	1,520	1,489	1,228		1,260
1857/58	938	97	751	2,669	665	1,331	1,446	1,144		
1858/59	1,098	106	777	3,025	565	1,359	1,497			
1859/60	705	67	305	2,084	799	1,289	1,281	846		950
1860/61	861	104	147	1,798	416	722	1,267			949

Appendix A —*continued*

Year	Imports				Exports Value (Rs '000s)		Ivory trade			
	Ivory	Copal	Cloves	Total	Cotton goods	Total	Total imports	Re-export to London	Home market¹	Total exports
1861/62	856	167	704	2,099	583	868	1,472	1,073		1,186
1862/63	825	305	456	2,275	1,028	1,437	1,354	487		576
1863/64	575	192	780	2,090	1,075	1,471	1,004	609		768
1864/65	901	121	472	1,773	1,222	1,753	1,451	490		741
1865/66	848	26	690	2,174	2,391	2,759	1,211	653		894
1866/67	705	60	323	1,826	1,286	1,544	1,045	521		722
1867/68	769	13	624	1,946	1,255	1,573	1,167			
1868/69	654	37	318	1,702	1,461	1,967	1,243	1,110		1,222
1869/70	854	21	543	1,727	1,324	1,660	1,149			

Note: ¹Home market: including re-export from Bombay and Surat to Gujarat and Kutch, and the difference between import and export at Surat.

Sources: IOR: P/419/39–106; 66 (1148), 1858/9–1869/70.

Appendix B Prices of ivory and *merekani* sheeting, 1802/3–1873/74

Year	*Ivory* (MT\$ per frasela)					*merekani*[1] (MT\$ per 30 yd)
	Zanzibar[1]	Salem[1]	Bombay[2]	Surat[2]	London[3]	
1802/3			26.54	32.96		
1803/4			23.97	30.81		
1804/5			29.11	35.10	39.13	
1805/6			31.24	42.80	36.71	
1806/7					44.80	
1807/8			34.24	36.38	31.69	
1808/9			36.38	62.92	32.70	
1809/10			30.39	54.36		
1810/11			34.24	59.92		
1811/12			31.67	32.10		
1812/13			29.96	27.82		
1813/14			23.54	26.54		
1814/15			27.39	24.82		
1815/16			25.25	23.54		
1816/17			27.39	22.26		
1817/18			27.39	25.68		
1818/19			26.54	24.40		
1819/20			26.96	28.68		
1820/21			25.68	23.54		
1821/22			26.11	29.11		

Appendix B—*continued*

Year	Ivory (MT\$ per frasela)					*merekani*[1] (MT\$ per 30 yd)
	Zanzibar[1]	Salem[1]	Bombay[2]	Surat[2]	London[3]	
1822/23			24.40	26.54		
1823/24	22.00		25.68	27.82		
1824/25			29.11	27.82		
1825/26			27.39	24.40		
1826/27		26.25	28.25	24.40		
1827/28	19.50		27.39	29.11		3.00
1828/29	22.00	37.10	29.11			
1829/30		31.85	29.11			
1830/31		36.75	27.82			
1831/32	24.40		29.96			
1832/33	25.40		31.24			
1833/34	27.25	45.50	32.10			
1834/35			33.38			3.38
1835/36		44.90	34.24			3.68
1836/37	29.40	45.35	37.61			3.54
1837/38		44.10	33.61			3.50
1838/39			34.16			3.83
1839/40	29.65	44.20	29.32			3.34
1840/41	29.85	42.75	35.32			3.66
1841/42	29.65	43.70	36.47			2.40
1842/43	30.40	42.35	24.02		37.48	2.20
1843/44	29.60	42.00	35.89			3.26

1844/45	31.70	43.75	43.33		2.70
1845/46	43.45	48.55	26.17		2.19
1846/47	36.00	47.25	32.89		2.68
1847/48	35.00	49.00	34.32		2.25
1848/49	32–35.15	49.00	33.75	44.53	2.54
1849/50	35.35	49.00	30.61	38.45	2.14
1850/51	38.00	50.75	36.32	47.95	1.97
1851/52	36.60		35.89	47.20	1.97
1852/53	39.80		38.18	50.84	1.95
1853/54	45.50	50.15	41.04		
1854/55	47.00	59.50	48.33	37.85	
1855/56	45.90	63.00	46.48	39.34	
1856/57	40.25		40.18	52.92	
1857/58	50.00	61.25	56.20	63.68	
1858/59	52.85	66.50	49.65	49.87	
1859/60	52.50	62.15	53.63	46.46	
1860/61	48.65		52.91	45.57	
1861/62	44.00		44.33	39.63	
1862/63	49.25		46.19	33.77	
1863/64	45.25		44.76	41.12	2.33
1864/65	46.75		48.33	47.20	
1865/66	47.60		44.57	47.13	
1866/67	54.35		43.19	55.44	
1867/68	55.00		30.89	52.10	
1868/69	60.35		33.89	50.84	2.88
1869/70	54.00		30.89	52.77	

Appendix B—*continued*

Year	Ivory (MT$ per frasela)					merekani[1] (MT$ per 30 yd)
	Zanzibar[1]	Salem[1]	Bombay[2]	Surat[2]	London[3]	
1870/71	57.85		32.46		52.92	
1871/72	54.25		32.60		39.56	3.25
1872/73	56.25		33.46		46.09	
1873/74	89.65		34.17		56.18	

Notes: [1]Prices are given for the calendar year.

[2]Prices are given by financial years and have been converted to MT$ per *frasela*, at the rate of Rs2.18 per MT$.

[3]Prices for London given in Appendix C have been converted to MT$ per *frasela*, at the rate of MT$4.75 per £1.

[4]'Hard' ivory, probably coming from eastern Zaire, began to appear at Zanzibar, and was lower priced, MT$32, compared to MT$35.15 for 'soft' ivory.

Sources: 1. EI, SCHR, Inward Manifests, 1826–40, 1855–75; Ward Papers; PM, Papers of Shepard, West, Waters, Fabens, and Ropes; BHS, Lefavour Papers; RIHS, Custom House Records; MAE, CCZ, Vol. II, pp. 205–10, 232–7, 263, 299, 364; Vol. III, pp. 14, 51, 79, 108. Compare with Bennett (1963), p. 89, which is based on same sources, but is not as precise.

2. IOR, P/419/39–106; 66 (1148), 1858/9–1869/70.

3. PRO, Cust. 5, Vols. 1–161; Cust. 4, Vols. 5–7, 9–11, 37.

Appendix C   Ivory imports into the United Kingdom, 1792–1875

Year	W. Africa	S. Africa	E. Africa[1]	N. Africa[2]	India[3]	Total	Price (£/ton)
			Quantities (in tons)				
1792	118	–	–	–	–	131	
1800	97	3	–	–	20	119	
1806	93	–	–	–	18	113	
1807	88	2	–	–	7	111	
1810	133	4	–	–			
1811	99	1					
1812	89	–	–	–	3	131	
1813							
1814	105	1	–	–	–	137	
1815	126	2	–	–	21	185	
1816	90	9	–	–	9	138	
1817	65	1	–	–	15	104	
1818	96	2	–	–	–	118	
1819	104	1	–	–	8	130	
1820	109	5	–	–	28	154	
1821	134	1	–	–	33	190	
1822	74	6	–	–	20	102	
1823	101	14	–	–	46	163	
1824	133	9	–	–	108	269	
1825	123	44	–	–	128	302	
1826	115	14	–	–	81	224	
1827	81	22	–	–	60	168	
1828	85	11	–	–	45	180	
1829	110	15	1	–	61	217	
1830	154	12	–	–	77	274	
1831	130	10	–	–	106	264	
1832	87	4	–	–	48	150	
1833	108	4	–	–	51	252	
1834	128	17	–	–	116	337	
1835	104	10	6	–	113	260	
1836	119	5	25	–	87	325	
1837	112	3	25	–	109	292	
1838	105	8	12	–	105	244	
1839	82	3	11	–	132	257	
1840	97	5	5	2	114	270	
1841	106	15	11	–	118	286	
1842	77	13	1	–	131	314	505[4]
1843	89	12	11	–	106	267	
1844	84	9	7	–	151	260	

Appendix C—*continued*

Year	W. Africa	S. Africa	E. Africa[1]	N. Africa[2]	India[3]	Total	Price (£/ton)
			Quantities (in tons)				
1845	75	21	2	10	198	314	
1846	72	15	2	33	133	263	
1847	71	23	1	10	195	315	
1848	49	22	–	57	84	229	600[4]
1849	63	29	15	46	203	365	518[4]
1850	72	56	–	75	172	458	646[4]
1851	64	50	–	29	129	302	636[4]
1852	73	44	2	86	221	453	685[4]
1853	105	54	–	118	156	498	
1854	68	37	–	113	158	440	510
1855	82	39	4	111	130	409	530
1856	61	29	–	83	239	463	713
1857	80	59	–	109	162	482	858
1858	92	67	–	142	255	599	672
1859	73	57	–	165	113	504	626
1860	77	61	–	158	142	526	614
1861	68	65	–	93	217	544	534
1862	67	60	–	174	171	556	455
1863	70	112	–	97	126	455	554
1864	89	56	40	166	131	557	636
1865	107	45	80	82	103	501	635
1866	126	26	64	215	76	593	747
1867	102	32	42	230	25	510	702
1868	82	28	1	211	4	490	685
1869	111	38	62	364	7	693	711
1870	96	59	5	274	11	601	713
1871	145	55	42	306	20	640	533
1872	136	51	23	294	12	561	621
1873	156	56	17	294	60	669	757
1874	125	77	46	140	197	668	863
1875	152	72	160	167	178	813	950

Notes:[1] Includes Aden from 1871 which began to handle East African as well as Ethiopian ivory after the opening of the Suez Canal.

[2] The area from Egypt to Morocco, and including Malta.

[3] Described as East India Company Territories until the 1850s.

[4]Prices for 1842–52 are derived from PM, Waters Papers, I; Fabens Papers, IV; and Shepard Papers, 31, 33, 36 & 37.

Blank spaces indicate no data.

Sources: PRO: Cust. 5, Vols. 1–161; Cust. 4, Vols. 5–7, 9–11, 37; unless otherwise marked.

Sources

Introduction

Although Zanzibar was the seat of the Omani empire in East Africa from the middle of the eighteenth century onwards, the period of Omani rule did not give rise to a continuous series of indigenous archival records. Arabic documents are scattered among other, generally later, series in the Zanzibar Archives, and consist of letters and deeds of various land and commercial transactions which have been examined by Naqar. A useful beginning in collecting indigenous records has been made by the Eastern African Centre for Research on Oral Traditions and African National Languages (Eacrotanal) which has assembled more than 140 'ancient manuscripts' in Arabic and Kiswahili. A resumé of the first twenty-five was published in 1981.[1]

Hitherto records created by the British Consulate at Zanzibar had formed the bedrock of historical analysis of East Africa during the nineteenth century. Established in 1841 under the control of the Bombay government as a consequence of the dominance of British Indian interests in the Persian Gulf, they naturally betray their imperial and generally political bias. The Zanzibar Archives, unfortunately, were not accessible to me during the period of my research, but the records are to a considerable extent duplicated at the Maharashtra Government Archives in Bombay. A selection of these records of wider political significance was forwarded to the British Indian government whose records are now located in the National Archives of India at New Delhi, and, in smaller numbers, in the India Office Records in London. Simultaneously, in view of the wider British interests in the suppresion of the slave trade, the British Consul in Zanzibar was required to communicate directly with the Foreign Office in London on matters connected with the slave trade. These records, as well as consular records on Muscat and Zanzibar, are located in the Public Record Office, Kew. Also housed there are the United Kingdom customs records which have provided very useful statistics on the African ivory trade as a whole.

[1]Naqar, passim; Eacrotanal, Vol. 1.

French interest in East Africa was largely a product of its connection with its sugar colonies in the Mascarenes, in particular with the French demand for slaves from the second half of the eighteenth century. Although their political ambitions in the region were curbed after the end of Anglo-French warfare early in the nineteenth century, a revival of their wider commercial and political interests was to give birth to admirable surveys by F. Albrand in the 1810s and by C. Guillain and Captain Loarer in the 1840s. These records are located in the Archives Nationales, Section Outre-Mer, in Paris. They are supported by French consular records housed in the Archives du Ministère des Affaires Etrangères.

Perhaps the most crucial records for an economic history of East Africa during the nineteenth century, however, are American sources. American interest in Zanzibar was almost exclusively commercial. The papers of Edmund Roberts, who negotiated the first commercial treaty with Zanzibar, are located in the Library of Congress, Washington, DC. The official records of the mission are housed in the National Archives in Washington, DC, which, more importantly, also preserve American consular records from Zanzibar, part of which are available on microfilm.

The records that offer information unobtainable elsewhere, however, are the unofficial papers of American merchants located particularly in the Peabody Museum and the Essex Institute in Salem, Massachusetts. These sources, consisting of letters, account books, logbooks and the custom house records, have yielded the most authentic raw data on the commerce of Zanzibar, particularly statistical, without which an economic history would have been difficult to write. A selection of these records has been published by N.R. Bennett and George Brooks.[2] Unfortunately, these records suffer from serious gaps from 1852 after the retirement of some of the early merchants.

[2]Bennett and Brooks (eds) (1965).

Archival sources

Public Record Office, Kew, Surrey (PRO)

1. Foreign Office Records

FO 54 (Muscat), Vols 1–24. This series contains a large part of the consular correspondence relating to Zanzibar until the late 1850s that does not directly relate to the slave trade.

FO 84 (Slave Trade). A very large series containing correspondence not always exclusively about the slave trade. Vols 425 (1842) to 1393 (1873) are the most useful for Zanzibar.

FO 403 (Foreign Office Confidential Prints – Africa). A selection of records printed for contemporary use in the Foreign Office, fairly complete for certain periods and topics, and containing documents sometimes missing from the above series.

2. Admiralty Records
Adm. 1/62–63. Admiral's Despatches, Cape of Good Hope, 1809–11. These Contain Captain Fisher's and Captain Tomkinson's reports, 1809.

Adm. 52/3940. Journal of Lieutenant J.B. Emery, 1824–6.

3. Customs Records
Cust. 4, Vols 5–70. Ledger of Imports: Countries, 1809–75.

Cust. 5, Vols 1A–114. Ledger of Imports: Commodities, 1792–1875.

Cust. 8, Vols 33–116. Ledger of Exports of British Merchandise: Countries, 1831–75.

Cust. 10, Vols 22–73. Ledger of Exports of Foreign and Colonial Merchandise: Countries, 1831–75.

India Office Records, London (IOR)

1. Marine Records
Miscellaneous (MR, Misc. 586). 'Steam Communication with East Coast of Africa'. Contains original journals and papers of the 1811 visit by Smee and Hardy. A report by the former was published in the *Transactions of the Bombay Geographical Society* and republished in Burton (1872), Vol. 2.

2. Political and Secret Department
L/P&S/9, Vols 12, 37, 40–3, 48–50. This series contains copies of consular correspondence from Zanzibar, duplicated in Bombay and New Delhi, and partly in the PRO.

Proceedings of the Government of India and of the Presidencies and Provinces.

Bombay Commerce: Internal and External Reports (P/419/Vols 39–106). This series, continued under *Bombay, Annual Statement of the Trade and Navigation of the Presidency*, (66–1148), 1848/9–1869/70, contains tabulated trade figures, prices and general comments. It provides statistics for the trade between Zanzibar and Bombay.

National Archives of India, New Delhi (NAI)

1. Proceedings of the Government of India in the Foreign Department
This series contains copies of consular records from Zanzibar forwarded from Bombay, arranged in files. It can be consulted by using the excellent decennial indexes from 1830.

2. Indian and Bombay Political Despatches to the Court of Directors

This series contains despatches forwarded to the India Office in London.

Maharashtra State Archives, Bombay (MA)

1. Proceedings of the Government of Bombay in the Political Department, 1820–73

This contains the most complete series of the British consular correspondence from Zanzibar outside the island, partly duplicated in the NAI, the IOR and the PRO.

2. Diaries

These were consulted for the period before 1820.

Archives du Ministère des Affaires Etrangères, Paris (MAE)

1. Correspondance Consulaire et Commerciale

Vols I–III of this series cover the period 1828 to 1874. It contains French consular correspondence relating particularly to commercial matters.

2. Correspondance Politique: Zanzibar

Vols I–IV of this series cover 1844–76.

Archives Nationales: Section Outre-Mer, Paris (ANSOM)

Océan Indien

1/1 Mission Henry Lambert dans l'Océan Indien, 1858.

1/9 Mission Livingstone en Afrique centrale.

2/10 Mission de M. Guillain à la côte orientale d'Afrique, 1845–58. Includes Captain Loarer's 'Ports au sud et au nord de Zanguebar', A to D.

5/23 'Memoire sur la population, l'organisation et l'économie de l'île de Zanguebar', including Captain Loarer's:

No. 1 Ile de Zanguebar: Population commerciale; Poids, mesures et monnaies.

No. 2 Lois et coutumes de douane: commerce sous les divers pavillons: Arabe, Nord Americain, Anglais.

Nos. 3–6 Commerce d' exportation.

No. 7 Merchandises d'importation.

14/55 Affaires politiques: consulat de France à Zanzibar, 1841–1859.

15/59 ibid., 1842–4.

15/60 Affaires commerciales: Propositions de M. Aubert Roche relatif au développement du commerce français en Asie et dans l'Afrique orientale, 1842–53.

15/61 Quiloa, 1778.

15/62 Affaires sanitaires: Topographie medicale des îles de Zanguebar et de Quiloa, 1820.

15/63 Constitution de Zanzibar du 20.4.1843.

15/64 Commerce: Renseignements sur le commerce à la côte orientale d'Afrique, 1850–73.

15/65 Renseignements politiques et commerciaux sur Zanzibar et Mascate, 1844–91.

17/89 Projet d'acquisition par le France de l'île de Pemba, 1822.

21/108 Missions françaises et étrangères, 1846–1892.

22/124 Rapport de consul de Zanzibar sur l'arraisonnement des boutres arabes par les croiseurs anglais, 1863.

National Archives, Washington, DC (NAW)

1. Record Group 59 (RG 59)

This group contains American consular correspondence from Zanzibar accumulated at the State Department for 1836–1915. It is microfilmed in eleven reels (T 100) to which reference is made in this book.

2. Record Group 84 (RG 84)

This group contains incomplete consular records collected at Zanzibar, partly duplicating RG 59, but also containing some documents missing from it, especially:

.c.3 Misc. Record Books, 1836–1910.

.c.8.2 Instructions from the State Department 1834–1911.

.c.8.3 Misc. Letters Received, 1840–1912.

.c.17 Invoice Book, 1861–1909, containing important statistics on American trade.

.c.20 Arrivals and Departures of American Vessels, 1846–1916.

.c.24.1 Ships' Daily Journals, 1857–1916.

3. Special Missions (Micro. 77, Roll 152)

This contains letters from the State Department.

4. Special Agents (Micro. 37, Roll 10)

This contains letters from Edmund Roberts to the State Department.

5. Domestic Letters of the State Department

Vols 125–136 (Micro. 40, Roll 90) were used. These contain letters from the State Department to the Navy Department.

Library of Congress, Washington, DC (LC)

Papers of E. Roberts
These cover his visits to Zanzibar and Muscat, 1827/8–1833.

Peabody Museum, Salem, Massachusetts (PM)

1. Papers of M. Shepard (1836–53)
This is one of the most important collections.

2. Letter of M.W. Shepard (1844)
This letter, inserted in the logbook of the *Star*, gives an intimate account of the history and conditions of Zanzibar.

3. Papers of B.F. Fabens (1843–7)
The papers of one of the resident agents in Zanzibar.

4. West papers
The papers of a partner in the West-Pingree group trading with Zanzibar.

5. Papers of R.P. Waters (1836–47)
The papers of the first United States Consul and commercial agent at Zanzibar.

6. Papers of E.D. Ropes
The papers of one of the later consuls and commercial agents. They contain a very important table of exports from Zanzibar, 1863–7.

7. Papers of F. Brown (1825–90)
Miscellaneous papers, including a copy of the table of exports from Zanzibar, 1863–7.

8. Papers of Ahmed b. Nooman
He was Seyyid Said's emissary to the US in 1840. The papers include a photostat copy of his Arabic accounts with an English translation, and comments by H.F. Eilts. See Eilts, for further details.

Essex Institute, Salem, Mass.

1. Papers of M. Shepard
These include his account books.

2. Papers of R.P. Waters
These contain Arabic letters; daily meteorological observations incorporating details of shipping; and a list of foreign vessels at Zanzibar, 1832–7.

3. Papers of C. Ward
The papers of the second United States Consul and commercial agent at Zanzibar.

4. Salem Custom House Records (SCHR)
These comprise several hundred linear feet of documents, containing inward and outward manifests.

Beverley Historical Society, Beverley, Massachusetts (BHS)

Ms. 16,977
A. Lefavour, 'Directions and Remarks on the Coast of Sumatra, So. Madagascar, the Red Sea, the Persian Gulf, East Coast of Africa, Zanzibar, Mombasa and other Iss.' Extracts published in Tagnery (1964).

Rhode Island Historical Society, Providence, Rhode Island (RIHS)

1. Papers of J. R. Congdon (1811–1900)
See Tanner (1953).

2. US Custom House Papers

Pennsylvania Historical Society, Philadelphia, Pennsylvania

Journal, logbook and letters of S. Drinker
Drinker navigated Seyyid Said's vessel, *Sultana*, back to Zanzibar in 1840–1. Drinker's 'Private Journal of events and scenes, 1838–41', giving a graphic account of life on a Zanzibari naval ship, is in the possession of H.M. Drinker in Philadelphia. A typed copy is in the Peabody Museum and in the possession of the author. See Eilts.

Harvard School of Business Administration: Baker Library, Cambridge, Massachusetts (HSBA)

Emerton Papers
Miscellaneous documents of one of the early merchant captains in East African waters.

Printed and unpublished works

Abir, M. (1970), 'Southern Ethiopia', in Gray and Birmingham (eds), pp. 119–38

Akinola, G.A. (1972), 'Slavery and slave revolts in the Sultanate of Zanzibar in the nineteenth century', *Journal of the Historical Society of Nigeria*, vol. 6, pp. 215–28

Akinola, G.A. (1973), 'The Sultanate of Zanzibar, 1870–1890' (unpublished PhD thesis, University of London)

Abrahams, R.G. (1967a), *The Political Organisation of Unyamwezi* (Cambridge: Cambridge University Press)

Abrahams, R.G. (1967b), *The Peoples of Greater Unyamwezi, Tanzania* (London: International African Institute)

Albrand, F. (1838), 'Extrait d'une mémoire sur Zanzibar et sur Quiloa', *Bulletin de la Société de Géographie*, 2ᵉ Serie, vol. 10, pp. 65–84

Alexis, M.G. (1890), *Stanley l'Africain* (Liège)

Alpers, E.A. (1966), 'The role of the Yao in the trade of East Central Africa' (unpublished PhD thesis, University of London)

Alpers, E.A. (1967), *The East African Slave Trade* (Historical Association of Tanzania, Paper No. 3, Nairobi)

Alpers, E.A. (1969), 'The coast and the development of the caravan trade', in Kimambo and Temu (eds), pp. 35–56

Alpers, E.A. (1970), 'The French slave trade in East Africa (1721–1810)', *Cahiers d'Etudes Africaines*, vol. 10, no. 37, pp. 80–124

Alpers, E.A. (1975), *Ivory and Slaves in East Central Africa* (London: Heinemann)

Alpers, E.A. (1983), 'Muqdisho in the nineteenth century: a regional perspective', *Journal of African History*, vol. 24, no. 4, pp. 441–59

Anon. (1888). *R.P. Waters: A Sketch* (Salem: reprinted from vol. 20 of the *Bulletin of the Essex Institute*)

Austen, R.A. (1977), 'The Islamic slave trade out of Africa (Red Sea and Indian Ocean): an effort at quantification' (Paper presented at the Conference on Islamic Africa: Slavery and Related Institutions, Princeton)

Bathurst, R.D. (1967), 'The Ya 'rubi dynasty of Oman' (unpublished DPhil thesis, University of Oxford)

Bathurst, R.D. (1972), 'Maritime trade and imamate government: two principal themes in the history of Oman to 1728', in Hopwood (ed.), pp. 98–106

Baur and LeRoy (1886), *A Travers le Zanguebar: voyage dans l'Oudoe, l'Ouzigoua, l'Oukwere, l'Oukami et l'Ousagara* (Tours: Mame et Fils)

Baxter, H.C. (1944), 'Pangani: the trade centre of ancient history', *Tanganyika Notes and Records*, no. 17, pp. 15–25

Beachey, R.W. (1967), 'The East African ivory trade in the nineteenth century', *Journal of African History*, vol. 8, no. 2, pp. 269–90

Beachey, R.W. (1976a), *The Slave Trade of Eastern Africa* (London: Collings)

Beachey, R.W. (1976b), *A Collection of Documents on the Slave Trade of Eastern Africa* (London: Collings)

Bennett, N.R. (1959), 'Americans in Zanzibar, 1825–45', in Essex Institute *Historical Collections*, vol. 95, pp. 239–62

Bennett, N.R. (1961a), 'Americans in Zanzibar, 1845–65', Essex Institute *Historical Collections*, vol. 97, pp. 31–56

Bennett, N.R. (1961b), 'The Arab power of Tanganyika in the nineteenth century' (unpublished PhD dissertation, Boston University)

Bennett, N.R. (1963), *Studies in East African History* (Boston: Boston University Press)

Bennett, N.R. (1966), 'Charles de Vienne and the Frere mission to Zanzibar', in J. Butler (ed.), *Boston University Papers on Africa*, Vol. 2, pp. 107–121 (Boston: Boston University Press)

Bennett, N.R. (ed.) (1968), *Leadership in Eastern Africa: Six Political Biographies* (Boston: African Studies Center)

Bennett, N.R. (1969), 'France and Zanzibar, 1776–1844', in D. McCall (ed.), *Eastern African History* (New York: Praeger)

Bennett, N.R. (1971), *Mirambo of Tanzania, ca.1840–1884* (New York: Oxford University Press)

Bennett, N.R. (1973), 'The Arab impact', in Ogot (ed.), pp. 210–28

Bennett, N.R. (1978), *A History of the Arab State of Zanzibar* (London: Methuen)

Bennett, N.R. and Brooks, G.E. (eds) (1965), *New England Merchants in Africa* (Boston: Boston University Press)

Bennett, N.R., Brooks, G.E. and Booth, A.R. (1962), 'Materials for African history in the Peabody Museum and the Essex Institute', *African Studies Bulletin*, vol. 5, no. 3, pp. 13–41

Berg, F.J. (1968), 'The Swahili community of Mombasa, 1500–1900', *Journal of African History*, vol. 9, no. 1, pp. 35–56

Berg, F.J. (1971), 'Mombasa under the Busaidi sultanate: the city and its hinterland in the nineteenth century' (unpublished PhD dissertation, University of Wisconsin)

Berg, F.J. (1973), 'The coast from the Portuguese invasion', in Ogot (ed.), pp. 115–34.

Bhatia, B.M. (1963), *Famines in India* (London: Asia Publishing House)

Boteler, T. (1835), *Narrative of a Voyage of Discovery to Africa and Arabia* (2 vols, London: Bentley)

Boxer, C.R. and Azevedo, C. de (1960), *Fort Jesus and the Portuguese in Mombasa, 1593–1729* (London: Hollis & Carter)

Brady, C.T. (1950), *Commerce and Conquest in East Africa* (Salem: Essex Institute)

Bridges, R.C. (1963), 'British exploration of East Africa, with special reference to the Royal Geographical Society, 1788–1885' (unpublished PhD thesis, University of London)

Brode, H. (1907), *Tippoo Tib* (London: Arnold)

Brode, H. (1911), *British and German East Africa* (London: Arnold)

Brown, B. (1971), 'Muslim influence on trade and politics in the Lake Tanganyika region', *African Historical Studies*, vol. 4, no. 3, pp. 617–29

Brown, W.T. (1971a), 'The politics of business: relations between Zanzibar and Bagamoyo in the late nineteenth century', *African Historical Studies*, vol. 4, no. 3, pp. 631–43

Brown, W.T. (1971b), 'A pre-colonial history of Bagamoyo' (unpublished PhD dissertation, Boston University)

Browne, J.R. (1846), *Etchings of a Whaling Cruise with Notes of a Sojourn on the Island of Zanzibar* (New York: Harper and Bros.)

Burgess, E. (1840), 'Probable openings for missionaries at Zanzibar', *Missionary Herald*, vol. 31, pp. 118 *et seq.*

Burnes, A. (1835), *Travels into Bakhara* (London: Carey)

Burnes, A. (1836), 'On the maritime communications of India, as carried on by the natives, particularly from Kutch, at the mouth of the Indus', *Journal of the Royal Geographical Society*, vol. 6, pp. 23–9

Burns, C.L. (1902), 'A monograph on ivory carving', *Journal of Indian Art and Industry*, vol. 9, nos. 70–80

Burton, R.F. (1859), 'The lake regions of Central Equatorial Africa', *Journal of the Royal Geographical Society*, vol. 29, pp. 1–464

Burton, R.F. (1860), *The Lake Regions of Central Africa* (2 vols, London: Longman)

Burton, R.F. (1872), *Zanzibar: City, Island and Coast* (2 vols, London: Tinsley)

Burton, R.F. (1873), *The Lands of Cazembe* (London: Murray)

Cameron, V.L. (1877), *Across Africa* (London: Daldy, Isbister)

Capen, N. (ed.) (1852), *Writings of Levi Woodbury* (Boston: Little Brown)

Cashmore, T.H.R. (1961), 'A note on the chronology of the Wanyika of the Kenya coast', *Tanganyika Notes and Records*, no. 57, pp. 153–72.

Cassanelli, L.V. (1982), *The Shaping of Somali Society: Reconstructing the History of a Pastoral People, 1600–1900* (Philadelphia: University of Pennsylvania Press)

Chau Ju Kua, (1911), *Chau Ju-Kua, his Work on the Chinese and Arab Trade in the Twelfth and Thirteenth Centuries, entitled Chu-fan-chi*; tr. by F. Hirth and W.W. Rockhill (St Petersburg: Imperial Academy of Sciences)

Chaudhuri, K.N. (1965), *The English East India Company: The Study of an Early Joint-Stock Company, 1600–1640* (London)

Chittick, H.N. (1959), 'Notes on Kilwa', *Tanganyika Notes and Records*, no. 53, pp. 179–203

Chittick, H.N. (1969), 'A new look at the history of Pate', *Journal of African History*, vol. 10, no. 4, pp. 375–91

Chittick, H.N. and Rotberg, R.I. (eds) (1975), *East Africa and the Orient* (New York: Africana Publishing)

Christie, J. (1871), 'Slavery in Zanzibar as it is', in Fraser, Tozer and Christie, pp. 31–64

Christie, J. (1876), *Cholera Epidemics in East Africa* (London: Macmillan)

Sources

Christopher, W. (1843), 'Extracts from a journal kept during a partial inquiry into the present resources and state of northeastern Africa', *Transactions of the Bombay Geographical Society*, vol. 4, pp. 383–409

Christopher, W. (1844), 'Commanding HMS Tigris on the East Coast of Africa', *Journal of the Royal Geographical Society*, vol. 14, pp. 76–104

Colomb, P.H. (1873), *Slave Catching in the Indian Ocean* (London: Longmans, Green)

Commissariat, M.S. (1938), *A History of Gujarat* (Bombay: Longmans, Green)

Commission of Disputes between the Rulers of Muscat and Zanzibar (1861), *Proceedings* (Bombay: Government Printer)

Cooley, W.D. (1845), 'The geography of N'yassi', *Journal of the Royal Geographical Society*, vol. 15, pp. 185–235

Cooley, W.D. (1852), *Inner Africa Laid Open* (London: Longman)

Cooley, W.D. (1854), 'Notice of a caravan journey from the east to the west coast of Africa', *Journal of the Royal Geographical Society*, vol. 24, pp. 269–70

Cooley, W.D. (1855), 'Journey from Benguela to Mozambique', *Proceedings of the Royal Geographical Society*, vol. 1, pp. 75–6

Cooper, F. (1974), 'Plantation slavery on the east coast of Africa in the nineteenth century' (unpublished PhD dissertation, Yale University)

Cooper, F. (1977), *Plantation Slavery on the East Coast of Africa* (New Haven: Yale University Press)

Cooper, J. (1875), *The Lost Continent* (London: Longmans, Green)

Coupland, R. (1938), *East Africa and Its Invaders* (Oxford: Clarendon Press)

Coupland, R. (1939), *The Exploitation of East Africa, 1856–1890* (London: Faber)

Crofton, R.H. (1929), *Statistics of the Zanzibar Protectorate, 1893–1928* (London: Eastern Press)

Crofton, R.H. (1936), *A Pageant of the Spice Islands* (London: Bale & Danielsson)

Cruttenden, I.N. (1848), 'On eastern Africa', *Journal of the Royal Geographical Society*, vol. 18, pp. 136–9

Cunnison, I. (1961), 'Kazembe and the Portuguese', *Journal of African History*, vol. 2, no. 1, pp. 61–76

Cunnison I. (1966), 'Kazembe and the Arabs', in E. Stokes and R. Brown (eds), *The Zambezian Past* (Manchester: Manchester University Press) pp. 226–37

Dale, G. (1920), *The Peoples of Zanzibar* (London: Universities' Mission to Central Africa)

Datoo, B.A. (1968), 'Selected phases of the historical geography of major eastern African ports' (unpublished PhD thesis, University of London)

269

Datoo, B.A. (1970), 'Misconceptions about the use of monsoons by dhows in East African waters', *East African Geographical Review*, vol. 8, pp. 1-10

Datoo, B.A. (1974), 'Influence of monsoons on movement of dhows along the East African coast', *East African Geographical Review*, vol. 12, pp. 23-33

Datoo, B.A. (1975), *Port Development in East Africa: Spatial Patterns from the Ninth to the Sixteenth Centuries* (Nairobi: East African Literature Bureau)

Datoo, B.A. and Sheriff, A.M.H. (1971), 'Patterns of ports and trade routes in different periods', in L. Berry (ed.), *Tanzania in Maps* (London: University of London Press), pp. 102-5

Delf, G. (1963), *Asians in East Africa* (London: Oxford University Press)

Devereux, W.C. (1869), *A Cruise in the 'Gorgon'* (London: Bell & Daldy)

Duignan, P. (ed.) (1967), *Handbook of American Resources for African Studies* (Stanford: Hoover Institution, Stanford University)

Dundas, C.C.F. (1913), 'History of Kitui', *Journal of the Royal Anthropological Society*, vol. 43, pp. 480-549

Dundas, C.C.F. (1924), *Kilimanjaro and its People* (London: Witherby)

Dutt, R. (1882), *The Economic History of India under Early British Rule, 1757-1837* (2 vols, Reprinted, 1960, Delhi)

Eacrotanal [Eastern African Centre for Research on Oral Traditions and African National Languages] (1981) *Resumé of Old Arabic Manuscripts*, Vol. 1 (Zanzibar)

Eilts, H.F. (1962), 'Ahmed bin Na'man's mission to the United States in 1840. The voyage of Al-Sultanah to New York City', *Essex Institute Historical Collections*, vol. 98, pp. 219-77

Ellis, T.P. (1902), 'Ivory carving in the Punjab', *Journal of Indian Art and Industry*, nos 70-80

Emery, J.B. (1833), 'A short account of Mombasa and the neighbouring coast of Africa', *Journal of the Royal Geographical Society*, vol. 3, pp. 280-3

Encyclopaedia Britannica (1910) (11th edition, New York) (1970) (New edition, Chicago)

Erhardt, Rev. J. (1855), 'Report respecting central Africa, as collected in Mambara and the East coast', *Proceedings of the Royal Geographical Society*, vol. 1, pp. 8-10

Farrant, L. (1975), *Tippu Tip and the East African Slave Trade* (London: Hamilton)

Farsy, A.S. (1942), *Seyyid Said bin Sultan* (Zanzibar)

Farsy, A.S. (1944), *Tarehe ya Imam Shafi na Wanavyuoni Wakubwa wa Mashariki ya Afrika* (Zanzibar)

Feierman, S. (1974), *The Shambaa Kingdom* (Madison: University of Wisconsin Press)

Fitzgerald, W.W.A. (1898), *Travels in the Coastlands of British East Africa and the Islands of Zanzibar and Pemba* (London: Chapman & Hall)

Fraser, H.A. (1871), 'Zanzibar and the slave trade', in Fraser, Tozer and Christie, pp. 9–19

Fraser, H.A., Tozer, Bishop and Christie, J. (1871), *The East African Slave Trade* (London: Harrison)

Freeman-Grenville, G.S.P. (1960), 'Historiography of the East African coast', *Tanganyika Notes and Records*, no. 55, pp. 279–89

Freeman-Grenville, G.S.P. (ed.) (1962a), *The East African Coast: Select Documents* (Oxford: Clarendon Press)

Freeman-Grenville, G.S.P. (1962b), *The Medieval History of the Coast of Tanganyika* (London: Oxford University Press)

Freeman-Grenville, G.S.P. (1963), 'The coast, 1498–1840', in Oliver and Mathew (eds), pp. 129–68

Freeman-Grenville, G.S.P. (1965), *The French at Kilwa Island* (Oxford: Clarendon Press)

Frere, B. (1874), *Eastern Africa as a Field for Missionary Labour* (London: Murray)

Garlake, P.S. (1966), *The Early Islamic Architecture of the East African Coast* (London: Oxford University Press)

Gavin, R.J. (1962), 'The Bartle Frere expedition and Zanzibar, 1873', *Historical Journal*, vol. 5, pp. 122–48

Gavin, R.J. (1965), 'Seyyid Said', *Tarikh*, vol. 1, pp. 16–29

Gavin, R.J. (1968), 'Middle Africa', in J.D. Omer-Cooper, *et al.*, *The Growth of African Civilisation: The Making of Modern Africa*, Vol. 1 (London: Longman), pp. 271–305

Gazetteer of the Bombay Presidency (1880), vol. 5 (Bombay: Government Printer)

Germain, A. (1868), 'Note sur Zanzibar et la côte orientale d'Afrique', *Bulletin de la Société de Géographie*, 5ᵉ serie, vol. 16, pp. 530–59

Giraud, V. (1890), *Les Lacs de l'Afrique Equatoriale* (Paris: Hachette & Cie)

Glassman, C. (1977), 'A quantitative social history of the illegal, seagoing, East African slave trade, 1873–1900' (Research paper, Columbia University)

Gobineau, A. de (1859), *Trois Ans en Asie (de 1855 à 1858)* (Paris: Hachette)

Graham, G.S. (1967), *Great Britain in the Indian Ocean* (Oxford: Clarendon Press)

Grant, D.K.S. (1938), 'Mangrove woods of Tanganyika Territory, their silviculture and dependent industries', *Tanganyika Notes and Records*, no. 5, pp. 5–16

Grant J.A. (1864), *A Walk Across Africa* (London: Blackwood)

Gray, J.M. (1947), 'Ahmed b. Ibrahim – the first Arab to reach Buganda', *Uganda Journal*, vol. 11, pp. 80–97

Gray, J.M. (1952), 'A history of Kilwa: Part II', *Tanganyika Notes and Records*, no. 32, pp. 11–37

Gray, J.M. (1956a), 'The French at Kilwa, 1776-1784', *Tanganyika Notes and Records*, no. 44, pp. 28-49

Gray, J.M. (1956b), *Report on the Inquiry into claims to certain lands at or near Ngezi, Vitongoji, in the mudiria of Chake Chake, in the District of Pemba* (Zanzibar: Government Printer)

Gray, J.M. (1957), *The British in Mombasa, 1824-1826* (London: Macmillan)

Gray, J.M. (1958), 'Trading expeditions from the coast to lakes Tanganyika and Victoria before 1857', *Tanganyika Notes and Records*, no. 49, pp. 226-46

Gray, J.M. (1961), 'The Diaries of Emin Pasha', *Uganda Journal*, vol. 25, n. 1.

Gray, J.M. (1962a), *History of Zanzibar* (London: Oxford University Press)

Gray, J.M. (1962b), 'The French at Kilwa in 1797', *Tanganyika Notes and Records*, nos 58 and 59, pp. 172-3

Gray, J.M. (1964a), 'The recovery of Kilwa by the Arabs in 1785', *Tanganyika Notes and Records*, no. 62, pp. 20-4

Gray, J.M. (1964b), 'A French account of Kilwa at the end of the eighteenth century', *Tanganyika Notes and Records*, no. 63, pp. 222-8

Gray, J.M. (n.d.), 'History of Zanzibar, 1856-1886' (unpublished ms. at the University of Dar es Salaam)

Gray, R. and Birmingham, D. (eds) (1970), *Pre-Colonial African Trade* (London: Oxford University Press)

Grefulhe, H. (1878), 'Voyage de Lamoo à Zanzibar', *Bulletin de la Société de Géographie et d' Etudes Coloniales de Marseille*, vol. 2, pp. 209-17, 327-60.

Guillain, C. (1856), *Documents sur l'histoire, la géographie et le commerce de l'Afrique orientale* (3 vols and album, Paris: Bertrand)

Hafkin, N.J. (1973), 'Trade, society and politics in northern Mozambique, c. 1753-1913' (unpublished PhD dissertation, Boston University)

Haight, M.V.J (1967), *European Powers and South-East Africa* (rev. edn, London: Longmans)

Hall, C. (1967), 'Dutch navigation off the East African coast', *Tanzania Notes and Records*, no. 67, pp. 39-48

Halliday, F. (1979), *Arabia without Sultans* (Harmondsworth: Penguin)

Hamerton, A. (1855), 'Brief notes containing information on various points connected with H.H. the Imam of Muscat', *BR*, vol. 24, pp. 250-60

Harkema, R.C. (1964), 'Het achterland van Zanzibar in de tweede helft van de negentiende eeuw', *Tijdschrift voor Economische en Sociale Geografie*, vol. 55, no. 2, pp. 42-8

Harkema, R.C. (1967), 'De stad Zanzibar in tweede helft van de negentiende eeuw en enkele oudere Oostafrikaanse kuststeden' (unpublished PhD, thesis, University of Groningen)

Hart, Captain (1855), 'Extracts from brief notes of a visit to Zanzibar', *BR*, vol. 24, pp.274-83

Hawley, D. (1970), *The Trucial States* (London: Allen & Unwin)

Heanley, R.M. (1888), *A Memoir of Edward Steere* (London: Bell)

Holmes, C.F. (1971), 'Zanzibari influence at the southern end of Lake Victoria: the lake route', *African Historical Studies*, vol. 4, no. 3, pp. 477-503

Hopkins, A.G. (1973), *An Economic History of West Africa* (London: Longman)

Hopwood, D. (ed.) (1972), *The Arabian Peninsula* (London: Allen & Unwin)

Hourani, G.F. (1951), *Arab Seafaring in the Indian Ocean in Ancient and Early Medieval Times* (Princeton: Princeton University Press)

Hoyle, B.S. (1967), *The Seaports of East Africa,* (Nairobi: East African Publishing House)

Hutchinson, E. (1874), *The Slave Trade of East Africa* (London: Sampson Law)

Ingham, K. (1962), *A History of East Africa* (London: Longmans)

Ingrams, W.H. (1931), *Zanzibar, its History and its People* (London: Witherby)

Isaacs, N. (1936), *Travels and Adventures in Eastern Africa* (2 vols, Cape Town: Van Riebeeck Society)

Jabir, M.H. (1977), 'Plantation economy during the Protectorate period in Zanzibar' (unpublished MA thesis, University of Dar es Salaam)

Jackson, K.A. (1972), 'An ethnohistorical study of the oral traditions of the Akamba of Kenya' (unpublished PhD dissertation, University of California, Los Angeles)

Jiddawi, A.M. (1951), 'Extracts from an Arab account book, 1840-1854', *Tanganyika Notes and Records*, no. 31, pp. 25-31

Johnson, F. (1945), *A Standard Swahili-English Dictionary* (London: Oxford University Press)

Johnson, H.H. (1886), *The Kilima-Njaro Expedition* (London)

Kaniki, M.H.Y. (ed.) (1980), *Tanzania Under Colonial Rule* (London: Longman)

Kelly, J.B. (1968), *Britain and the Persian Gulf, 1795-1880* (Oxford: Clarendon Press)

Kelly, J.B. (1972), 'A prevalence of furies: tribes, politics and religion in Oman and Trucial Oman', in Hopwood (ed.), pp. 107-41

Kimambo, I.N. and Temu, A.J. (eds.) (1969), *A History of Tanzania* Nairobi: East African Publishing House)

Kirk, W. (1962), 'The north-east monsoon and some aspects of African History', *Journal of African History*, vol. 3, no. 2, pp. 263-7

Kjekshus, H. (1977), *Ecology Control and Economic Development in East African History* (London: Heinemann)

Klein, H.S. and Engerman, S.L. (1975), 'Shipping patterns and mortality in the African slave trade to Rio de Janeiro, 1825–1830', *Cahiers d'Etudes Africaines*, vol. 15, no. 59, pp. 381–98

Krapf, J.L. (1860), *Travels, Researches and Missionary Labours in Eastern Africa* (London: Trübner)

Krumm, B. (1940), *Words of Oriental Origin in Swahili* (London: Sheldon Press)

Kumar, R. (1965), *India and the Persian Gulf Region* (London: Asia Publishing House)

Lambert, H.E. (1957), *Ki-Vumba. A dialect of the Southern Kenya Coast* (Kampala: East African Swahili Committee)

Lamphear, J. (1970), 'The Kamba and the northern Mrima coast', in Gray and Birmingham (eds), pp. 75–101

Leech, Lt. R. (1856), 'Sketch of the trade of the port of Mandvie . . . in Cutch', in *BR*, vol. 15, pp. 211–26

Leigh, J.S. (1980), 'The Zanzibar diary of' (ed. by J.S. Kirkman), *International Journal of African Historical Studies*, vol. 13, pp. 281–312, 492–507

Livingstone, D. (1857), *Missionary Travels and Researches in South Africa* (London: Murray)

Livingstone, D. (1874), *Last Journals*, ed. by H. Waller (2 vols, London: Murray)

Livingstone, D. (1963), *Livingstone's African Journal, 1853–1856* (2 vols, London: Chatto & Windus)

Lloyd, C. (1949), *The Navy and the Slave Trade* (London: Longmans, Green)

Loarer, Captain (1851), 'L'Ile de Zanzibar', *Revue de l'Orient*, vol. 9, pp. 240–99

Lodhi, A. (1973), *The Institution of Slavery in Zanzibar and Pemba* (Uppsala: Scandinavian Institute of African Studies)

Lofchie, M.F. (1965), *Zanzibar, Background to Revolution* (Princeton: Princeton University Press)

Lorimer, J.C. (1908–15), *Gazetteer of the Persian Gulf, 'Omān and Central Arabia* (2 vols, Calcutta)

Low, D.A. (1963), 'The northern interior, 1840–84', in Oliver and Mathew (eds), pp. 297–351

Lyne, R.N. (1905), *Zanzibar in Contemporary Times* (London: Hurst & Blackett)

Mackenzie, D. (1895), 'A report on slavery and the slave trade in Zanzibar, Pemba and the mainland of the British Protectorate of East Africa', *Anti-Slavery Reporter*, 4th ser., vol. 15, pp. 69–96

Sources

McMaster, D.N. (1966), 'The ocean-going dhow trade to East Africa', *East African Geographical Review*, vol. 4, pp. 13–24

MacMurdo, Captain J. (1820), 'An account of the province of Cutch', *Transactions of the Literary Society of Bombay*, vol. 2

MacQueen, J. (1845), 'Notes on African geography: visit of Lief Ben Saed to the Great African Lake', *Journal of the Royal Geographical Society*, vol. 15, pp. 371–6

Mangat, J.S. (1969), *A History of the Asians in East Africa* (Oxford: Clarendon Press)

Martin, B.G. (1971), 'Notes on some members of the learned classes of Zanzibar and East Africa in the nineteenth century', *African Historical Studies*, vol. 4, pp. 525–45

Martin, E.B. (1973), *The History of Malindi: A Geographical Analysis of an East African Coastal Town from the Portuguese Period to the Present* (Nairobi: East African Literature Bureau)

Martin, E.B. and Martin, C.P. (1978), *Cargoes of the East* (London: Elm Tree Books)

Martin, E.B. and Ryan, T.C.I. (1977), 'A quantitative assessment of the Arab slave trade of East Africa, 1770–1896', *Kenya Historical Review*, vol. 5, pp. 71–91

Marx, K. (1962), *Capital* (3 vols, Moscow: Progress Publishers)

Marx, K. and Engels, F. (1969), *Selected Works* (3 vols, Moscow: Progress Publishers)

Mathew, G. (1963), 'The East African coast until the coming of the Portuguese', in Oliver and Mathew (eds), pp. 94–127

Maurizi, V. (Shaikh Mansur) (1819), *History of Seyd Said* (London: Booth)

Menon, R. (1978), 'Zanzibar in the nineteenth century: aspects of urban development in an East African coastal town' (unpublished MA dissertation, University of California, Los Angeles)

Meteorological Office (1943), *Weather in the Indian Ocean*, Vol. 1 (London: Meteorological Office)

Meteorological Office (1949), *Monthly Meteorological Charts of the Indian Ocean* (London: Meteorological Office)

Middleton, J. (1961), *Land Tenure in Zanzibar* (London: HMSO)

Middleton, J. and Campbell, J. (1965), *Zanzibar, its Society and its Politics* (London: Oxford University Press)

Middleton, J. and Kershaw, G. (1965), *The Central Tribes of the North-Eastern Bantu: the Kikuyu, including Embu, Meru, Mbere, Chuka, Mwimbi, Tharaka and the Kamba of Kenya* (rev. edn, London: International African Institute)

Milburn, W. (1813), *Oriental Commerce* (2 vols, London: Black, Parry)

Miles, S.B. (1919), *The Countries and Tribes of the Persian Gulf* (London: Harrison)

275

Mondevit, Saulnier de (1820), 'Observations sur la carte de Zanzibar, 1787', *Nouvelles Annales des Voyages* (Paris)

Morgan, W.T.W. and Shaffer, N.M. (1966), *Population of Kenya* (Nairobi: Oxford University Press)

Morris, H.S. (1968), *The Indians in Uganda* (London: Weidenfeld & Nicolson)

Mukherjee, R. (1974), *The Rise and Fall of the East India Company* (New York: Monthly Review Press)

Al-Naqar, U. (1978), 'Arabic materials in the Government Archives of Zanzibar', *History in Africa*, vol. 5, pp. 377–82

New, C. (1873), *Life, Wanderings and Labours in Eastern Africa* (London: Hodder & Stoughton)

Nicholls, C.S. (1971), *The Swahili Coast, Politics, Diplomacy and Trade on the East African Littoral, 1798–1856* (London: Allen & Unwin)

Niebuhr, C. (1792), *Travels Through Arabia* (2 vols, Edinburgh: R. Morison & Son)

Northway, P.H. (1954), 'Salem and the Zanzibar-East African trade, 1825–1845', Essex Institute *Historical Collections*, vol. 90, pp. 123–53, 261–73, 361–88

Ogot, B. (ed.) (1973), *Zamani: A Survey of East African History* (Nairobi: East African Publishing House)

Oliver, R. (1963), 'Discernible developments in the interior, c. 1500–1840', in Oliver and Mathew, (eds), pp. 169–211

Oliver, R. and Mathew, G. (eds) (1963), *History of East Africa*, vol. 1, (Oxford: Clarendon Press)

Osgood, J.F. (1854), *Notes of Travel; or, Recollections of Majunga, Zanzibar, Muscat, Aden, Mocha and Other Eastern Ports* (Salem: G. Creamer)

O'Swald (W.) & Co. (1931), *Aus der Geschichte des Hauses Wm O'Swald and Co; Hamburg* (Hamburg: O'Swald and Co.)

Owen, I.R. (1856), 'The ivory and teeth of commerce', *Journal of the Society of Arts*, vol. 5, no. 213, pp. 65–8

Owen, W.F. (1833), *Narrative of Voyages to Explore the Shores of Africa, Arabia and Madagascar* (2 vols, London: Bentley)

Paine, R.D. (1924), *The Ships and Sailors of Old Salem* (Boston: Lauriat)

Palgrave, W.G. (1865), *Narrative of a Year's Journey through Central and Eastern Arabia* (London: Macmillan)

Panikkar, K.M. (1953), *Asia and Western Dominance: A Survey of the Vasco da Gama Epoch of Asian History, 1498–1945* (London: Allen & Unwin)

Pearce, F.B. (1920), *Zanzibar, the Island Metropolis of East Africa* (London: Unwin)

Philby, H. St. J.B. (1939), 'African contact with Arabia', *Journal of the Royal African Society*, vol. 38, pp. 33–46

Philips, C.H. (ed.) (1951), *Handbook of Oriental History* (London: Royal Historical Society)

Phillips, J.D. (1947), *Salem and the Indies* (Boston: Houghton Mifflin)

Phillips, W. (1967), *Oman: A History* (London: Longmans)

Pickering, C. (1850), *The Races of Man and Their Geographical Distribution* (London: Bohn)

Piggott, R.J. (1961), *A School Geography of Zanzibar* (London: Macmillan)

Playfair, R.L. (1865), 'Report on . . . the various countries around Zanzibar', *Transactions of the Bombay Geographical Society*, vol. 18

Plekhanov, G.V. (1974), *Selected Philosophical Works* (5 vols, Moscow: Progress Publishers)

Plowden, W.C. (1868), *Travels in Abyssinia and the Galla Country* (London: Longmans, Green)

Postans, Lt.T. (1839/40), 'Some account of the present state of the trade between the port of Mandvie in Cutch, and the East Coast of Africa', *Transactions of the Bombay Geographical Society*, vol. 3

Prins, A.H.J. (1958), 'On Swahili historiography', *Journal of the East African Swahili Committee*, vol. 28, pp. 26–41

Prins, A.H.J. (1961), *The Swahili-Speaking Peoples of Zanzibar and the East African Coast* (London: International African Institute)

Prins, A.H.J. (1965), *Sailing from Lamu* (Assen: Van Gorcum)

Putnam, G.G. (1924–30), *Salem Vessels and Their Voyages* (Salem, Mass.: Essex Institute)

Rabaud, A. (1879), 'Zanzibar', *Bulletin de la Société de Géographie de Marseille*, vol. 3, pp. 158–77

Ranger, T.O. (1969), *The Recovery of African Initiative in African History* (Inaugural Lecture, University of Dar es Salaam)

Rebmann, J. (1849), 'Narrative of a journey to Jagga, the snowy country of Eastern Africa', *Church Missionary Intelligencer*, vol. 1, no. 1, pp. 12–23

Roberts, A.D. (1967), 'The History of Abdullah ibn Suliman', *African Social Research*, vol. 4, pp. 241–70

Roberts, A.D. (ed.) (1968), *Tanzania before 1900* (Nairobi: East African Publishing House)

Roberts, A.D. (1970), 'Nyamwezi trade', in Gray and Birmingham (eds), pp. 39–74

Roberts, E. (1837), *Embassy to the Eastern Courts of Cochin-China, Siam and Muscat in the U.S. Sloop-of-War Peacock, . . . 1832-3-34* (New York: Harper)

Rodney, W. (1972), *How Europe Underdeveloped Africa* (London: Bogle-L'Ouverture)

Ross, R. (tr. and ed.) (1984), 'The Dutch on the Swahili Coast, 1776–8. Two journals of slaving voyages' (unpublished)

Rowley, H. (1884), *Twenty Years in Central Africa* (London: Wells Gardner, Darton)

Ruete, E. (1888), *Memoirs of An Arabian Princess* (London: Ward & Downey)

Ruschenberger, W.S.W. (1838), *Narrative of a Voyage round the World* (2 vols, London: Bentley)

Russell, C.E.B. (Mrs) (1935), *General Rigby, Zanzibar and the Slave Trade* (London: Allen & Unwin)

Sacleux, C. (1939–40), *Dictionnaire Swahili–Français* (Paris: Institut d'Ethnologie)

Said b. Habeeb (1860), 'Narrative of an Arab inhabitant of Zanzibar', *Transactions of the Bombay Geographical Society*, vol. 15, pp. 146–8

Said-Ruete, R. (1929), *Said b. Sultan* (London: Alexander-Ousley)

St. John, C. (1970), 'Kazembe and the Tanganyika–Nyasa corridor, 1800–1890', in Gray and Birmingham (eds), pp. 202–28

Sakkarai, L. (1977), 'Indian merchants in East Africa' (Paper presented at the Conference on Islamic Africa: Slavery and Related Institutions, Princeton)

Salil b. Razik (1871), *History of the Imams and Seyyids of Oman*, tr. by G.P. Badger (London: Hakluyt Society)

Salt, H. (1814), *A Voyage to Abyssinia, 1809–10* (London: Rivington)

Schweinfurth, G. (1888), *Emin Pasha in Central Africa* (London: Philip)

Schweitzer, G. (1898), *Emin Pasha, His Life and Work* (2 vols, London: Constable)

Sheriff, A.M.H. (1971), 'The rise of a commercial empire: an aspect of the economic history of Zanzibar, 1770–1873' (unpublished PhD thesis, University of London)

Sheriff, A.M.H. (1975a), 'Trade and underdevelopment: economic history of the East African coast from the 1st to 15th century', *Hadith*, vol. 5, pp. 1–23

Sheriff, A.M.H. (1975b), 'Social formations in pre-colonial Kenya', in A.J. Temu and B. Swai (eds), *Kenya Under Colonial Rule*, forthcoming

Sheriff, A.M.H. (1980), 'Tanzanian societies at the time of the partition', in Kaniki (ed.), pp. 11–50

Sheriff, A.M.H. (1981), 'The East African coast and its role in maritime trade', in G. Mokhtar (ed.), *Unesco General History of Africa*, Vol. 2 (London: Heinemann), pp. 551–67

Sheriff, A.M.H. (1986a), 'Ivory and commercial expansion in East Africa in the nineteenth century', in G. Liesegang (ed.), *Import and Export Trade in the 19th century*

Sheriff, A.M.H. (1986b), 'The Zanzibar peasantry under imperialism, 1873–1963', in A. Sheriff and D.E. Ferguson (eds.), *Zanzibar Under Colonial Rule* (Dar es Salaam: Tanzania Publishing House), forthcoming

Shorter, A. (1968a), 'Ukimbu and the Kimbu chiefdoms of southern Unyamwezi' (unpublished DPhil thesis, University of Oxford)

Shorter, A. (1968b), 'The Kimbu', in Roberts (ed.) (1968), pp. 96–116

Shorter, A. (n.d.), 'The grand design of Amran Masudi' (unpublished mimeo.)

Smee, T. (1811), 'Observations during a voyage of research on the East Coast of Africa, from Cape Guardafui to the Island of Zanzibar, in the Honourable Company's Cruisers *Ternate*, Capt. T. Smee and *Sylph* Schooner, Lieut. Hardy', in Burton (1872), Vol. 2

Smith, Alan (1969), 'The trade of Delagoa Bay as a factor in Nguni politics, 1750–1835', in L. Thompson (ed.), *African Societies in Southern Africa* (London: Heinemann), pp. 171–89

Smith, Alan (1970), 'Delagoa Bay and the trade of South-Eastern Africa', in Gray and Birmingham (eds), pp. 265–90

Smith, Alison (1963), 'The southern section of the interior, 1840–84', in Oliver and Mathew (eds), pp. 253–96

Spear, T. (1974), 'The Kaya complex: a history of the Mijikenda peoples of the Kenya coast to 1900' (unpublished PhD dissertation, University of Wisconsin)

Speke, J.H. (1862), 'On the commerce of Central Africa', *Transactions of the Bombay Geographical Society*, vol. 15, pp. 145–8

Speke, J.H. (1863), *Journal of the Discovery of the Sources of the Nile* (London: Blackwood)

Speke, J.H. (1864), *What Led to the Discovery of the Sources of the Nile* (London: Blackwood)

Stahl, K.M. (1964), *History of the Chagga People of Kilimanjaro* (The Hague: Mouton)

Stanley, H.M. (1872), *How I Found Livingstone* (2nd edn, London: Low, Marston)

Stanley, H.M. (1878), *Through the Dark Continent* (2 vols, London: Low, Marston)

Stanley, H.M. (1961), *The Exploration Diaries of H.M. Stanley*, ed. by R. Stanley and A. Neame (London: Kimber)

Stigand, C.H. (1913), *The Land of Zinj* (London: Constable)

Strandes, J. (1899), *The Portuguese Period in East Africa*, tr. by J.F. Wallwork (Nairobi: 1961)

Sulivan, G.L. (1873), *Dhow Chasing in Zanzibar Waters* (London: Low, Marston)

Sutton, J.E.G. (ed.) (1969), *Dar es Salaam: City, Port and Region, Tanzania Notes and Records*, Special Number (no. 71), Dar es Salaam

Sutton, J.E.G. (1973), *Early Trade in Eastern Africa* (Nairobi)

Sykes, Colonel (1853), 'Notes on the possessions of the Imaum of Muskat, on the climate and productions of Zanzibar, and the prospects of African discovery', *Journal of the Royal Geographical Society*, vol. 23, pp. 101–19

Tagnery, P. (1964), 'Archives and manuscript collections: Beverley

(Mass.) Historical Society', *Africana Newsletter*, vol. 11, pp. 65–8

Tanganyika (1959), *Annual Report of the Department of Antiquities, 1958* (Dar es Salaam: Government Printer)

Tanner, E.C. (1953), 'The Providence Federal Custom House Papers as a source of maritime history since 1790', *New England Quarterly*, vol. 26, pp. 88–100

Theal, G.M. (ed.) (1898–1903), *Records of South Eastern Africa* (9 vols, London: Government of the Cape Colony)

Thomas, B. (1938), *Arab Rule Under the Al-Bu Sa'id Dynasty of Oman, 1741–1937* (London: Milford)

Tidbury, G.E. (1949), *The Clove Tree* (London: Lockwood)

Tippu Tip (1958–9), *Maisha ya Hamed b. Muhammed el Murjebi Yaani Tippu Tip*, tr. by W.H. Whiteley, historical introduction by Alison Smith, supplement to the *Journal of the East African Swahili Committee*, 28/ii and 29/i

Topan, M.T. (1962–3), 'Biography of Sir Tharia Topan Kt' (Manuscript in the possession of Farouk Topan)

Tosh, J. (1970), 'The northern inter-lacustrine region', in Gray and Birmingham (eds), pp. 103–18

Troup, R.S. (1932), *Report on Clove Cultivation in the Zanzibar Protectorate* (Zanzibar: Government Printer)

Unomah, A.C. (1973), 'Economic expansion and political change in Unyanyembe, c. 1840–1900' (unpublished PhD thesis, University of Ibadan)

Villiers, A. (1940), *Sons of Sindbad* (New York: Scribner)

Villiers, A. (1948), 'Some aspects of the Arab dhow trade', *Middle East Journal*, vol. 11, pp. 398–416

Vogel, (1855–6), 'Ivory trade of central Africa', *Proceedings of the Royal Geographical Society*, vol. 1, pp. 215–16

Wakefield, Rev. T. (1870), 'Routes of native caravans from the coast to the interior of Eastern Africa', *Journal of the Royal Geographical Society*, vol. 40, pp. 303–39

Walji, S.R. (1969), 'Ismailis on mainland Tanzania, 1850–1948' (unpublished MA dissertation, University of Wisconsin)

Warden, F., *et al.* (1856), 'Arab tribes of the Persian Gulf'; 'Historical sketch of Muskat, 1694/5–1819' *BR*, vol. 24, pp. 168–234, 300–6

Weber, M. (1923), *General Economic History* (London: Allen & Unwin)

Werner, A. (1914–15), 'A Swahili history of Pate', *Journal of African Society*, vol. 14, pp. 148–61; vol. 15, pp. 278–96

Wheatley, P. (1975), 'Analecta Sino-Africana Recensa', in Chittick and Rotberg (eds), pp. 76–114

Whiteley, W.H. (1956), *Ki-Mtangata, a dialect of the Mrima Coast* (Kampala: East African Swahili Committee)

Whiteley, W.H. (1969), *Swahili: The Rise of a National Language* (London: Methuen)

Wilkinson, J.C.W. (1964), 'Historical geography of Trucial Oman to the beginning of the sixteenth century', *Geographical Journal*, vol. 130, pp. 337–49

Wilkinson, J.C.W. (1972), 'The origins of the Omani state', in Hopwood (ed.), pp. 67–88

Williams, E. (1964), *Capitalism and Slavery* (London: André Deutsch)

Wilson, A. (1970), 'Long distance trade and the Luba-Lomami empire' (unpublished MA thesis, University of London)

Winder, R.B. (1965), *Saudi Arabia in the Nineteenth Century* (London: Macmillan)

Windham, Sir R. (ed.) (1961), *Law Report*, vol. 8 (Zanzibar: Government Printer)

Woolf, L.S. (1920), *Empire and Commerce in Africa* (reprinted 1968, London: Cass)

Wrigley, C.C. (1957), 'Buganda: an outline economic history', *Economic History Review*, 2nd ser., vol. 10, pp. 60–80

Ylvisaker, M. (1971), 'Shamba na Konde: Land usage in the hinterland of the Lamu archipelago, 1865–95' (Seminar paper, Nairobi)

Ylvisaker, M. (1979), *Lamu in the Nineteenth Century: Land, Trade and Politics* (Boston: African Studies Center)

Ylvisaker, M. (1982), 'The ivory trade in the Lamu area, 1600–1870', *Paideuma*, vol. 28, pp. 221–31

Yule, H. and Burnell, A.C. (1903), *Hobson-Jobson* (London: Murray)

Zanzibar (1960), *Report on the Census of the Population of Zanzibar Protectorate* (Zanzibar: Government Printer)

Zanzibar Gazette (1892-), (Zanzibar: Government Printer)

Zevin, R.B. (1965), 'The growth of manufacturing in early nineteenth century New England' (unpublished PhD thesis, University of California, Berkeley), Abstract in *Journal of Economic History*, vol. 25, pp. 680–2

Index